SOLAR AND LUNAR RETURNS

Personal calculable astrology for
the individual

D1741653

SOLAR AND LUNAR RETURNS

An introduction to the use of personal return charts in astrological interpretation

by

John Filbey
D.F.Astrol.S.

THE AQUARIAN PRESS

First published 1988

British Library Cataloguing in Publication Data

Filbey, John
Solar and lunar returns.
1. Astrology
I. Title
133.5   BF1708.1

ISBN 0-85030-606-X

The Aquarian Press is part of the Thorsons Publishing Group, Wellingborough, Northamptonshire, NN8 2RQ, England

Printed in Great Britain by Biddles Limited, Guildford, Surrey

1   3   5   7   9   10   8   6   4   2

CONTENTS

The Solar Cycle

ACKNOWLEDGEMENTS

In the preparation of, and the researches for, this book, the works and writings of the siderealists, particularly Cyril Fagan, proved to be of inestimable value, and I gladly acknowledge with gratitude my indebtedness to them.

Although this work is designed as an introduction to return techniques, principally those applicable to the tropical zodiac, it is hoped that it will prove useful in promoting further research into 'both zodiacs', thereby leading to a better understanding of the fundamental basis of astrological symbolism and the relationship which man has with the universe.

Finally, I acknowledge, with thanks, the assistance given by friends and relatives in supplying so much useful personal data. For permission to reproduce the logarithm tables, I am indebted to the publishers, W. & R. Chambers Ltd, and I extend my thanks to them.

INTRODUCTION

The reappraisal of some areas of astrological thought which has occurred during the last few decades has resulted in a greater awareness of what astrology and its symbolism actually represents. This awareness has, among other things, contributed to the rejection of fatalism and superstition with which astrology was often associated. Prediction and prognostication are no longer the principal objectives of more enlightened consultants. Instead, the accent has shifted toward personal counselling in order that an individual may achieve a fuller life according to his needs and abilities. Although we may not be able to predict precisely, we can often assess future trends from a study of the relevant charts. The dividing line between fate and free will is extremely thin and, although we may think that we are responding to events and conditions in a free and untrammelled way, we may occasionally be the victims of a capricious fate.

Among the advances made concerning astrological techniques (and the realization that astrology needs to be approached in an active and dynamic manner), are those concerning return charts. The theory of returns and cyclic charts is not new. Like so many 'new' discoveries in astrology they are really rediscoveries whose value for assessing probable trends and conditions during a particular period are considerable. As with all transit charts (for this is what returns are), their indications require to be considered in conjunction with the personal natal chart, or if dealing with mundane data, any other relevant mundane charts.

The 'renaissance' of solar and lunar return techniques was in the early 1950s, although the theory and practice of the solar return chart had always been considered in a somewhat limited manner. It was the sidereal astrology advocates, notably Fagan, Bradley and a few others, whose indefatigable researches paved the way towards establishing firm foundations concerning the sidereal zodiac and the techniques applicable to it.

The various types of returns, as proposed by Fagan and his colleagues, are discussed in this work, some of which have been applied in terms of the tropical zodiac. In presenting a work such as this, which is mainly concerned with return charts computed in terms of the tropical zodiac, the object has been (a) to introduce the theory and practice of the return techniques in order that those who wish to do so can investigate further, (b) to ascertain whether in fact return charts calculated according to the usual tropical system are valid. In studies such as this, the emphasis is on events at a particular time, but there is doubtlessly the psychological element present, the nature of which would be in accordance with the return and its indications.

The evidence for the validity of return charts, whether computed in the tropical system or the sidereal is, I think, well and truly established. 'Both zodiacs', in their own right, have value provided they are not 'mixed up' together. And this is the important point which appears to be misunderstood by some astrologers. The practice of expunging precession from tropical longitudes and then using the tropical zodiac appears illogical. When precession is expunged, the tropical zodiac is no longer tropical; we cannot have it both ways!

1.

THE THEORY AND PRINCIPLES
OF RETURN CHARTS

The Solar Return

The Solar Return is a 'revolution' chart erected for the exact time when the Sun, in its yearly progress, returns to the same longitude that it held at birth. This occurs each year on or within a day or so of the birthday. It is a personal chart as distinct from other types of return charts, such as the ingress, solstice or New Moon charts, which are mundane figures cast for the commencement of a new cycle.

The effectiveness of any predictive system must have a correlation with the events and conditions experienced by an individual, and these must conform both in time and in nature with the planetary symbolism of the appropriate charts. The solar return chart is the 'base chart' from which other types of returns can be calculated in order to assess the current patterns which may be operating at any given time. These subsidiary charts and their significance are discussed in Chapter 2.

Basically, solar return charts are based on transits, i.e. the transiting Sun forming a conjunction with the natal Sun. The chart calculated for the exact time of the conjunction denotes the 'pattern of the year' and indicates the events which are likely to occur, or the conditions and circumstances which will be experienced during the year in which the return is operative, the year, of course, commencing from the date of the return. Essentially a transit-based technique, the solar return chart operates from birth to death; as one return ends, another commences. This continuous cycle indicates the potentialities which may be expressed, or the events likely to be experienced during the 'return year'.

In discussing events, circumstances and conditions, we should note that it is the intrinsic nature of the planet(s) and their mutual configurations with each other, coupled with their mundane (house) positions, that determines how a particular event or condition may materialize. The indications contained in the return chart will only be activated when the planets are brought into major aspect with either the natal, solar (planets in the return chart) or transiting planets.

The key to return charts and their indications lies in the progression of the chart, and the maximum effect is experienced when one or more planets, natal, solar or transiting are conjunct either the angles of the progressed return, or those of the natal or return chart. The solar return chart is a kinetic instrument in a perpetual state of fluctuation and it cannot be studied in isolation or as a static entity. The planetary positions and their aspects at the time of the return remain 'impressed' throughout the length of the solar return year, but the daily movement subsequent to the solar return day, will result in various aspects and configurations being formed during the course of the year. Not every contact will correlate with a major event or condition, for it is the nature of the contact and its closeness to an angle which will determine how a person will respond.

Research with solar return charts tends to confirm that the solar planets correlate with actions which are initiated by the person, whereas the transiting planets (those positions on the day under review) relate to events and conditions which stem from the actions of self and others combined. The solar planets indicate independent actions and responses, in contrast to the transiting planets, which show reactions associated with or instituted by others. As with all astrological charts which are personal, the solar return chart and its implications need to be studied and interpreted in the light of the person's temperament, environment and general approach to life.

The tropical solar return as an astrological technique has never been adequately explored and it is only in the last few decades that serious attention has been given to it. Many notable astrologers of the past either gave it superficial attention or ignored it completely. With the advent and discoveries of the sidereal system of returns as advocated by Cyril Fagan, Donald Bradley and others, the whole question of cyclic charts and their significance began to command greater interest and attention. Many of the fine techniques introduced by Fagan and Bradley and publicized by Firebrace in the sidereal astrology journal *Spica*—now defunct—were for use with the sidereal zodiac. However, many of these techniques are applicable using the tropical zodiac.

Irrespective of which zodiac one favours, the proof of any astrological system or technique depends on whether the results obtained conform with the life experiences at any given time. Using well-attested data we should, if the method is valid, be able to correlate planetary action and symbolism, with everyday life. We need 'commonsense astrology' geared to the requirements and needs of human beings in order that individuals may seek a greater understanding of themselves and others and in doing so achieve some form of fulfilment.

The Lunar Return
This is a chart calculated for the time and date when the Moon in its monthly progress returns to the same longitude that it held at birth. This occurs every twenty-seven days or so and the indications in the return are effective for the subsequent four weeks of its operation.

In the same manner as the solar return chart indicates the 'pattern of the year', so the lunar return shows the 'pattern of the month'— the month commencing from the date of the return. It is against the 'backdrop' of the solar return that the lunar return should be studied. Although the lunar chart can be assessed on its own without recourse to other charts, its indications are often more apparent when related to the natal chart and the solar return chart. Often that which is shown in the solar return will be activated by appropriate lunar contacts. Even when the progressed solar return and the lunar return show great disparity with each other, and appear to be at odds concerning likely conditions or events, it is often noted that their indications manifest on different levels or in different modes.

In all assessments of lunar returns it has to be remembered that like the solar returns these are kinetic instruments and their transitive effects need evaluating in conjunction with the natal chart and the current solar return. In dealing with solar and lunar return charts and their significance for a particular year/month we need to analyse them firstly as independent charts, then in relation to the natal chart, and finally compare them with any other kind of subsidiary chart which may be appropriate to the period under review.

The solar return chart holds good for a complete year from the date of the return, and the lunar return holds sway for about four weeks from the date of the return. Research, particularly with sidereal returns indicates that these periods of time can be subdivided so that additional returns are possible. These periods of time and the type of subsidiary chart associated with them are discussed in Chapter 2.

The Zodiac and Precession

When dealing with solar and lunar returns we have to differentiate between those calculated in terms of the tropical zodiac and those using the sidereal zodiac. It is important that the difference which exists concerning the 'two zodiacs' is understood. In no way should the tropical and sidereal become 'mixed up', for they are two entirely separate systems.

If we consider the Earth as the fixed point, the Sun appears to move around it once a year, passing through the twelve signs of the zodiac along a line known as the Ecliptic (the Sun's apparent path in the heavens). Alternatively, if we consider the Sun as fixed, then the Earth is in orbit around it and the plane containing the orbit is the plane of the Ecliptic. The Earth's axis of rotation, roughly at right angles to this plane, is inclined at an angle of 23½ degrees— *inclination of the axis*—or as it is usually described *the obliquity of the Ecliptic.*

When the Greek astronomer Hipparchus (second century BC) compared contemporary observations with those made about a century and a half earlier by Timocharis, he concluded that the longitude of the stars appeared to be increasing at the rate of 36 seconds per year (the modern value is about 50 seconds), while their latitudes showed no definite changes. There were two possible explanations that would account for this change: (a) the stars had real and identical motions, (b) the fundamental reference point, the Vernal Equinox, was not a fixed reference point on the Ecliptic. The fact that the latitudes of stars showed no appreciable changes led to the conclusion that the Equator and, in consequence, the Vernal Equinox moved in such a manner that the longitudes of the stars increased uniformly. The cause of this displacement of stars remained unknown for many centuries, and it was Newton who first gave a correct explanation of precession.

In discussing the cause of precession, we need to understand two distinct and unrelated motions, namely: (a) the motion of the solar system in our galaxy, (b) the motion of the Celestial Pole around the Pole of its own orbit, i.e., the Pole of the Ecliptic. Our galaxy and solar systems are whirling around a common centre in their own galactic orbits at different rates of motion, such motions being technically termed *proper motions*. Each of the stars which form the pattern of the constellations, (zodiacal and non-zodiacal) is a sun. As all the stars are moving at gigantic but different speeds around the centre of the galaxy, all the constellations will completely lose their familiar patterns in the course of time.

Our Sun with its planets is moving in its own galactic orbit around the centre of the galaxy, and will take an estimated 220 million years to complete the circuit. The direction of the path in the galaxy taken by the Sun and planets is known as the 'apex', and according to astronomical determinants, it lies in Sagittarius 29°. Geocentrically, the Sun comes to the Ecliptic conjunction of its apex about 14 January each year. The phenomenon of 'precession', the dating of 'zodiacal ages' and the question of 'zodiacs' have nothing to do with the Sun's proper motion in space.

The Precession of the Equinoxes is the annual occurrence of the Vernal Equinox about 21 March, nearly 20½ minutes before the Earth has made a complete orbital revolution around the Sun, so that each year at that instant, the Sun crosses the Celestial Equator at a slightly different point. As the result of precession, every star—except those less than 23½° from the Ecliptic Poles—passes through every hour of Right Ascension from 0 to 24 hours, once every 25,800 years; also the declinations, every 12,900 years swing to and fro 47° (23½ × 2) greatly changing the stars visible at a given place and season.

The Vernal Equinoctial point (0° Aries) is that point on the Ecliptic intersected by the Celestial Equator. As the Equator is always at right angles to its own pole, it follows that the movement of the Celestial Pole around the Pole of the Ecliptic will cause the vernal-equinoctial point to slip backward along the Ecliptic at the rate of approximately 1° in 71½ years. Precession is therefore a purely terrestrial effect related to the Earth itself. If the Earth were not an oblate spheroid, but a perfect sphere, there would be no precession and the tropical zodiac would be fixed.

The continuous minute tilting of the Earth's axis by the Sun and Moon causes the Celestial Poles and Equator to change their places continuously among the stars in harmony, so that each successive moment, the Celestial Equator intersects the Ecliptic at a slightly different point—in the opposite direction of the Earth's orbital motion—of the one it would occupy if left undisturbed. Thus precession is continuous, not a sudden yearly occurrence.

The gravitational forces of the Sun and Moon pull on the Earth's equatorial bulge, as though trying to bring the Earth into an upright position. However, the spinning Earth behaves like a gyrostat causing the Earth's axis (which would otherwise always point to the same position on the star sphere) and the Celestial Poles to rotate round the poles of her orbit (those of the Ecliptic) in circles 23½° distant from them in a period of 25,800 years, displacing the Vernal Equinox in the opposite direction to her orbital motion.

As Precession is continuous, the Celestial Equator intersects the Ecliptic at a point about one-seventh second of arc west of the position the day before at the same hour, so that Right Ascension is measured from a slightly different point on the star sphere each day. About 21 March each year, the Vernal Point is approximately 50 seconds west of its position a year before, or about 3 seconds of right ascension (1° in 71.62 years).

The Ecliptic is the fundamental plane of reference and, as longitude is measured along the Ecliptic from the Vernal Equinox, it changes with precession, but latitude which is measured north or south of the Ecliptic, does not change. At the present time, the North Celestial Pole is near the star Ursae Minoris (Pole Star) and its nearest approach (less than half a degree) will be in the year 2100.

The position of the stars is listed for a definite epoch, e.g. 1 January 1950. This is done because it is not possible to produce maps and catalogues to keep abreast with precession. In plotting the positions of celestial objects observed before or after the epoch date, astronomers must calculate the amount of precessional change in right ascension and declination for the appropriate interval of time. In the ephemerides used by astrologers, the tabulations of planetary positions are given in celestial longitudes which have been converted from right ascension.

The Zodiac

The majority of Western astrologers use the tropical zodiac which commences with the vernal-equinoctial point and which retrogrades along the Ecliptic at the rate of 1° of longitude in 71½ years, resulting in the tropical zodiac, as a whole, to retrograde. The twelve signs of the zodiac are counted from the Vernal Point with each sign permanently allotted thirty degrees of the complete circle of the Ecliptic. Aries, the first sign, commences at 0° of celestial longitude—the Vernal Point, with the other signs each allocated a 30° span or one-twelfth of the Ecliptic circle. As the twelve tropical signs are fixed with reference to the Vernal Point, they are in motion because the Vernal Point is in motion (Precession of the Equinoxes). This 'Moving Zodiac' is in constant motion against the order of the zodiacal constellations, whereas the sidereal, starry zodiac is aligned to the fixed stars and is consequently non-moving and non-precessional.

When considering the relative merits of one system as compared with another, it is essential to understand what each represents. The term 'zodiacs' is misleading and confusing, for there is only one circle of the zodiac, and whether we call it 'tropical' or 'sidereal', will depend solely on the point from which it is measured. The *tropical cycle* is the cycle of the seasons, corresponding to the Sun's yearly return each March to the Vernal Equinox—the intersection of the Celestial Equator with the Ecliptic—which we call the First Point of Aries; and the solar monthly progress is measured through the signs along the Ecliptic in degrees of longitude. The *sidereal cycle* is that of the retrogression of the Vernal Point through the twelve zodiacal constellations (at present from Pisces to Aquarius) during an era of some 25,800 years. It is measured from a fixed reference point on the same ecliptic circle which locates the fixed star Spica (Alpha Virginis) permanently in 29° Virgo.

In about AD 221 'both zodiacs' coincided; i.e. the Vernal Point had retrogressed to the exact conjunction with its sidereal counterpart. However, owing to the continual shift of the Vernal Point in relation to the fixed stars, the difference between 0° Aries tropical and 0° Aries sidereal is now approximately 24°. This difference termed the *ayanamsa* by the sidereal advocates has to be subtracted from all tropical longitudes in order to convert to sidereal longitudes (see Calculations: Chapter 3). In subtracting this difference, the precession which has accrued since AD 221 is expunged from the tropical longitudes. The ayanamsa for a given date is found by subtracting the sidereal longitude of the Vernal Point for the same date from 360°. Tables to facilitate the conversion from tropical longitudes are available.

Many of the techniques utilized in sidereal astrology may, at first sight, appear rather involved and complicated. Basically, the computations needed to set up the various charts are not difficult, but the sidereal system has a wide terminology and uses a variety of charts, many of which, are based on solar and lunar returns of one kind or another.

The sidereal approach regarding interpretation of charts differs from the traditional tropical view, particularly in relation to natal charts. Aspects are considered according to the intrinsic nature of the planets involved, and mundane position (house position) varies in importance according to whether planets are angular (foreground) or enfeebled (background). Planetary significance and associated matters are discussed in Chapter 4.

Critics of astrology argue that it is a pseudo-science, because its advocates (or at least those who use the tropical zodiac) fail to take into account the phenomenon of precession. The argument is that 'astrology is not based on fact because the Vernal Equinox no longer corresponds with the constellation Aries, but has moved in relation to the stars'. Consequently, the division of the zodiac no longer coincides with the constellations, and although the Sun 'enters' Aries at the Vernal Equinox, it is in fact in the constellation Pisces. Whether this criticism has validity or not depends on which cycle is considered the more important. If the yearly solar cycle, which is seasonal, is considered to have greater significance, then the tropical or moving zodiac is more important. Likewise, the sidereal or fixed zodiac merits consideration if the precession of the Equinoctial Points is regarded as being significant.

Many of the methods associated with the sidereal techniques are, of course, applicable to the tropical system, and are not necessarily unique to the sidereal system. Researchers need to approach astrology and its symbolism with an open-minded awareness and in the true spirit of enquiry. The tropical and sidereal techniques regarding return charts both require unbiased investigation. It seems illogical to state, as some do, that because one method 'works' fairly well, all other methods must be wrong. Whatever astrological symbolism is adopted, it has to portray life and all that life encompasses in a realistic and timely manner. Life is experienced at many levels and in a variety of ways and this interaction can be related to, and expressed by, various kinds of astrological patterns and techniques.

As we study astrology and its workings in relation to life experiences, we realize that nothing exists in isolation and that we are part of the greater whole.

2.
TYPES OF RETURNS
MAJOR AND SUPPLEMENTARY

Return charts can be divided into two main categories: (a) those that can be classified as major; (b) those that are derived from the major returns and are based upon factors connected with the major returns.

The principal return is the solar return, which is a chart computed for the date and exact time when the Sun returns to the exact natal longitude that it held at birth. The other major return is the lunar return, which is computed for the date and time when the Moon returns to the same natal longitude that it held at birth. These two returns, one yearly (solar) and the other monthly (lunar) are based on the natal position of the Sun and Moon.

In addition to these two principal factors, Sun and Moon, we can extend the solar return to obtain the demi-solar return, which is a chart cast for the date and time during the solar return year when the transiting Sun reaches its natal opposition point, approximately six months subsequent to the date of the solar return. A further series of charts can also be obtained by taking the date and time when the transiting Sun is 90° (square) its radical place. The term used by siderealists for this type of chart is quarti-solar.

The solar Moon (the Moon's position in the solar return) can also be used for two kinds of returns: (a) the *anlunar*, which is a lunar return computed for each month that the solar Moon transits the longitude that it held in the solar return, (b) the *kinetic lunar return*, which is based on the solar Moon's progressed position.

Lunar returns based on the Moon's natal position can also be supplemented with *demi-lunar* returns and *quarti-lunar* returns. These returns are cast for the time when the Moon reaches the opposition (demi) or square (quarti) of its natal position. So, in addition to the two principal return charts based on the radical

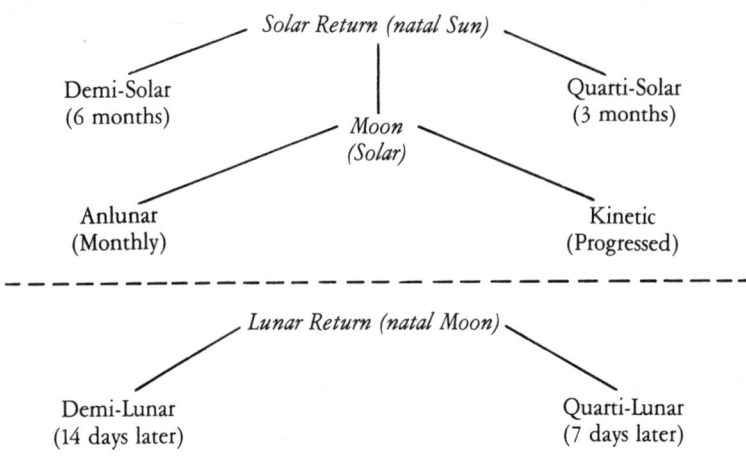

position of the Sun and Moon, we have several subsidiary returns which are 'offshoots' of the two main returns:

All these return charts are applicable to the person, based as they are upon the individual natal chart. With mundane astrology other techniques are used and these along with the appropriate calculations are shown in Chapter 7.

The advocates of the sidereal system also use the 'secondary' or 'day for a year' system similar to that used by those who favour the tropical zodiac. There is, however, an important difference in that the siderealists allow for the daily progression of the angles and not merely for the advance of the MC by approximately one degree per day-year. This technique, termed *natal quotidian* is the same as the ordinary secondary progressions as used by tropicalists. The calculation of these quotidians (discussed in Chapter 3) differs from the normal method used by tropicalists, but the technique is not a special sidereal one and can be used by tropical astrologers.

The *solar quotidian* is a chart based on the difference of the *Mean Sun* for the date and time of an event and the date and time of the solar return. *Converse returns* are, as the term implies, charts based upon the natal data and calculated for a date and time prior to the birthdate. These returns often prove as effective as those computed in the usual manner, i.e. direct. A few examples of some of these returns and the method of calculation are given in Chapter 3.

Although some of the techniques associated with return charts may at first sight appear difficult, a little practice will soon confirm that any effort expended on return charts is well worth while. Even without modern calculating aids, most of the charts can be erected without too much labour, although if many charts are to be studied, then a computer program or a calculator would be an asset.

A criticism can, of course, be made that if one uses enough charts and a multiplicity of directions, aspects and involved figuring, one is almost certain to find some form of appropriate correlation for a particular period, event or condition. However, experience with the various return techniques indicates that the subsidiary charts require to be compared with their 'parent' chart as well as the natal chart. Even though different return charts for a given period may show conflicting indications, it is often noted that their significance can be related to different levels of experience. As with most planetary action in relation to personal charts, there will be the psychological undercurrents governing the attitudes, moods and responses and these will reflect the planetary action operating at the time. This being so, one type of return may appear passive in so far as definite actions or events are concerned and be indicative of psychological changes, whereas another return covering the same period of time will manifest in an active, vigorous manner. Even though separate return charts covering the same period may show a wide divergence regarding their probable effects, there is really no contradiction, for both are functioning in the manner appropriate to the current planetary pattern. One may be motivated to act in a certain manner, compelled as it were, by some inner force and at the same time be confronted by environmental factors over which one has little or no control.

The personal return charts are admirable for the way they 'highlight' a definite period. Prominent aspects, configurations and patterns in return charts always indicate important experiences in accordance with the charts as a whole. It is not always easy to ascertain whether the planetary indications will 'act' decisively in the form of events or whether their action will be 'low key', mainly affecting the feelings and moods without any significant outer impact. Sometimes, of course, there is a combination of both 'inner and outer' in that psychological conditions impel action of one kind or another, the results of which may have far-reaching consequences.

Although astrology is not solely concerned with what has been termed 'event-orientated astrology', there has been a tendency in recent years to go to extremes and relate all astrological principles to some form of psychological manifestation. All well and good provided the correlation is viewed realistically and not in some vague abstract way. The study of a person's life in relationship to the events and happenings which have occurred will often prove extremely valuable. By comparing patterns at the time, or during a period, with actual events and conditions, we are able to confirm or to deny many of astrology's traditional tenets.

One needs to 'think' astrology and to approach all its techniques with an open mind, with the realization that we have as yet, scratched only the surface of astrological science. For the newcomer to return techniques it is probably advisable to make haste slowly; otherwise there is a danger of becoming 'swamped' with a multiplicity of charts, figures and symbols. If attention is concentrated on the solar return chart and its progressions in conjunction with the monthly lunar returns, this will form a sound base for branching out into other areas of return techniques. Although each return chart has its own individual significance and can be studied independently, it has to be related to its 'parent or master' chart. For example, the solar and lunar returns to the natal chart; the kinetic chart to the appropriate return of which it is a derivative and also to the actual natal chart. Although there may be, at first sight, many apparently contradictory indications in various charts covering the same period, it is often found that there is a subtle interaction of influences which, although operating at different levels, coincide with the life experiences at that period.

The only way to test return charts is through empirical study. Bearing in mind that 'one swallow does not make a summer' we can, provided we study enough cases, form some indication of whether the return techniques have validity and also by implication the truth of astrological symbolism.

3.

CALCULATIONS (1)
THE TROPICAL ZODIAC

The solar return chart is cast for the exact moment when the Sun each year returns to its birth longitude. This occurs on or close to the birthday. As the Sun moves approximately one minute of arc in about twenty-four minutes of time, its position requires to be calculated accurately, using either a calculating device, logarithms or apportionment tables. The log tables given in Raphael's ephemerides and elsewhere (diurnal proportional logarithms) are not sufficiently accurate for finding the Sun's position accurate to seconds. If logs are used, then Ternary and Diurnal tables are necessary. The use of logs is quite simple and merely involves simple addition or subtraction. The easiest method is, however, to use a calculator which incorporates a sexagesimal function.

The initial procedure prior to computing any kind of solar or lunar return is to ascertain the exact natal longitude of the Sun to the nearest second, and in the case of lunars, the Moon's position to the nearest minute. Normally, a natal chart shows the Sun's position to the nearest minute of longitude, but this is insufficient for solar returns, which must be calculated to the nearest second.

The following examples are given in some detail in order that the 'mechanics' of the calculations can be understood and that reference to the data can be made when dealing with the various return charts. All the data are as given personally or from official records and no attempt has been made to rectify or adjust in any way the birthtimes as quoted.

Example No. 1:
Required: the Sun's natal longitude.
Birth data: 9.05 UT (GMT) 12.6.1929, 51.31N 0.20W.

Working:

	D	M	S	
Sun's long. noon 12.6.29	21	00	39	Gemini
Sun's long. noon 11.6.29 less	20	03	18	
(a) Sun's daily motion (24 hours)	00	57	21	

	H	M	S	
Birthtime	9	05	00	UT
(b) Time to noon (12.6.29)	2	55	00	

Using calculator:

$$(2.55.00) = \frac{2.916 \times 0.9558}{24} (57' \ 21'') = 0.116 = \underline{6' \ 58''}$$

Noon position 12.6.29	21°	00' 39"
Less	00	06 58
Sun's natal longitude	20	53 41 Gemini.

Using logs:

	D	M	S	Log	
Sun's motion 11/12 June 1929	0	57	21	.49674	Ternary
Interval to noon	2	55	00 +	.91533	Diurnal
Motion during interval	0	06	58	1.41207	Ternary

6 min. 58 sec. deducted from noon position 21° 00' 39"
= Sun's natal longitude   20 53 41

Example No.1a:
Find the Ascendant and MC for Example No.1.

Working:

	H	M	S
Sidereal time (ST) 0 hr UT 12.6.29	17	19	20
Time elapsed	+ 9	05	00
Mean time correction (9.86 sec. per hour)	+ 0	01	29
ST at Greenwich	2	25	49
Longitude Equiv. (West)	− 0	01	20
RAMC (ST at birth)	2	24	29

Asc. 22° Leo: MC 8° Taurus

Using a noon-based ephemeris:

	H	M	S
ST at noon 12.6.29		5	21	18
Interval to noon	−	2	55	00
Correction (9.86 sec. per hour)	−	0	00	29
Longitude Equiv. (West)	−	0	01	20
RAMC		2	24	29

Example No.2:
Required: The Sun's natal longitude.
Birth data: 11.50 UT 29.8.1928, 48.47N. 9.11E.

Working:

		D	M	S	
Sun's long. noon 29.8.28		5	52	35	Virgo
Sun's long. noon 28.8.28	less	4	54	37	
(a) Sun's daily motion (24 hours)		0	57	58	

	H	M	S	
Birthtime	11	50	00	UT
(b) Time to noon (29.8.28)	00	10	00	

Calculator:

$$(0.10) = \frac{0.166 \times 0.966}{24} \ (57' \ 58'') = 0.0066 = \underline{24 \text{ sec.}}$$

Noon position 29.8.28	5° 52′ 35″
Less	0 00 24
Sun's natal longitude	5 52 11 Virgo

Using logs:

	D	M	S	Log	
Sun's motion 28/29 Aug. 1928	0	57	58	0.49209	Ternary
Interval to noon	0	10	00	+ 2.15836	Diurnal
Motion during interval	0	00	24	2.65045	Ternary

24 sec. deducted from noon position	5° 52′ 35″
= Sun's natal longitude	5 52 11

Example No.2a:
Find the Ascendant and MC for Example No.2.

Working:

	H	M	S
ST 0 hr UT 29.8.28	22	27	48
Time elapsed	+ 11	50	00
Correction	+ 00	01	57
ST at Greenwich	10	19	45
Longitude Equiv. (East)	+ 00	36	44
RAMC	10	56	29

Asc. 24 Scorpio: MC 13 Virgo

Using a noon-based ephemeris:

	H	M	S
ST at noon 29.8.28	10	29	46
Interval to noon	− 00	10	00
Correction	− 00	00	01
ST at Greenwich	10	19	45
Longitude Equiv. (East)	+ 00	36	44
RAMC	10	56	29

Example No.3:
Required: the Sun's natal longitude.
Birth data: 9.08 UT 28.6.1925, 51.10N 7.04E

Working:

	D	M	S	
Sun's long. noon 28.6.25	6	14	49	Cancer
Sun's long. noon 27.6.25	5	17	36	
(a) Sun's daily motion (24 hours)	0	57	13	

	H	M	S
Birthtime	9	08	00
(b) Time to noon	2	52	00

Calculator:

$$(2.52) = \frac{2.866 \times 0.954}{24} \ (57' \ 13'') = 0.114 = \underline{6' \ 50''}$$

Noon position 28.6.25		6° 14′ 49″
Less		0 06 50
Sun's natal longitude		6 07 59 Cancer

Using logs:

	D	M	S	Log	
Sun's motion 27/28 June 1925	0	57	13	.49775	Ternary
Interval to noon	2	52	00 +	.92284	Diurnal
Motion during interval	0	06	50	1.42059	Ternary

6 min. 50 sec. deducted from noon position		6° 14′ 49″
= Sun's natal longitude		6 07 59

Example No.3a:
Find the Ascendant and MC for Example No.3.

Working:

	H	M	S
ST 0 hr. UT 28.6.25	18	22	17
Time elapsed	+ 9	08	00
Correction	+ 0	01	30
ST at Greenwich	3	31	47
Longitude Equiv. (East)	+ 0	28	16
RAMC	4	00	03

Asc. 9° Virgo: MC 2° Gemini

Using a noon-based ephemeris:

	H	M	S
ST at noon 28.6.25	6	24	15
Interval to noon	− 2	52	00
Correction	− 0	00	28
ST at Greenwich	3	31	47
Longitude Equiv. (East)	+ 0	28	16
RAMC	4	00	03

Example No.4:
Required: the Sun's natal longitude.
Birth data: 06.45 UT 23.3.1899, 51.10N 7.04E.

Working:

	D	M	S
Sun's long. noon 23.3.1899	2	39	15
Sun's long. noon 22.3.1899	1	39	47
(a) Sun's daily motion (24 hours)	0	59	28

	H	M	S
Birthtime	6	45	00
(b) Time to noon	5	15	00

Calculator:

$$(5.15) = \frac{5.25 \times 0.991}{24} (59' \ 28'') = 0.217 = \underline{13'}$$

Noon position 23.3.1899	2° 39′ 15″	
Less	0 13 00	
Sun's natal longitude	2 26 15	Aries

Using logs:

	D	M	S	Log	
Sun's motion 22/23 March 1899	0	59	28	.48100	Ternary
Interval to noon	5	15	00 +	.66005	Diurnal
Motion during interval	0	13	00	1.14105	Ternary

13 min. deducted from noon position	2° 39′ 15″
= Sun's natal longitude	2 26 15

Example No.4a:
Find the Ascendant and MC for Example No.4.

Working:

		H	M	S
ST 0 hr. UT 23.3.1899		12	01	04
Time elapsed	+	6	45	00
Correction	+	0	01	06
ST at Greenwich		18	47	10
Longitude Equiv. (East)	+	0	28	16
RAMC		19	15	26

Asc. 11 Taurus: MC 17 Capricorn

Using a noon-based ephemeris:

	H	M	S
ST at noon 23.3.1899	0	03	02
Interval to noon	− 5	15	00
Correction	− 0	00	52
ST at Greenwich	18	47	10
Longitude Equiv. (East)	+ 0	28	16
RAMC	19	15	26

Example No.5: H.M. Queen Elizabeth II
Required: the Sun's natal longitude.
Birth data: 1.40 UT 21.4.1926, Bruton St, London W1. 51.30N 0.08W.

Working:

	D	M	S	
Sun's long. noon 21.4.26	0	37	33	Taurus
Sun's long. noon 20.4.26	29	39	01	Aries
(a) Sun's daily motion (24 hours)	0	58	32	

	H	M	S
Birthtime	1	40	00
(b) Time to noon	10	20	00

Calculator:

$$(10.20) = \frac{10.333 \times 0.975}{24} \ (58' \ 32'') = 0.420 = \underline{25' \ 12''}$$

Noon position 21.4.26	0° 37′ 33″
Less	0 25 12
Sun's natal longitude	0 12 21 Taurus

Using logs:

	D	M	S	Log	
Sun's motion 20/21 April 1926	0	58	32	.48787	Ternary
Interval to noon	10	20	00	+ .36597	Diurnal
Motion during interval	0	25	12	.85384	Ternary

25 mins. 12 secs. deducted from noon position	0° 37′ 33″
= Sun's natal longitude	0 12 21

Example No.5a:
Find the Ascendant and MC for Example No.5.

Working:

	H	M	S
ST 0 hours UT 21.4.26	13	53	14
Time elapsed	+ 01	40	00
Correction	+ 00	00	16
ST at Greenwich	15	33	30
Longitude Equiv. (West)	− 0	00	32
RAMC	15	32	58

<u>Asc. 21 Capricorn: MC 25 Scorpio</u>

Using a noon-based ephemeris:

	H	M	S
ST at noon 21.4.26	01	55	12
Interval to noon	− 10	20	00
Correction	− 00	01	42
ST at Greenwich	15	33	30
Longitude Equiv. (West)	− 0	00	32
RAMC	15	32	58

Example No.6: HRH The Duke of York
Required: the Sun's natal longitude.
Birth data: 15.30 UT 19.2.1960, Buckingham Palace, 51.30N 0.08W.

Working:

	D	M	S	
Sun's long. noon 20.2.60	0	51	49	Pisces
Sun's long. noon 19.2.60	29	51	20	Aquarius
(a) Sun's daily motion (24 hours)	1	00	29	

	H	M	S
Birthtime	15	30	00
(b) Time after noon	3	30	00

Calculator:

$$(3.30) = \frac{3.5 \times 1.008}{24} (60'\ 29'') = 0.147 = \underline{8'\ 49''}$$

Noon position 19.2.60		29° 51′ 20″	
Add		00 08 49	
Sun's natal longitude		00 00 09 Pisces	

Using logs:

	D	M	S		Log	
Sun's motion 19/20 Feb. 1960	1	00	29		.47364	Ternary
Interval from noon	3	30	00	+	.83614	Diurnal
Motion during interval	0	08	49		1.30978	Ternary

8 min. 49 sec. added to noon position	29° 51′ 20″
= Sun's natal longitude	00 00 09 Pisces

Example No.6a:
Find the Ascendant and MC for Example No.6.

Working:

	H	M	S
ST at 0 hours UT 19.2.60		9	51	50
Time elapsed	+	15	30	00
Correction	+	00	02	33
ST at Greenwich		01	24	23
Longitude Equiv. (West)	−	00	00	32
RAMC		01	23	51

Asc. 11 Leo: MC 23 Aries

Using a noon-based ephemeris:

	H	M	S
ST at noon 19.2.60		21	53	48
Interval from noon	+	03	30	00
Correction	+	00	00	35
ST at Greenwich		01	24	23
Longitude Equiv. (West)	−	00	00	32
RAMC		01	23	51

Example No.7: HRH The Duchess of York
Required: the Sun's natal longitude.
Birth data: 9.03 UT 15.10.1959, London W1 51.31N 0.09W.

Working:

	D	M	S	
Sun's long. noon 15.10.59	21	22	56	Libra
Sun's long. noon 14.10.59	20	23	29	
(a) Sun's daily motion (24 hours)	00	59	27	

	H	M	S
Birthtime	9	03	00
(b) Time to noon	2	57	00

Calculator:

$$(2.57) = \frac{2.95 \times 0.991}{24} (59' \ 27'') = 0.122 = \underline{7' \ 18''}$$

Noon position 15.10.59	21° 22' 56"
Less	00 07 18
Sun's natal longitude	21 15 38 Libra

Using logs:

	D	M	S	Log	
Sun's motion 14/15 October 1959	00	59	27	.48112	Ternary
Interval to noon	02	57	00 +	.91039	Diurnal
Motion during interval	00	07	18	1.39151	Ternary

7 min. 18 sec. deducted from noon position	21° 22' 56"
= Sun's natal longitude	21 15 38

Example No.7a:
Find the Ascendant and MC for Example No.7.

Working:

		H	M	S
ST at 0 hr. UT 15.10.59		1	31	07
Time elapsed	+	9	03	00
Correction	+	0	01	29
ST at Greenwich		10	35	36
Longitude Equiv. (West)	−	00	00	36
RAMC		10	35	00

Asc. 18 Scorpio: MC 7 Virgo

Using a noon-based ephemeris:

	H	M	S
ST at noon 15.10.59	13	33	05
Interval to noon	− 2	57	00
Correction	− 0	00	29
ST at Greenwich	10	35	36
Longitude Equiv. (West)	− 0	00	36
RAMC	10	35	00

The foregoing examples of how to calculate the natal Sun's position with an accuracy required for solar return charts, have been given in detail, as these data will be used to illustrate some of the case histories in Chapter 6. In the use of logs, degrees and hours are synonymous and therefore the time interval of the calculation has been listed under degrees, minutes and seconds (DMS).

In addition to the Examples 1–7 given in detail, the following examples are listed without detailed calculations, but the procedure for finding the Sun's longitude, Ascendant and MC is the same for all natal charts.

Example No.8
Birth data: 20.22 UT 21.8.1930, 56.57N 3.0W.
Sun 28° 01′ 43″ Leo. Asc. 6 Aries: MC 2 Capricorn.

Example No.9
Birth data: 23.07 UT 2.6.1953, 34.21N 119.04W.
Sun 12° 04′ 56″ Gemini: Asc. 24 Libra: MC 27 Cancer.

Example No.10
Birth data: 04.00 UT 17.10.1949, 34.09N 118.09W.
Sun 23° 26′ 57″ Libra: Asc. 15 Gemini: MC 25 Aquarius.

Example No.11
Birth data: 09.00 UT 11.5.1953, 51.37N 0.17W.
Sun 20° 21′ 53″ Taurus: Asc. 29 Cancer: MC 4 Aries.

Example No.12
Birth data: 23.10 UT 4.3.1956, 51.30N 0.08W.
Sun 14° 21′ 50″ Pisces: Asc. 12 Scorpio: MC 28 Leo.

Calculation of the Solar Return Chart (Tropical Zodiac)
The date and time of the Tropical Solar Return (TSR) will always differ from the Sidereal Solar Return (SSR) and the reasons for this

will be explained later when sidereal solar return charts are considered. At this stage we need to understand the calculation procedures for setting up the usual tropical returns. The Sun returns to the longitude that it held at birth on or near to the birthdate each year. The following examples, using different methods, illustrate how the date and time of the return is determined.

Example No.1:
Find the date and time of the solar return for 1973/74:
Birth data: 9.05 UT 12.6.29, London.
Natal Sun 20° 53′ 41″ Gemini.

Working:

From the 1973 ephemeris:	D	M	S	
Sun's long. 12.6.73	21	22	11	Gemini
Sun's long. 11.6.73	20	24	52	
Suns motion in 24 hours	0	57	19	
Sun's natal long.	20	53	41	
Sun's long. noon 11.6.73	20	24	52	
Difference	0	28	49	

$$
\begin{array}{lcl}
57'\ 19'' & = & 24\ \text{hours} \\
28\ \ 49 & = & \dfrac{0.4802 \times 24}{} \\
57\ \ 19 & = & 0.9553
\end{array}
$$

= 12.04 after noon on 11 June = <u>0.04 UT 12.6.73</u> = 1973/74 <u>solar return.</u>

Using logs:

	D	M	S	Log
Sun's motion 11/12 June 1973	0	57	19	.49699 Ternary
Difference	0	28	49	.79563 Ternary

		Log	
Then log of difference		0.79563	Ternary log
less log of motion		0.49699	Ternary log
= Time of return		0.29864	Diurnal log

= 12.04 = <u>0.04 UT 12.6.73</u>

Example No.1a:
Using same birth data, find the date and time of the solar return for 1979/80.

Working:

	D	M	S	
1979 Ephemeris				
Sun's long. 12.6.79	20	55	54	Gemini
Sun's long. 11.6.79	19	58	34	
Sun's motion in 24 hours	0	57	20	
Sun's natal long.	20	53	41	
Sun's long. noon 12.6.79	20	55	54	
Difference	0	02	13	

Therefore $\begin{matrix} (2'\ 13'') \\ (57'\ 20'') \end{matrix}$ $\dfrac{0.037 \times 24}{0.955} = 0.9279 = \underline{56'}$

12.00 less 56 min. = 11.04 UT 12.6.79 = date and time of 1979/80
solar return.

Using logs:

	D	M	S	Log	
Sun's motion 11/12.6.79	0	57	20	0.49687	Ternary
Difference	0	02	13	1.90957	Ternary
Then log of difference			1.90957	Ternary log	
less log of motion			0.49687	Ternary log	
Time of return			1.41270	Diurnal log	

= 56 mins. before noon 12.6.79 = 11.04 UT = date and time of
1979/80 solar return.

Example No.1b:
Using same birth data, find the date and time of the solar return
for 1967/68.

Working:

	D	M	S	
1967 Ephemeris				
Sun's long. 13.6.67	21	47	29	Gemini
Sun's long. 12.6.67	20	50	08	
Sun's motion in 24 hours	00	57	21	
Sun's natal long.	20	53	41	
Sun's long. noon 12.6.67	20	50	08	
Difference	00	03	33	

Therefore $(3'\ 33'')$ $\dfrac{0.059 \times 24}{0.9558}$ = 1.4856 = 1.29 =
$(57'\ 21'')$

1 hr. 29 min. after noon on 12.6.67 = date and time of the solar return 13.29 UT 12.6.67

Example No.2:
Find the date and time of the solar return for 1949/50.
Birth data: 11.50 UT 29.8.28, 48.47N 9.11E.
Natal Sun 5° 52′ 11″ Virgo.

Working:

From the 1949 ephemeris	D	M	S	
Sun's long. 30.8.49	6	46	07	Virgo
Sun's long. 29.8.49	5	48	06	
Sun's motion in 24 hours	0	58	01	
Sun's natal long.	5	52	11	
Sun's long. noon 29.8.49	5	48	06	
Difference	0	04	05	

$$
\begin{aligned}
58'\ 01'' &= 24 \text{ hours} \\
04\ \ 05 &= \qquad \frac{0.068 \times 24}{} \\
58\ \ 01 &= \qquad\quad 0.967
\end{aligned}
$$

= 1.689 = 1 hr. 41 min. after noon on the 29.8.49. Solar return occurred at 13.41 UT 29.8.49

Using logs:

	D	M	S	Log
Sun's motion 29/30.8.49	0	58	01	.49172 Ternary
Difference	0	04	05	1.64426 Ternary
Then log of difference			1.64426	Ternary log
less log of motion			0.49172	Ternary log
= Time of return			1.15254	Diurnal log

= 1.41 = 13.41 UT 29.8.49

Example No.2a:
Using same birth data find the date and time of the solar return for 1952/53.

Working:

1952 Ephemeris	D	M	S	
Sun's long. 29.8.52	6	04	20	Virgo
Sun's long. 28.8.52	5	06	21	
Sun's motion in 24 hours	0	57	59	
Sun's natal long.	5	52	11	
Sun's long. noon 29.8.49	6	04	20	
Difference	0	12	09	

57' 59"	= 24 hours	
12 09	=	0.2025×24
57 59	=	0.9663

= 5.029 = 5.02 before noon on the 29.8.52 =
06.58 UT 29.8.52 = date and time of the solar return for 1952/53

Using logs:

	D	M	S	Log	
Sun's motion 28/29.8.52	0	57	59	.49197	Ternary
Difference	0	12	09	1.17070	Ternary
Then log of difference				1.17070	Ternary log
less log of motion				0.49197	Ternary log
= Time of return				0.67873	Diurnal log

= 5.02 before noon = 06.58 UT 29.8.52

Example No.2b:
Using same birth data: find the date and time of the 1955/56 solar return.

Working:

1955 Ephemeris	D	M	S	
Sun's long. 30.8.55	6	20	32	Virgo
Sun's long. 29.8.55	5	22	33	
Sun's motion in 24 hours	0	57	59	
Sun's natal long.	5	52	11	
Sun's long. noon 29.8.55	5	22	33	
Difference	0	29	38	

$$\begin{array}{llll} 57' & 59'' & = 24 \text{ hours}\cdot \\ 29 & 38 & = & 0.4939 \times 24 \\ 57 & 59 & = & \overline{0.9663} \end{array}$$

= 12.265 = 12.16 = 00.16 UT 30.8.55 = date and time of the solar return 1955/56

Using logs:

	D	M	S	Log
Sun's motion 29/30.8.55	0	57	59	.49197 Ternary
Difference	0	29	38	.78349 Ternary
Then log of difference			0.78349	Ternary log
less log of motion			0.49197	Ternary log
= Time of return			0.29152	Diurnal

= 12.16 = 00.16 UT 30.8.55 = date and time of the solar return 1955/56.

Example No.3:
Find the date and time of the solar return for 1951/52.
Birth data: 09.08 UT 28.6.1925, 51.10N 7.04E.
Natal Sun 6° 07′ 59″ Cancer.

Working:

1951 Ephemeris	D	M	S	
Sun's long. 29.6.51	6	56	14	Cancer
Sun's long. 28.6.51	5	59	01	
Sun's motion in 24 hours	0	57	13	
Sun's natal long.	6	07	59	
Sun's long noon 28.6.51	5	59	01	
Difference	0	08	58	

$$\begin{array}{llll} 57' & 13'' & = 24 \text{ hours} \\ 08 & 58 & = & 0.1494 \times 24 \\ 57 & 13 & = & \overline{0.9536} \end{array}$$

= 3.761 = 3.46 after noon = 15.46 UT 28.6.1951 = date and time of the 1951/52 solar return.

Using logs:

	D	M	S	Log
Sun's motion 28/29.6.51	0	57	13	0.49775 Ternary
Difference	0	08	58	1.30264 Ternary

Then log of difference	1.30264	Ternary log
less log of motion	0.49775	Ternary log
= Time of return	0.80489	Diurnal log

= 3.46 after noon = 15.46 UT 28.6.51

Example No.3a:
Using same birth data: find the date and time of the 1954/55 solar return.

Working:

1954 Ephemeris	D	M	S
Sun's long. 28.6.54	6	14	40 Cancer
Sun's long. 27.6.54	5	17	26
Sun's motion in 24 hours	0	57	14
Sun's natal long.	6	07	59
Sun's long. noon 28.6.54	6	14	40
Difference	0	06	41

$$57'\ 14'' = 24 \text{ hours}$$
$$06\ 41 = \underline{0.111 \times 24}$$
$$57\ 14 = 0.954$$

= 2.802 = 2.48 before noon 28.6.54. = 09.12 UT 28.6.54 = date and time of 1954/55 solar return.

Using logs:

	D	M	S	Log
Sun's motion 27/28.6.54	0	57	14	0.49762 Ternary
Difference	0	06	41	1.43028 Ternary

Then log of difference	1.43028	Ternary log
less log of motion	0.49762	Ternary log
= Time of return	0.93266	Diurnal log

= 2.48 before noon on the 28.6.54 = 09.12 UT 28.6.54.

Example No.4:
Find the date and time of the solar return for 1922/23.
Birth data: 06.45 UT 23.3.1899, 51.10N 7.04E.
Natal Sun 2° 26′ 15″ Aries.

Working:

1922 Ephemeris	D	M	S
Sun's long. 24.3.22	03	03	59 Aries
Sun's long. 23.3.22	02	04	30
Sun's motion in 24 hours	00	59	29
Sun's natal long.	02	26	15
Sun's long. noon 23.3.22	02	04	30
Difference	00	21	45

$$
\begin{array}{lll}
59'\ 29'' & = & 24 \text{ hours} \\
21\ \ 45 & = & \underline{0.3625 \times 24} \\
59\ \ 29 & = & 0.9914
\end{array}
$$

= 8.46 after noon on the 23.3.22
= 20.46 UT 23.3.1922 = date and time of the 1922/23 solar return.

Using logs:

	D	M	S	Log	
Sun's motion 23/24.3.22	0	59	29	0.48088	Ternary
Difference	0	21	45	0.91781	Ternary

Then log of difference			0.91781	Ternary
less log of motion			0.48088	Ternary
= Time of return			0.43693	Diurnal

= 20.46 UT 23.3.1922

Example No.5:
Find the date and time of the solar return for 1951/52.
Birth data: 01.40 UT 21.4.1926, 51.30N 0.08W.
Natal Sun 0° 12′ 21″ Taurus.

Working:

1951 Ephemeris	D	M	S	
Sun's long. 21.4.51	00	34	38	Taurus
Sun's long. 20.4.51	29	36	06	Aries
Sun's motion in 24 hours	00	58	32	
Sun's natal long.	00	12	21	Taurus
Sun's long. noon 20.4.51	29	36	06	Aries
Difference	00	36	15	

$$58' \ 32'' \quad = 24 \text{ hours}$$
$$36 \quad 15 \quad = \quad \frac{0.6042 \times 24}{}$$
$$58 \quad 32 \quad = \quad 0.9755$$

= 14.863 = 14.52 after noon on the 20.4.51
= 02.52 UT 21.4.51 = date and time of the 1951/52 solar return.

Using logs:

	D	M	S	Log	
Sun's motion 20/21.4.51	0	58	32	.48787	Ternary
Difference	0	36	15	.69596	Ternary
Then log of difference				0.69596	Ternary log
less log of motion				0.48787	Ternary log
= Time of return				0.20809	Diurnal

= 14.52 after noon on the 20.4.51 = 02.52 UT 21.4.51.

Example No.5a:

Using the same birth data find the date and time of the solar return for 1952/53.

Working:

1952 Ephemeris	D	M	S	
Sun's long. 20.4.52	00	20	28	Taurus
Sun's long. 19.4.52	29	21	54	Aries
Sun's motion in 24 hours	00	58	34	
Sun's natal long.	00	12	21	
Sun's long. noon 20.4.52	00	20	28	
Difference	00	08	07	

58' 34"   = 24 hours

08 07   = $\dfrac{0.1353 \times 24}{0.976}$

58 34   =

= 3.326 = 3.20 before noon on the 20.4.52
= 08.40 UT 20.4.52 = date and time of the 1952/53 solar return.

Using logs:

	D	M	S	Log
Sun's motion 19/20.4.52	00	58	34	.48762 Ternary
Difference	00	08	07	1.34589 Ternary

Then log of difference	1.34589	Ternary log
less log of motion	0.48762	Ternary log
Time of return	0.85827	Diurnal log

= 3.20 before noon on the 20.4.52 = 08.40 UT 20.4.52

Example No.5b:
Using same birth data find the date and time of the solar return for 1947/48.

Working:

1947 Ephemeris	D	M	S	
Sun's long. 21.4.47	00	32	34	Taurus
Sun's long. 20.4.47	29	33	59	Aries
Sun's motion in 24 hours	00	58	35	
Sun's natal long.	00	12	21	Taurus
Sun's long. noon 21.4.47	0	32	34	
Difference	00	20	13	

58' 35"   = 24 hours

20 13   = $\dfrac{0.3369 \times 24}{0.976}$

58 35   =

= 8.2822 = 8.17 before noon on the 21.4.47
= 03.43 UT 21.4.47 = date and time of the 1947/48 solar return.

Using logs:

	D	M	S	Log
Sun's motion 20/21.4.47	00	58	35	.48750 Ternary
Difference	00	20	13	.94956 Ternary

Then log of difference	0.94956	Ternary log
less log of motion	0.48750	Ternary log
Time of return	0.46206	Diurnal log

= 8.17 before noon on the 21.4.47. = 03.43 UT 21.4.47

Example No.5c:
Using the same birth data, find the date and time of the solar return for 1948/49.

Working:

1948 Ephemeris	D	M	S	
Sun's long. 20.4.48	00	18	30	Taurus
Sun's long. 19.4.48	29	19	58	Aries
Sun's motion in 24 hours	00	58	32	
Sun's natal long.	00	12	21	Taurus
Sun's long. noon 20.4.48	00	18	30	
Difference	00	06	09	

$$
\begin{array}{ll}
58'\ 32'' = 24\ \text{hours} \\
06\ \ 09\ = & 0.1025 \times 24 \\
58\ \ 32\ = & 0.976
\end{array}
$$

= 2.522 = 2.31 before noon on the 20.4.48
= 09.29 UT 20.4.48 = date and time of the 1948/49 solar return.

Using logs:

	D	M	S	Log	
Sun's motion 19/20.4.48	00	58	32	.48787	Ternary
Difference	00	06	09	1.46640	Ternary

Then log of difference	1.46640	Ternary log
less log of motion	0.48787	Ternary log
Time of return	0.97853	Diurnal log

= 2.31 before noon on the 20:4.48 = 09.29 UT 20.4.48

Example No.6:
Find the date and time of the solar return for 1986/87.
Birth data: 15.30 UT 19.2.1960, 51.30N 0.08W.
Natal Sun 00° 00′ 09″ Pisces.

Working:

1986 Ephemeris	D	M	S	
Sun's long. 19.2.86	00	32	52	Pisces
Sun's long. 18.2.86	29	32	21	Aquarius
Sun's motion in 24 hours	01	00	31	
Sun's natal long.	00	00	09	Pisces
Sun's long. noon 18.2.86	29	32	21	Aquarius
Difference	00	27	48	

$$
\begin{array}{rcl}
60' \ 31'' & = & 24 \text{ hours} \\
27 \ \ 48 & = & 0.4633 \times 24 \\
60 \ \ 31 & = & 1.0086
\end{array}
$$

= 11.025 = 11.02 after noon on the 18.2.86 = 23.02 UT 18.2.86

= date and time of the 1986/87 solar return.

Using logs:

	D	M	S	Log	
Sun's motion 18/19.2.86	01	00	31	.47340	Ternary
Difference	00	27	48	.81123	Ternary

Then log of difference	0.81123	Ternary log
less log of motion	0.47340	Ternary log
= Time of return	0.33783	Diurnal

= 11.02 after noon = 23.02 UT 18.2.86

Example No.7:
Find the date and time of the solar return for 1985/86.
Birth data: 09.03 UT 15.10.59, 51.31N 0.09W.
Natal Sun 21° 15′ 38″ Libra.

Working:

1985 Ephemeris	D	M	S	
Sun's long. 15.10.85	22	04	33	Libra
Sun's long. 14.10.85	21	05	03	
Sun's motion in 24 hours	00	59	30	
Sun's natal long.	21	15	38	
Sun's long. noon 14.10.85	21	05	03	
Difference	00	10	35	

```
59' 30"     = 24 hours
10   35     =                    0.1764 × 24
59   30     =                    0.9916
```

= 4.269 = 4.16 = 16.16 UT 14.10.85 = date and time of the 1985/86 solar return.

Using logs:

	D	M	S	Log
Sun's motion 14/15.10.85	00	59	30	0.48076 Ternary
Difference	00	10	35	1.23065 Ternary

Then log of difference	1.23065	Ternary log
less log of motion	0.48076	Ternary log
= Time of return	0.74989	Diurnal log

= 4.16 after noon = 16.16 UT 14.10.85

Example No.8:
Find the date and time of the solar return for 1959/60.
Birth data: 20.22. UT 21.8.1930, 56.57N 3.0W.
Natal Sun 28° 01′ 43″ Leo.

Working:

1959 Ephemeris	D	M	S	
Sun's long. 22.8.59	28	38	46	Leo
Sun's long. 21.8.59	27	41	00	Leo
Sun's motion in 24 hours	00	57	46	
Sun's natal long.	28	01	43	
Sun's long. noon 21.8.58	27	41	00	
Difference	00	20	43	

```
57' 46"     = 24 hours
20   43     =                  0.345 × 24
57   46     =                  0.963
```

= 8.607 = 8.36 after noon on the 21.8.59
= 20.36 UT 21.8.59 = date and time of the 1959/60 solar return.

Example No.9:
Find the date and time of the solar return for 1976/77.

Birth data: 23.07 UT 2.6.1953, 34.21N 119.04W.
Natal Sun 12° 04′ 56″ Gemini.

Working:

1976 Ephemeris	D	M	S	
Sun's long. 3.6.76	13	01	29	Gemini
Sun's long. 2.6.76	12	04	00	Gemini
Sun's motion in 24 hours	00	57	29	
Sun's natal long.	12	04	56	
Sun's long. noon 2.6.76	12	04	00	
Difference	00	00	56	

$$
\begin{aligned}
57′\ 29″ &= 24\ \text{hours} \\
00\ \ 56 &= \quad \frac{0.016 \times 24}{} \\
57\ \ 29 &= \quad 0.958
\end{aligned}
$$

= 0.389 = 23 min. after noon on the 2.6.76
= 12.23 UT 2.6.76 = date and time of the 1976/77 solar return.

Example No.10:
Find the date and time of the solar return for 1973/74.
Birth data: 04.00 UT 17.10.1949, 34.09N 118.09W.
Natal Sun 23° 26′ 57″ Libra.

Working:

1973 Ephemeris	D	M	S	
Sun's long. 17.10.73	23	58	16	Libra
Sun's long. 16.10.73	22	58	44	Libra
Sun's motion in 24 hours	00	59	32	
Sun's natal long.	23	26	57	
Sun's long. noon 16.10.73	22	58	44	
Difference	00	28	13	

$$
\begin{aligned}
59′\ 32″ &= 24\ \text{hours} \\
28\ \ 13 &= \quad \frac{0.4703 \times 24}{} \\
59\ \ 32 &= \quad 0.992
\end{aligned}
$$

= 11.375 = 11.23 after noon on the 16.10.73
= 23.23. UT 16.10.73 = date and time of the 1973/74 solar return.

Example No.11:
Find the date and time of the solar return for 1980/81.
Birth data: 09.00 UT 11.5.1953, 51.37N 0.17W.
Natal Sun 20° 21′ 53″ Taurus.

Working:

1980 Ephemeris	D	M	S	
Sun's long. 11.5.80	20	56	02	Taurus
Sun's long. 10.5.80	19	58	04	
Sun's motion in 24 hours	00	57	58	
Sun's natal long.	20	21	53	
Sun's long. noon 10.5.80	19	58	04	
Difference	00	23	49	

$$
\begin{array}{lll}
57'\ 58'' & = 24\ \text{hours} \\
23\ \ 49 & = & \underline{0.397 \times 24} \\
57\ \ 58 & = & 0.966
\end{array}
$$

= 9.861 = 9.52 = 21.52 UT 10.5.80 = date and time of the 1980/81
solar return.

Using logs:

	D	M	S	Log	
Sun's motion 10/11.5.80	0	57	58	0.49209	Ternary
Difference	0	23	49	0.87839	Ternary
Then log of difference				0.87839	Ternary log
less log of motion				0.49209	Ternary log
= Time of return				0.38630	Diurnal log

= 9.52 after noon on the 10.5.80 = 21.52 UT 10.5.80

Example No.11a:
Using same birth data find the date and time of the solar return
for 1986/87.

Working:

1986 Ephemeris	D	M	S	
Sun's long. 11.5.86	20	30	09	Taurus
Sun's long. 10.5.86	19	32	10	
Sun's motion in 24 hours	00	57	59	
Sun's natal long.	20	21	53	
Sun's long. noon 11.5.86	20	30	09	
Difference	00	08	16	

$$
\begin{array}{rcl}
57'\ 59'' & = & 24\ \text{hours} \\
08\ \ 16 & = & \dfrac{0.137 \times 24}{} \\
57\ \ 59 & = & 0.966
\end{array}
$$

= 3.422 = 3.25 before noon on the 11.5.86
= 08.35 UT 11.5.86 = date and time of the 1986/87 solar return.

Using logs:

	D	M	S	Log	
Sun's motion 10/11.5.86	0	57	59	0.49197	Ternary
Difference	0	08	16	1.33794	Ternary
Then log of difference			1.33794	Ternary log	
less log of motion			0.49197	Ternary log	
= Time of return			0.84597	Diurnal log	

= 3.25 before noon = 08.35 UT 11.5.86

Example No.12:
Find the date and time of the solar return for 1981/82.
Birth data: 23.10 UT 4.3.1956, 51.30N 0.08W.
Natal Sun 14° 21′ 50″ Pisces.

Working:

1981 Ephemeris	D	M	S	
Sun's long. 5.3.81	14	49	46	Pisces
Sun's long. 4.3.81	13	49	38	
Sun's motion in 24 hours	01	00	08	
Sun's natal long.	14	21	50	
Sun's long. noon 5.3.81	14	49	46	
Difference	00	27	56	

60′ 08″   = 24 hours
27 56   =   0.4655 × 24
60 08   =   ─────────────
                                            1.002

───
= 11.148 = 11.09 before noon on the 5.3.81 = 00.51 UT 5.3.81
───
= date and time of the 1981/82 solar return.

Using logs:

	D M S	Log
Sun's motion 4/5.3.81	01 00 08	.47616 Ternary
Difference	00 27 56	.80915 Ternary

Then log of difference	0.80915	Ternary log
less log of motion	0.47616	Ternary log
= Time of return	0.33299	Diurnal log

=11.09 before noon 5.3.81 = 00.51 UT 5.3.81

Solar Return Charts: Finding the Ascendant and MC
Having determined the date and time of the solar return, the return chart is calculated exactly as if it were a natal chart. It is useful when calculating the date and time of a solar return chart to find, in addition, the date and time of the subsequent return. It is the difference between returns which form the basis for progressing the return. This is discussed under 'The Progressed Sidereal Solar Return' (page 99).

    In calculating any type of chart it is always preferable to work with universal time, which commences at 0 hours (midnight), but as many students are taught to use the sidereal time at Greenwich noon and work from that, examples using that method are given below.

Example No.1:
Find the Asc. and MC for the solar return which occurred at 0.04 UT 12.6.73, London.

Working:

		H	M	S
ST 0 hr. UT 12.6.73		17	20	42
Time elapsed	+	00	04	00
Correction (9.86 sec.)	+	00	00	01
ST at Greenwich		17	24	43
Long. Equiv. (0.20W)	−	00	01	20
RAMC		17	23	23
RA Mean Sun*		05	20	43
RA Apparent Sun*		05	20	21

* See Progressed Tropical Returns (page 54).

Example No.1:
Using a noon-based ephemeris:

		H	M	S
ST at noon 12.6.73		05	22	41
Interval to noon	−	11	56	00
Correction	−	00	01	58
ST at Greenwich		17	24	43
Long. Equiv. (West)	−	00	01	20
RAMC		17	23	23

= Ascendant 8° Pisces: MC 21 Sagittarius: at London as required.

Example No.2:
Solar return occurred at: 13.41 UT 29.8.49, London.

Working:

		H	M	S
ST 0 hr. UT 29.8.49		22	27	28
Time elapsed	+	13	41	00
Correction	+	00	02	15
ST at Greenwich		12	10	43
Long. Equiv. (0.20W)	−	00	01	20
RAMC		12	09	23
RA Mean Sun		10	29	43
RA Apparent Sun		10	30	38

Example No.2:
Using a noon-based ephemeris:

	H	M	S
ST at noon 29.8.49	10	29	27
Interval from noon	+ 01	41	00
Correction	+ 00	00	16
ST at Greenwich	12	10	43
Long. Equiv. (West)	− 00	01	20
RAMC	12	09	23

= Ascendant 5° Sagittarius: MC 2° Libra: at London as required.

Example No.3:
Solar return occurred at 15.46 UT 28.6.51, London.

Working:

	H	M	S
ST 0 hr. UT 28.6.51	18	21	08
Time elapsed	+ 15	46	00
Correction	+ 00	02	35
ST at Greenwich	10	09	43
Long. Equiv. (0.20W)	− 00	01	20
RAMC	10	08	23
RA Mean Sun	06	23	43
RA Apparent Sun	06	26	43

Example No.3:
Using a noon-based ephemeris:

	H	M	S
ST at noon 28.6.51	06	23	06
Interval from noon	+ 03	46	00
Correction	+ 00	00	37
ST at Greenwich	10	09	43
Long. Equiv. (West)	− 00	01	20
RAMC	10	08	23

= Ascendant 13° Scorpio: MC 0° Virgo: at London as required.

Example No.4:
Solar return occurred at: 16.16 UT 14.10.85, London.

Working:

	H	M	S
ST 0 hr. UT 14.10.85	01	29	56
Time elapsed	+ 16	16	00
Correction	+ 00	02	40
ST at Greenwich	17	48	36
Long. Equiv. (0.09W)	− 00	00	36
RAMC	17	48	00
RA Mean Sun	13	32	36
RA Apparent Sun	13	18	35

Example No.4:
Using a noon-based ephemeris:

	H	M	S
ST at noon 14.10.85	13	31	54
Interval from noon	+ 04	16	00
Correction	+ 00	00	42
ST at Greenwich	17	48	36
Long. Equiv. (West)	− 00	00	36
RAMC	17	48	00

= Ascendant 23° Pisces: MC 27° Sagittarius: at London as required.

Example No.5:
Solar return occurred at. 02.52 UT 21.4.51, London.

Working:

	H	M	S
ST 0 hr. UT 21.4.51	13	53	02
Time elapsed	+ 02	52	00
Correction	+ 00	00	28
ST at Greenwich	16	45	30
Long. Equiv. (0.08W)	00	00	32
RAMC	16	44	58
RA Mean Sun	01	53	30
RA Apparent Sun	01	52	25

Example No.5:
Using a noon-based ephemeris:

	H	M	S
ST at noon 21.4.51	01	55	00
Interval to noon	− 09	08	00
Correction	− 00	01	30
ST at Greenwich	16	45	30
Long. Equiv. (West)	− 00	00	32
RAMC	16	44	58

= Ascendant 18° Aquarius: MC 12° Sagittarius: at London as required.

The above example (No.5) is the calculation for Princess Elizabeth's solar return prior to the death of her father (George VI) and her accession to the throne as Queen Elizabeth II. This return has been cast for London but I seem to recall that on her twenty-fifth birthday she was, in fact, in Rome. If so, the question arises whether the return should be calculated for the place of residence at the time of the return, or whether it should be for London, her birthplace. This case, along with other examples will be discussed further in the chapter dealing with case studies. When the place of residence is doubtful, the return is calculated for the birthplace.

4.

THE PROGRESSED
TROPICAL RETURN

The Mean Sun

The Right Ascension of the Mean Sun, often abbreviated to RAMS or just MS is a factor used in the calculation of certain return and progressed charts. The first column of a noon-based ephemeris lists the sidereal time at noon and this listing, such as that found in Raphael's ephemerides, is the Mean Sun expressed in time for Greenwich mean noon. It increases at the constant rate of 9.855 seconds per hour or a daily motion of 3 minutes 56.556 seconds. In publications which list the sidereal time for 0 hours (midnight), the tabulated sidereal time, plus or minus 12 hours is the Mean Sun for 0 hours UT. The easiest way to avoid errors in chart calculation is to use the 24-hour clock commencing from 0 hours UT thereby making all the calculation steps additive, except for the entry when the longitude is west.

Example No.1:
Using a 0 hr.-based ephemeris, find the MS for 09.05 UT 12.6.29.

Working:

	H	M	S
ST 0 hr. UT 12.6.29	17	19	20
Interval (09.05) at 9.855 sec.	+ 00	01	29
Less	− 12	00	00
Right Ascension of the Mean Sun	5	20	49

Example No.1a:
Using a noon-based ephemeris: Data as for example No.1.

Working:

	H	M	S
ST noon 12.6.29	05	21	18
Interval (12.00 – 9.05)			
= 2.55 × 9.855 sec.	− 00	00	29
RAMS	05	20	49

Example No.2:
Using a 0 hr.-based ephemeris find the MS for 01.40 UT 21.4.26.

Working:

	H	M	S
ST 0 hr. UT 21.4.26	13	53	14
Interval (1.40) at 9.855 sec.	+ 00	00	16
Less	− 12	00	00
RAMS	01	53	30

Example No.2a:
Using a noon-based ephemeris

Working:

	H	M	S
ST at noon 21.4.26	01	55	12
Interval (12.00 – 1.40)			
= 10.20 × 9.855 sec.	− 00	01	42
RAMS	01	53	30

The Apparent Sun

The Apparent Sun is the 'True Sun' which moves along the Ecliptic at a varying rate, whereas the Mean Sun (first column of a noon-based ephemeris) moves along the Celestial Equator at a mean or average rate. The Mean Sun, which is really a fictitious body, has a motion which is the average rate throughout the year and the difference between this motion and that of the Apparent Sun is known as the Equation of Time, which varies throughout the year. As the progression of the solar return is not strictly a mean rate matter we use the Right Ascension of the Apparent Sun (RAAS). If the Mean Sun was taken it would entail corrections for the Equation of Time, either plus or minus depending on the time of the year.

There are several methods for finding the Right Ascension of the

Apparent Sun of which the following are a few examples:

Example No.1:
Sun's long. 20° 53′ 41″ Gemini

Working:

From any Tables of Houses 10th cusp:	H	M	S
21° Gemini	5	20	49
20 Gemini	5	16	29
1° (60 min.)	0	04	20

Calculator:

$$(53′\ 41″)\ \frac{53.68\ \times\ 4.33}{60}\ (4′\ 20″)\ =\ 3.87\ =\ 3′\ 52″$$

	H	M	S
which added to (20° Gemini) ST	5	16	29
	0	03	52
Right Ascension of Apparent Sun =	5	20	21

Example No.2:
Sun's long. 0° 12′ 21″ Taurus

Working:

From any Tables of Houses 10th cusp:	H	M	S
1° Taurus	1	55	27
0 Taurus	1	51	37
1 (60 min.)	0	03	50

Calculator:

$$(12′\ 21″)\ \frac{12.35\ \times\ 3.83}{60}\ (3′\ 50″)\ =\ 0.788\ =\ 48″$$

	H	M	S
which added to (0 Taurus) ST	1	51	37
	0	00	48
RA Apparent Sun	1	52	25

Example No.3:
Sun's long. 5° 52′ 11″ Virgo.

Working:

From any Tables of Houses 10th cusp:	H	M	S
6° Virgo	10	31	08
5 Virgo	10	27	22
1 (60 min.)	0	03	46

Calculator:

$$(52'\ 11'')\ \frac{52.183\ \times\ 3.76}{60}\ (3'\ 46'') = 3.27 = 3'\ 16''$$

	H	M	S
Which added to (5° Virgo) ST	10	27	22
	0	03	16
RA Apparent Sun	10	30	38

An alternative method for finding the RA of the Apparent Sun is to use the trigonometric formula:

Tan A = Cos E. Tan L.

where A = the required RA, E, the Obliquity of the Ecliptic (23° 27') , and L, the Sun's longitude.

Example No. 3 has the Sun's longitude as 5° 52' 11'' Virgo. Measuring from 0° Cancer to Virgo = 65° 52' 11''.

Deg.	Min.	Sec.	
65	52	11	= Tan 2.232362
23	27	00	= Cos 0.917407 (E) Obliquity of Ecliptic
			= Tan 2.433337
			= 67.65938
			+ 90.
			157.65938 over 15

= 10.5106 = 10.30.38 sidereal time = RA of Apparent Sun.

Calculation of the Progressed Tropical Return

The length of the tropical year from equinox to equinox is 365.24219 days (365 days, 5 hours, 48 minutes 46 seconds). The sidereal year (fixed star to fixed star) is 365.25636 days (365 days, 6 hours. 09 minutes 09 seconds) or about 20 minutes longer than the tropical year.

If we average out the differences in the sidereal times of several pairs of consecutive solar returns for the same Sun's position we will obtain a value of 5.813 hours for the tropical zodiac and 6.153 hours for the sidereal. This difference is the basis of the progressed solar return.

The progressed solar return completes one full rotation from the date of the return until the commencement of the next return plus the approximate six-hour difference. In other words, as one return ends, another commences; the process repeating from birth to death. The natal chart is, in fact, the solar return for the first year of life.

As the progression of the return is based on the *Right Ascension of the Apparent Sun* (RAAS) this factor has to be determined according to the methods already outlined. In addition, the date and time of the succeeding return needs to be ascertained. As the ending of one return marks the commencement of the next, it follows that any method of progression must incorporate the total period for which a particular return is valid, which in the case of solar returns, is approximately 365¼ days.

For accurate timing of the progressed solar return the following formula applies, but if the original birth data does not warrant detailed calculations, the incremental tables (see Appendix 1) can be used in lieu.

The formula for progressing the solar return consists in determining the RA of the Midheaven (RAMC) at the time of the solar return and at the time of the succeeding return. The difference between the times of the two returns, plus 24 hours and divided by 24 hours 0 minutes 3.5 seconds, will give the *year constant*. By multiplying the difference between the Sun's RA at the date under review and its RA at the time of the return by this constant, we obtain the *sidereal time increment* which — added to the RAMC of the solar return — gives the RAMC of the progressed return.

In other words, the progressed solar return's ratio is a proportion of 24.00.3.5 to 29.48.46 (tropical) or 30.09.13 (sidereal). This is the average from birthday to birthday — the Sun's RA moving ahead at 24.00.3.5 while the return's sidereal time has advanced 24 hours plus the additional 5.812 hours (tropical) or 6.153 hours (sidereal).

In all astrological calculations, detailed work should correspond with the degree of accuracy of the original data. There is little point in precise calculations if there is uncertainty regarding the birth time, etc. Alternatively, if the data are well-authenticated, accurate calculations are required. The formula for accurately progressing the solar return is as follows:

(a) S1: RAMC (sidereal time) succeeding solar return
— S2: RAMC (sidereal time) preceding solar return
                    = Difference
+ 24 hr. and divided by 24 hr. 0 min. 3.5 sec.
                    = 'Y' = Year Constant

(b) R1: Sun's RA at date and time required
— R2: Sun's RA at preceding solar return
                    = Difference
                    x 'Y' = Increment of Sidereal Time (I)

(c) S2: RAMC of preceeding solar return
            + Increment (I) = RAMC of the progressed return

This procedure entails calculating the date and time of two returns (current and succeeding year) in order to arrive at the differences between the two returns. If the birth data are accurate the effort, using the above formula, is worthwhile.

Example No.1:
Birth data: 09.05 UT 12.6.29, 51.31N 0.20W.
Solar return 1973/74: 00.04 UT 12.6.73.
Event: Death of husband: 29.6.73, London.

Progressed Return	H	M	S
(A) RAMC 1974 return 05.50 UT 12.6.74	23	09'	23
RAMC 1973 return 00.04 UT 12.6.73	17	23	23
Difference	05	46	00
Add	24	00	00
	29	46	00

H	M	S	
29	46	00	

$$\div \frac{29\ 46\ 00}{24\ 00\ 03} = 1.2402 = \text{Year constant}$$

(B) Sun's RA 29.6.73 21.00 UT   06 34 37
     Sun's RA 12.6.73 00.04 UT   05 20 21

		H	M	S
(B)	Sun's RA 29.6.73 21.00 UT	06	34	37
	Sun's RA 12.6.73 00.04 UT	05	20	21
	Difference	01	14	16
	1.14.16 × 1.2402 = Increment	01	32	06
(C)	RAMC solar return	+ 17	23	23
	RAMC progressed solar return	18	55	29
	Asc. 1° Taurus: MC 12 Capricorn.			

Example No.2:
Birth data: 11.50 UT 29.8.28 48.47 N 9.11E.
Solar return 1949/50: 13.41 UT 29.8.49.
Event: Marriage 14.30 UT 13.5.50, London.

Progressed Return	H	M	S
(A) RAMC 1950 return 19.22 UT 29.8.50	17	50	30
RAMC 1949 return 13.41 UT 29.8.49	12	09	23
Difference	05	41	07
Add	24	00	00
	29	41	07

$$\div \frac{\begin{array}{ccc} \text{H} & \text{M} & \text{S} \\ 29 & 41 & 07 \end{array}}{24 \quad 00 \quad 03} = \underline{1.2367} = \text{Year constant}$$

		H	M	S
(B)	Sun's RA 13.5.50 14.30 UT	03	19	21
	Sun's RA 29.8.49 13.41 UT	10	30	38
	Difference	16	48	43
	16.48.43 × 1.2367 = Increment	20	47	29
(C)	RAMC solar return	+ 12	09	23
	RAMC progressed solar return	08	56	52
	Asc. 1° Scorpio: MC 12 Leo.			

Example No.3:
Birth data: 09.08 UT 28.6.25 51.10N 7.04E.
Solar return 1954/55: 09.12 UT 28.6.54.
Event: Birth of son. 21.32 UT 18.11.54, London.

Progressed Return

	H	M	S
(A) RAMC 1955 return 14.50 UT 28.6.55	09	12	22
RAMC 1954 return 09.12 UT 28.6.54	03	34	25
Difference	05	37	57
Add	24	00	00
	29	37	57

$$\div \frac{\begin{array}{ccc} H & M & S \\ 29 & 37 & 57 \end{array}}{24 \quad 00 \quad 03} = \underline{1.2346} = \text{Year constant}$$

	H	M	S
(B) Sun's RA 18.11.54 21.32 UT	15	34	46
Sun's RA 28.6.54 09.12 UT	06	26	43
Difference	09	08	03
09.08.03 × 1.2346 = Increment	11	16	37
(C) RAMC solar return	+ 03	34	25
RAMC progressed solar return	14	51	02
Asc. 9° Capricorn: MC 15° Scorpio.			

Example No.4:
Birth data: 01.40 UT 21.4.26 51.30N 0.08W.
Solar return 1951/52: 02.52 UT 21.4.51.
Event: Death of father and accession to the throne: 6.2.52.

Progressed Return

	H	M	S
(A) RAMC 1952 return 08.40 UT 20.4.52	22	32	59
RAMC 1951 return 02.52 UT 21.4.51	− 16	44	58
Difference	05	48	01
Add	24	00	00
	29	48	01

$$\div \frac{\begin{array}{ccc} H & M & S \\ 29 & 48 & 01 \end{array}}{24 \quad 00 \quad 03} = \underline{1.2416} = \text{Year constant}$$

(B) Sun's RA 6.2.52 11.45 UT   21 16 23
    Sun's RA 21.4.51 02.52 UT   − 01 52 25
    Difference   19 23 58
    19.23.58 × 1.2416 = Increment   00 05 11

(C) RAMC solar return   + 16 44 58
    RAMC progressed solar return   16 50 09
    Asc. 21° Aquarius: MC 14° Sagittarius.

5.

LUNAR RETURNS

The Natal Moon

There are several types of returns based on the Moon's position, either in the natal chart or in some subsidiary chart. The calculation of a lunar return based on the Moon's natal longitude is similar to that used for the solar return except that where the Sun's position is required exactly, the Moon's longitude need only be computed to the nearest minute. If precision is required, and this will be governed by how accurate the birth data has been recorded, the Moon's longitude needs to be corrected by means of second differences. For normal purposes it is sufficient to compute the Moon's position using its twelve-hour motion.

Example No.1:
Find the Moon's natal longitude.
Birth data: 9.05 UT 12.6.29, 51.31N 0.20W.

Working:

	D	M	S	
Moon's long. noon 12.6.29	29	13	28	Leo
Moon's long. 0 hr. 12.6.29	22	09	43	Leo
Moon's motion in 12 hours	07	03	45	

	H	M	S
Birthtime	09	05	00
Time to noon	02	55	00

Calculator:

$$(2.55) = \underline{2.916 \times 7.0625} \; (7° \; 03' \; 45'')$$
$$12$$

= 1.7165 = 1° 43'

Noon position 12.6.29	29°	13'	28"		
Less	01	43	00		
Natal Moon's longitude	27	30	28	Leo	27° 31' Leo

Example No.2:
Birth data: 11.50 UT 29.8.28, 48.47N 9.11E.

Working:

	D	M	S	
Moon's long. noon 29.8.28	15	45	11	Aquarius
Moon's long. 0 hr. 29.8.28	09	10	59	
Moon's motion in 12 hours	06	34	12	

	H	M	S
Birthtime	11	50	00
Time to noon	00	10	00

Calculator:

$(0.10) = \dfrac{0.166 \times 6.5699}{12}$ (6° 34' 12")

$= 0.0912 = 5'\ 28"$

Noon position 29.8.28	15° 45' 11"				
Less	00 05 28				
Natal Moon's longitude	15 39 43	Aquarius	15° 40' Aquarius		

Example No.1:
Using Diurnal Proportional Logs

			Log
Moon's daily motion 11/12.6.29	14° 13' 45" (14°14')		.2269
Time to noon	2 55 00	+	.9153
Moon's motion during interval	1 44 00		1.1422

Noon position 12.6.29	29°	13'	28"
Less	1	44	00
	27	29	28 = within a minute or so of

the position found by the calculator.

Example No.2:

						Log
Moon's daily motion 28/29.8.28	13°	02'	58"	(13°03')		.2646
Time to noon	00	10	00		+	2.1584
Moon's motion during interval	00	05	00			2.4230

Noon position 29.8.28	15°	45'	11"		
Less	00	05	00		
	15	40	11	=	15° 40' Aquarius

The exact natal longitudes of the Sun and Moon should be recorded on all natal charts to form a reference for calculating the various types of returns. In addition, two other important factors should be noted, namely the Right Ascension of the Mean and of the Apparent Sun.

THE TROPICAL LUNAR RETURN

The tropical lunar return relates to the natal chart in a manner similar to that of the solar return. Every twenty-seven days or thereabouts the Moon will transit its natal position. The time and date when this occurs marks the commencement of the lunar return for that particular period.

The procedure for calculating these returns is similar to that used for the solar returns without the necessity of using extensive logs. If logs. are preferred, then the usual Diurnal logs. are sufficient. The following examples, which will be referred to under case studies, show the ease with which these returns can be calculated.

Example No.1:
Natal Moon: 27° 31' Leo.
Lunar return required for June 1973.

Working:

1973 Ephemeris — June:	D	M	S	
Moon's position noon 6th	28	22	20	Leo
Moon's natal position	27	31	00	
Difference	00	51	20	(0.855)
Moon's daily motion 5/6th June	13	55	33	(13.925)

Calculator:

$$\frac{0.855 \times 24}{13\cdot925} = 1.474 = 1 \text{ hr. } 28 \text{ min.}$$

before noon on the 6th = <u>10.32 UT 6.6.73. = Lunar return</u>

Using Diurnal logs:

	D	M		
Log. of difference	0	51	1.4508	
Log. of motion	13	56	0.2362	less
Time required	01	28	1.2146	

= 1 hr. 28 min. before noon =
<u>10.32 UT 6.6.73 = time and date of Lunar return</u>

Additional check: Moon's longitude 10.32 UT

$$= \frac{13° \; 55' \; 33''}{24} \times 1 \text{ hr. } 28 \text{ min.} = 0.851 = 51 \text{ min.}$$

from noon longitude 28° 22' = 27° 31' Leo = natal longitude.

Example No.2:
Natal Moon: 27° 31' Leo.
Lunar return required for Oct./Nov. 1979.

Working:
1979 Ephemeris — Oct.:	D	M	
Moon's position 16 Oct.	02	02	Virgo
Moon's natal position	27	31	Leo
Difference (nearest minute)	04	31	(4.516)
Moon's daily motion 15/16 Oct.	11	47	(11.783)

Calculator:

$$\frac{4.516 \times 24}{11.783} = 9.2 = 9 \text{ hr. } 12 \text{ min.}$$

before noon on the 16th = <u>02.48 UT 16.10.79 = time and date of</u>
<u>lunar return.</u>

Using Diurnal Logs.

	D	M	Log
Log of difference	4	31	.72539
Log of motion	11	47	.30894 less
Time required			.41645

= 09 hr. 12 min. before noon =
02.48 UT 16.10.79 = time and date of lunar return

Additional check: Moon's longitude 02.48 UT

$$= \frac{11° \ 47'}{24} \times 14 \ hr. \ 48 \ min. = 7.266 = 7° \ 16'$$

which added to noon position (15th) 20° 15′ Leo = 27° 31′ Leo
= Moon's natal longitude.

Example No.3:
Natal Moon 27° 31′ Leo.
Lunar return required for December 1967.

Working:

1967 Ephemeris — Dec.:	D	M	
Moon's natal long.	27	31	Leo
Moon's position noon 21st	22	04	Leo
Difference	05	27	(5.45)
Moon's daily motion 21/22nd	13	18	(13.30)

Calculator:
$$\frac{5.45 \times 24}{13.3} = 9.834 = 9 \ hr. \ 50 \ min.$$

= time after noon on the 21st = 21.50 UT 21.12.67 = time and
date of lunar return.

Using Diurnal logs:

	D	M	Log.
Log. of difference	5	27	.64382
Log. of motion	13	18	.25636 less
Time required			.38746

= 9 hr. 50 min. after noon =

21.50 UT 21.12.67 = time and date of lunar return.

Additional check: Moon's longitude 21.50 UT

$$= \frac{13° \ 18'}{24} \times 9 \ hr. \ 50 \ min. = 5.45 = 5° \ 27'$$

which added to noon position (21st) 22° 4' Leo = 27° 31' Leo = Moon's natal longitude.

Example No.4:
Natal Moon 15° 40' Aquarius.
Lunar return required for May 1950.

Working:

1950 Ephemeris — May:	D	M	
Moon's natal long.	15	40	Aquarius
Moon's position noon 8th	12	01	Aquarius
Difference	03	39	(3.65)
Moon's daily motion 8/9th	12	56	(12.93)

Calculator:
$$\frac{3.65 \times 24}{12.93} = 6.773 = 6 \ hr. \ 46 \ min.$$

after noon on the 8th = 18.46 UT 8.5.50 = time and date of the lunar return.

Example No.5:
Natal Moon 15° 40' Aquarius.
Lunar return required for December 1979.

Working:

1979 Ephemeris — Dec.:	D	M	
Moon's natal long.	15	40	Aquarius
Moon's position noon 22nd	11	07	Aquarius
Difference	04	33	(4.55)
Moon's daily motion 22/23	14	14	(14.23)

Calculator:
$$\frac{4.55 \times 24}{14.23} = 7.672 = 7 \ hr. \ 40 \ min.$$

after noon on the 22nd = <u>19.40 UT 22.12.79</u> = <u>time and date of</u>
<u>the lunar return.</u>

Using Diurnal logs:

	D	M	Log
Log of difference	4	33	.72220
Log of motion	14	14	.22691 less
Time required			.49529

= 7 hr. 40 min. after noon =
<u>19.40 UT 22.12.79 = time and date of lunar return.</u>

Example No.6:
Natal Moon 15° 40′ Aquarius.
Lunar return required for May 1953.

Working:

1953 Ephemeris — May:	D	M
Moon's natal long.	15	40 Aquarius
Moon's position noon 6th	15	28 Aquarius
Difference	00	12 (0.2)
Moon's daily motion 6/7th	14	05 (14.08)

Calculator:

$$\frac{0.2 \times 24}{14.08} = 0.341 = 0 \text{ hr. } 20 \text{ min.}$$

after noon on the 6th = <u>12.20 UT 6.5.53</u> = <u>time and date of lunar</u>
<u>return.</u>

Example No.7:
(Same data as Example No.6)
Lunar return required for February/March 1956.

Working:

1956 Ephemeris Feb.:	D	M
Moon's position noon 11th	17	14 Aquarius
Moon's natal long.	15	40 Aquarius
Difference	01	34 (1.56)
Moon's daily motion 10/11th	12	09 (12.15)

Calculator:

$$\frac{1.56 \times 24}{12.15} = 3.095 = 3 \text{ hr. } 06 \text{ min.}$$

before noon on the 11th = 08.54 UT 11.2.56 = time and date of lunar return.

Lunar Return Charts: Finding the Ascendant and MC

A lunar return chart is calculated exactly in the same manner as a natal or solar return chart.

Example No.1:
Lunar return data:
10.32 UT 6.6.73. 51.31N 0.20W.

Working:

	H	M	S
ST 0 hr. UT 6.6.73	16	57	03
Time elapsed	+ 10	32	00
Correction (9.86 sec. per hour)	+ 00	01	44
ST at Greenwich	03	30	47
Long. Equiv. (0.20W)	− 00	01	20
RAMC	03	29	27
RA Mean Sun	04	58	47

Asc. 3° Virgo: MC 25° Taurus: at London as required.

Example No.2:
Lunar return data:
02.48 UT 16.10.79. 51.31N 0.20W.

Working:

	H	M	S
ST 0 hr. UT 16.10.79	01	35	40
Time elapsed	+ 02	48	00
Correction	+ 00	00	27
ST at Greenwich	04	24	07
Long. Equiv. (0.20W)	− 00	01	20
RAMC	04	22	47
RA Mean Sun	13	36	07

Asc. 13° Virgo: MC 8° Gemini: at London.

Example No.3:
Lunar return data:
21.50 UT 21.12.67. 51.31N 0.20W.

Working:

	H	M	S
ST 0 hr. UT 21.12.67	05	55	31
Time elapsed	+ 21	50	00
Correction	+ 00	03	35
ST at Greenwich	03	49	06
Long. Equiv. (0.20W)	− 00	01	20
RAMC	03	47	46
RA Mean Sun	17	59	06

Asc. 6° Virgo: MC 29° Taurus: at London.

Example No.4:
Lunar return data:
18.46 UT 8.5.50. 51.31N 0.20W.

Working:

	H	M	S
ST 0 hr. UT 8.5.50	15	01	01
Time elapsed	+ 18	46	00
Correction	+ 00	03	05
ST at Greenwich	09	50	06
Long. Equiv. (0.20W)	− 00	01	20
RAMC	09	48	46
RA Mean Sun	03	04	06

Asc. 10° Scorpio: MC 25° Leo: at London.

N.B. Place of residence at the time of the return was London, but
birthplace was abroad so the Asc. and MC will be at:

Birth Lat: 48.47N Long. 9.11E

	H	M	S
ST at Greenwich as found	09	50	06
Long. East 9° 11′	+ 00	36	44
RAMC at birthplace at the time of the return.	10	26	50

Asc. 20° Scorpio: MC 5° Virgo.

When transposed to the birth latitude, the natal Sun is conjunct the lunar return MC.

Example No.5:
Lunar return data:
19.40 UT 22.12.79. 51.31N 0.20W.

Working:

	H	M	S
ST 0 hr. UT 22.12.79	05	59	49
Time elapsed	+ 19	40	00
Correction	+ 00	03	14
ST at Greenwich	01	43	03
Long. Equiv. (0.20W)	− 00	01	20
RAMC	01	41	43
RA Mean Sun	18	03	03

Asc. 14° Leo: MC 27° Aries: at London.
Asc. 20° Leo: MC 7° Taurus at birthplace.

Example No.6:
Lunar return data:
12.20 UT 6.5.53. 51.31N 0.20W.

Working:

	H	M	S
ST 0 hr. UT 6.5.53	14	54	13
Time elapsed	+ 12	20	00
Correction	+ 00	02	01
ST at Greenwich	03	16	14
Long. Equiv. (0.20W)	− 00	01	20
RAMC	03	14	54
RA Mean Sun	02	56	14

Asc. 1° Virgo: MC 21° Taurus: at London.

Asc. 7° Virgo: MC 0° Gemini: at birthplace.

Example No. 7:
Lunar return data:
08.54 UT 11.2.56. 51.30N 0.08W.

Working:

	H	M	S
ST 0 hr. UT 11.2.56	09	20	11
Time elapsed	+ 08	54	00
Correction	+ 00	01	28
ST at Greenwich	18	15	39
Long. Equiv. (0.08W)	− 00	00	32
RAMC	18	15	07
RA Mean Sun	21	21	39

Asc. 8° Aries: MC 3° Capricorn: at London.

Asc. 27° Aries: MC 12° Capricorn: at birthplace.

Example No. 8:
Birth data: 1.40 UT 21.4.26, London.
Natal Moon 12° 07' Leo:
Lunar return required for Jan/Feb. 1952.

Working:
1952 Ephemeris — Jan.:

	D	M	S	
Moon's position noon 13th	06	14	57	Leo
Moon's natal position	12	07	00	Leo
Difference	05	52	03	(5.867)
Moon's daily motion 13/14 Jan.	11	50	42	(11.844)

Calculator:

$$\frac{5.867 \times 24}{11.844} = 11.89 = 11.53 \text{ after noon}$$

on the 13th = 23.53 UT 13.1.52 = Lunar return.

Example No.8:
Lunar return data:
23.53 UT 13.1.52. 51.30N 0.08W.

Working:

	H	M	S
ST 0 hr. UT 13.1.52		07	25	43
Time elapsed	+	23	53	00
Correction	+	00	03	55
ST at Greenwich		07	22	38
Long. Equiv. (0.08W)	−	00	00	32
RAMC		07	22	06
RA Mean Sun		19	29	38

Asc. 14° Libra: MC 19° Cancer: at London.

6.

SUBSIDIARY RETURN CHARTS

Demi and Quarti Returns
The solar return chart and the lunar return chart are based on the natal longitudes of the Sun and Moon. These two types of returns can be supplemented with additional return charts based on the time and date when the Sun or Moon transits its opposition point (demi-solar or lunar) or its square (90°) position (quarti-solar or lunar). These techniques, initially introduced by the sidereal researchers in terms of the sidereal zodiac, are an extremely useful adjunct for reviewing or studying a particular period.

In addition to these supplementary charts based on the natal longitudes of the Sun and Moon, other returns can be calculated using the longitude of the 'solar Moon', i.e. the Moon's position in the solar return chart. The value of many of these additional return charts is that they often highlight important factors and time periods relative to the main solar or lunar return.

A realistic approach is required concerning the number of return charts being considered at any given time, otherwise one is liable to sink into a quagmire of figures and symbols which have little meaning.

The calculation of subsidiary return charts is similar to that used for the principal return charts with the exception that the solar Moon return requires greater detail as it is based on the Moon's progressed position. The following examples illustrate the calculation procedures:

The Demi-Solar Return

Example No.1:
Required: the demi-solar return for 1951/52.
Natal Sun 0° 12′ 21″ Taurus.

Demi-solar Sun = 0 12 21 Scorpio.

Working:

1951 Ephemeris:	H	M	S	
Sun's long. 24.10.51	00	15	56	Scorpio
Sun's long. 23.10.51	29	16	10	Libra
Sun's motion in 24 hours	00	59	46	
Sun's long (opposition)	00	12	21	Scorpio
Sun's long. noon 24.10.51	00	15	56	
Difference	00	03	35	(0.059)

$$59' \ 46'' \ = 24 \text{ hours}$$
$$03 \ \ 35 \ \ = \ \ \underline{0.059 \times 24}$$
$$59 \ \ 46 \ \ = \ \ \ \ \ \ 0.996$$

= 1.439 = 1.27 before noon on the 24.10.51
= 10.33 UT 24.10.51 = time and date of demi-solar return.

Using logs:

	D	M	S	Log	
Sun's motion 23/24.10.51	0	59	46	.47881	Ternary
Difference	0	03	35	1.70099	Ternary

Then log of difference	1.70099	Ternary	
less log of motion	0.47881	Ternary	
Time of return	1.22218	Diurnal	

= 1.27 before noon on the 24.10.51. = 10.33 UT 24.10.51.

Find the Asc. and MC.

Working:

	H	M	S
ST 0 hr. 24.10.51	02	06	22
Time elapsed	+ 10	33	00
Correction	+ 00	01	44
ST at Greenwich	12	41	06
Long. Equiv. (0.08W)	− 00	00	32
RAMC	12	40	34
RA Mean Sun	14	08	06
RA Apparent Sun	13	52	25

Asc. 11° Sagittarius: MC 11° Libra: at London.

The Quarti-Solar Return

Example No.1:
Required: the quarti-solar returns for 1951/52.
Natal Sun 0° 12′ 21″ Taurus.
Quarti-solar Sun = 0 12 21 Leo.
Quarti-solar Sun = 0 12 21 Aquarius.

The first quarti-solar return occurs when the transiting Sun squares its natal position, approximately three months after the commencement of the solar return. The second quarti-solar return will occur approximately midway between the date of the demi-solar return and the commencement of the next Solar return.

Working:

1951 Ephemeris	H	M	S	
Sun's long. 24.7.51	00	46	55	Leo
Sun's long. 23.7.51	29	49	38	Cancer
Sun's motion in 24 hours	00	57	17	
Sun's long. (square 90°)	00	12	21	Leo
Sun's long. noon 23.7.51	29	49	38	Cancer
Difference	00	22	43	(0.378)

$$57′\ 17″ = 24 \text{ hours}$$
$$22\ 43 = \frac{0.378 \times 24}{}$$
$$57\ 17 = 0.9547$$

= 9.517 = 9.31 after noon on the 23.7.51
= 21.31 UT 23.7.51 = time and date of quarti-solar return.

Find the Asc. and MC:

Working:

	H	M	S
ST 0 hr. UT 23.7.51	19	59	42
Time elapsed	+ 21	31	00
Correction	+ 00	03	32
ST at Greenwich	17	34	14
Long. Equiv. (0.08W)	− 00	00	32
RAMC	17	33	42
RA Mean Sun	08	03	14
RA Apparent Sun	08	09	35

Asc. 14° Pisces: 24° Sagittarius: at London.

Quarti-solar Sun: 0.12.21 Aquarius.

Working:
1952 Ephemeris:

	H	M	S	
Sun's long. 21.1.52	00	23	49	Aquarius
Sun's long. 20.1.52	29	22	44	Capricorn
Sun's motion in 24 hours	01	01	05	
Sun's long. (square 90°)	00	12	21	Aquarius
Sun's long. noon 20.1.52	29	22	44	Capricorn
Difference	00	49	37	(0.827)

61′ 05″	= 24 hours	
49 37	=	0.827 × 24
61 05	=	1.018

= 19.49 = 19.30 after noon on the 20.1.52 =
07.30 UT 21.1.52. = time and date of quarti-solar return.

Find the Asc. and MC:

Working:

	H	M	S
ST 0 hr. UT 21.1.52	07	57	15
Time elapsed	+ 07	30	00
Correction	+ 00	01	14
ST at Greenwich	15	28	29
Long. Equiv. (0.08W)	− 00	00	32
RAMC	15	27	57
RA Mean Sun	19	58	29
RA Apparent Sun	20	09	35

Asc. 19° Capricorn: 24° Scorpio: at London.

The foregoing examples are the demi-solar and quarti-solar return charts for the Princess Elizabeth, as she was then, covering the period of the death of her father (George VI) and her accession to the British throne as Queen Elizabeth II. These returns are interesting when related to the natal chart.

The Annual Lunar Return

This return, termed the *anlunar* by the sidereal advocates, is a return which uses the Moon's position in the solar return chart. This lunar return is related to the solar return chart in the same way that the ordinary lunar return relates to the natal chart. These charts are calculated in the usual manner as the ordinary lunar return.

Example No.1:
Required the anlunar return for the period covering the accession of Queen Elizabeth II.
Solar Return 1951/52: 02.52 UT 21.4.51.
Solar Moon 19° 43′ Libra.
Death of father 6.2.52.
The solar Moon transited Libra 18/19.1.52. Therefore the return appropriate to this period will be as follows:

	D	M	
Solar Moon's long.	19	43	Libra
Moon's long. noon 19.1.52	19	17	Libra
Difference	00	26	(0.433)
Moon's daily motion 19/20.1.52	13	04	(13.066)

Calculator:

$$\frac{0.433 \times 24}{13.066} = 0.795 = 0 \text{ hr. 48 min.}$$

after noon = 12.48 UT 19.1.52 = Anlunar Return

	H	M	S
ST 0 hr. 19.1.52	07	49	22
Time elapsed	+ 12	48	00
Correction	+ 00	02	07
ST at Greenwich	20	39	29
Long. Equiv. (0.08W)	− 00	00	32
RAMC	20	38	57
RA Mean Sun	19	51	29

Asc. 13° Gemini: MC 8° Aquarius: at London.

The Demi-Lunar Return

This return chart is calculated for the return of the Moon to the opposition longitude of its natal position. This occurs each month, approximately fourteen days from the date of the lunar return that is based on the natal Moon. Queen Elizabeth's natal Moon is 12° 07′ Leo, so the demi-lunar longitude will always be 12° 07′ Aquarius.

Example No.1:
Find the demi-lunar return for the period covering the death of her father and her accession to the throne: 6.2.52.
The Moon transited Aquarius during the 26/27 Jan. 52, so the appropriate demi-lunar is found as follows:

	D	M	
Demi-lunar long.	12	07	Aquarius
Moon's long. 27.1.52	14	30	Aquarius
Difference	02	23	(2.383)
Moon's daily motion 26/27.1.52	15	13	(15.216)

Calculator:

$$\frac{2.383 \times 24}{15.216} = 3.76 = 3.45 \text{ before noon}$$

= 08.15 UT 27.1.52 = time and date of demi-lunar return.

Find the Asc. and MC for the demi-lunar return.

Working:

	H	M	S
ST 0 hr. UT 27.1.52	08	20	55
Time elapsed	+ 08	15	00
Correction	+ 00	01	21
ST at Greenwich	16	37	16
Long. Equiv. (0.08W)	− 00	00	32
RAMC	16	36	44
RA Mean Sun	20	22	16

Asc. 15° Aquarius: MC 11° Sagittarius: at London.

The Quarti-Lunar Return

This return is calculated for the time and date when the transiting Moon, each month, squares (90°) its natal position. In the foregoing example the natal Moon is Leo 12° 07′ so the quarti-lunar returns will occur when the Moon reaches the same longitude (12° 07′) in Taurus/Scorpio. The nearest quarti-lunar for the period covering 6 February 1952 is sometime during 1/2 February when the transiting Moon was in Taurus.

	D	M	
Quarti-lunar long. 12° 07′ Taurus	12	07	Taurus
Moon's long. 2.2.52	08	41	Taurus
Difference	03	26	(3.43)
Moon's daily motion 2/3.2.52	12	36	(12.60)

Calculator:

$$\frac{3.43 \times 24}{12.60} = 6.54 = 6.32 \text{ after noon on the 2.2.52}$$

= 18.32 UT 2.2.52 = time and date of quarti-lunar return.

Find the Asc. and MC for the quarti-lunar return:

Working:

	H	M	S
ST 0 hr. UT 2.2.52	08	44	34
Time elapsed	+ 18	32	00
Correction	+ 00	03	03
ST at Greenwich	03	19	37
Long. Equiv. (0.08W)	− 00	00	32
RAMC	03	19	05
RA Mean Sun	20	47	37

Asc. 2° Virgo: MC 22° Taurus: at London.

The other quarti-lunar return (12° 07′ Scorpio), prior to the period of her accession, occurred in January 1952. These quarti-lunar returns which occur midway between the periods of the lunar and demi-lunar returns, often confirm the indications present in the lunar return.

The Moon transited Scorpio on the 20/23 January so the appropriate quarti-lunar will be:

	D	M	
Quarti-lunar long.	12	07	Scorpio
Moon's long. 20.1.52	02	21	Scorpio
Difference	09	46	(9.76)
Moon's daily motion 20/21.1.52	13	29	(13.48)

Calculator:
$$\frac{9.76 \times 24}{13.48} = 17.384 = 17.23$$

17 hr. 23 min. after noon on the 20th =
05.23 UT 21.1.52. = time and date of quarti-lunar return.

Find the Asc. and MC.

Working:

	H	M	S
ST 0 hr. UT 21.1.52	07	57	15
Time elapsed	+ 05	23	00
Correction	+ 00	00	53
ST at Greenwich	13	21	08
Long. Equiv. (0.08W)	− 00	00	32
RAMC	13	20	36
RA Mean Sun	19	58	08

Asc. 19° Sagittarius: MC 22° Libra: at London.

Quotidians

Solar Quotidians (SQ)

The solar return chart can be progressed by using either the Right Ascension of the Apparent Sun or the Right Ascension of the Mean Sun. The quotidian method uses the RA of the Mean Sun moving at a constant rate of 3 mins. 56.6. secs. per day. It may seen strange that two different methods can be used to progress the angles of the solar return, but experience has shown that both have validity.

This technique is extremely simple to apply and consists of extracting the increase of the RAMS between the date of the return and the date and time under review. The difference in the Mean Sun is added to the sidereal time (RAMC) of the return. The sum is the RAMC of the SQ.

Example No.1:
Required: SQ for 10.50 UT 23.7.86.
Solar return 1985/6: 16.16 UT 14.10.85.
Mean Sun 13.32.36: RAMC 17.48.00. at London.

Working:

	H	M	S
Mean Sun 23.7.86. 10.50 UT	08	03	31
Mean Sun solar return	− 13	32	36
Difference	18	30	55
RAMC solar return	+ 17	48	00
RAMC solar quotidian	12	18	55

At London: Asc. 7° Sagittarius: MC 5° Libra.

Lunar Quotidians (LQ)

The lunar return can be progressed by the quotidian method in a manner similar to the solar quotidian. The method of calculation is the same as for the solar quotidian, i.e. the difference between the RAMS for the date required and the RAMS at the time of the return. The addition of the difference means that the sidereal time will advance daily by 3 minutes 56.6 seconds.

Example:
Lunar return data:
Moon 15° 40′ Aquarius: 18.46 UT 8.5.50. 51.31N 0.20W
RAMC 9.48.46: Mean Sun 3.04.06.
Lunar quotidian for 14.30 UT 13.5.50 London.

	H	M	S
Mean Sun 13.5.50. 14.30 UT	03	23	07
Mean Sun 8.5.50. 18.46 UT	− 03	04	06
Difference	00	19	01
RAMC Lunar return	+ 09	48	46
RAMC Lunar quotidian	10	07	47

At London: Asc. 13° Scorpio: MC 0° Virgo:

At birthplace: Lat. 48° 47′N. Long. 9° 11′E the lunar return RAMC is 10.26.50: Asc. 18° Scorpio: MC 5° Virgo:
Lunar quotidian at birthplace: RAMC 10.45.51.
Asc. 21° Scorpio: MC 10° Virgo.

Natal Quotidians

Natal quotidian charts (NQ) are the familiar 'day for a year' or secondary progressions which are used by most astrologers. There is, however, an important difference, which is, that the daily progression of the angles is allowed for and not merely the advance of the MC by about one degree per day. The RAMC is at the rate of 24 hours, 3 minutes, 57 seconds per day and it is this progress on which the quotidian or daily chart is based.

It has been suggested that the usual method of calculating secondary directions is incorrect (see Fagan and Firebrace, *Primer of Sidereal Astrology*) and that the reckoning for the progressed day requires to be adjusted. To this end a correction termed the *bija* was introduced by Fagan. This bija measure for one day or one year of life is 3 minutes, 55.91 seconds and this quantity is always negative (i.e. subtractive) when computing progressed charts but always positive (i.e. additive) when dealing with regressed charts.

The usual day-for-a-year measure appears to work satisfactorily in most cases, although there can be 'time-lags concerning the progressions operating at a particular time and their correlation with events and conditions.

Kinetic Returns

The Kinetic Solar Return (KSR)

This type of return is based on the progressed Sun's longitude, or if using regressions on the Sun's regressed position. It can be used as an adjunct to the other types of returns such as the solar return based on the Sun's natal longitude or other auxiliary returns.

Example No.1:
Birth data: 09.05 UT 12.6.29, London.
Natal Sun 20° 53′ 41″ Gemini.

12 June 1929	09.05 UT		163 days	
12 June 1949	09.05 UT	+	20 days	(20 years)
2 July 1929	09.05 UT		183	

Prog. Sun's longitude 9° 58′ 30″ Cancer: =
Kinetic Sun
Solar return 1949/50

	D	M	S	
Sun's long. noon 2.7.49	10	15	10	Cancer
Kinetic Sun	− 09	58	30	
Difference	00	16	40	(0.277)
Sun's daily motion 1/2.7.49	00	57	13	(0.9536)

$$\frac{16' \ 40''}{57 \ 13} \qquad \frac{0.277 \times 24}{0.9536} = 6.99 = 6 \text{ hr. } 59 \text{ min. before noon}$$

on 2 July = 05.01 UT 2.7.49 = KSR.

		H	M	S
ST 0 hr. UT 2.7.49		18	38	48
Time elapsed	+	05	01	00
Correction	+	00	00	49
ST at Greenwich		23	40	37
Long. Equiv. (0.20W)	−	00	01	20
RAMC		23	39	17

	H	M	S
RA Mean Sun	06	39	37
RA Apparent Sun	06	43	24

Asc. 23° Cancer: MC 24° Pisces: at London.

		H	M	S
RAMC Kinetic return 1950/51		05	25	14
RAMC Kinetic return 1949/50		23	39	17
		05	45	57
	+	24	00	00
		29	45	57

$$\frac{29.45.57}{24} = 1.2402 \text{ Constant}$$

Progress 1949/50 kinetic for 24 June 1950.

		H	M	S
RAAS noon 24.6.50		06	10	28
RAAS KSR	−	06	43	24
Difference		23	27	04
x constant	=	05	05	03
RAMC KSR	+	23	39	17
RAMC Prog. return		04	44	20

Asc. 16° Virgo: MC 12° Gemini: at London.

Using the RA Mean Sun we have:

	H	M	S
Mean Sun 24.6.50 noon	06	08	17
Mean Sun 2.7.49 05.01 KSR	− 06	39	37
Difference	23	28	40
Add RAMC KSR 1949	23	39	17
RAMC Prog.	23	07	57

Asc. 16° Cancer: MC 16° Pisces: at London.

The Lunar Kinetic

This type of return was introduced by Cyril Fagan in the 1960s. Although it is, initially, a sidereal technique, the principles of its calculation can be adapted for use with tropical charts.

Basically, it is a moving or dynamic lunar return. Whereas the usual lunar returns are static because they are related to solar or lunar positions that are fixed, the kinetic lunar is computed for a date and time when the Moon transits its progressed longitude in the solar return. The calculations for this type of return requires the use of the Mean Sun (RAMS) (q.v.) but the procedure is not difficult. A few examples of this kind of return may prove useful.

If we took the lunar position in the solar return chart and computed a return for the time and date each month that the Moon transited this position, we would have an anlunar return (q.v.). But if we use the longitude of the progressed Moon we can compute the kinetic or solar Moon return and also progress it.

Example No.1:
Required: the solar Moon return for January 1952.
Solar return data: 02.52 UT 21.4.51.
RAMC 16.44.58. Moon 19° 43′ Libra.
Event: date 6.2.52.

In order to compute the lunar kinetic or solar Moon return we need to know in what longitude the progressed Moon will be in January 1952. From the ephemeris for January 1952, the date required is the 20th as this is the date on which it will transit its progressed longitude.

Working:

		H	M	S	
(A) 0.0 hr. UT 19.1.52*	Mean Sun	19	49	22	
Solar return 21.4.51	Mean Sun	01	53	30	–
Difference		17	55	52	
Correction		00	02	57	–
Mean solar hours		17	52	55	
UT of solar return		02	52	00	+
UT of progressed SR 21.4.51		20	44	55	

* The date when the Moon transits the longitude that it has in the solar return:

(B) Moon's longitude at 20.45 UT 21.4.51: = 0° 30′ Scorpio

(C) Moon's progressed longitude 0° 30′ Scorpio:
    Moon transits this longitude on 20 January 1952:

	D	M	
Moon's prog. long.	00	30	Scorpio
Moon's long. at 0 hr. 20th Jan.	25	46	Libra
Difference	04	44	(4.73)
Moon's 12 hr. motion (0–12 hr.) 20th	06	35	(6.58)

$$\frac{4.73 \times 12}{6.58} = 8.63 = 8.38 \text{ UT } 20.1.52$$

		H	M	S	
UT of lunar kinetic		08	38	00	
Correction (9.86 sec.)	*	00	01	25	+
ST at 0 hr. UT 20 Jan.	**	07	53	19	+
RAMC at Greenwich		16	32	44	
Long. Equiv. (0.08W)		.00	00	32	–
RAMC of lunar kinetic or solar Moon return		16	32	12	
Mean Sun = * + ** + 12 hr.		19	54	44	

RAMC of return gives Ascendant of 13° Aquarius:
                        Midheaven of 10° Sagittarius:

As this return covers the period when George VI died and his daughter Elizabeth became queen, we can progress the return to the date of the event, namely 6 February 1952.

Working:

		H	M	S	
6.2.52. 12.00 UT	Mean Sun	21	02	18	
Solar Moon return	Mean Sun	19	54	44	–
Difference		01	07	34	
RAMC of return		16	32	12	+
RAMC of progressed return		17	39	46	

Ascendant 18° Pisces: MC 25° Sagittarius.

As an additional check on our calculations we can take the increment of solar time from the date of the return to the date under review (1 hour 07 minutes), which added to the UT of the return (8 hours 38 minutes) will give 9 hours 45 minutes. On 20 January at noon the sidereal time is 19.55.17. Deducting the difference between 12.00 and 9.45 = 2.15. Taking this from the sidereal time at noon gives 17.40 which is the sidereal time or RAMC of the progressed return.

This particular return, set for London, appears to support the opinion of those who state that all returns should be cast for the birthplace. However, there is no firm agreement on this point and only intensive studies will show whether birthplace or residence should have priority. It is often difficult to ascertain where a person was residing at a particular time, particularly public figures who are frequently on the move.

In this work there are some cases of foreign births and an effort has been made to list the return factors which alter with locality, namely the Ascendant and house cusps, in order that some indication can be obtained concerning the birthplace/residence question. Very often the matter is of little consequence as the distances apart are comparatively slight. But when vast distances are involved, such as being born in the United States and subsequently residing in Britain, the mundane positions of a chart will be completely different.

Example No.2:
Required the solar Moon return for May 1950.
Solar return data: 13.41 UT 29.8.49.
RAMC 12.09.23. Moon 19° 53′ Scorpio.
Event: Marriage 13.5.50. London.

(A) *Working*:

		H	M	S
3.5.50. 00.00 UT	Mean Sun	02	41	18
Solar return 29.8.49	Mean Sun	10	29	43 −
Difference		16	11	35
Correction		00	02	40 −
Mean solar hours		16	08	55
UT of solar return		13	41	00 +
UT of prog. SR 30.8.49		05	49	55

(B) Moon's long. 05.50 UT 30.8.49 = 29° 18′ Scorpio.

(C) Moon's progressed long. 29° 18′ Scorpio:
Moon transits this longitude on May 3rd.

	D	M
At noon 3.5.50. Moon's long.	00	44 Sagittarius
Moon's prog. long.	29	18 Scorpio
	01	26 (1.43)
Moon's daily motion 2/3 May 50.	15	15 (15.25)

$$\frac{1.43 \times 24}{15.25} = 2.26 = 2.15 \text{ before noon} =$$

09.45 UT 3.5.50.

		H	M	S
ST 0 hr. UT 3.5.50		14	41	18
Time elapsed	+	09	45	00
Correction	+	00	01	36
ST at Greenwich		00	27	54
Long. Equiv. (0.20W)	−	00	01	20
RAMC solar Moon return.		00	26	34
Mean Sun		02	42	54

Solar Moon return: Asc. 1° Leo: MC 7° Aries: at London.

Progressed for 13.5.50 14.30 UT London.

		H	M	S	
13.5.50: 14.30 UT	Mean Sun	03	23	07	
Solar Moon return	Mean Sun	02	42	54	−
Difference		00	40	13	
RAMC of return		00	26	34	+
RAMC of prog. return		01	06	47	

Asc. 8° Leo: MC 18° Aries: at London.

This example can be compared with the birthplace which was 48° 47′N, 9° 11′E.

Asc. at birthplace	=	6° Leo Solar Moon return
MC at birthplace	=	17 Aries Solar Moon return
Asc. at birthplace	=	13 Leo Prog. SM return
MC at birthplace	=	28 Aries Prog. SM return

7.

CALCULATIONS (2)
THE SIDEREAL ZODIAC

The majority of Western astrologers use the tropical zodiac and although the term 'zodiacs' has crept into astrological terminology, there is only one zodiac, its designation depending on the point from which it is measured.

The tropical zodiac commences with the Vernal (Spring) equinoctial point, which is in retrograde motion along the Ecliptic at the rate of one degree of longitude in about 71½ years. As this point is retrograding so also is the tropical zodiac, this motion being termed the Precession or Regression of the Equinoxes. This 'Moving or Precessional' zodiac is constantly moving against the order of the zodiacal constellations. In contrast to the tropical zodiac, the sidereal (starry) zodiac which was, according to Fagan, Bradley and others the zodiac of antiquity, is permanently aligned to the fixed stars and therefore non-moving and non-precessional.

The 'zero-year' when 'both zodiacs' coincided was, according to Fagan, AD 221. Since that time the continual shift of the tropical zodiac has resulted in a divergence between the tropical and sidereal starting points. This difference, which is now approximately 24° is known by the Sanskrit word *ayanamsa*. The sidereal zodiac, like the usual tropical zodiac is divided into twelve equal divisions of 30° each. These divisions have the same familiar names as the tropical zodiac, Aries, Taurus, Gemini, etc.

The ayanamsa for a given date is found by subtracting the sidereal longitude of the vernal point—Synetic Vernal Point (SVP)—for the same date, from 360°. From AD 221 the ayanamsa can be found by subtracting the numerical value of the SVP from 30°. For the entire period 221–2376, the SVP is in Pisces.

The calculation of charts using the sidereal zodiac has been made easier through the publication of sidereal ephemerides which reduce the work involved in converting from one zodiac to another. The *American Sidereal Ephemeris* compiled by Neil Michelsen is particularly valuable for charting in the sidereal zodiac (see References).

Conversion of Tropical to Sidereal

The sidereal longitude of the SVP (numerical value) deducted from 30° will give the ayanamsa and this amount subtracted from the tropical longitude will give the sidereal longitude.

Example No.1:
Find the sidereal longitude of the Sun 1.1.87. 12.00 UT.

Sun's long. (tropical)	10° 31′ 48″		Capricorn
30° − SVP 5° 26′ 33″ =	24 33 27	−	
Sun's sidereal longitude =	15 58 21		Sagittarius

Alternatively, an easier method:

Sun's tropical long.	10° 31′ 48″		Capricorn
SVP	+ 5 26 33		
	15 58 21		
Less 1 sign or 30°	30 00 00		
Sidereal long.	15 58 21		Sagittarius

To convert a sidereal longitude to tropical,
reverse the process:

15 58	21	sidereal Sagittarius
+ 30 00	00	
15 58	21	
− 5 26	33	SVP
10 31	48	tropical Capricorn

To convert a tropical chart into a sidereal chart the ayanamsa for the *date of the chart* must be deducted from all tropical longitudes, including the cusps of the twelve mundane houses. As precession is always negative, the addition of the SVP or the deduction of the ayanamsa expunges from the tropical chart all the precession that has accrued since AD 221.

For the benefit of those readers who may not be too familiar with the sidereal techniques, it may be useful to list a natal chart using both tropical and sidereal placements and to compute a solar and lunar return using 'both zodiacs'.

Example No.1:
Natal data: 1.40 UT 21.4.1926 London, 51.30N 0.08W

Tropical Long.					*Sidereal Long.*			
	°	′	″		°	′	″	
Sun	00	12	21	Taurus	06	29	58	Aries
Moon	12	07		Leo	18	25		Cancer
Mercury	04	40		Aries	10	57		Pisces
Venus	13	58		Pisces	20	15		Aquarius
Mars	20	53		Aquarius	27	10		Capricorn
Jupiter	22	30		Aquarius	28	47		Capricorn
Saturn	24	26		Scorpio	00	43		Scorpio
Uranus	27	22		Pisces	03	39		Pisces
Neptune	22	02		Leo	28	20		Cancer
Pluto	12	42		Cancer	18	59		Gemini
Asc.	21	25		Capricorn	27	42		Sagittarius
MC	25	35		Scorpio	01	52		Scorpio

RAMC 15.32.58...
Mean Sun 01.53.30..
Apparent 01.52.25..
Sun
SVP..6° 17′ 37″.....................

Sidereal Calculation

Example No.1 shows how the tropical Sun to be 0° 12′ 21″ Taurus.
Our next step is to convert this longitude into terms of the sidereal
zodiac. To do this, we merely add to it the sidereal longitude of the
Vernal Point (VP) on the date of birth. From the ephemeris* for
21.4.26 this is found to be 6° 17′ 37″:

Tropical long. of Sun	30°	12′	21″
VP 21.4.26. Pisces 6° 17′ 37″	336	17	37 +
	366	29	58
Less circle	360	00	00 −
Sidereal long. natal Sun	6	29	58

* *The American Ephemeris for the Twentieth Century* or *The American Sidereal Ephemeris.*

<u>Aries 6° 29′ 58″</u>

An easier and quicker method for conversions such as this is to add the VP to the Sun's tropical longitude and deduct one whole sign or 30°:

Sun's tropical long.	Taurus	0°	12′	21″	
VP		6	17	37	+
	Taurus	6	29	58	
Less one sign (30°)		30	00	00	−
Sun's sidereal long.	Aries	6	29	58	

   To calculate the Sidereal Solar Return (SSR) for our subject's twenty-fifth birthday (21.4.51) we first have to find the VP for this date. From the ephemeris this is 5° 56′ 21″. To find the date of the month in 1951 on which the SSR will occur, the precession that has accrued since the date of birth must be added to the tropical longitude of the natal Sun. The accrued precession is the difference between the VP on the birthdate and the date of the SSR:

Birthdate 21.4.26	VP	6°	17′	37″	
Estimated date SSR 21.4.51	VP	5	56	21	−
Accrued precession		0	21	16	
Tropical long. natal Sun	Taurus	0	12	21	+
Precessed long. natal Sun	Taurus	0	33	37	

   From the ephemeris (April 1951) the Sun will be in 0° 33′ 37″ Taurus sometime prior to noon on 21 April. The calculation to find the exact time is as follows:

1951

April 21 Noon UT Sun's long.	00°	34′	38″	Taurus
April 20 Noon UT Sun's long.	29	36	06	Aries
Daily motion (DM)	00	58	32	
	00	34	38	
Precessed long. natal Sun	00	33	37	−
Difference	00	01	01	

The exact time of the return will be when the sun is in 0° 33′ 37″ Taurus (tropical). Therefore if the Sun moves 58′ 32″ in 24 hours, it will move 1′ 01″ in: $\dfrac{(1'\ 01'')}{(58\ 32)}\ \dfrac{0.017 \times 24}{0.976} = 0.417 = 25$ min.

The Sidereal Solar Return for 1951/52 occurred at 11.35 UT 21.4.1951.
The RAMC is found as follows:

	H	M	S
UT SSR		11	35	00
Correction 9.86 sec. per hour	+	00	01	54
ST 0 hr. UT 21.4.51	+	13	53	02
ST at Greenwich		01	29	56
Long. Equiv. (0.08W)	−	00	00	32
RAMC. SSR at birthplace*		01	29	24

At London the Ascendant is 18° Cancer: MC 0° Aries.

A chart should now be calculated in the normal manner, the
tropical longitudes of the planets being computed for 11.35 UT
21.4.51 with the cusps of houses for a sidereal time of 1.29.24. All
longitudes, including the cusps of the houses, should then be reduced
to the sidereal zodiac by adding the VP Pisces 5° 56′ 21″.

The Natal Chart (Sidereal)
If a sidereal ephemeris for the year required is available the calculation
of a chart is a simple matter. However, if conversion has to be made
using a tropical ephemeris the work takes a little longer.

Example No.1:
Using a tropical ephemeris calculate a natal chart and convert into
the sidereal zodiac.
Birth data: 1.40 UT 21.4.26. London 51.30N 0.08W.

1926 Ephemeris	H	M	S	
ST 0 hr. UT 21.4.26		13	53	14	*
Time elapsed	+	01	40	00	
Correction 9.86 sec. per hour	+	00	00	16	**
ST at Greenwich		15	33	30	
Long. Equiv. (0.08W)	−	00	00	32	
RAMC		15	32	58	
Mean Sun * + ** less 12 hours		01	53	30	
Apparent Sun		01	52	25	

* If the Queen was not residing in London on her twenty-fifth birthday, then the
question of locality versus residence arises.

Asc. 21° Capricorn: MC 25° Scorpio: at London.
These are the tropical longitudes of the ascendant and Midheaven.
To convert to the sidereal zodiac we add the SVP for 21.4.26 (6° 17′
37″) and reduce by one sign.

Asc. in degrees and minutes = 21° 25′ + 6° 17′ less 30° = 27°
42′ Sagittarius sidereal: MC 25° 35′ Scorpio + 6° 17′ less 30° =
1° 52′ Scorpio sidereal.

The cusps of the houses, irrespective of the house system, are found
in a similar manner. Add to the tropical longitude shown on the
appropriate cusp the SVP value and deduct 30°.

The planetary positions are calculated for the birthtime in the
usual manner and are then converted into sidereal longitudes using
the SVP for the birth date. For example, the Sun's position at 1.40
UT 21.4.26. is 0° 12′ 21″ Taurus tropical. Convert to sidereal equals
0.12.21 + SVP 6.17.37 = 6.29.58 Taurus less 1 sign or 30° = 6°
29′ 58″ Aries = sidereal longitude. The Moon and the planets are
dealt with in the same way.

The Sidereal Solar Return

This return, computed in terms of the sidereal zodiac, is not the
same as the tropical return. The time of the return will always be
different and sometimes the day. This is due to the elimination of
precession which, in a period of seventy-two years, amounts to a full
degree. Although there may be little difference with the slower-
moving planets, the time difference between the two types of return
greatly affects the position of the Moon and angles.

Using a sidereal ephemeris the calculation of a sidereal solar return
(SSR) is the same as for the tropical return. When no sidereal
ephemerides are available the tropical ephemerides can be used.
In using tropical ephemerides we have to add to the tropical longitude
the accrued value of precession in order to eliminate it, and then
calculate the time of the Sun's return to this position and not to
its natal tropical longitude. The use of logs., for those that prefer
this method, or the use of a calculator enables the Sun's position
to be found quite easily.

Example No.1:
Find the date and time of the Sidereal Solar Return for 1951/52.
Birth data: 1.40 UT 21.4.26. London, 51.30N 0.08W.

Sidereal Sun	6°	29'	58"	Aries
Tropical Sun	0	12	21	Taurus
SVP	6	17	37	

Accrued precession:

Birthdate 21.4.26 SVP		6	17	37	
21.4.51 SVP		5	56	21	–
Precession		0	21	16	
Sun's tropical long.	Add	0	12	21	
		0	33	37	Taurus

This tropical longitude restores the Sun to its place amongst the fixed stars. The next step is to calculate the date and time when the Sun reaches 0° 33' 37" Taurus.

Working:

1951 Ephemeris		D	M	S	
Sun's long. 21.4.51. noon UT		00	34	38	Taurus
Sun's long. required		00	33	37	
Difference		00	01	01	(0.017)
Sun's daily motion 20/21.4.51		00	58	32	(0.975)

Calculator:

$$\begin{matrix} (1'\ 01") \\ (58\ 32) \end{matrix} \quad \frac{0.017 \times 24}{0.975} = 0.417 = 0 \text{ hr. } 25 \text{ min.}$$

0.25 before noon = 11.35 UT 21.4.51 = Date and time of SS Return 1951/52.

Using logs:

	D	M	S	Log	
Sun's motion 20/21 April	0	58	32	0.48787	Tern.
Difference	0	01	01	2.24809	Tern.
Then log of difference			2.24809	Ternary	
less log of motion			0.48787	Ternary	
25 minutes			1.76022	Diurnal	

= 11.35 UT 21.4.51 = SS Return

	H	M	S
ST at noon 21.4.51.	1	55	00
Interval to noon	− 0	25	00
Correction	− 0	00	04
Longitude Equiv. (0.08W)	− 0	00	32
RAMC at London	1	29	24

As the return occurred at 11.35 UT all the planetary positions are calculated for this time with the cusps taken out for London. As a tropical ephemeris was used all cusps and planetary positions must be transposed into the sidereal zodiac by the addition of the SVP for 21 April 1951 (5° 56′ 21″) and the deduction of one sign or 30°.

Tropical long.				*Sidereal long.*			
	°	′	″		°	′	″
Sun	00	33	37 Taurus	06	29	58	Aries
Moon	24	58	Libra	00	54		Libra
Mercury	06	28	Taurus	12	24		Aries
Venus	07	15	Gemini	13	11		Taurus
Mars	08	12	Taurus	14	08		Aries
Jupiter	29	58	Pisces	05	54		Pisces
Saturn	26	41	Virgo	02	37		Virgo
Uranus	06	02	Cancer	11	58		Gemini
Neptune	17	49	Libra	23	45		Virgo
Pluto	17	25	Leo	23	21		Cancer
Asc.	12	33	Leo	18	29		Cancer
MC	24	08	Aries	00	04		Aries
RAMC	01.	29.	24				
Mean Sun	01.	54.	56				
Apparent Sun	01.	53.	47				

The Progressed Sidereal Solar Return (PSSR)

There are two main methods of progression which can be applied to the SSR (a) the mean daily increase in sidereal time which is added to the sidereal time of the return, (b) the solar quotidian, which is dependent on the increase of the Right Ascension of the Mean Sun (MS) between the date of the return and the date under review. With method (a) the difference in sidereal time between two consecutive solar returns plus 24 hours and divided by the mean length of the sidereal year (365.25636) will give the daily increase in sidereal time to be added to the sidereal time of the return. A fairly accurate progression can be achieved by taking the average difference between the sidereal time of consecutive returns, namely 30 hours, 9 minutes and 13 seconds, which gives a daily advance of 4 minutes 57 seconds sidereal time.

Example No.1:
Find the RAMC of the PSSR for the 6.2.1952.
Solar Return data: 11.35 UT 21.4.1951. London.
RAMC 1.29.24

Date required 6.2.52 =		37	day of year
	+	365	ease of deduction
		402	
Date of SSR 21.4.51	−	111	day of year
Days elapsed		291	

$$\frac{291 \times 30.1536}{366}\ 23.58.28\ \text{Increment of sidereal time.}$$

RAMC SR =   01.29.24 +
RAMC PSSR   01.27.52 (approx.)

For a more precise calculation we take the actual difference between two consecutive returns and work with those figures.

Example No.2:
SSR 1952.

Accrued Precession:

		D	M	S	
Birthdate 21.4.26 SVP		6	17	37	
21.4.52 SVP		5	55	24	−
Precession		0	22	13	
Sun's tropical long.	Add	0	12	21	
		0	34	34	Taurus

Calculation:

1952 Ephemeris	D	M	S	
Sun's long. 20.4.52. noon UT	00	20	28	Taurus
Sun's long. required	00	34	34	
Difference	00	14	06	(0.235)
Sun's daily motion 20/21.4.52	00	58	33	(0.976)

Calculator:

$$\frac{0.235 \times 24}{0.976}\ 5.78\ = \qquad 5\text{hr. } 47 \text{ min. after noon}$$

= 17.47 UT 20.4.52 = date and time of 1952/53 Sidereal solar return: The RAMC is found as follows:

		H	M	S
ST 0 hr. UT 20.4.52		13	52	05
Time elapsed	+	17	47	00
Correction	+	00	02	55
ST at Greenwich		07	42	00
Longitude Equiv. (0.08W)	−	00	00	32
RAMC at London		07	41	28

		H	M	S
RAMC 1952/53 Return		07	41	28
RAMC 1951/52 Return		01	29	24
		06	12	04
	+	24	00	00
		30	12	04

$$\frac{30.12.04}{24.00.03} = \frac{30.2011}{24.0009} = 1.2583 \text{ Constant}$$

		H	M	S
RA Apparent Sun 6.2.52. Noon UT		21	16	26
RA Apparent Sun 21.4.51. 11.35 UT		01	53	47 −
Difference		19	22	39
x constant 1.2583	=	00	22	58
RAMC SR	+	01	29	24
RAMC Prog. solar return		01	52	22

The approximate sidereal time of 1.30, found by taking the average advance over the year, requires the equation of time adjustment to compensate for the difference between apparent and mean time. This correction, which is a plus in this case, will bring the approximate sidereal time fairly close to the sidereal time as found by exact calculation.

An alternative method of calculation which will give a rough approximation of the progressed sidereal solar return is to multiply the number of days elapsed from the date of the return by the average advance in sidereal time. The average advance of sidereal time is 4 minutes 57 seconds per day, so using tables (day of year) and Sidereal Increment (see Appendix 1) we have:

Day of year 6 Feb.   37 + 365* = 402
Day of year 21 April   111   −
Days elapsed   291

		H	M	S
291 × 4.95 min. =		24	00	27
Add RAMC SSR	+	01	29	24
Mean RAMC of PSSR		01	29	51
Equation of time (see below)	+	00	15	00
True RAMC of PSSR		01	44	51

The difference between apparent time and mean time means that the sidereal time must be corrected; the amount of the correction depending upon the dates involved. In the above example the value for 6 February = −14 minutes, and 21 April = +1: Therefore the date of the SSR 21.4.51 = + 1
            PSR   6.2.52 = −14
Subtract algebraically by changing the sign of the lower figure and add: Plus 1
        Plus 14 = 15 minutes to be added to the RAMC (sidereal time) to give the sidereal time of the PSSR based on the average difference of sidereal time between solar returns.

If the person is residing at the place for which the solar return was computed no correction to the sidereal time (RAMC) as found is needed. If the residence is different, then the time difference between the respective longitudes has to be applied. In the methods outlined above there is a slight difference between the two sidereal times of a couple of minutes which is insignificant. However, for accurate progression, the method using the apparent Sun should be used.

The Queen's father, King George VI, died at Sandringham, Norfolk in the early hours of 6.2.52, while Princess Elizabeth (as she then was) was in Nyeri, Kenya. The news of her father's death and her accession to the throne was conveyed to her at 2.45 p.m. local time (11.45 UT) 6.2.52.* The standard time −3 hours was unfortunately given in some astrological magazines as −2 hours. The geographical latitude of Nyeri is 0° 25′ South: Longitude 36° 56′ East.

The Midheaven of the SSR progresses at the rate of about five minutes of sidereal time per day so we can always obtain a rough approximation of the progressed angles by multiplying the number of days elapsed from the date of the return by about five minutes and adding the result to the sidereal time (RAMC) of the return. However, for accurate progression we need to take the length of the sidereal year and calculate the progressed sidereal solar return (PSSR) for the actual date under review, in this case, the 6 February 1952.

SSR	UT	RAMC (Greenwich)
20 April 52	17.47	7.42.00
21 April 51	11.35	1.29.56
Difference in time	06.12	6.12.04
Add one day (24 hours)		24.00.00
True length of sidereal year		30.12.04

$$\frac{30.12.04}{24.00.03.5} = 1.2583 \text{ Constant.}$$

This constant is applicable for the whole of this particular return year. Using the Right Ascension of the Apparent Sun we can now progress the return to the date required:

		H	M	S	
6 Feb. 1952 11.45 UT	RAA Sun	21	16	23	
SSR 1951	RAA Sun	01	53	47	
Difference		19	22	36	
times constant (1.2583)	=	24	22	54	
Increment	=	00	22	54	
RAMC SSR Greenwich meridian		01	29	56	+
Longitude Equiv. (0.08W)		00	00	32	–
RAMC Prog. SSR		01	52	18	

On or about the 290th day after the date of the return the Midheaven will return to its original position in the solar return. In certain cases this means that some planets will come twice to the Midheaven in the course of the return year.

The sidereal version of Queen's Elizabeth's solar return for 1951/52 and its progression for the death of her father and her accession to the throne is notable in that it portrays the events and conditions of 6 February 1952. The first factor which is all-apparent is the transiting Sun opposed to the solar Pluto and separating from an opposition of the natal Moon. This could be construed symbolically as a 'full moon' indicating an end of one cycle and the commencement of a new phase. Plutonian contacts invariably coincide with altering the status quo, losses, farewells and, although death is only one of the manifestations associated with Pluto, its prominence in this return is extremely apt.

Another major factor in this solar return is the Midheaven in exact conjunction with the solar Sun while the transiting Sun opposes the Ascendant. The Sun, symbol of honours and acclaim, is thus 'doubly reinforced' through its conjunction with the tenth and seventh angles. The transiting Venus is opposed to the natal Pluto and the transiting Uranus, indicating the emotional shock and loss at the death of her father. So, we have Sun, Moon, Pluto and Venus either angular or prominently aspected, all of which are appropriate for the events experienced at that time. The natal Neptune is an additional testimony to the sense of loss, confusion and worry paramount at this time, due to its closeness to the progressed Ascendant, opposition the transiting Sun.

The Solar Return chart, with its progressions, is the major instrument, but many of the indications contained in it can be confirmed through the use of the lunar return chart or other subsidiary charts. As an illustration, we can compute and study the Queen's lunar return immediately preceding her accession.

Her natal Moon is 12° 07′ Leo (tropical) and 18° 25′ Cancer (sidereal). The calculation for the *sidereal zodiac* is as follows:

Working:
Required: Date and time of the sidereal lunar return for the period Jan./Feb. 1952.

SVP 21.4.26		6°	17′	37″
SVP 1.1.52	−	5	55	40
Accrued precession		0	21	57
Tropical long. natal Moon Leo		12	07	00 +
Precessed long. natal Moon Leo		12	28	57

From the ephemeris (January 1952) the Moon will be in 12° 29′ Leo sometime in the early hours of 14 January. The exact time is found as follows:

1952

14 Jan. 0 hr. UT Moon's long.	12°	10′	02″ Leo
14 Jan. 12 hr. UT Moon's long.	18	05	40
Motion in 12 hours	05	55	38
Precessed long. natal Moon	12	28	57
Moon's long. 0 hr. 14 Jan.	12	10	02
Difference	00	18	55

The exact time of the lunar return will be when the Moon is in 12° 29′ Leo (tropical). If 12 hours = 5° 55′ 38″, then 18′ 55″ will = ?

$$(18′ \ 55″) = \frac{0.315 \times 12}{5.927} = 0.638 = 38 \text{ min. after}$$

0 hr. 14 Jan. = 00.38 UT 14.1.52 = time and date of Lunar return:

	H	M	S
UT lunar return		00	38	00
Correction	+	00	00	06
ST 0 hr. 14 Jan.	+	07	29	40
ST at Greenwich		08	07	46
Long. Equiv. (0.08W)	−	00	00	32
RAMC (birthplace)		08	07	14

Asc. 28° Virgo: MC 5° Cancer: (sidereal).

The procedure for calculating the chart is the same as for the solar return, the planets being calculated for the universal time of the return and the houses for the sidereal time (RAMC).

In the Queen's solar return, Pluto was prominent and at the time of the demise of her father the Sun was in major aspect to it. If we study the lunar return (based on her natal sidereal Moon) for the period covering Jan./Feb. 1952, we find confirmation that this period will be anything but joyful. Saturn, Neptune and Mars are astride the Ascendant with the Moon closing to a conjunction with the lunar Pluto. The presence of Neptune and Saturn on an angle square the lunar Sun shows the tremendous emotional tension, fear and sense of isolation which these two planets, acting in concert, often symbolize. The tendency for Pluto to 'catapult' one into the limelight is adequately shown in the solar return and its progressions. In the lunar chart it reinforces the sense of loneliness through its lunar contact. The significance of Pluto and its reputation for the dramatic can be shown by progressing this lunar chart at the quotidian rate (3 minutes 57 seconds per day).

	H	M	S	
Mean Sun of event 6.2.52 11.45 UT	21	02	16	
Mean Sun of LR 14.1.52 00.38 UT	19	29	46	−
Difference	01	32	30	
Add RAMC LR	08	07	14	+
RAMC lunar quotidian (London)	09	39	44	

Asc. 14° Libra: MC 28° Cancer.
At this rate the lunar Pluto is conjunction the MC and the natal Neptune, ecliptically, is precisely on the MC.

These contacts are impressive and comply with the essential criteria that events, conditions or experiences must correspond both in time and in nature with the appropriate astrological patterns.

So far we have dealt with the sidereal version using two major return charts. In fairness we should look at the tropical returns for this period and see whether, in fact, they are indicative of the period under review.

The tropical solar return occurred at:
02.52 UT 21.4.51: RAMC 16.44.58: RAAS 1.52.25:

Mean Sun 1.53.30: Constant 1.2416:

Natal Sun 0° 12′ 21″ Taurus: Natal Moon 12° 07′ Leo:

The tropical return, like the sidereal version, has Pluto close to an angle (seventh) but unlike its sidereal counterpart it lacks the powerful solar contacts normally associated with increased status and prestige. It does have, however, a close conjunction of Moon/Neptune on the eighth cusp (Placidus) which may be symbolic of the shape of things to come during the return year. The emphasis on the second/eighth house sectors may be indicative of the increased power and patronage which is the prerogative of monarchs. However, when the solar return chart is 'married up' with the natal chart, and is progressed for the period required, namely 6 February 1952, a very different picture emerges. The progressed angles are almost identical with those of the return, thereby bringing the natal Mars/Jupiter to the Ascendant opposition the transiting Pluto. The Sun on the day was close to the solar and progressed Ascendants opposition Pluto and applying to the conjunction of Mars/Jupiter opposition natal Neptune, which was exactly on the seventh angle. Both the returns, sidereal and tropical are, in their own fashion, extremely interesting in that the sidereal chart with its 'double' angular Sun shows the honour and prestige, while the tropical chart with its Sun/Pluto, Mars/Jupiter and Neptunian contacts aptly describe the events and conditions at that time.

The lunar returns preceding this period are also noteworthy in that both returns have Saturn/Neptune on the Ascendant. In the tropical return Saturn is exactly conjunction the Ascendant, while in the sidereal chart it is Neptune which is closest. Saturn, of course, signifies restructuring and responsibilities, so its presence on an angle would be highly appropriate for the accession of a monarch. Likewise, Neptune would show the apprehension, sorrow and feelings of unreality present at that time.

Sidereal Lunar Returns (SLR)

These returns are based on the return of the natal Moon each lunar month to its place among the fixed stars. The calculations are similar to those for the solar return, but owing to the Moon's rapid motion no complicated calculations are required. If logs. are used, then the Diurnal table (see Appendix 1) will suffice. The easiest method, as with all return calculations, is to use a calculator in conjunction with the tables listed in Appendix 1 to this work.

Example No.1:

Required the lunar return for Jan./Feb. 52.

Natal Moon-Tropical 12° 07′ Leo
Precession   + 0 22

                       12 29 Leo
13.1.52 noon UT   − 06 15 Leo
Difference   06 14   Diurnal log. 0.58549

Moon's daily
motion 13/14.1.52   11 51   Diurnal log. 0.30649 −
                                      12.38   0.27900

12 hr. 38 min. after noon = 00.38 UT 14.1.52 =
date and time of SL Return

	H	M	S
ST 0 hr. UT 14.1.52	07	29	40
Time elapsed	+ 00	38	00
Correction	+ 00	00	06
Longitude Equiv. (0.08W)	− 00	00	32
RAMC at London	08	07	14

This RAMC at London (8.07.14) gives the following:
Asc. 22° Libra: MC 29° Cancer: Tropical
Asc. 28 Virgo: MC 5 Cancer: Sidereal

The corresponding *Tropical lunar return* is found as follows:
Natal Moon 12° 07′ Leo:

                       °   ′

Moon's long. 14.1.52
noon UT   18 06 Leo
Moon's natal long.   12 07
Difference   05 59   Diurnal log. 0.60327

Moon's daily motion
13/14.1.52   11 51   Diurnal log. 0.30649 −
                                     12.07   0.29678

12 hr. 07 min. before noon on the 14.1.52 =
11.53 = 23.53 UT 13.1.52 = date and time of tropical lunar return.

	H	M	S
ST 0 hr. UT 13.1.52		07	25	43
Time elapsed	+	23	53	00
Correction	+	00	03	55
Longitude Equiv. (0.08W)	−	00	00	32
RAMC at London		07	22	06

Asc. 14° Libra: MC 19° Cancer: at London.

Solar quotidian (sidereal)
Birth data: 1.40 UT 21.4.26. London.
Solar return 1951/52. 11.35 UT 21.4.51 London.
Mean Sun 1.54.56. RAMC 1.29.24.
    The solar quotidian (SQ) method is dependent on the increase of the Right Ascension of the Mean Sun (MS) between the date of the return and the date of the event or day under review.
    The method of calculation is simple. Add the difference in Mean Sun (MS) to the sidereal time (ST) of the return. The sum is the ST or RAMC of the solar quotidian (SQ).

Example No.1:
SQ required for 6.2.52. Data as above.

	H	M	S
Mean Sun Noon UT 6.2.1952		21	02	18
Mean Sun solar return	−	01	54	56
Difference		19	07	22
RAMC (ST) of SR	+	01	29	24
RAMC (ST) of SQ		20	36	46

Asc. 11° Gemini: MC 7° Aquarius: Tropical
Asc. 17° Taurus: MC 13° Capricorn: Sidereal

For correctness, the quotidian planets should be calculated for the progressed time i.e. 19.07.22 less acceleration 3 minutes 8 seconds later than the UT of the solar return (6.39 UT 22.4.51). The difference will be slight except for the Moon.
    Note: All the computer-calculated charts are in terms of the tropical zodiac.

Event: Death of father and accession to the throne.
6.2.52

ELIZABETH II. S/R   *No.1*
Gmt 2 52 21 4 1951
51 30N 0 8W

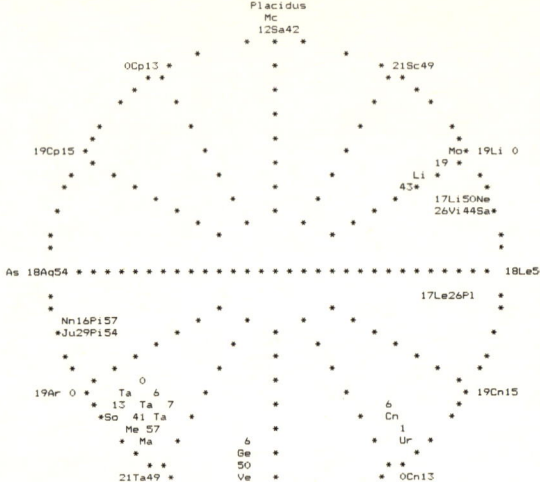

Ref:
Natal Chart No.5

SOLAR RETURN

No.2   ELIZABETH II
Gmt 23 55 13 1 1952
51 30N 0 8W

Event: Death of father
6.2.1952

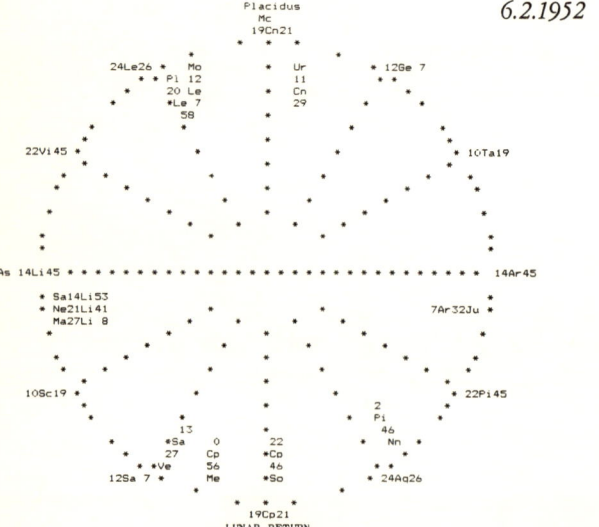

LUNAR RETURN

Ref:
Natal Chart No.5

ELIZABETH II: SOLAR/MOON
Gmt 8 38 20 1 1952   *No.3*
51 30N 0 8W

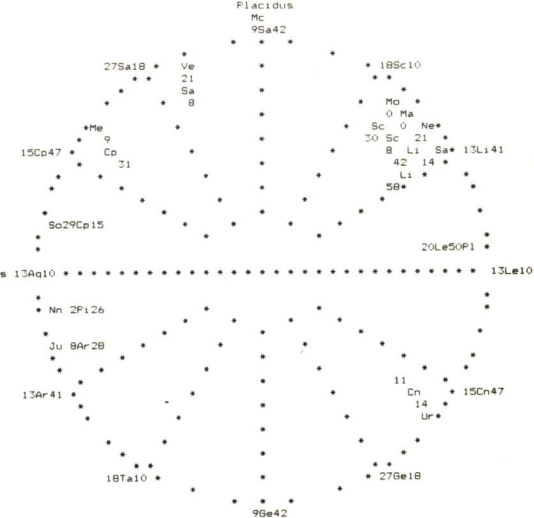

SOLAR MOON RETURN (kinetic lunar)
Preceding death of father
6 February 1952

Ref:
Natal Chart No.5

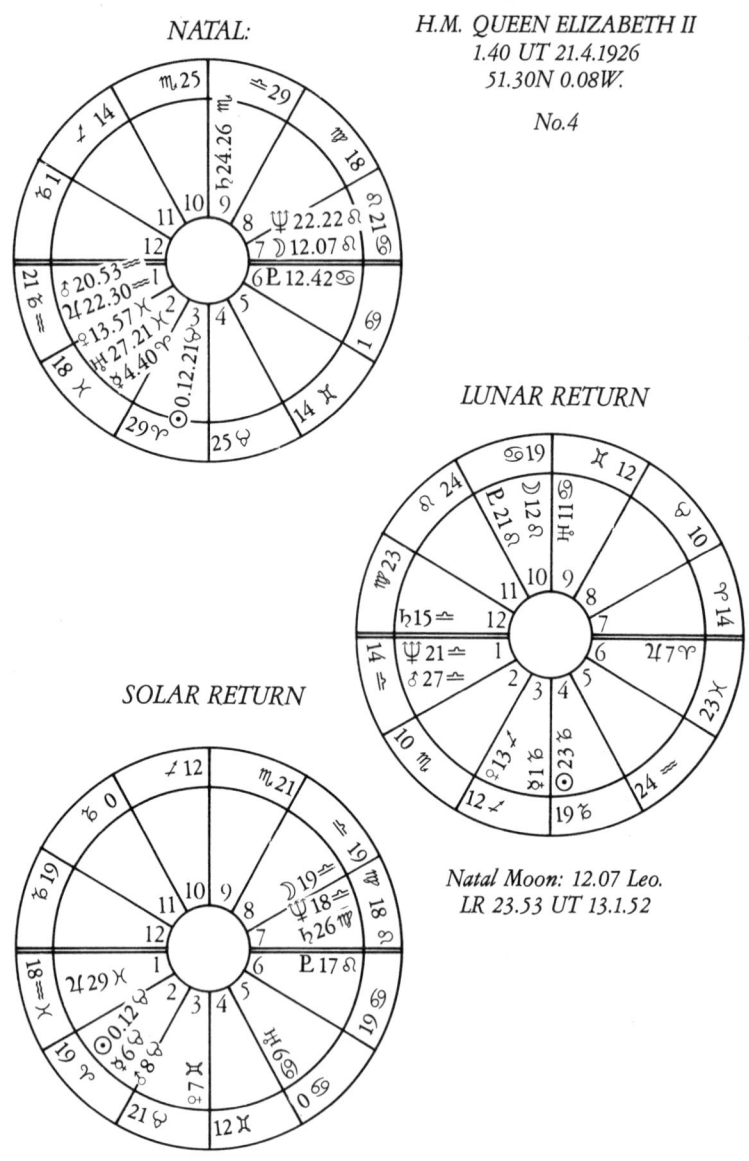

NATAL:

H.M. QUEEN ELIZABETH II
1.40 UT 21.4.1926
51.30N 0.08W.

No.4

LUNAR RETURN

SOLAR RETURN

Natal Moon: 12.07 Leo.
LR 23.53 UT 13.1.52

Natal Sun: 0.12.21 Taurus.
SR 02.52 UT 21.4.51

Returns preceding the death of father and accession 6.2.52 (tropical zodiac)

NATAL: H.M. QUEEN ELIZABETH II

No.4(a)

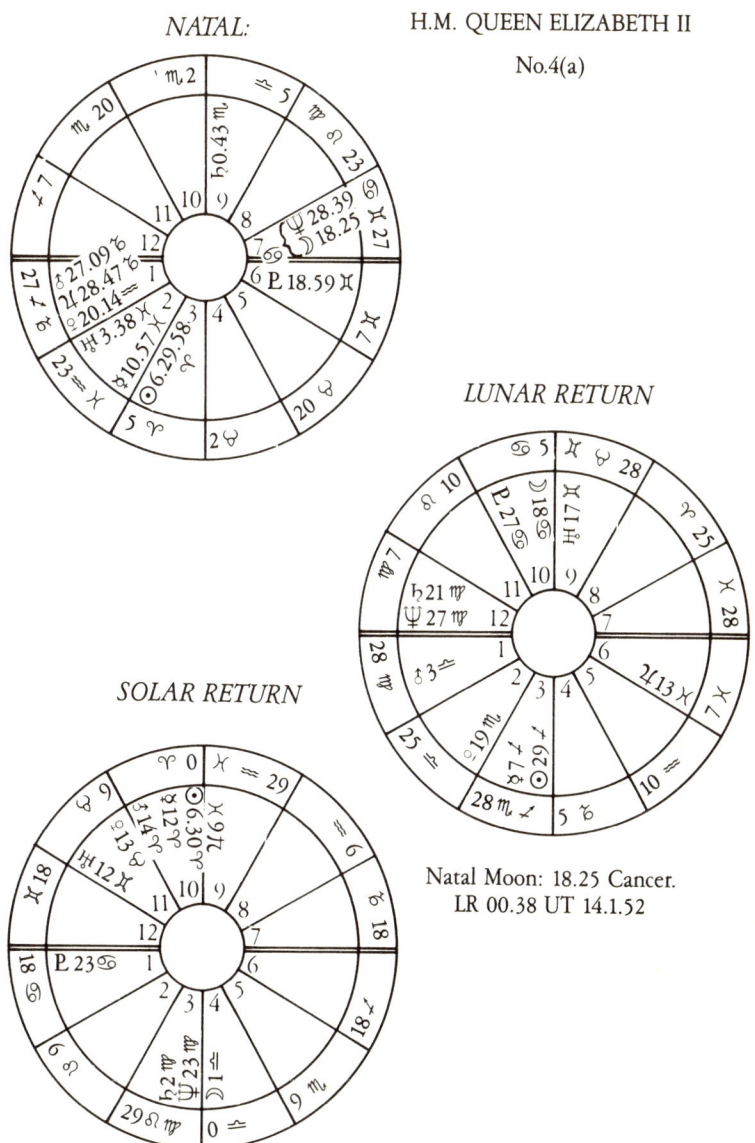

LUNAR RETURN

SOLAR RETURN

Natal Moon: 18.25 Cancer.
LR 00.38 UT 14.1.52

Natal Sun: 6.29.58 Aries.
SR 11.35 UT 21.4.51

Returns preceding the death of father and accession 6.2.52 (sidereal zodiac)

NATAL   ELIZABETH II   *No.5*
Gmt 1 40 21 4 1926
51 30N 0 8W

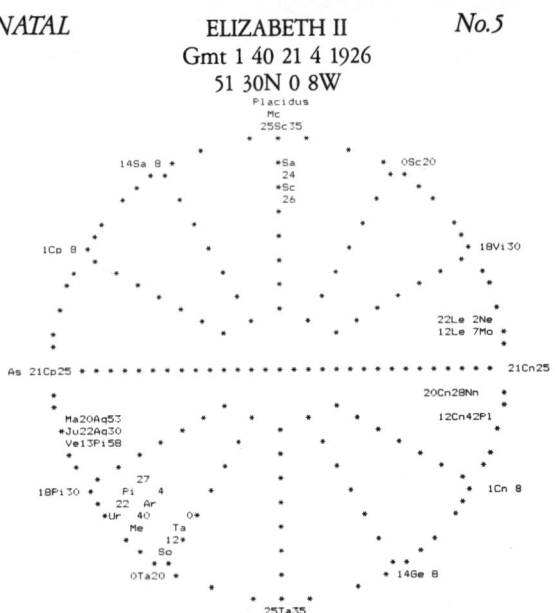

```
                    Placidus
                      Mc
                    25Sc35
                     *  *  *
              *            *              *
   14Sa 8 *          *Sa        *  0Sc20
        *  *          24        *  *
      *              *Sc              *
                      26
     *            *        *        *
                         *              *
  1Cp 8 *      *        *        *         * 18Vi30
     *            *        *        *
     *                  *              *
        *            *        *        22Le 2Ne
     *                  *        *      12Le 7Mo *
As 21Cp25 * * * * * * * * * * * * * * * * * * * 21Cn25
     *                                  20Cn28Nn  *
   Ma20Aq53     *        *        *      12Cn42P1
   *Ju22Aq30                *        *            *
   Ve13Pi58  *        *        *        *
      *  *            *        *        *
   18Pi30 *    27        *        *        * 1Cn 8
        *   Pi  4      *        *        *
        * 22  Ar                *
        *Ur  40    0*
          Me    Ta        *
        *   12*         *
          *  So      *
        *  *        *        * 14Ge 8
    0Ta20 *      *        *
              *  *  *
              25Ta35
```

PROGRESSED SOLAR RETURN   *No.5(a)*

TROPICAL

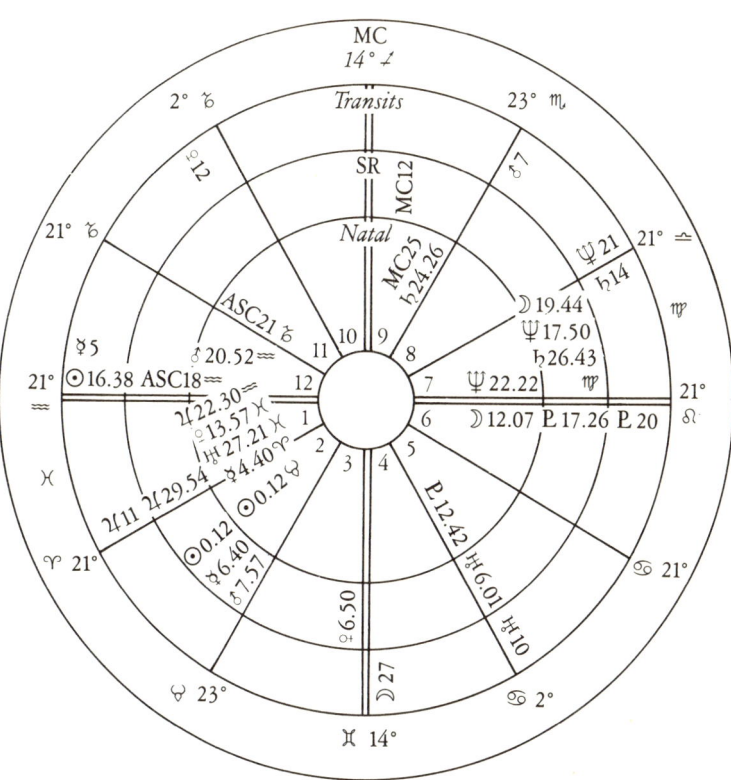

SOLAR RETURN				PROGRESSED RETURN			
Date 21.4.51 Time 02.52				Date 6.2.52 Time 11.45			
	H	M	S		H	M	S
RA Sun	1	52	25	RA Sun PSR	21	16	23
RAMC	16	44	58	RA Sun SR −	1	52	25
Constant	1.2416			= Difference	19	23	58
Queen Elizabeth II				× Constant =	00	05	11
				RAMC SR +	16	44	58
				RAMC PSR	16	50	09

PROGRESSED SOLAR RETURN   No.5(b)

SIDEREAL

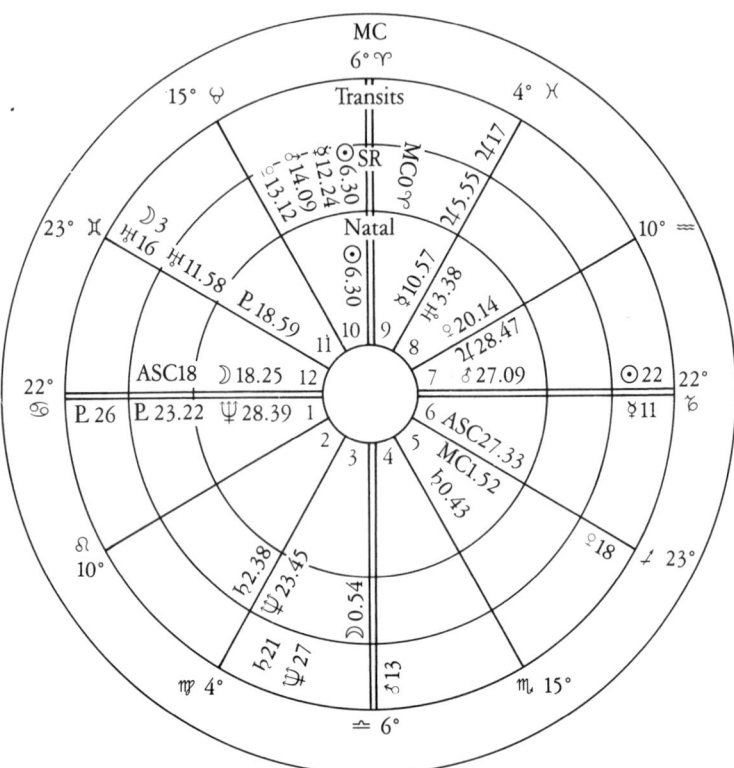

SOLAR RETURN				PROGRESSED RETURN			
Date 21.4.51 Time 11.35				Date 6.2.52 Time 11.45			
	H	M	S		H	M	S
RA Sun	01	53	47	RA Sun PSR	21	16	23
RAMC	01	29	24	RA Sun SR −	01	53	47
Constant	1.2583			= Difference	19	22	36
Queen Elizabeth II				× Constant =	00	22	54
				RAMC SR +	01	29	24
				RAMC PSR	01	52	18

ELIZABETH II: SM PROG.   *No.5 (c)*
Gmt 9 45 20 1 1952
51 30N 0 8W

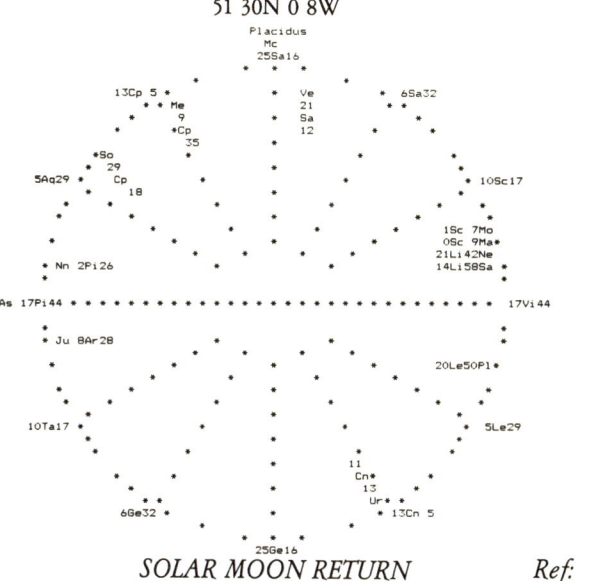

SOLAR MOON RETURN   *Ref:*
PROGRESSED   *Natal Chart No.5*

8.

PLANETARY SIGNIFICATORS, ASPECTS AND HOUSES

The return of the Sun each year to the natal longitude that it held at birth marks the commencement of the solar return year. Millions of people share the same birthday although born in different years. Their solar returns will occur on, or within a day of, their birthday and all will have the same, or almost the same, planetary longitudes. This being so, should they not all experience the same conditions and circumstances during the ensuing solar year? Obviously they do not have identical years because (a) their natal charts are individual to them and them alone, (b) the mundane (house) positions of the planets will differ according to the locality of residence, and (c) the aspects and contacts with the major angles will indicate the tone and pattern of the ensuing year.

The houses are fields of action or experiences and the planetary principles are expressed via the signs occupied and through matters associated with the appropriate houses. The degree of this expression is accentuated or modified according to the aspectual pattern(s) which a planet may have. Planets 'operate' in accordance with their intrinsic nature. Mars is always Mars—active, energetic, aggressive—but it is not only Mars considered in isolation. It is Mars/Gemini or Mars/Virgo or whatever sign the planet happens to occupy. As with Mars, so with all the other planets. So, although Mars is basically active or even tough, as befits its basic nature, it will display its qualities through the mode of the occupied sign. If the planet is well-integrated and strong by house and aspect, the more favourable attributes of the planet will be in evidence. Ill-conditioned by house, sign or aspect, the less attractive qualities of the planet will be displayed. Mars/Virgo, for example, is an active, orderly combination with the ability to use the energies in a practical and detailed manner.

The expression of this placement could, of course, be on several levels, but however it is expressed it will always be energy tempered with the Virgo qualities.

In return charts the same configurations will be common to many thousands of people sharing the same birthday return, but they will not all have the same mundane positions because these are dependent on geographical location. 'The face of the heavens' is different according to the place from which it is viewed. The same planetary patterns for a specified time and place apply worldwide, but their 'fields of action' (houses) are different according to the place for which the chart has been set.

The question of whether a return chart should be set for the birthplace or for the place of residence at the date of the return is debatable. Some researchers suggest that the solar return should be erected for the place of residence, others that it should always be set for the birthplace. This is a very important point, because there can be a wide divergence between charts for those who have settled far from their birthplace. The planetary positions will, of course, not alter, but the Ascendant and house positions can alter very substantially, depending on the location. So far as lunar returns are concerned, there appears to be firm evidence that these should be set for the birthplace, irrespective of where the person happens to be at the date and time of the return. This applies to lunar returns based on the natal Moon. Other lunars derived from the 'parent' solar return should be set in conformity with the solar return, i.e. either the place of residence or the birthplace, depending upon which locality has been used initially.

My own investigations over many years, appears to confirm that solar returns should be set for the place of residence at the date and time of the return, while lunars based on the natal Moon should be set for the birthplace. As with so much of astrology, only detailed research using well-attested data will indicate whether this is correct or not.

The conditions, experiences and psychological responses which are likely to be active and dominant during a solar return year are shown, initially, by the placement of planets and their aspects closely configurating one or more of the major angles (first, tenth) and to a lesser extent the seventh and fourth angles. These angular contacts will be expressed during the course of the year, particularly when, by progression, the planets involved contact or form some major aspect with the angles.

In the study of personal return charts two important factors are in constant interplay, (a) the individual and his motivations (his inner self) and (b) the impact of the environment with which he needs to come to terms. We carry our 'natal pattern' throughout life and our actions, responses and experiences are all governed by this natal 'make-up'. During the operation of a particular return our reactions will reflect the current pattern of the return in association with, and influenced by, the natal potentialities.

Many of the responses connected with the action of returns are not always as clear-cut as one would expect. Often there is a subtle, imperceptible response of a psychological nature which, although not apparently associated with any particular condition or event is, nevertheless, the forerunner of subsequent conditions and/or events. It is, therefore, not easy to pinpoint the exact type of experience which a particular planetary combination may signify. What one can discern, and this with remarkable clarity at times, is that major configurations will, when they are in contact with the angles, coincide with responses which reflect the intrinsic nature of the bodies involved. If Saturn is brought to an angle in the return, I may feel depressed, soulful, apprehensive or restricted, the cause of which may be a variety of things. What the Saturn symbolism is indicating is the negative reactions associated with this planet. Alternatively, I may accept some form of responsibility—get married, buy land—or commit myself to some form of long-term project. How and in what way this Saturn contact will operate will depend on the return chart and its implications and my own natal pattern.

It would appear that the natal positions and the solar (those in the return chart) are intimately connected with actions and behaviour initiated by the individual, while the transiting (those at the period under review) planets are often indicative of that which originates from 'outside' as the result of the environment and the actions or decisions of other persons. The distinction between natal, solar and transiting planets is important. The transits are positions of the planets subsequent to the date of the return and are indicative of transient factors which, for a short period, affect the individual and his relationship with the environment. The natal planets' 'influence' is imprinted at birth and lasts throughout the lifetime. The natal chart can be progressed or regressed by various methods, such as one day before or after birth being equivalent to one year of life. This method works fairly well and often acts as a 'backcloth' indicating the important periods of the life. However, for bringing into sharp focus the 'pattern of the year', the solar return and its subsidiary charts need to be consulted.

In the study of return charts, comparison with the natal positions is essential. The natal chart shows the basic drives and urges which seek expression. The house and sign position will show where and how this can be achieved. If the natal positions form some major relationship with the return chart, then the natal indications relative to matters and conditions signified by the planets involved will be to the forefront during the return year. In other words, a natal planet prominent in a return chart, either through being close to one of the angles or in major aspect with a solar planet, will express its intrinsic nature subject to the indications contained in the return chart.

Natal planets are always important when, by progression, they are 'carried' to the angles of the return chart. Their significance can be assessed by their natal relationship (house, sign and aspects) and how this relationship combines with the current return chart under review. The practice of noting where natal planets 'fall' in the various houses of the return chart does not, in itself, appear significant.

Experience has shown that the solar return chart has three well-defined areas regarding mundane position. Firstly, the angular houses and the areas closely adjacent to them are the most important. The sidereal researchers designated these areas as the *Foreground* and planets located there operate at their maximum efficacy, either for 'good or ill'. The succedent houses (second, fifth, eighth and eleventh) are termed the *Middleground*, and planets located there are considered to be of secondary importance. The four cadent houses (third, sixth, ninth and twelfth) comprise the *Background* and planets in these areas are said to be inactive and unable to operate effectively either for good or ill. It is doubtful whether any planet is ever inactive, although cadency may diminish or conceal the true nature of the planet and its operation.

Angularity is certainly most important, as traditional astrology has always maintained. The practice of relegating the other houses, particularly the cadent ones, to an 'inferior position' requires additional research in so far as tropical returns are concerned.

The drives, urges and behaviour patterns which characterize all human beings in a greater or lesser degree are represented by the natal planets and their condition. Throughout life we respond and react according to our natal patterns, but these patterns are affected, if only temporarily, by various astrological progressions, of which the returns are a very important and prime example. Natal positions are 'permanent imprints' whereas returns are of a temporal nature, lasting only for the period for which they cover.

Each chart, natal or return is individual to the person concerned and requires assessment according to the circumstances of the person and his environment. The natal chart and its degree of integration shows how well we are able to cope with life situations. Planets strong aspectually and mundanely enable one to 'survive' crises more or less intact, whereas a less well integrated chart may show a lack of determination in confronting difficulties.

Many complex factors govern attitudes and responses but if we are aware of the intrinsic nature of the planets and the forces which they represent, we can accept the challenges with which we are, sooner or later, presented. A realistic assessment of the natal chart is the first priority before any attempt can be made regarding the likely effect of progressions, returns or other forecasting techniques.

The approach to analysis demands an acceptance of the fact that one must interpret the configurations dynamically and not in a materialistic manner. Although the key to a proper understanding of solar returns lies with the evaluation of the progressed return we should be aware that directions, progressions, transits and the like indicate periods of time when we will experience the effects of a particular configuration and our reactions and responses will be governed by, and will correlate with, the type of aspect(s) operating at that particular time.

Good astrology demands good sense. It is in the practical application of astrological symbolism and principles in relation to real life and not in theoretical abstractions, that we can observe the relationship between heaven and earth. The interplanetary patterns and cosmic phenomena operate in a pulsating and rhythmic sequence, and each of us responds according to our own individual impulses.

The planets represent, symbolically, the urges, drives and life impulses which we all seek to express according to our 'natal pattern'. Traditionally, the planets are said to 'rule' matters and conditions appropriate to their nature. It is doubtful whether the term 'rule' really conveys the true nature of the planets whose symbolism is so wide-ranging and all-embracing.

Each of us—in our natal chart—has ten planets (including the Sun and Moon), twelve zodiacal signs, twelve houses and usually a variety of aspects or configurations. This astrological 'mix' will determine how, and in what manner, we seek to express ourselves in the quest for self-fulfilment.

THE PLANETS

Sun

The Sun is, of course, a star, but for astrological purposes it is referred to, along with the Moon, as a planet. Astronomically, the Sun is not particularly important, but to us it is the centre of the solar system and symbolizes the all-pervading life-force.

Well placed and aspected it gives a proper sense of pride and a magnanimous approach. It signifies all activities connected with achieving a sense of 'self-identity'. It is highly individual and self-assertive with a genuine sense of pride in its accomplishments and achievements.

Natally, a well-placed Sun denotes an easy 'outflow' of the energies and, even if the chart contains difficult or challenging patterns, a 'good Sun' will assist in minimizing their effects. There is a natural outgoing creativity associated with the Sun—the Sun always wants to shine—and this desire to create, in one form or another, has connotations with power, superiority and self-esteem. An 'obscure' Sun will still have all the innate solar qualities, but their expression is curtailed with the energies being directed towards the enhancement of self often as a compensatory factor.

In return charts, the Sun prominent and well-placed denotes attention being focused on the individual, and he will become the recipient of favours, honours, acclamation and congratulations. His sense of self-awareness, self-assurance, self-promotion and prestige is greatly enhanced. Self-assertive and confident, he is stimulated to plan and formulate projects which satisfy his need for creativity. Ill-placed or obscurely placed in a return chart, the Sun's energies flow spasmodically so that there is a lack of integration—one feels in the shadows—and the solar qualities lack full expression. There is an inability to project the personality to the best advantage with a consequent retreat from mainstream activities.

Moon

The Moon, always an important body, is the significator of fluctuation, emotional responses, moods and cravings. As the Sun is outgoing and positive, so the Moon is withdrawn and negative. It denotes the protective instinct and the desire for security. Although unassertive it is tenacious, and its rhythms and cycles are influential in determining human behaviour. The Moon and its motions are responsible for the ebb and flow that characterize all forms of life. It is significantly associated with human sexuality, parturition, health and emotional responses.

Basically, the Moon represents habit and emotion; the caring, protective instinct that nourishes and sustains life. Even though it is associated with change and movement it has a constancy which is more real than one would suppose. In solar return charts the Moon indicates sensation and is the chief activator of conditions, and the responses which it generates will be of the nature of the planet(s) with which it has a relationship. Its action in return charts is to galvanize into life the planets with which it comes into contact. If the angles of the progressed return form an aspect (notably the conjunction) with the Moon, the effects are all the more pronounced. When well-placed, angular or favourably aspected it denotes movement, changes, travelling and altered conditions, usually caused by external forces and to which the individual reacts favourably. An ill-conditioned Moon signifies fearfulness, lowered vitality and sometimes unwelcome publicity concerning one's private affairs. One's emotions seem to be paraded publically for the curiosity of the masses!

Mercury

The communicative principle which embraces all forms of knowledge, contacts, information, speech, writing and exchanges of all kinds is Mercurial. It is the inquisitive factor that wishes to 'know' the why and wherefore of everything. It denotes our ability to comprehend the outside world and how we express our need to know about and relate to that which is external to us. The ability to understand and respond to our environment, to communicate at all levels, to acquire and absorb knowledge and ideas, to co-ordinate learning and experience and thereby be able to adapt to changing circumstances as and when required, are all aspects of the Mercury principle.

Relating and interpreting enables us to project ourselves in an intelligible and co-ordinated manner. Mercury well placed in return charts shows that the communicatory facilities will be employed to the full. There will be considerable activity both mentally and physically and the nervous energy will be expended to the maximum. It is a period when a variety of activities are either planned or commenced, the nature of which will depend on Mercury's contact and the return as a whole. Mercurial action results in an inability to remain still but to be constantly 'on the move', either physically or mentally. The same restlessness is apparent when Mercury is not well placed but in these instances the restlessness degenerates into indecisiveness and carelessness. It may denote nervous reactions and an overcritical attitude accompanied by a lack of definite purpose and co-ordination. The energy is wasted on trivialities and inconsequential matters.

Venus
Planet of love, beauty, unity and co-operation, Venus signifies all forms of relationships. Love, marriage, intimacy, affections, partnerships, social contacts are all expressions of the Venus principle. In the same way that Mercury indicates our desire to communicate via the mental processes, so Venus is associated with relationships that involve the expression of the feelings. All matters that require co-operative effort and which enhance our feelings depend upon the responses that we extend to, or receive from, others. Without the Venus principle no social intercourse is possible. It is through compromise and harmonious interchanges that we experience the goodwill and affection of others.

The aspects that Venus has are all-important, as indeed are all the aspects between various planets, but in the case of Venus the expression of the feelings is governed to some degree by its placement, either strong or weak, and the planets with which it is in aspect. The element is also important and shows how the principles of unity and harmony are displayed. In Water, Venus is emotional and caring and capable of great sacrifice. In Earth, it is practical and realistic and may present an appearance of independence in order to protect the feelings. This, of course, is totally alien to the true nature of Venus, which is so much dependent on relationships, co-operation and mutual sharing. In Fire, the Venus principle burns bright and clear and it is in this element that the warmth and exuberance of relationships can be observed at their best. In Air, there is often a detached attitude and the feelings are expressed somewhat intellectually. There appears no surrender to the emotions and the approach to personal relationships, love and affection is cold and matter of fact. However, all this is deceptive for Air is just as needful for affection as the other three elements, but like Earth needs to be reassured and stimulated before it responds to its maximum capacity.

In return charts, Venus prominent and well-placed will indicate periods when relationships, attachments and social gatherings will command the attention. As Venus is the significator of all that tends to beautify and embellish life, its prominence often coincides with periods of relaxation, comfort and feelings of contentment. It is a time when tokens of friendship and affections are given or received. Ill-placed or aspected in return charts, Venus denotes a lethargic attitude and relationships tend to become strained. Hurt feelings, sudden separations and embarrassment are the order of the day; obstacles occur which prevent the continuance or development of relationships and associations. There may be sorrow and a feeling of rejection, particularly if Saturn or Pluto contact Venus.

Mars

The energy of Mars can be crude and primitive or it can be, when channelled into constructive outlets, a vigorous and effective factor. Mars represents the principle of initiative and action. It indicates how and in what manner we project our energies, meet challenges and seek to overcome obstacles. An uncontrolled Mars is a violent, primitive, destructive factor, particularly when in contact with Saturn, whose unbridled energies wreak havoc and disaster. A controlled Mars, on the other hand, enables one to assess the difficulties of a particular situation and confront the problem or the challenge with courage and determination. The Mars force helps us to overcome adversity, protect ourselves and our interests, and by exertion initiate actions against that which threaten to endanger or injure us.

In many ways, Mars is similar to the Sun, inasmuch as it is concerned with self, the ego and self-assertion. Unlike the Sun, however, it often lacks creativity. Although it is associated with the dominant, pioneering spirit which is essential for the commencement of projects and enterprises, it is impatient, rash and often destructive.

Well-placed in return charts with constructive aspects it indicates a period when the energies will be utilized to their maximum capacity in an objective and assertive manner. One seeks to project one's image to overcome difficulties and endeavours to obtain a sense of achievement through the use of physical and emotional energy. When poorly placed, or not well-integrated in return charts, Mars indicates that the energies may be expended in an uncoordinated and misdirected way. Overactivity without well-defined aims can result in wasteful efforts which in turn cause a sense of frustration, recklessness, impatience and a lack of achievement. These factors are not conducive for harmonious relationships and often conflict and antagonisms are experienced. When Mars is operating at a negative level, frustration and impatience often lead to carelessness and hasty actions with the result that accidents can occur, damaging to both self and others.

The Mars force has to be expressed and our energies expended but unless this is done in a controlled and constructive manner we will always be at 'odds' with our environment and liable to suffer in one way or another from abrasive actions initiated by ourselves or others.

Jupiter

As the largest planet in the solar system, Jupiter symbolizes the desire to 'be greater than'. It signifies how we attempt to reach out beyond our immediate environment and strive to expand our consciousness—the far horizons of the mind—and of the physical world.

Jupiter's action is similar to that of Mercury, but whereas Mercury is curious and concerned with the immediate present, Jupiter looks to the future and its action is related to gaining depth and breadth from experiences which can enlarge and expand our knowledge. Faith, hope, vision, growth and development are Jupiterian expressions. It denotes the 'opportunity factor' which when Jupiter is active in progressions or returns, enables us to expand according to our needs and inclinations. How, and in what manner, and with what result will depend on Jupiter's condition by sign, house and aspect.

An activated Jupiter invariably promotes confidence, presents opportunities, preserves us from injury—often at the eleventh hour—and assists in the realization of aims and objectives. As a 'luck factor' it is often prominent at the time of sudden and unexpected wins in lotteries, contests, etc.

Well-placed in return charts it indicates joy, elation and acquisition. Acquisition in a Jupiterian sense relates to those things or conditions which increase our sense of well-being, preserve us from injury and contribute to a widening of our knowledge and understanding. Saturn, the very antithesis of Jupiter, denotes a different form of acquisition, namely the desire to have and to hold for security reasons. Whereas Jupiter is all-embracing expansiveness, Saturn is restrictive, controlled consolidation.

Obscurely placed or conditioned, Jupiter is symptomatic of over-optimism, lack of forethought and exaggerated actions. Although the essential nature of Jupiter is concerned with progress and development, this can only be achieved by co-ordinated action and an appreciation of the obstacles to be overcome. Trusting in luck is not always the wisest course. Even a poorly contacted Jupiter will exhibit the urge towards advancement and improvement, but the final results may not match the original expectations. However, Jupiter is a protective influence and even at the worst of times it seems to operate miraculously, often at the last moment, to preserve us from injury or from the results of our own follies.

Saturn

Jupiter and expansiveness need control, and it is Saturn which provides the limits. Unlimited freedom can lead to excesses. Saturn despite its gloomy reputation and its association with negativity, fear, inadequacy and restriction, is essential if we are to develop.

This planet denotes the urge to consolidate the values which appear important, and these values will, naturally, differ according to the needs and the awareness of the individual. Hence the cautious and responsible attitudes often associated with Saturnian action. The conservative, restraining and even limiting influence of Saturn, pessimistic though it may be, does enable us to approach life in a constructive manner and be prepared to accept events and conditions over which we have little or no control. Many of the 'fateful' experiences of life coincide with Saturnian action. Adversity and challenge, however painful, are necessary for moral growth and even if our aspirations do not always equal our achievements, we can become stronger as the result of striving and the acceptance of disturbing experiences. In doing so, we can gain an insight into the broader aspects of life and of the values that we, as persons, consider important. Through hindrances, delays, disappointments, defeats and losses, we can observe the action of Saturn.

Despondency, gloom, loneliness and isolation mark the periods when Saturn is active in progressions or return charts. It is time when we tend to throw up barriers, either physical or psychological, as a form of protection to prevent the intrusion of those things which frighten us or are liable to reveal our weaknesses or fears. If the placement of Saturn indicates where and how we exhibit negative attitudes, or feel inferior, then we can—by facing up to them— acquire greater strength and learn that by coming to terms with our limitations we can achieve a more structured existence.

We learn through experience and, however difficult or painful the process may be, the results usually justify the efforts. Venus enables us to 'forget self' usually voluntarily, but Saturn forces us to conform and accept reality through personal or collective self-denial.

Uranus

Saturn denotes our orthodox and conservative approaches and reactions to events and conditions, but Uranus indicates our urge to be 'different'. It shows the desire to cast off restrictive bonds and to act, think and live in an unfettered and at times revolutionary manner.

Self-discovery is an essential feature of this planet. Our sense of originality and uniqueness impels us to experiment with the 'new'. In doing so, we have to change and adapt many of our preconceived ideas and haul ourselves out of comfortable ruts. Uranus symbolizes our desire to be free from all restraints, to act independently, sometimes wilfully, irrespective of the consequences of our actions. The Uranian urge demands complete freedom of expression; the need to experience novelty and change and the desire to relinquish the old and commonplace in favour of the new. Often this urge to embrace the 'new' is accompanied by much 'heart-searching' and although change is essential for progress and growth, the rejection of the old should not be undertaken merely in order to feel or appear differently.

Uranian action corresponds with events and conditions which occur with startling rapidity—very much in the nature of a volcanic eruption—and which, by their suddenness, shatter the foundations of established patterns. This planet represents the rebellious and independent factor by which we seek to be ourselves untrammelled by convention or rigid lines of demarcation. Hence its action is associated with the demolition of barriers and the rejection of outmoded practices and methods. The results may be either catastrophic, or they may be the prelude to establishing the 'new man' or the 'new order'.

In return charts, Uranus correlates with all manner of changes—new persons, new scenes, discovery and reappraisal of much which was formerly taken for granted. Familiar contacts, places and persons are viewed through different eyes. Well-placed and aspected this planet corresponds with an exciting and progressive period which is remarkable for the beneficial changes which occur. Ill-placed or poorly conditioned, it denotes drastic actions, the severance of ties, autocratic attitudes and unfortunate incidents and accidents.

Uranian action often coincides with an urge to challenge existing conditions either on a personal basis or in a collective manner. Discontent and disenchantment with people, places and things, prompt rebellious action. Although Uranus is often associated with the new and experimental and displays a unique and original approach to things, its action is often disruptive, authoritarian and destructive.

Neptune

Probably of all the planets, Neptune is one of the most difficult to understand in depth. There is a 'will-o'-the-wisp' nature with this planet which defies analysis. It appears to be related to that which is 'not of this world'. It often denotes idealistic and inspirational tendencies with an urge to surrender the self to some greater, indefinable power. Astrologically, it is the force that enables us to rise above the commonplace and by ignoring the ugly and the materialistic strive to reach the sublime heights.

The cold realities of life (signalled by Saturn) become bearable when we can indulge ourselves in Neptunian escapism. Through Neptunian 'forgetfulness' we can, if only for a brief spell, enter the romantic dreamworld where everything appears as we would wish it to be, not as it actually is. In our flight from reality or mundane existence, we retreat to a world of make-believe fantasy and embrace those things and conditions which take us 'out of this world'. Religion, music, acting and diguises of one kind or another permit us to escape the commonplace and to experience the delights and charms of an unreal world, safely cocooned in the webs of our own fantasies. In our dreamworld, we pose and posture and in our imaginings, seek compensation for what we lack.

Even though the Neptunian principles can be identified with the vague, subtle, illusory and deceptive elements of life, they are in many ways essential in that they act as a safety valve whereby the stresses and tensions of everyday life can be reduced or mitigated. Neptune assists in releasing the bonds of reality often through renunciation and withdrawal. When we cannot differentiate between fact and fiction our lives become chaotic and confused, but if we can strike a happy balance, we can acquire an inner 'Neptunian peace'.

In return charts, this planet coincides with romantic interludes, ecstatic experiences, falling in love or devotional attitudes. It indicates nervous excitement, fluster, flurry and a feeling of 'being out of this world'. Its less desirable attributes contribute to confused and treacherous conditions, entanglements, victimization, hysteria, rejection, humiliation, renunciation and embarrassments.

Pluto

This the outermost planet of the solar system yet discovered, is the planet of finality. Of all the planetary urges, drives and forces, those of Pluto are the most dramatic and, at times, the most shattering.

Symbolically, it denotes the transformation of life-patterns, the termination of existing structures, ways of thought, beliefs, relationships and established conditions. Its action is direct, often violent and destructive and results from an accumulation of tensions which over a long period of time have been held in check, but which eventually erupt with startling force. Pluto acts like a cleansing agent removing that which is obsolete, outmoded or obstructive, preparatory to establishing new foundations. Natally, it represents those things which we prefer to hide, forget or ignore. Due to its slow motion, it remains in the same sign for many years, but it is a highly individual planet and its mundane position and aspects are very important in all charts.

Pluto is remarkable in many ways, not least, for the manner in which it indicates singleness of purpose. This planet is a 'loner' and although naturally secretive and concealing, is paradoxical in that it rends aside the veil of mystery to reveal the true nature of persons, events and conditions. Anti-social by nature, it has, nevertheless, an association with organizing on a vast collective scale.

The disintegration and destruction which often corresponds with Plutonian action is invariably a prelude to rebuilding and renewing after the old, outworn or obsolete have been disposed. Not only are physical clearances associated with Pluto, but also psychological. Phoenix-like, from the ashes or the refuse of destruction it renews and transforms. As the planet of finality—nothing is ever the same after it has been subjected to Plutonian action—it corresponds with beginnings and endings, commencements and closures, birth and death, either actual or symbolic.

For a planet whose action is naturally concealing, it has the strange capacity to catapult one into the limelight with all the attendant glare of publicity—possibly another expression of its ability to 'bring to the light of day'. It is a planet which, without warning, exposes, disposes, regenerates and through revelation, change and renewal forces us to accept reality. In our efforts to hide or ignore that which we find uncongenial, frightening or unacceptable, we fail to realize that, sooner or later, nemesis will overtake us forcing us to face reality.

As the 'face of the forgotten past', Pluto, periodically, brings into sharp focus the memories, fears and guilt of things long past. The surfacing of Plutonian action, painful though it may be, forces us to re-examine our values and beliefs. In the upheavals which accompany this action, we become aware of the issues which are important to us as individuals. We are ready to reject the insignificant, the unimportant and to respond to the regenerative influence, and we become in a sense, tranformed or 'reborn'.

Plutonian aspects and contacts are synonymous with reality. Prominent contacts of this planet correspond with periods when we are compelled to accept the consequences of past actions and face up to those things which we would rather conceal or forget. It forces us to question our motives and our actions. Like some magic mirror, Pluto reflects our image, nakedly and unashamedly, revealing our true self. This revelation can result in a descent to the depths with all its attedant torments, or it can be a prelude to soaring to the heights of heaven. If we can accept the reality as portrayed by Pluto we can be transformed.

In return charts, this powerful planet marks the commencement or ending of phases, farewells, goodbyes and the severance of ties. The nature of its action will depend on the planets with which it is in contact and the condition of the chart considered as a whole.

ASPECTS

Simply stated, the term 'aspect' means view, look or appearance. Astrologically, aspects are angular relationships between two or more planets or important points, measured either zodiacally or mundanely.

The traditional teaching concerning aspects which grouped all contacts between benefic planets as 'good' and all contacts between malefic planets as 'bad' is not supported by modern research. The benefic planets according to classical astrologers, were the Moon, Venus and Jupiter, while the malefics were Mars and Saturn. The Sun and Mercury were classified either as benefics or neutrals depending upon their condition. The outer planets (Uranus, Neptune and Pluto) unknown in antiquity, are now considered to be challenging forces with Neptune a little less so.

This classification of benefic and malefic planets and 'good' and 'bad' aspects appears to be archaic, and fails to take into account the essential nature of astrological symbolism. Aspects represent a 'blending of energies' and it is the intrinsic nature of the bodies in aspect which has to be assessed. It is true that certain types of aspect appear more constructive than others, but the effect of any aspect is governed by the planets involved.

All aspects, broadly speaking, can be divided into two main categories (a) those that are constructive, and assist in the ease of expression, and (b) those that are challenging or difficult and act as tension-producing factors. Now, it does not follow that all constructive aspects will produce good and that all the difficult ones will coincide with evil. On the contrary, many so-called 'good' aspects may be detrimental in so far as effort and initiative are concerned, whereas the 'bad' aspects may be productive of good in that the challenges and difficult conditions often associated with them have to be resolved in one way or another.

Aspects are neither 'good nor bad'. What they do indicate is the manner in which the natal chart potentials will be expressed according to the planet(s), sign, and house(s) involved. The reappraisal of astrology and its concepts in the light of modern psychology has shown that the complexity of human behaviour is discernible from astrological charts; the natal chart showing the 'basic foundations' with returns, progressions and other subsidiary charts showing, under appropriate stimuli, the probable reactions and responses.

Terms used when dealing with aspects do not always convey the true meaning, nor do they adequately explain the 'core' significance of a particular configuration. To say that an aspect is good, bad, easy, challenging, hard, soft, harmonious or inharmonious means very little unless it is analysed and related to the chart as a whole, and with reference to the person concerned.

Although aspects have been classified into two main groups—major and minor—it is only the major aspects which are considered important in the analysis of return charts. Each chart requires to be studied in its totality and allowance made for aspects which are *applying* (approaching exactitude) and for those *separating* (departing from exactitude). The strength of the planets in aspect, their house position, particularly if angular, and whether they form part of a stellium or some other significant formation, all require assessment.

Aspects can be either zodiacal or mundane. Zodiacal aspects are measured along the Ecliptic in celestial longitude, whereas mundane aspects are measured along the Celestial Equator in right ascension. Mundane aspects are formed from the distance between the angles, and are often referred to as *in mundo* (in the world), while zodiacal aspects which are formed in the zodiac are termed *in zodiaco* (in the zodiac). If, for example, a planet is conjunct the Midheaven in 2° Pisces, and another planet is conjunct the Ascendant in 8° Cancer, they are in zodiacal trine (120° allowing for orb), but in mundane square. Mundane aspects depend upon the distance in mundane houses, and are measured, not by zodiacal degrees on the cusps of the houses, but by the proportional parts of a planets' semi-arc (the time it is above the horizon—diurnal semi-arc—or the time it is below the horizon—nocturnal semi-arc). A planet's semi-arc measures three mundane houses for that planet; two-thirds of its semi-arc, two houses; and one-third of its semi-arc, one house. Any planet which by the Earth's rotation arrives at the cusps of the twelfth, eleventh, tenth, etc. houses will be then in mundane semi-sextile, sextile or square to the Ascendant, as the case may be. Mundane aspects are based upon the Earth's diurnal rotation, whereas zodiacal aspects are based on the subdivision of the planets' orbits along the Ecliptic.

The division of the circle by a specified number gives a numerical value, and these values have been found to contain certain fundamental principles which are expressed in conformity with the planets involved. The principles associated with the various types of aspect can also be related to the starting points of the zodiac and to the commencement of the twelve mundane houses. When viewed in this way, an aspect has a basic correlation with a particular house(s) and sign(s). For example, the *conjunction* which occurs when two or more planets are in the same degree of longitude, has a basic correspondence with 0° Aries, Mars, the ruler, and the first house. Likewise, the trine aspect (120°) has two relationships, namely, 0° Leo, Sun, the ruler, and the fifth house, and with 0° Sagittarius, Jupiter, the ruler, and the ninth house. With the square aspect (90°), we have 0° Cancer, Moon, and the fourth house and also 0° Capricorn, Saturn and the tenth house. The other major aspects will all have a similar correspondence.

Major Aspects

The conjunction

This is the most powerful of all, and the blending of two or more planetary drives or energies can be highly constructive and beneficial or it can be very challenging, depending upon the planets in contact.

A well-integrated conjunction indicates much latent energy which, under appropriate stimuli, is expressed in an outgoing, active and enterprising manner. All aspects require to be examined in relation to the sign and house containing the planets in aspect.

The conjunction always has a subtle Aries, Mars/first house 'influence' in that it is concerned with personal interests and efforts. It is highly individual and self-motivated, and its action, depending upon the planets involved, will be thrusting, active and enterprising. Conjunctions falling in signs which have a natural affinity with the planet(s) concerned, as, for example, the Sun conjunct Saturn in Leo, or Sun/Saturn in Capricorn, are more powerful than conjunctions where there are no natural affinities. The question arises, will the Sun in Leo 'thaw' the Saturnian influence or will Saturn 'freeze' the solar power? The answer lies in the chart as a whole and how the conjunction is modified or accentuated by other planetary factors. The Leo example could indicate a denial or restricted expression of the natural Leo creativity, while the Capricorn placement may coincide with a desire to 'reach the top'—a form of personal aggrandisement. All conjunctions are related to 'self' and their condition in charts is always important.

The Sextile

The division of the circle by six gives 60° and this sextile aspect is generally considered beneficial. Using the analogy of the distance between signs, it can be related to the signs Gemini and Aquarius and the third and eleventh houses. This association with Air is often displayed as a versatility of mind, which is curious, enquiring and adaptable. It is an aspect of creativity and inventiveness but tends to disperse its forces too widely and without sustained application. Basically, a harmonious contact it assists in promoting a mental awareness and the ability to think quickly and clearly. This, of course, will depend on the planets and signs involved. Sextiles between benefic planets give ease of expression and a relaxed approach, while contacts with the major planets such as Saturn, Uranus or Pluto introduce greater motivations.

The Square

This aspect of 90° has a natural relationship with Cancer and the fourth house and with Capricorn and the tenth. It is an aspect which produces tension, stress and dis-harmony, the nature and conditions of which, depend on the planets and signs forming the contact. It is challenging and compulsive, causing confrontation, often as a means of relieving the intense feelings of frustration which bodies in square often generate. It is an 'effort-producing' contact in that the intense energies associated with it seek release. This is an incentive to confronting difficult situations and seeking to overcome the disturbing or threatening effects which we think may overwhelm us. The square, despite its so-called 'bad reputation' has much to offer in the way of progress and development. Cancer and Capricorn are both tenacious signs concerned with security and structures. In erecting barriers we can be secure but we can also block ourselves in and become prisoners of circumstances. Defensive attitudes, fear and guilt complexes need to be overcome and it is the nature of the square aspect which releases forces in order that more structured and stabilized foundations can be laid.

A chart containing many squares will show that there is a ceaseless battle to overcome adverse conditions—either personal or circumstantial—the nature of which will depend on the chart as a whole. However, most charts have some redeeming features which assist in mitigating even the most formidable of aspects.

The Trine

The circle divided by three gives 120°, the trine aspect. Counting from Aries it has a relationship with Leo/Sun and the fifth house, and with Sagittarius/Jupiter and the ninth. It is a positive aspect and, despite the suggestions sometimes made that it is a 'lazy influence', the fact is that it is an energetic, but at the same time, a tranquil and 'easy-flowing' contact. The effect of all aspects can be experienced either inwardly or outwardly, but the trine aspect gives a sense of inner harmony and contentment combined with feelings of optimistic expectations. It is a fortunate contact in so far as beneficial conditions, pure good luck or other tokens of esteem often coincide under a trine aspect. As always, the planets involved will show the nature of the condition or event. Too much good fortune can, of course, result in a lack of effort, self-indulgence and various other undesirable traits, but it is doubtful whether the trine aspect, considered in itself, is really inimical to sustained effort in the achievement of aims and objectives.

Again, as with all contacts, the nature of the bodies in aspect requires analysis. Sun trine Jupiter in Fire, could indicate vision, enthusiasm and a burning zeal, but this excess of Fire could also result in an over-optimistic, exaggerated and exclusive sense of self-importance, with the expectation that others will always pander to one's needs. Likewise, Sun trine Saturn in Earth may show the easy acquirement of assets, or how one views and relates to those things which have real value and structure.

The Opposition

With this aspect of 180° there is often an emphasis on self and how one relates to external conditions. There is a 'see-saw and tug-of-war' effect in that there is a constant struggle to maintain equilibrium and to avoid being pulled apart in two opposite directions. This aspect, like the square, is challenging and associated with tension and confrontation but, unlike the square, its imbalance often stems from indecisiveness on one hand, or from lack of co-ordinated actions on the other. It is an aspect of struggle in that the planets concerned require to be 'balanced' in order that their principles can be expressed in a well-integrated manner. The 'separative' nature of this aspect indicates that the principles of the planets in aspect need to be combined and evaluated according to the nature and requirements of the individual.

The Mars/Aries—Venus/Libra connection and their associated houses—first and seventh—illustrate the fundamental nature of the opposition aspect. Action and receptivity, in an attempt to achieve a balance between self and others, invariably governs the operation of this aspect. Some oppositions are easier to 'bear' than others. Moon/Venus is a far more passive and less demanding aspect than say Mars/Saturn, which could indicate conflict and power struggles damaging both to the person and to others. Planets coming to opposition in return charts seem to signify that the principles associated with them will manifest forcibly either as indicators of impending changes or the reappraisal of existing conditions or attitudes. With the benefic planets (Venus, Jupiter) these are accepted gladly and in some cases with much delight. The Sun or Moon often coincide with new phases of existence, while the contacts of the outer planets are always significant, especially if important areas of the chart are involved.

The kinetic nature of charts means that various patterns, configurations and aspects will always be in the process of forming and separating so that at any given time there will be some factors, at least, which under suitable excitation, will correlate with some internal or external response. Planets 'operate' according to their natures, so that in the assessment of planetary action this fact has to be always considered. Mars, for example, is a highly energetic force, often rash and impatient, hence it is often prominent at the times of accidents or when one suffers physical injury, but as with all the planets its mode of operation accords with its intrinsic nature. The severity or otherwise of its action depends upon its sign placement, its aspects and its house position. The constraints imposed by a prominent Saturn, however frustrating they may appear, are often beneficial in that one is prevented from acting ill-advisedly or hastily. Over-caution can, of course, lead to missed opportunities, delays and disappointments. It all depends on the planetary aspects, not only natally but also 'progressively', and how these patterns are responded to, either actively or passively.

Each aspect or planetary formation, both in the natal chart and in the return charts and their subsidiaries, requires to be evaluated according to the nature of the planets in aspect. It is therefore rather meaningless to speak of 'bad squares or oppositions' or 'good trines and sextiles' unless the formation is considered relative to the person and his environmental background.

The so-called 'difficult' aspects (square and opposition) often denote intense energy, depending upon the planets involved, while the 'easy' contacts are often indicative of tractability and moderation. The same type of energy exists with all aspects, but its expression differs according to the kind of aspect.

With a preponderance of difficult aspects there will be conflict and contention, with an inner sense of dissatisfaction often projected externally. An over-abundance of easy contacts promotes lethargy, and there is a tendency to 'glide along' without too much exertion. This inclination to flow with the tide would be more apparent with several Neptunian contacts rather than Saturnian ones which would introduce a stiffening element conducive to sustained effort.

Naturally, the responses to aspects will be governed to a greater or lesser degree by the nature of the personality and the environment. Each person will respond according to their own needs and behaviour patterns. In return charts the responses will 'lock in' with the natal potentialities, so that during the course of the return year, as the various natal planets are brought by progression to the angles, matters normally associated with the planet will be experienced.

Probably the only way to determine the nature of 'aspects in action' is through a detailed study of actual case histories, and it is here that return charts can be so valuable. Although external events and conditions can be observed and related to the current patterns operating in a chart, it is less easy to determine how a person felt and responded, particularly if the aspect(s) were of a stressful nature. Events such as marriage and the birth of children, normally joyous and happy occasions, will invariably show the benefic planets (Venus, Jupiter or the Moon) prominent in the appropriate return chart(s). Likewise, sorrowful or demanding situations often have Mars, Saturn or Pluto close to the angles in the appropriate chart(s).

HOUSES

Great Circles and House Systems

If we look at the sky, we see that it meets the Earth, and this is the great circle of the *horizon*. Immediately overhead is the *zenith* with the opposite point, the *nadir* immediately beneath our feet. If we look due south, we have due east on the left, with due west on the right. Now, if we imagine a great circle passing from the east point of the horizon, cutting through the zenith and passing down through the west point and continuing to rise once more at the east point, we have the great circle of the *Prime Vertical*. Again, if we imagine another great circle rising at the north point of the horizon, cutting through the Prime Vertical at right angles to the zenith, and descending at the south point of the horizon and continuing around under the Earth, we have the *Meridian Circle*.

These three great circles of the sphere (Horizon, Prime Vertical and Meridian) are the basis for house systems that have some claim for consideration. One of these systems is the Campanus system, of which the Prime Vertical is employed as the foundation circle. If the Prime Vertical is divided into twelve equal parts, with six great circles of the sphere from the north or south points of the horizon passing through the dividing points on the Prime Vertical, we obtain the cusps of the twelve Campanian houses. This division gives the six houses above the horizontal plane and six below, which appear like lunes, and in which all the bodies must be contained. As every place on Earth has its own horizon, zenith and nadir, so it has its own Campanian lunes. The method of Campanus is free from any suggestion of either zodiacal or mundane motion since the Prime Vertical is the basic circle. In this system, the horizon circle is one of the boundaries of the first and seventh houses.

The house system which is most frequently used, and for which Tables of Houses are readily available is the Placidus system listed in Raphael's ephemerides. Tables of Houses are necessary for all astrological charting in order to determine the Ascendant (Rising Sign), Midheaven (MC) and the cusps of the intermediate houses for a specified sidereal time and place.

Due to the Earth's rotation, all signs rise and set every twenty-four hours, the average time for the 30° of a sign to rise being about two hours, except at the polar latitudes where certain signs neither rise nor set. At the Equator, the signs rise evenly, but in the intermediate latitudes and as we approach the Poles, the signs do not rise uniformly, due to the angle which the Ecliptic makes with the Equator. Signs which take longer than average to ascend are termed 'signs of long ascension', while those that ascend quickly are known as 'signs of short ascension'. In the northern hemisphere at intermediate latitudes, the signs Cancer to Sagittarius are signs of long ascension; the short ascension signs are Capricorn to Gemini. In southern latitudes the reverse applies.

The intersection of the Ecliptic with the observer's horizon is the Ascendant or Rising Sign and marks the commencement of the first house; the opposite point is the Descendant or seventh house. The point due south is the upper meridian (*Medium Coeli*: MC)—the culminating point—while the opposite point to the Midheaven is the *Imum Coeli*: IC. The intersection of the axis of the horizon and the axis of the meridian define the four quadrants of a chart:

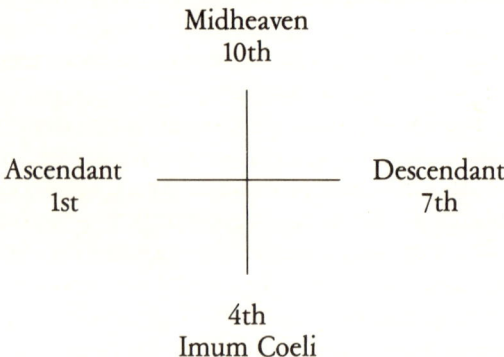

With the quadrant systems of house division, the four angles all correspond to house cusps; the Ascendant becomes the first house cusp, the Descendant, the seventh, the Midheaven, the tenth with its opposite point, the *Imum Coeli*, the fourth. Intermediate cusps are arrived at by a division of either time or space.

The twelvefold division of the heavens (houses) appears to have 'grown' from identifying the twelve signs of the zodiac with twelve divisions of the heavens. This division appears to have some validity in that the first house has a natural affinity with Aries (first sign) and all that it represents. Likewise, the other houses have a relationship with their appropriate signs.

In the quadrant systems, the houses are classified into three main divisions: Angular, succedent and cadent. The angular houses (the Foreground in sidereal astrology) are the most important. Next the succedent houses (the Middleground), and finally the cadent houses (Background). Although the cadent houses have been considered as 'inactive places', recent research has tended to disprove this theory, and confirm that areas of the cadent houses closely adjacent to the angles are highly important.

Houses in Return Charts

In dealing with return charts, the angles are all-important, but other sectors may be significant if there are unusual configurations, groupings or exact aspects, either between planets or important points in the chart.

It is not sufficient, nor is it desirable to assess return charts without considering the polarity which exists in astrology as in all things. Houses and signs are not 'watertight compartments' which have rigidly defined boundaries. On the contrary, there is a subtle interaction and blending with both signs and houses. All houses and signs require to be evaluated in conjunction with their opposites, and related to the chart as a whole.

The ramifications of a particular house can be extensive and far-reaching. Take, for example, a tenth house Jupiter which is activated in a return chart. This could promote an expansive attitude in general with favourable circumstances concerning work or other outside activities. The new work appointment may involve relocation in a different area and this in turn will have implications for home, family, friends and neighbours (fourth and eleventh houses). If a family is involved, then the children will be affected by new schooling, new friends, etc. So there is always some form of 'knock-on' effect emanating from one contact, the nature of which will be in accordance with the house(s), signs and aspects. This is an important point in all assessments. Sometimes the results of a particular contact are not easily discernible. One can respond 'internally' without very much outward effect. In so far as the psychological implications are concerned, these are always difficult to determine unless one is a professional counsellor and engaged in 'face-to-face' counselling with the person involved.

The division and classification of the twelve houses illustrates the polarity and correspondence which exists with each pair of houses and signs. The houses 1-6 are associated with the individual's perception and attitudes concerning his needs and requirements as a person and the manner in which he views and relates to those things which affect him on a personal level. Houses 7-12, are, broadly speaking, an extension of houses 1-6 in that they represent the integration, or lack of it, with others and the world at large.

The Houses Defined

The First and Seventh Houses

The first house (Ascendant) represents self and is, so to speak, the vantage point from which we view everything related to the world and our existence. The Rising Sign is the 'filter' through which all impressions, thoughts and feelings are interpreted. Virgo rising, will give the critical approach, analytical and detailed, with the knowledge that there is always room for improvement. As with Virgo, so with all the other signs according to their nature. The need to be of service, which Virgo typifies, is also expressed by the opposite sign (Pisces). Through service Virgo reaches out (seventh house) to others.

The Second and Eighth Houses

The second house refers to all kinds of assets and resources; how we regard them, use them, value them. The value we place upon an object, a skill or some other possession often enhances our 'sense of worth' and is conducive to feeling secure. The term wealth embraces all forms of assets, talents, capabilities—in fact, everything which we can fashion or utilize for the benefit of ourselves and others. The polarity of the second and eighth houses illustrates the 'wealth of others'—wealth taken in its widest terms—and shows how and in what way, the values and assets of others concern us. The second house is 'mine'; the eighth is 'theirs'. These two houses show how we regard possessions and the use to which they are put, either personally or in partnership with others. The Plutonian connection with the eighth house is expressed, in one way, through sex and death. To have and to hold, highly expressive of Taurus/Scorpio, can, on one hand, give a confident and secure approach combined with pleasurable experiences, but over-demanding attitudes in relation to others and their values can lead to destruction and loss. The values of the second house in combination with those of the eighth often undergo some form of reappraisal and transition during the course of a lifetime, and when these occur, it will be found that the eighth house and Pluto are prominent in the current charts.

The Third and Ninth Houses

The third house relates to perception and how we communicate with our immediate environment. Like Gemini which always 'wants to know', the third house shows how we discover by observing and questioning. As with all the houses, the sign on the cusp and any planets located there, will influence how we react and respond. It is the house where the dawn of learning and understanding commences and where we begin to comprehend those things which are external to us. We explore, often superficially, a variety of impressions in our quest for self-identity. In the same way that the third is concerned with what is local and at hand, so the ninth house is concerned with the broad horizons which stretch to infinity. The same questing, curious and speculative qualities which the third house and its natural sign and ruler (Gemini/Mercury) often display, are observable with the ninth house and its sign and ruler (Sagittarius/Jupiter). The same desire to know is apparent but it is directed towards the future and not the immediate present. Philosophical speculation, an endeavour to understand the meaning and laws of existence and an acquisition of learning and knowledge are all signified by the ninth house.

The desire to broaden one's horizons is expressed through travel, either mental or physical and through abstract thinking. Hence the relationship of this house with voyaging, higher learning and the 'shape of things to come'. Visions, dreams and prophecy are traditionally associated with this house and planets well placed here often give the ability to discern the outcome of events or conditions.

The Fourth and Tenth Houses

The fourth house, describes the place where we seek 'refuge' from the pressure of the outside world. Normally, it denotes the home or base where we feel most comfortable and secure and where life can be experienced in accordance with habitual patterns and conditions. The roots of our existence and all our inherited traits have some connection with this house. Traditionally associated with mother or mother figure, it symbolizes all the protective, nurturing instincts usually denoted by the Moon and Cancer. This house shows the ties of blood and family and how 'close' or otherwise we are to family and blood relations.

Although this house has associations with conditions at the close of life—womb to grave—its importance appears to be connected with training and upbringing, the quality of which has its origins in the moral attitudes displayed by the parents or guardians. Many of the conflicts which are associated with personal relationships can be traced in some measure, to this house and the sign and planets occupying it. Whether 'childhood shows the man as morning shows the day' has relevance or not, it is often apparent that the Moon/Cancer and the fourth house have a significant influence on the development and growth of an individual.

In contrast to the fourth house, its opposite the tenth (Capricorn/Saturn) signifies the 'image' we present to the world. It is the house where we seek to climb the highest mountain, whatever that mountain may be. The height and nature of the mountain will vary according to the person's aspirations.

With the tenth house we always present the image which will, we hope, impress others, make us look good, feel good. The Sun achieves recognition freely and easily, but Saturn always demands payment, and in our striving to reach the summit there is always a price to be paid. Whether the account is large or small will depend on the tenth in particular and the chart as a whole. Sometimes the account is delayed, but it is always rendered in full measure, and the scale of it can leave us shattered and impoverished. Triumph and tragedy often go hand in hand and what we accomplish via the tenth house is often a mere compensation for the failure and disappointments that we have experienced in other areas of our life.

These two houses are connected with 'authority figures' and all that they signify. Normally, the fourth is related to the mother and the tenth associated with the father. It is not always easy to verify this teaching and the answer probably lies in studying individual charts to ascertain, if possible, which parent exercised the greater influence. Also in return charts and progressions, the time of the demise of the parents may throw some light on the matter.

The Fifth and Eleventh Houses

The fifth house and its relationship with Sun/Leo describes the area of life where we employ our natural talents, assets and ideas in self-promotional activities. In order to enhance our sense of self-esteem and to 'shine' in some way, we become involved in creative enterprises, take chances and/or speculate, in order to acquire gains of one kind or another. Through self-promotion of our ideas we engage in 'game-playing' in the anticipation that we may gain prestige and acclamation.

The 'game-playing' syndrome is apt for this house because it is this sector of the chart which indicates the activities and pursuits which gives us the greatest pleasure and act as a vehicle for our creativity and self-expression. The fifth house and its connection with the projection of the self often conceals the person's vulnerability and weaknesses. Hence the desire to achieve some appreciation, however small, for his efforts and accomplishments. Superiority, typical of the Sun and Leo, is associated with this house in activities of a competitive nature such as sports, gambling, lotteries and beauty contests. It is a house where one can express one's 'true self' creatively or competitively.

In the same way that the fifth house symbolizes the 'individual man', so the eleventh house is related to the 'collective man'. No longer concerned with self as a separate entity, the eleventh house is associated with group identification, the development of social consciousness and reforming zeal. The concern for the welfare of the many, often in a detached manner, stems from the desire to subjugate the self for the benefit of the many. There is often a radicalism with this house, which is expressed in off-beat actions and attitudes. The current trends, whatever they may be, are either ignored or attacked as being 'old-fashioned' and outmoded. The Aquarian/Uranian influence of this house which is often displayed in an inventive and futuristic manner, can also be projected in an erratic and impracticable manner—Utopian ideals for a better world. Hopes, wishes, aspirations and expectations are associated with this house, and as with all the houses, its condition by sign, planet(s) and aspects will show how these may be realized.

The eleventh house is the house of 'detached relatedness' where the all-embracing feelings for humanity and their betterment have priority without the ties and bonds which bind us in more personal relationships.

The Sixth and Twelfth Houses

The sixth house and its relationships with Virgo/Mercury, is concerned with obligations and service. Whereas the fifth denotes play and leisure in all its aspects, the sixth is concerned with work in its broadest terms. Unlike the tenth house and its Saturnian connotations where we strive to project the best image, the sixth represents the approach to duty, obligations and service. The Virgo concern for 'perfection', often as a compensatory factor, enables us to use and exploit our skills and talents and in doing so, we achieve feelings of self-satisfaction, well-being and a sense of purpose.

The sixth house is a testing ground where we need to prove ourselves in order to feel good and useful. Through work and service we can meet the challenges necessary for overcoming any feelings of inadequacy or failure. If there is any lesson to be learned from the sixth house, it is that in order to be 'healthy' we require a balanced approach to work and service, neither too much, nor too little.

The sixth house is concerned with the practical realities of life, whereas the opposite house, the twelfth and its relationship with Pisces/Neptune, is more subtle in its indications. There is always something sacrificial about this house in that one is often compelled to renounce or deny the self for or on behalf of others. Virgo often sacrifices itself in practical forms of service, but Pisces and the twelfth refers to the service which is hidden and private. It is an area where one feels 'incarcerated' and where we struggle to free ourselves from the bondage of restrictive patterns. Feelings of guilt, ghosts of the past and all the mysterious elements which disturb us are part and parcel of this house. Hence the need to escape, either through dedicated unselfish service for others, generally the less fortunate, or through abstractions of one kind or another. It is the house which can denote the greatest inspirations and ideals; it can also denote the greatest suffering, often as the result of one's own follies.

SIGNS
The importance of the signs in relation to return charts is not always

apparent. Although the expression of a planet is governed to some extent by the sign occupied, it would appear that the importance of return charts depends more on the nature of the planets, their aspects and, very significantly, their house positions. This is not to suggest that the signs have no value in so far as return techniques are concerned—they do—but that their 'influence' has a more moderate and muted effect. The only exception to this is the sign containing the Sun or Moon. The Sun at the time of the solar return will, of course, be in its natal sign, so the influence of the sign will always be prominent. Likewise, the Moon at the time of a lunar return. The Sun and Moon in subsidiary return charts frequently display certain facets of the sign they occupy, often in a subtle manner, and which are a combination of their intrinsic natures and the sign occupied.

In studying sign emplacements in return charts experience suggests that the signs should be considered from a broad perspective and that the importance or otherwise of a particular sign(s) will depend on how prominent it is in the chart. Signs occupying the angles or containing the Sun, Moon or several planets will always exert their influence even though it may not be all that apparent. As always, the chart needs to be studied as a whole; how well is it integrated?, the degree of angularity of the planets and whether, during subsequent progressions, certain features of the chart will become prominent. All these factors require to be assessed before any deductions concerning the implications of the chart can be made.

The traditional meanings and matters of the twelve signs of the zodiac may have some relevance to return charts when considered within the context of the individual chart. If, for example, the sign Libra is prominent in the return, either through being angular or containing significant planets, then the return period will, among other things, be associated with those matters and responses which are of a Libran nature such as relationships, personal attachments, unity and harmony. As with Libra, so with all the other signs.

There is an ample supply of astrological literature dealing with planets, signs and houses from which one may proceed to study the more exciting aspects of astrology, not least of which is the technique of solar and lunar returns.

ASSESSMENT
The importance and significance of any return chart, irrespective

of the 'zodiac' used, depends upon the four main angles and how these points—Ascendant and Midheaven and their opposites—are 'conditioned' either by having planets in close conjunction or through being a factor of some major aspectual pattern. Although planets exert their maximum influence when 'bodily' on an angle, their ecliptical positions are just as important. It is true that a planet with considerable latitude may be in a different house when its mundane position is computed, and this requires to be considered when working with exact data. For the ordinary investigation and analysis of returns the normal delineation processes used with natal charts are sufficient, with the exception that less attention should be paid to house rulers, dispositors, parts and points and other forms of jugglery which contribute little towards clarity and a realistic interpretation.

Angularity means a planet on or within a specified distance of an angular cusp and the closer the planet is to the angle the greater its 'influence' for good or ill. Previously it was considered that planets in cadent houses (third, sixth, ninth and twelfth) were enfeebled and that the principles associated with the planet could not be expressed to their fullest capacity. Modern research has caused this somewhat bizarre approach to be overhauled and re-examined. The result is that planets which may be technically cadent, by being in one of the cadent houses, are just as active and significant but that the expression is less forceful or prominent than planets which are truly angular. A cadent planet within about 8–10 degrees of an angle can be classified as angular and its significance interpreted as such.

It appears rather strange that traditional astrology should demand that the houses have a rigid, watertight demarcation boundary whereby once past the cusp of one house and into the next, the significance of the former house ceases abruptly. All the houses are interrelated and research tends to confirm that the 'influence' of a particular house tends to wane gradually and that a planet close to a cusp has to be considered in terms of both houses.

Sometimes the angular contacts in return charts for a definite time and period, are not so pronounced as one would expect. There may be several reasons why this is so. It may be that the original data concerning the birthtime is not so exact and this would cause the angles to be 'off mark', particularly the Ascendant if a sign of short ascension is rising. Also it may be that our understanding of the 'orbs of influence'—the number of degrees that a planet is from exact aspect—may be faulty. However, there is little point in trying to justify ourselves if we find that the chart(s) under review do not meet our expectations. Provided we are satisfied that the data and calculations are correct, we have no alternative but to accept the idea that perhaps some of the astrological thinking is a 'grand illusion' and is unsupported by realistic astrological principles. It is not that astrology and its concepts are wrong but that we fail to understand the true nature of astrological symbolism and the various cosmic patterns with which we are intimately related.

In the interpretation of a chart there are many complex factors to consider, but a methodical 'breakdown' of the various factors will eventually show definite trends, some important, others less so. It is often found, as with several different return charts for the same period, that a particular planetary pattern will be repeated or accentuated in many different ways, so that what at first appeared to be a mass of unconnected and contradictory factors is seen to be of critical importance in the final analysis.

With return charts the assessment is twofold. Firstly, the return is analysed in isolation without recourse to the natal chart. Unusual groupings, planets angular, aspectual strength or weakness will all indicate the general 'tone' of the chart, which in turn will show the potentialities of the period under review—yearly for the solar return, monthly for the lunar. But the return chart is not a static instrument and its true significance becomes apparent when it becomes 'alive' through progression of one kind or another.

The analysis has to be consistent in terms of the planetary principles, the mundane position of the planet(s) and the various aspectual patterns. The nature of the sign containing the planet(s) will 'colour' the expression of the planet; it will not alter it. A planet will always be expressed according to its intrinsic nature and this expression will be accentuated or modified according to the sign position. The house position will highlight the area of life which will be activated in mundane experiences and conditions, although not all placements operate as hard and fast events or conditions but may be expressed as psychological undertones which eventually, under the appropriate stimuli, manifest in direct action as the result of other planetary contacts.

The Moon, the significator of moods and emotions, is always of paramount importance in the solar return chart. Her condition by sign, house and aspects set the emotional tone and responses for the year in question. Whereas the Sun will, by house and aspect, indicate the aims and direction of an individual in the quest for the realization of objectives, the motivation will be, to some extent, governed by the solar Moon and its condition. Therefore, all return chart assessments require the Sun/Moon relationship, singly and jointly, to be analysed in detail. The other planets will, according to their condition, indicate how they are likely to be expressed and this taken in conjunction with the Sun/Moon relationship, will show the probable unfoldment during the course of the return period.

The indications in any return chart, although initially studied in isolation, have to be related to the natal chart. The natal or birth chart is what we are 'born with' and the intrinsic natal pattern governs our responses, attitudes and approaches to life. Our reactions reflect the natal 'imprint' and this fact cannot be ignored in the analysis of progressions, return charts or other forecasting techniques and their probable effects. A solar or lunar return is a transit chart whose indications relate to a specified period of time such as a year or a month depending upon the type of return. The natal chart is with us always and its implications are life-long being manifested according to the particular natal pattern. The potentialities of the natal chart will be expressed under suitable and appropriate excitation. But this expression is subject to influences which can be either beneficial or detrimental. Hereditary and environmental factors cannot be deduced from any chart—a chart is merely a representation of a moment in time—but these two factors are all-important in astrological assessment. We need to evaluate the astrological symbolism in terms applicable to the individual's nature and environment.

We can, of course, gain very valuable information for research purposes through the study of returns without knowing too much about the person's private and personal life. However, if we wish to discover how a particular progression or transit in a return chart affected the person, we need to know how they felt at that time. It is here that the crux of the matter lies. What were the feelings at that time? Many contacts appear to form, reach exactitude and pass away without any noticeable outward effect. Subsequent investigation reveals that the person experienced an inner satisfaction from a 'sense of feeling good' or that they were quietly excited at the prospect of future expectations. Alternatively, the period may have been a time of confused conditions the effects of which only became apparent subsequently.

When the natal planets, by progression, are prominent in return charts the innate quality is expressed in accordance with their natal condition and with the pattern of the return chart. The angles are all-important and planets, natal, solar or transiting will always exert a major influence when close to or in major aspect with the angles. When the solar planets (those in the return) are brought to the angles, their action coincides with the indications contained in the return chart and with the basic natal chart. Transits (those positions on the date under review) often act as 'markers' and time the date, either by being close to an angle or by forming some prominent aspect involving an important area of the chart. Each chart has to be assessed methodically by analysing the parts and then endeavouring to combine the indications into a cohesive whole, in conjunction with the basic natal chart.

The general guidelines concerning the action and nature of planets when studied in relation to returns is given below. It must be emphasized that these are only guidelines for the benefit of beginners and that the only way to understand returns and their significance is to study them in relation to 'real life'. When prominent, i.e. on or near angles, a planet will reflect its nature in events and/or psychological conditions appropriate to its symbolism. The tendency to regard planetary contacts in a purely materialistic way will result in faulty analysis and error. More often than not, the contact will be expressed in a feeling of 'psychological awareness' which may coincide with, or be a prelude to, events or conditions which are symbolic of the planet concerned. Jupiter angular can signify joy, elation and an optimistic feeling of well-being which in turn can be conducive to expanding one's horizons in an advantageous manner. Assets of one kind or another are often acquired 'under Jupiterian contacts' but these often stem from the attitudes and actions of the person in seeking to promote the self.

When more than one planet is angular there is a 'mixture' of influences and the planet(s) nearest the angle should be given priority. The MC is the most important angle and planets close to it should always receive first consideration. Naturally, in any assessment of the probable effects of planetary contacts, the total chart including the natal positions must be considered.

Planets close to the Ascendant/Descendant generally signify events and conditions which have a bearing on the self and a person's personal interests. These are often affected through the involvement with others, either on a personal or non-personal basis. The lower angle (IC) often shows withdrawals and departures, the nature of which is indicated by the planet(s) involved.

Return charts always reflect the psychological implications current at a particular period. When a planet, natal, solar or transiting is active in a return, the response(s) to it will vary depending upon the strength or weakness of the planet in the return chart. A planet strong in the return chart with close aspects either to an angle or with other significant planets will exert maximum influence when by progression it is brought to an angle. In all return charts the orb (the distance from an exact aspect) should be narrow, no more than a few degrees.

The houses are always an important factor in the assessment of an astrological chart. Although there has been a tendency in some quarters to relegate the importance of house placements, experience has shown that all the houses are significant. Solar return houses have the same meaning and correlation as the natal houses and planets in the respective houses will operate in terms of the house and matters connected with it.

The chief factors regarding the houses are the four angles, which are of primary importance in return charts. The intermediate houses will, by having planetary placements, often indicate conditions and situations in broad terms, but it is the angles which, when progressed, bring to fruition the indications of the chart. The natal planets when brought to the angles of the progressed return act in accordance with their natal implications and in the 'field of experience' as denoted by the angle they contact.

The assessment and analysis of return charts provides a valuable introduction towards understanding the remarkable 'wheels within wheels' activity which characterizes cosmic motion. So far as return charts are concerned it would be misleading to list in 'cookbook fashion' all the possible combinations of planet, sign and house and what they signified. It is only by relating the individual return to the person concerned that its value can be discerned and appreciated. The following list illustrates the basic meanings of each of the planets when taken in isolation. Naturally, these indications will be modified or accentuated according to how the planet is placed or aspected in the return chart.

In judging the effects of progressions or transits in return charts the planetary configurations have to be interpreted not only in accordance with the fundamental nature of the bodies concerned, but also in relation to the nature of the contact. The significance of any contact requires to be considered on at least two levels: (a) the nature and meaning of the progressed or transiting body, and

(b) the intrinsic nature of the body being aspected, normally by conjunction or opposition. For example, Mars in transit to the natal Jupiter would not be expressed in the same way as Jupiter in transit to the natal Mars. The natal Jupiter represents, among other things, our status, opportunities for expansion and general well-being. Mars denotes initiative and energy but also hurt and destruction so its transit of Jupiter could be detrimental as the result of rash and aggressive action which in turn has a reactionary effect on matters requiring prudent and impartial judgement.

Jupiter in transit to Mars is a stimulating contact, denoting progress and growth often as the result of accepting challenging conditions and through enterprise and initiative achieving success. So whereas Mars in transit can be detrimental, its action when being transited is inclined to be more controlled and structured.

Naturally, the expression of planets in transit or by progression will be subjected to the pattern of the chart as a whole, but a clear distinction is needed when judging the effects of transiting bodies. The natal positions are 'with us always' but the transiting and progressed positions are comparatively short-lived factors which relate to external influences which impinge upon our basic foundations, i.e. the natal chart. These influences may be expressed in the form of active events or conditions or they may act as subtle overtones of a psychological nature without any apparent effect. It is doubtful whether any contact is a 'dumb note'. Even when there is no definite outward manifestation there is usually some form of inner expression taking place which is in conformity with the astrological patterns active at that particular time.

The most important thing in so far as return chart analysis is concerned is not to become 'bogged down' with irrelevant factors and details. A methodical approach which concentrates on the major factors such as angularity, exact aspects, unusual groupings and the fundamental nature of the planets involved, will do much towards achieving a commonsense analysis. Precise prediction is never possible and to attempt it is merely courting disaster. Future trends manifest in a variety of ways and it will be often seen that several charts covering the same period have much in common and frequently 'speak the same language'. Even when there appears to be some disparity regarding the indications of one chart compared with another, the differences are often more apparent than real. The coming of the sombre Saturn to an angle could coincide with a death or a loss which could have a dramatic and sorrowful effect depending upon the nature of the relationship. If, during the same period, Jupiter was prominent in another type of return, the indications might suggest some form of gain or the opportunity for advancement, the source of which was related to a combination of Jupiterian and Saturnian action. A typical instance of this could be the death of a parent and the subsequent inheritance of assets.

Obviously, it is impossible to treat of all the variable combinations, groupings and patterns which occur, in one way or another, in the various kinds of returns. Provided that the fundamental natures of the planets and what they signify are related to the person and his natal pattern, the appropriate returns can be analysed with some confidence.

Planetary Concepts

Sun   Self, desire, creativity, authority, the 'urge to power', honour and acclaim, the 'heart of the matter', self-awareness, the 'life-flowing' energies.

Moon   Moods, emotions, habit and instinctual behaviour, nurture, protection, sustenance, ebb and flow, sexuality, parturition, health, rhythm and change.

Mercury Communications, ideas, exchange, perception, intellect, learning, co-ordination, relating and interpreting, comprehension.

Venus   Unity, co-operation, sociability, empathy, affection, values, harmony, intimacy, beauty, love and romance, victory and peace.

Mars   Initiative, energy, war and strife, self-assertion, hurt and destruction, action, challenges, dominance, enterprise.

Jupiter Faith, hope, growth, expansion, knowledge, under-standing, wisdom, opportunities, judgement, 'luck', joy and elation, far horizons, the future, status, progress and advancement.

Saturn   Consolidation, restructuring, conservatism, 'fate', isolation, fears, limitations, frigidity, responsibilities, apprehensiveness, delays, disappointments, defeat and losses.

Uranus   Originality, uniqueness, independence, self-discovery, inventiveness, contrariness, freedom, modernity, novelty, change, deviation, wilfulness, rebelliousness, 'the new man or order', severances and disruptions, the unexpected.

Neptune The intangible, dream-states, unreality, 'not of this world', inspirational, escape, 'the quest for perfection and the ideal', fantasy, mortification, victimization, devotional, artificiality, falsehood, illusion and deception, fluster, flurry, hysteria.

Pluto   Termination or transformation of existing patterns, birth, death, resurrection, recycling, rebuilding, renewing, finality, 'ghosts from the past', regeneration, resurfacing, rebirth, farewells, goodbyes and exits.

When a planet is prominent in a return chart it will function in accordance with its strength or weakness as determined by any aspect pattern it may have. Well-integrated, a planet will 'display' the finer and more desirable qualities associated with it. When the planet has an incompatible placement the less desirable traits may be expressed, the degree of expression depending on the integration of the chart as a whole.

Signs and Symbols

Sign	Symbol	Name	Ruler	Symbol
1st Aries	♈	The Ram	Mars	♂
2nd Taurus	♉	The Bull	Venus	♀
3rd Gemini	♊	The Twins	Mercury	☿
4th Cancer	♋	The Crab	Moon	☽
5th Leo	♌	The Lion	Sun	☉
6th Virgo	♍	The Virgin	Mercury	☿
7th Libra	♎	The Balance or Scales	Venus	♀
8th Scorpio	♏	The Scorpion	Mars	♂
			Pluto	♇
9th Sagittarius	♐	The Archer	Jupiter	♃
10th Capricorn	♑	The Goat	Saturn	♄
11th Aquarius	♒	The Waterbearer	Uranus	♅
			Saturn	♄
12th Pisces	♓	The Fishes	Neptune	♆
			Jupiter	♃

The Moon's Nodes:

North	☊	Caput draconis	(dragon's head)
South	☋	Cauda draconis	(dragon's tail)

Part of Fortune: ⊕

See Appendix 3 for signs and symbols in computer-drawn charts.

Elements and Qualities

Sign	Element	Quality	House
Aries ♈	Fire (Positive)	Cardinal	1 Angular
Leo ♌		Fixed	5 Succedent
Sagittarius ♐		Mutable	9 Cadent
Capricorn ♑	Earth (Negative)	Cardinal	10 Angular
Taurus ♉		Fixed	2 Succedent
Virgo ♍		Mutable	6 Cadent
Libra ♎	Air (Positive)	Cardinal	7 Angular
Aquarius ♒		Fixed	11 Succedent
Gemini ♊		Mutable	3 Cadent
Cancer ♋	Water (Negative)	Cardinal	4 Angular
Scorpio ♏		Fixed	8 Succedent
Pisces ♓		Mutable	12 Cadent

Houses

Angular	(1, 10, 7 and 4).
Succedent	(2, 11, 8 and 5).
Cadent	(3, 12, 9 and 6).

Table of Aspects
(Major)

360° circle divided by:	Degree	Aspect	Symbol
1	360 or 0	Conjunction	☌
2	180	Opposition	☍
3	120	Trine	△
4	90	Square	□
6	60	Sextile	✳

(Minor)

	Degree	Aspect	Symbol
$5/12$	150	Quincunx	⊼
$2/5$	144	Bi quintile	±
$3/8$	135	Sesquiquadrate	⊡
5	72	Quintile	Q
8	45	Semi-square	∟
10	36	Decile	⊥
12	30	Semi-sextile	⋁

9.

RETURNS IN ACTION

Introduction

The various methods and techniques employed and which have been discussed in relation with the different types of returns require to be assessed in the light of actual experiences. Theory and hypothesis may act as a spur to our investigations and provide the necessary impetus to pursue our enquiries with enthusiasm and vigour but our findings must be related to reality.

If the techniques of return charts, particularly solar and lunar returns, are valid, then they must reflect the events and conditions of life as experienced at any given time. The dividing line between events and conditions, in so far as astrological symbolism is concerned, can be somewhat tenuous. The way in which a particular contact or pattern will be experienced is not as easy or clear-cut as one would wish. There are many reasons why this is so, but perhaps two of the main factors are that many conditions are psychological in nature, or that many events 'just happen' without apparent cause and seem to stem from the workings of a capricious fate.

The study of a few charts using return techniques will not prove anything statistically, but it will show that events, conditions and how we respond to them are related, in no small measure, to cosmic patterns operating at a particular time. The constant action and reaction which characterizes all forms of life is mirrored by these cosmic patterns and the appropriate astrological symbolism.

The study of various events which a person has experienced is probably the most practical way in deciding the validity of return charts. The ideal is, of course, to know exactly how the event or condition affected the person concerned and what were their responses. Unless intimately acquainted, this is difficult to discern but at least we have a starting point with the event and how it correlates with astrological indications.

The case studies which are discussed in the following pages relating to marriage and the birth of children are of friends (No.1) or relatives (2, 3, 4). None of them are professional astrologers and their knowledge of astrological techniques—except No.1, is slight. The data given by them concerning their marriages and children and also their own natal data have been used without any attempt at rectification or adjustments of any kind. It was very pleasing to know that all these mothers were most definite about the birthtimes of their children, even though they were not astrologers. The marriage times where they are quoted are fairly accurate but not necessarily exact. One needs an independent observer at weddings to note the time of 'I will'; one can hardly expect the participants to consult their watches.

Weddings and Births

A brief examination of the returns covering these events fully justifies the traditional tenets relating to planetary symbolism. The returns preceding marriage often have the following planets prominent:

1. Saturn, probably denoting the contractual basis of partnership in association with the increased sense of responsibility and obligations.
2. Venus, the significator of partnerships, love and affection and mutual undertakings.
3. Jupiter, for joy, opportunity and expansion.
4. Pluto, the planet of severance and departures is appropriate as it signifies the commencement of a new independent existence and the relinquishment of, in some instances, old ties and familiar surroundings.
5. The Moon and Neptune which are associated with moods and emotional excitement are indicative of the feelings which are normally experienced at the time of marriage.

All these planets may be active or significant, either in the return chart or through having some form of contact natally or by progression.

The birth of children, normally a happy and emotional event, is often associated with a strong Moon or Pluto contact. The symbolism is apt, for the Moon denotes the nurturing instinct and Pluto the 'new birth'. Normally, it is the angles which are all-important in judging the indications of return charts, but in the

NATAL   DUKE OF YORK   *No.6*

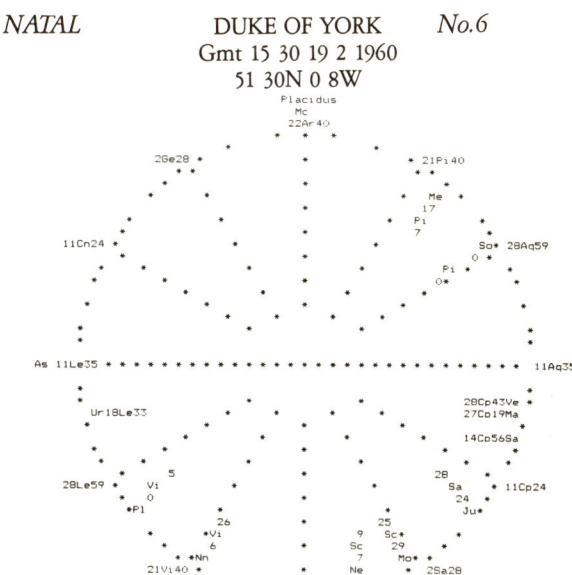

No.7   DUCHESS OF YORK   *NATAL*

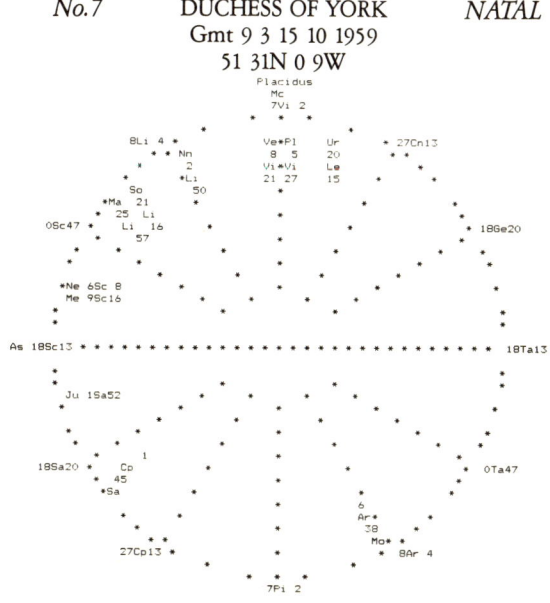

NATAL   PRINCESS MARGARET   *No.8*
Gmt 20 22 21 8 1930
56 57N 3 0W

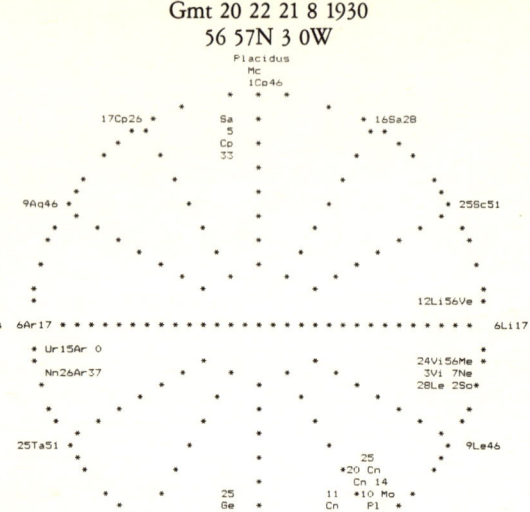

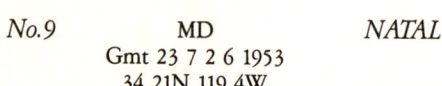

No.9   MD   *NATAL*
Gmt 23 7 2 6 1953
34 21N 119 4W

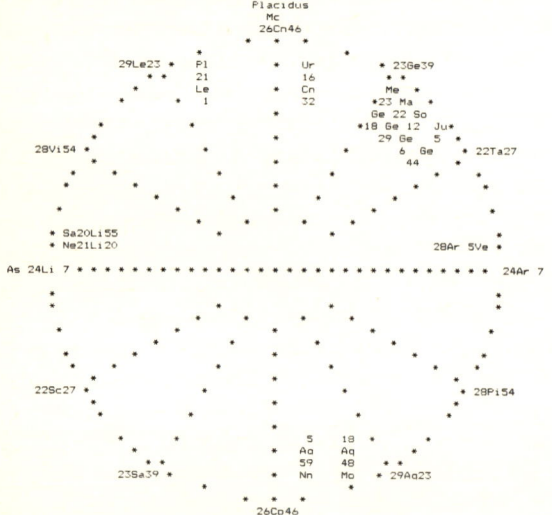

NATAL   ND   *No.10*
Gmt 4 0 17 10 1949
34 9N 118 9W

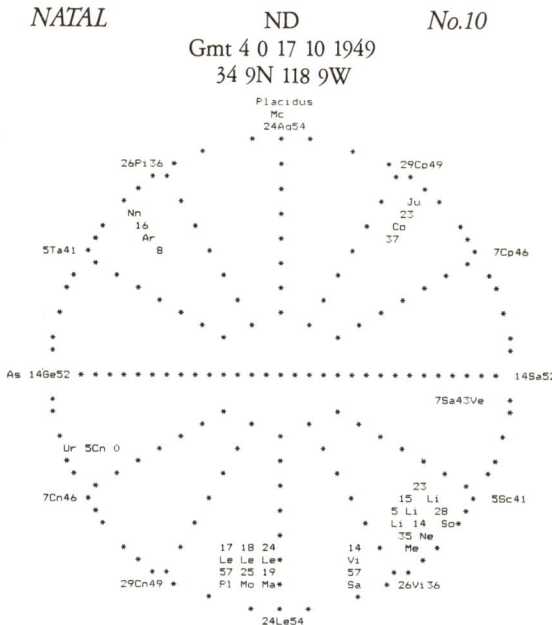

few cases under review there is a marked preponderance of planets occupying the fifth and eleventh houses, areas which are traditionally related to children (fifth) and hopes, wishes and expectations (eleventh). This may be coincidental in the cases studied or it may have some important implications which only detailed investigation using a considerable number of cases will confirm or deny.

A thorough analysis of any return chart requires that its indications are judged in conjunction with the appropriate natal chart. Often it will be found, that a natal planet is prominent in a return chart, either by being on an angle of the return or by coming to an angle by progression.

As has been stated elsewhere, no firm conclusions can be drawn from a cursory inspection of a few charts. What can be deduced is whether the event can be related to the astrological factors prominent at the time. If the symbolism of the chart is relative to the event then we have a starting-point for further studies.

(Tropical)
Princess Margaret (Countess of Snowdon), the sister of Queen
Elizabeth II, was born at:
9.22 p.m. British Summer Time = 20.22 UT
21 August 1930, Glamis Castle, 56° 37′ N, 3° 01′ W.
Natal Sun: 28° 01′ 43″ Leo: Natal Moon 25° 16′ Cancer:
RAMC 18.07.39: Mean Sun 9.57.43: Apparent Sun 10.00.49.
Asc. 6° Aries: MC 2° Capricorn (birth data as recorded).

The Princess was married at Westminster Abbey on the 6 May 1960
at 10.45 UT Lat. 51.30N 0.07W.
The solar return for 1959/60 occurred at:
20.36 UT 21.8.59 and the RAMC was (for her assumed place of
residence—London) 18.33.12 Mean Sun 9.57.40

Marriage data:		*Solar return* 1959/60	*Lunar return* (25° 16′ Cancer)
Time UT	10.45	20.36	12.28
Date	6.5.60	21.8.59	2.5.60
Lat.	51.30N	51.30N	51.30N
Long.	00.07W	00.07W	00.07W
Sun	15.54.09 Taurus	28.01.43 Leo	12.06 Taurus
Moon	13.39 Virgo	8.18 Aries	25.16 Cancer
RAMC	1.41.42	18.33.12	3.09.12
Mean Sun	2.57.10	9.57.40	2.41.40
App. Sun	2.53.44	10.00.49	2.38.36
Asc.	14 Leo	19 Aries	0 Virgo
MC	27 Aries	7 Capricorn	20 Taurus

Solar Moon Return: 09.29 UT 24.4.60. London

Progressed Solar Return: 6.5.60. London

Solar Quotidian: 6.5.60. London

The progressed solar return for the date of the marriage (6 May 1960)
fulfils all the criteria that are associated with weddings and the like.
The Solar Moon in Aries is conjunct the natal Ascendant, opposition
the natal Venus and square the return MC. The seventh house,
traditionally associated with partnerships and contracts, has a stellium
which includes Venus with Mars close to the eighth cusp. By
progression the natal Moon and Pluto are conjunct the seventh angle

and the solar Jupiter is on the Midheaven of the progressed return. As an added testimony, the transiting Moon in Virgo on the day of the wedding is exactly conjunct the solar Venus. The prominence of Saturn—conjunct solar MC and close to the progressed Ascendant—is quite fitting for an event which has contractual obligations and responsibilities.

The lunar return which occurred a few days prior to the date of marriage has Pluto, the significator of 'beginnings and endings' closely contacting the Ascendant and the lunar sun opposed to the lunar Neptune. This Sun/Neptune contact coupled with the Moon/Saturn opposition probably coincided with a sense of nervous excitement at the prospect of the event shortly to take place, but also overshadowed by the realization that an altered life-style with certain limitations was also to be accepted.

The solar Moon return which occurred in April prior to the marriage has Moon conjunct Venus—an apt contact for the forthcoming event—with Mars close to the upper meridian. The tight square of Saturn to the Aries planets (Mercury, Moon and Venus) introduces a 'sense of reality' regarding the acceptance of responsibilities. The exact trine of Moon to Uranus is symbolic of the anticipated thrill and excitement shortly to be experienced. The Cancer Ascendant is significant because the degree rising (22 Cancer) is the midpoint of the natal Moon/Pluto. Again we have a prominent Pluto indicating the severance of old ties and a 'new beginning'.

When the chart is progressed to 6 May, we have the natal Uranus/Venus close to an angle (tenth/fourth) and the transiting Mercury/Venus conjunct the return Sun (4 Taurus). The transiting Moon on the day was separating from a conjunction with Pluto and applying to the opposition of return Mars. The transiting Jupiter, which was passing over the natal Midheaven during this period formed a grand trine, in the return, with Sun and Pluto. On the date of the wedding it was exactly trine Mercury and Venus.

The solar quotidian progression for this period is found thus:

	H	M	S
6.5.60 Mean Sun		2	57	10
Solar return Mean Sun	−	9	57	40
Difference		16	59	30
Add RAMC solar return	+	18	33	12
RAMC solar quotidian		11	32	42

Asc. 28° Scorpio: MC 22° Virgo: at London.
This progression brings the solar return Mars to the MC and the solar
return Jupiter close to the Ascendant.

The Sidereal Return

The Sidereal Solar return for 1959/60 occurred at:
06.46 UT 22.8.59. Lat. 51.30N 0.08W.
RAMC 4.44.48. Sidereal Sun 4° 15′ 31″ Leo:
Sidereal Moon 19° 23′ Pisces:

In this return we find Venus and Mars, in the constellation Leo,
conjunct the Ascendant. These contacts are extremely appropriate
for marriage, particularly as the solar Moon in Pisces is in exact
opposition to the natal Venus in Virgo. As with all return charts,
their true import is not always apparent until they are galvanized
into life by some form of progression. Progressing this sidereal return,
using the right ascension of the apparent Sun, for the date of her
marriage, we have Uranus exactly on the Ascendant with Venus and
Mercury on the upper angle in exact trine to Jupiter and Pluto. As
an added testimony, the transiting Moon in Leo is precisely conjunct
the solar Venus and applying to the conjunction of the solar
Ascendant and Mars. Not only are the traditional significators of
marriage (Mars/Venus) to the fore, but Jupiter and Saturn aspect
the natal Midheaven; Jupiter by transit and Saturn in the return.
The solar Neptune close to the lower angle and the rising Uranus
denote excitement and novelty and the feeling of being in a 'whirl'.
There is little doubt that the symbolism of these returns is in keeping
with the event and conditions of 6 May, and although 'both zodiacs'
portray firm indications of marriage or partnership, the sidereal
version, in this case, appears more definite.

Using the solar quotidian for this period we have:

	H	M	S
6.5.60 Mean Sun	2	57	10
Sidereal Solar Return Mean Sun −	9	59	20
Difference	16	57	50
Add RAMC solar return +	4	44	48
RAMC solar quotidian	21	42	38

Asc. 5° Gemini: MC 0° Aquarius: (sidereal).

This progression brings Saturn and Jupiter to the seventh cusp, highly appropriate, with the Sun and Pluto close to the lower angle. These contacts probably denote the increased status and assets that royalty generally acquire at the time of marriage.

The progression of the solar return using the RA of the Apparent Sun, is the most accurate method, but for a rough approximation for any day during the return year, the following example may be useful.

Princess Margaret's wedding:

6 May Event	=	127 day of year (leap year)
22 Aug. SSR	=	234 day of year

127 + 365	=	492
less		234
		258 days elapsed

258 × 4 min. 57 sec. sidereal time = 21 hr. 18 min.

Equation of time 22.8	− 3 min.	
Equation of time 6.5	+4	= 00 07 min. minus
		21 11

add RAMC S/R 4.45 = 1.56 approx. Prog. S/R

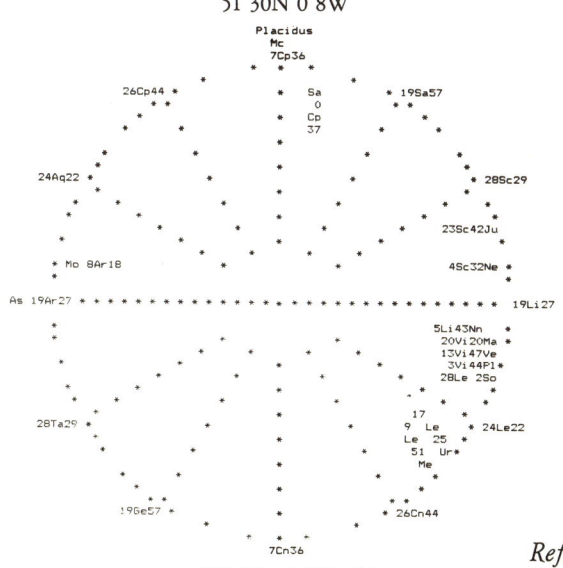

Event:
Marriage 6.5.60

PRINCESS MARGARET:
Gmt 20 36 21 8 1959
51 30N 0 8W

No.11

Placidus
Mc
7Cp36

26Cp44

Sa
0
Cp
37

19Sa57

24Aq22

28Sc29

23Sc42Ju

Mo 8Ar18

4Sc32Ne

As 19Ar27

19Li27

5Li43Nn
20Vi20Ma
13Vi47Ve
3Vi44Pl
28Le 2So

28Ta29

17
9 Le   24Le22
Le 25
51 Ur
Me

19Ge57

26Cn44

7Cn36

SOLAR RETURN

Ref:
Natal Chart No.8

Event:
Marriage, 6.5.60

PRINCESS MARGARET   *No.12*
Gmt 12 25 2 5 60
56 57N 3 0W

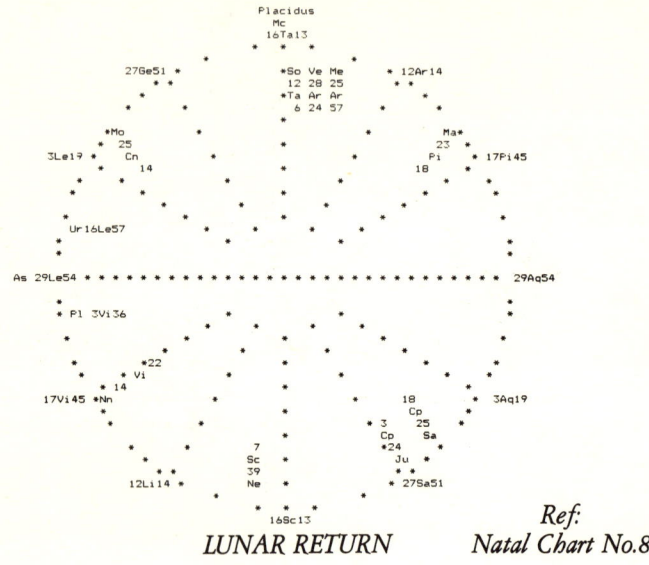

```
                          Placidus
                          Mc
                          16Ta13
                           *  *  *
                  *                        *
       27Ge51 *                 *So Ve Me      * 12Ar14
           * *                   12 28 25        * *
        *            *          *Ta Ar Ar             *
       *          *              6 24 57        *         *
     *Mo              *                  *         *
     *   25                      *                 23  *
   3Le19 *     Cn               *            *     Pi  * 17Pi45
     *    14       *            *            *    18   * *
      *        *           *        *         *      *
     *      *         *         *       *        *       *
    *                *         *       *       *          *
    Ur16Le57               *         *       *           *
    *                                                     *
   As 29Le54 * * * * * * * * * * * * * * * * * * * * * * * * 29Aq54
    *                                                     *
    *  Pl 3Vi36                                           *
     *                    *       *      *                *
     *          *    *         *        *       *         *
      *      *22          *         *        *      *    *
       *    * Vi               *         *        *    *
      * 14                     *              18    * 3Aq19
   17Vi45 *Nn                  *                 Cp     *
       *                  *         *       * 3    25  *
        *            *         *         * Cp   Sa *
         *      *        7          *     *24      *
          *   * *      Sc      *           Ju  *
           * *        39                  * *  *
        12Li14 *      Ne    *           * 27Sa51
             *      *  *  *         *
                   16Sc13
```

LUNAR RETURN   *Ref:*
Natal Chart No.8

PROGRESSED SOLAR RETURN   No.13

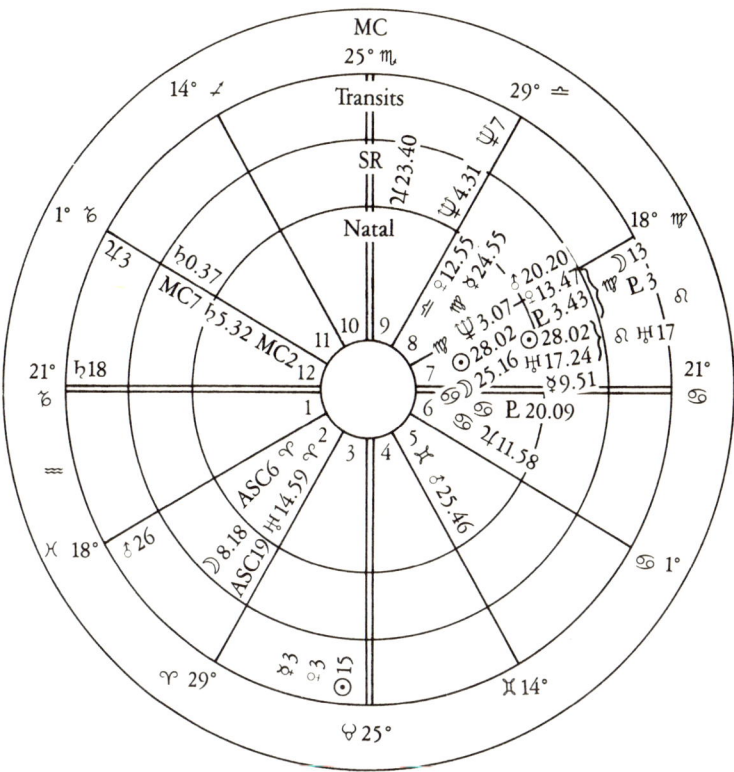

SOLAR RETURN				PROGRESSED RETURN			
Date 21.8.59 Time 20.36				Date 6.5.60 Time 10.45			
	H	M	S		H	M	S
RA Sun	10	00	49	RA Sun PSR	02	53	44
RAMC	18	33	12	RA Sun SR −	10	00	49
Constant	1.2454			= Difference	16	52	55
Princess Margaret				× Constant =	21	01	29
(Tropical)				RAMC SR +	18	33	12
				RAMC PSR	15	34	41

No.14   PRINCESS MARGARET   *Event: Marriage, 6.5.60*
Gmt 9 29 24 4 1960
51 30N 0 7W

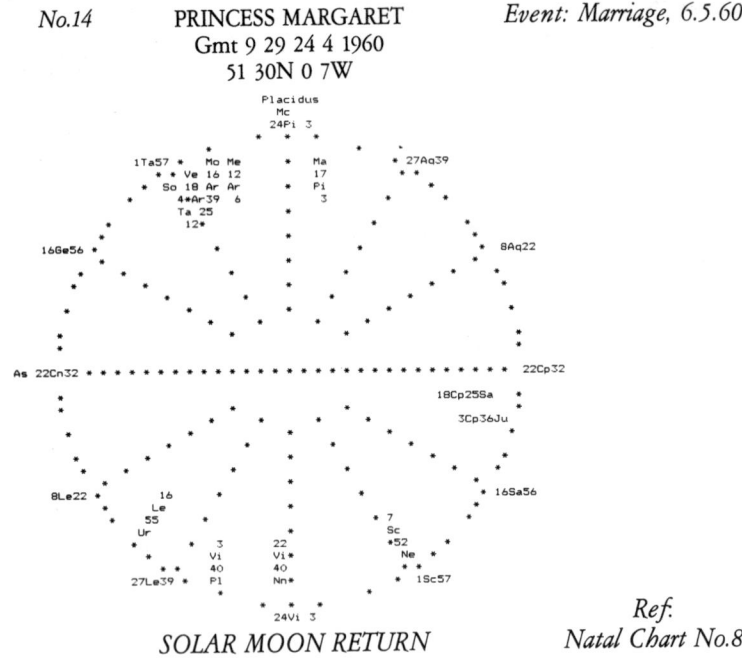

SOLAR MOON RETURN

Ref:
Natal Chart No.8

No.14(a)   *PROGRESSED SOLAR MOON RETURN*
MAY 1960

PRINCESS MARGARET
(Tropical)

Princess Margaret: *No.15*
  Natal Chart

NATAL CHART   *SIDEREAL*

20.22 UT   RAMC 18.07.39
21.8.1930   RAAS 10.00.49
56.37N   RAMS 09.57.43
3.01W

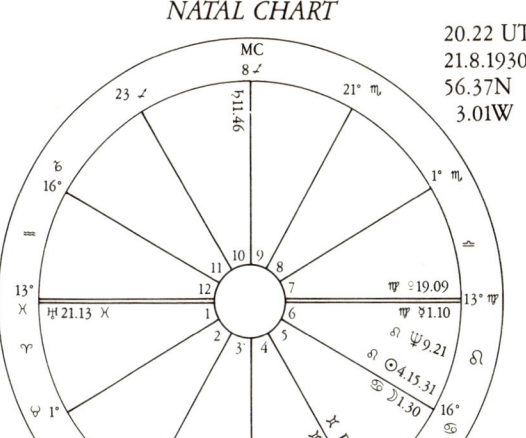

SOLAR RETURN

Princess Margaret   *No.16*

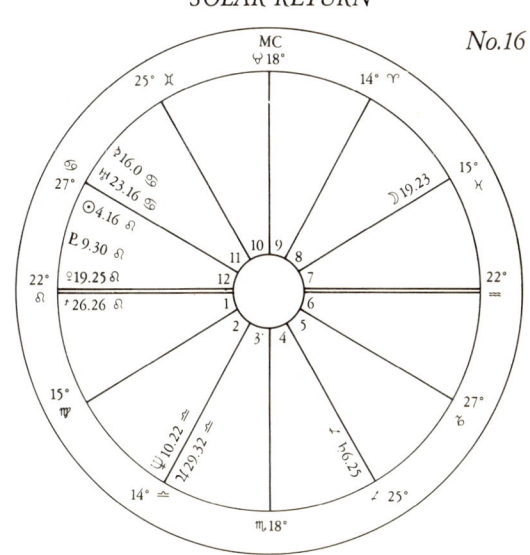

SIDEREAL

Natal Sun
4° 15' 31" Leo

S/R 06.46 UT
22.8.1959
RAMC 4.44.48
RAAS 10.00.49
RAMS 09.59.20
SVP 5.49.21

SIDEREAL PROGRESSED SOLAR RETURN   No.17

Princess Margaret

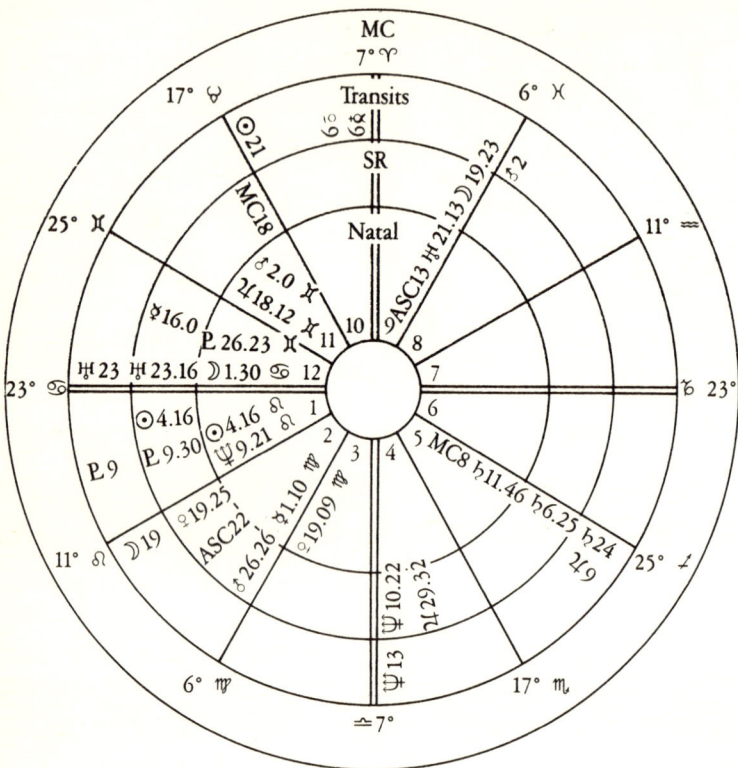

SOLAR RETURN				PROGRESSED RETURN			
Date 22.8.59 Time 6.46				Date 6.5.60 Time 10.45			
	H	M	S		H	M	S
RA Sun	10	00	49	RA Sun PSR	2	53	44
RAMC	4	44	48	RA Sun SR −	10	0	49
Constant	1.2576			= Difference	16	52	55
				× Constant =	21	13	50
				RAMC SR +	4	44	48
				RAMC PSR	1	58	38

SOLAR MOON RETURN

	H M S
(A) Date 24.4.60 Time 00.00 Required: Mean Sun	02 08 06
Date 21.8.59 Time 20.36 Solar Return − Mean	
Sun	9 57 40
Difference	16 10 26
Correction for Mean Solar Time minus −	00 02 39
Mean Solar Hours	16 07 47
UT of Solar Return Add +	20 36 00
Progressed Solar Return	12 43 47

UT 12.44. Date 22.8.59

(B) Progressed Solar Return: Moon's Longitude: Sign Deg. Min.
12.44 UT: 22.8.59 Date:

Sign	Deg.	Min.
♈	16	39

(C) Moon Transits progressed Longitude:
    = Solar Moon Return

Date	UT
24.4.60	09.29

	H M S
(D) ST at 0 hr. UT on Transit date	* 14 08 06
UT of Moon's Return Add +	09 29 00
Correction 9.86 sec. per hour Add + **	00 01 33
RAMC at Greenwich	23 38 39
Long. Equiv. −W:	00 00 28
RAMC Solar Moon Return	23 38 11
Mean Sun = * + ** + 12 hours	02 09 39

(E) *PROGRESSED SOLAR MOON RETURN*

Date 6.5.60 Time 10.45 Required:	Mean Sun	02 57 10
Solar Moon Return minus −	Mean Sun	02 09 39
Difference		00 47 31
RAMC Solar Moon Return Add +		23 38 11
RAMC Progressed Solar Moon Return		00 25 42

Solar Returns covering the period preceding weddings (W) and the birth of children (C)

Chart

No.18   Example No.1 Birth data: 9.05 UT 12.6.29, 51.31N 0.20W
                                Natal Sun. 20° 53' 41" Gemini.
                                Natal Moon. 27° 31' Leo.
         Event: Marriage 24.6.50. London.

No.19   Solar return 1950/51. 10.48 UT 12.6.50. London
                                RAMC 4.06.26
         Event: Birth of son 5.30 UT 12.9.53 London.

No.20   Solar return 1953/54 4.05 UT 12.6.53 London
                                RAMC 21.29.27
         Event: birth of son. 21.50 UT 28.3.56 London.

No.21   Solar return 1955/56 15.40 UT 12.6.55 London
                                RAMC 9.1.25

No.22   Example No.2 Birth data: 11.50 UT 29.8.28, 48.47N 9.11E
                                Natal Sun. 5° 52' 11" Virgo
                                Natal Moon. 15° 40' Aquarius
         Event: Marriage 13.5.50. 14.30 UT London.

No.23   Solar return 1949/50. 13.41 UT 29.8.49. London
                                RAMC 12.09.23
         Event: Birth of 1st daughter. 9.0 UT 11.5.53. London.

No.24   Solar return 1952/53. 6.58 UT 29.8.52. London
                                RAMC 5.26.22
         Event: Birth of 2nd daughter. 23.10 UT 4.3.56. London.

No.25   Solar return 1955/56. 00.16 UT 30.8.55. London
                                RAMC 22.44.22
         Event: Birth of 3rd daughter. 19.22 UT 16.3.63. London.

No.26   Solar return 1962/63. 17.07 UT 29.8.62. London
                                RAMC 15.28.28

No.27   Example No.3 Birth data: 9.08 UT 28.6.25. 51.10N 7.04E
                                Natal Sun. 6° 07' 59" Cancer
                                Natal Moon. 24° 14' Virgo
         Event: marriage 1.9.51. 13.30 UT.

No.28   Solar return 1951/52. 15.46 UT 28.6.51. London
                                RAMC 10.08.23
         Event: birth of 1st son 21.31 UT 18.11.54. London.

No.29   Solar return 1954/55. 9.12 UT 28.6.54. London
                                RAMC 3.34.25
         Event: birth of 2nd son 21.19 UT 15.5.57. London.

No.30   Solar return 1956/57. 20.47 UT 27.6.56. London
RAMC 15.9.24

No.31   *Example No.4 Birth data: 6.45 UT 23.3.1899. 51.10N 7.04E*
Natal Sun. 2° 26' 15" Aries
Natal Moon. 17° 22' Leo
Event: marriage. 13.1.23. 51.10N 7.04E.

No.32   Solar return 1922/23. 20.46 UT 23.3.22.
(Birthplace) RAMC 9.16.28
Event: birth of 1st daughter. 9.08 UT 28.6.25.

No.33   Solar return 1925/26. 14.09 UT 23.3.25.
(Birthplace) RAMC 2.39.27
Event: birth of 2nd daughter. 11.50 UT 29.8.28. 48.47N
9.11E.

No.34   Solar return 1928/29. 7.41 UT 23.3.28
51.10N 7.04E = RAMC 20.11.28 Asc. 3° Gemini
MC 1 Aquarius
48.47N 9.11E = RAMC 20.19.56 Asc. 3 Gemini
MC 3 Aquarius

No.35   *Example No.5 Birth data: 9.0 UT 11.5.53. 51.37N 0.17W*
Natal Sun. 20° 21' 53" Taurus
Natal Moon. 25° 37' Aries
Event: birth of daughter 3.45 UT 17.10.80. London.

No.36   Solar return 1980/81. 21.52 UT 10.5.80. London
RAMC 13.6.14
Event: birth of son 15.07 UT 8.10.86. West London.

No.37   Solar return 1986/87. 8.35 UT 11.5.86.
RAMC 23.49.13

No.38   *Example No.6 Birth data: 23.10 UT 4.3.56. West London*
Natal Sun. 14° 21' 50" Pisces.
Natal Moon. 19° 29' Sagittarius
Event: birth of son. 22.20 UT 20.10.81. 51.30N 0.05W.

No.39   Solar return 1981/82. 00.51 UT 5.3.81.
RAMC 11.41.25

For an event such as a wedding, normally a happy and joyous occasion, the benefic planets Venus and Jupiter, the significators of harmony and joy are often prominent, either in the return covering the period or by transit on the actual day. In addition, the Moon, which is associated with moods and physical responses and often acts as a 'marker' of solar return indications, will be active close to the time of the event. Partnership entails mutual responsibilities, so we could

Note: In all computer-calculated charts the position of the sun and moon are 'rounded' to the minute.

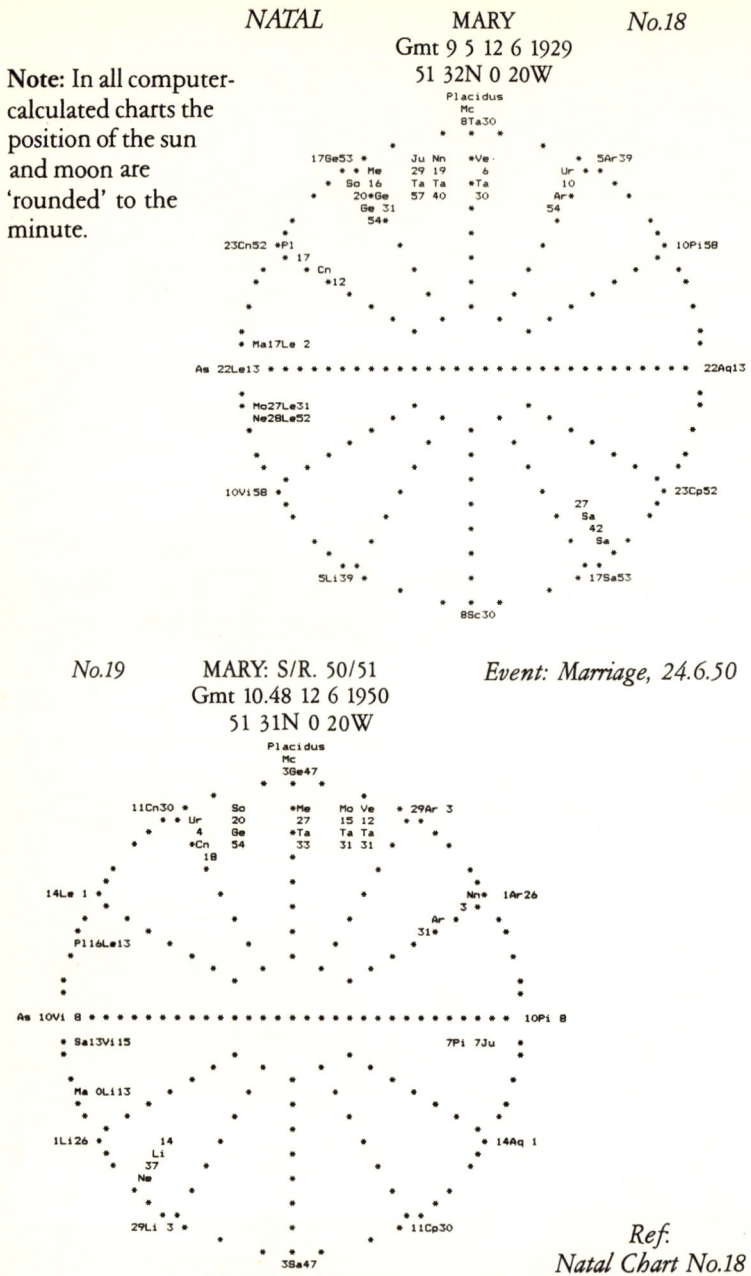

SOLAR RETURN

Event: Birth of son, 12.9.53   MARY: S/R. 53/54   *No.20*
Gmt 4 5 12 6 1953
51 31N 0 20W

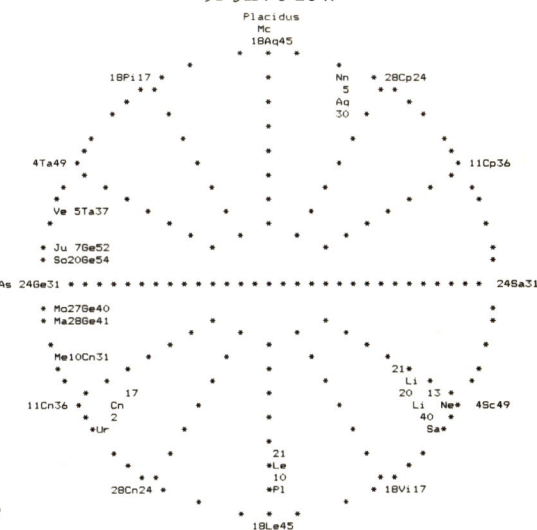

Ref.
Natal Chart No.18

SOLAR RETURN

No.21   MARY: S/R. 55/56   *Event: Birth of son, 28.3.56*
Gmt 15 40 12 6 1955
51 31N 0 20W

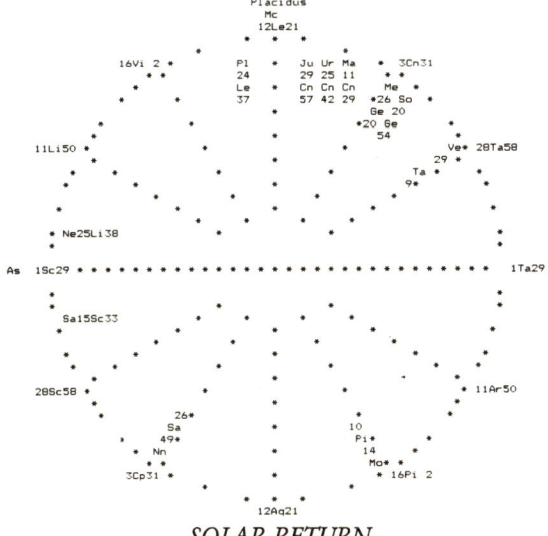

SOLAR RETURN   *Ref.*
Natal Chart No.18

NATAL   SUSI   *No.22*

Gmt 11 50 29 8 1928
48 47N 9 11E

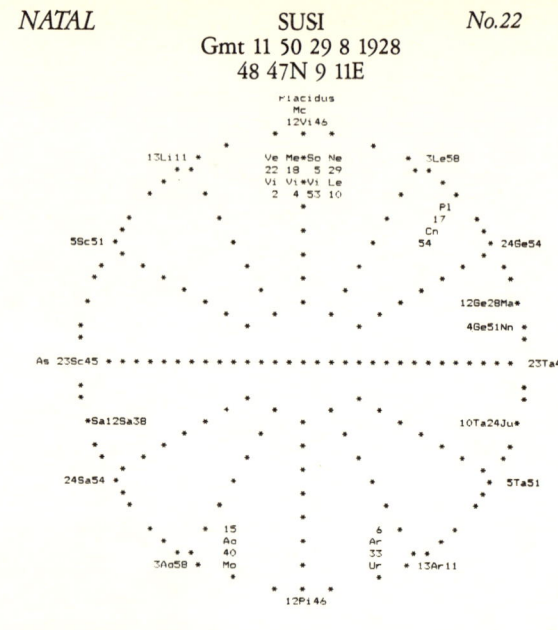

No.23   SUSI: S/R. 49/50   *Event: Marriage, 13.5.50*

Gmt 13 41 29 8 1949
51 31N 0 20W

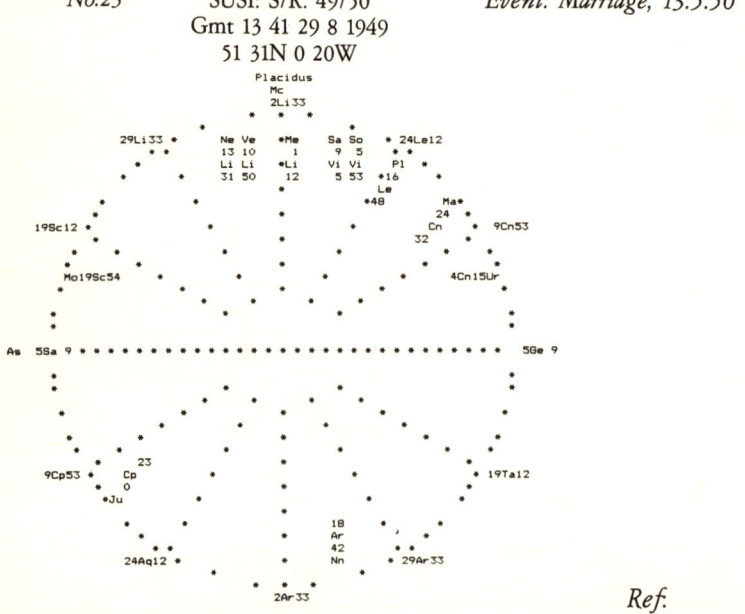

SOLAR RETURN   *Ref:*
Natal Chart No.22

Event: Birth of daughter,
11.5.53

SUSI: S/R. 52/53   *No.24*
Gmt 6 58 29 8 1952
51 31N 0 20W

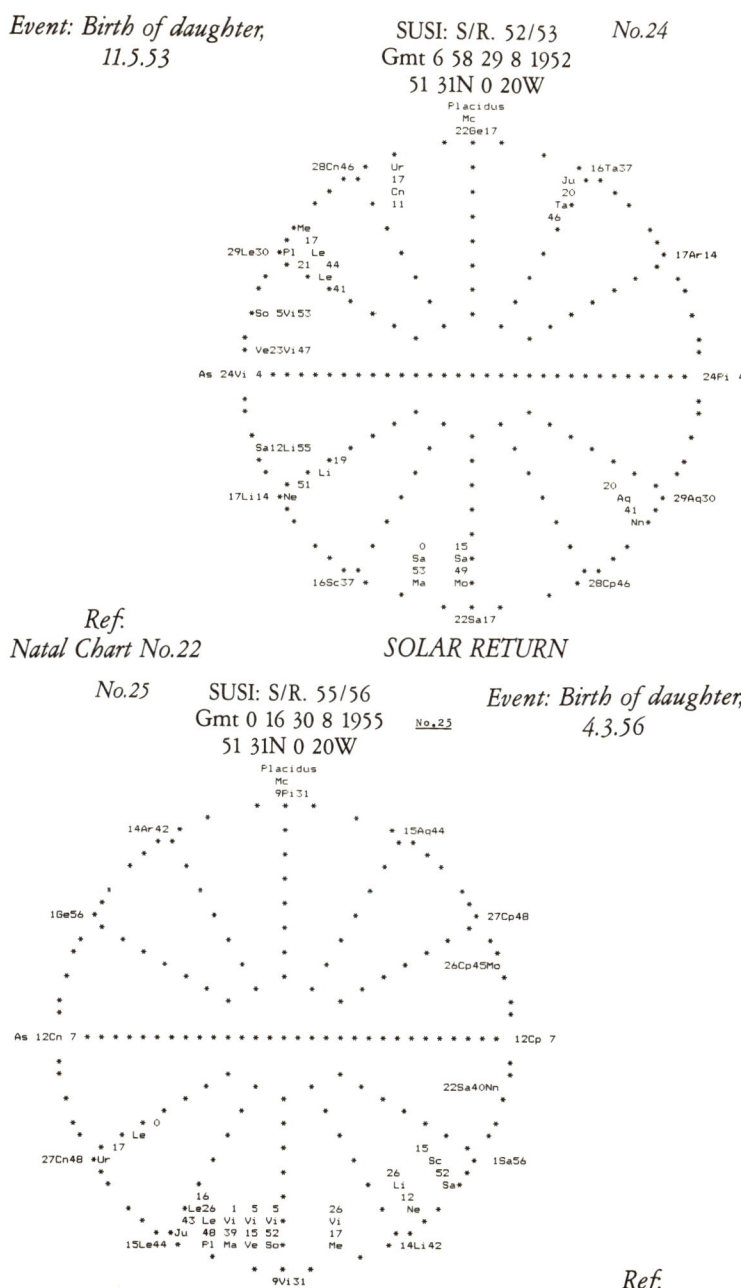

Placidus
Mc
22Ge17

28Cn46 ∗ Ur   ∗ 16Ta37
        17   Ju
        Cn   20
        11   Ta∗
                  46

∗Me
  17
29Le30 ∗Pl Le   17Ar14
      ∗ 21 44
         ∗ Le
         ∗41

∗So 5Vi53

∗ Ve23Vi47

As 24Vi 4 ∗ 24Pi 4

Sa12Li55
      ∗19
      ∗ Li
      ∗ 51   20
17Li14 ∗Ne   Aq ∗ 29Aq30
                              41
                              Nn∗

        0   15
        Sa   Sa∗
        53   49
16Sc37 ∗   Ma   Mo∗   ∗ ∗ 28Cp46

        22Sa17

Ref:
Natal Chart No.22   *SOLAR RETURN*

No.25   SUSI: S/R. 55/56   *Event: Birth of daughter,*
       Gmt 0 16 30 8 1955   No.25   *4.3.56*
       51 31N 0 20W

Placidus
Mc
9Pi31

14Ar 42 ∗   ∗ 15Aq44

1Ge56 ∗   ∗ 27Cp48

                          26Cp45Mo

As 12Cn 7 ∗ 12Cp 7

                          22Sa40Nn

        0
      ∗ Le
      ∗ 17   15
27Cn48 ∗Ur   Sc   ∗ 1Sa56
                              26   52
      16   Li   Sa∗
      ∗Le26 1 5 5   26   12
      43 Le Vi Vi Vi∗   Vi   ∗ Ne
      ∗ Ju 48 39 15 52   17   ∗ ∗
15Le44 ∗ Pl Ma Ve So∗   Me   ∗ 14Li42

        9Vi31

       SOLAR RETURN   *Ref:*
                              Natal Chart No.22

Event: Birth of daughter, 16.3.63   SUSI: S/R. 62/63   *No.26*
Gmt 17 7 29 8 1962
51 31N 0 20W

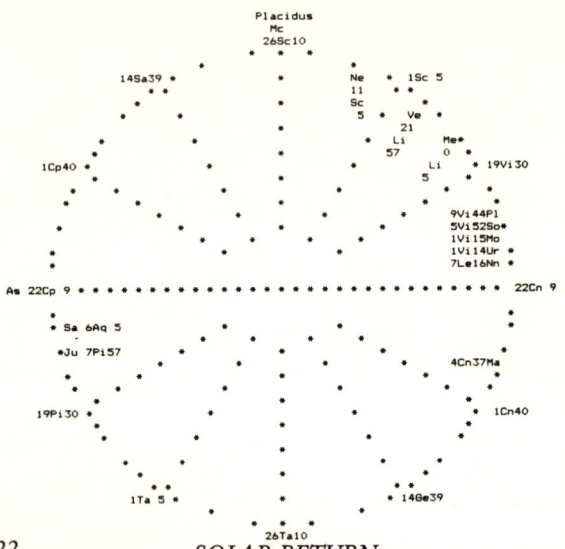

SOLAR RETURN

Ref:
Natal Chart No.22

No.27   ANN   *NATAL*
Gmt 9 8 28 6 1925
51 10N 7 4E

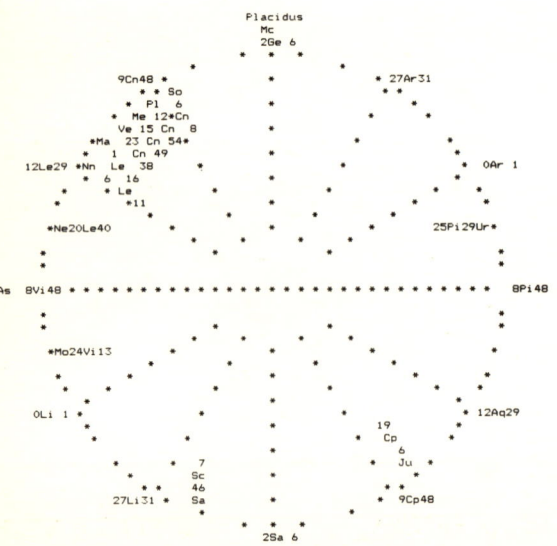

Event: Marriage, 1.9.51

ANN: S/R. 51/52   *No.28*
Gmt 15 46 28 6 1951
51 31N 0 20W

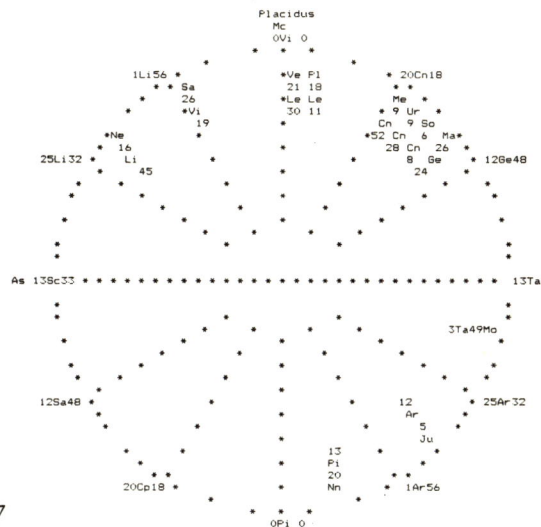

Ref:
Natal Chart No.27

SOLAR RETURN

No.29   ANN: S/R. 54/55   *Event: Birth of son, 18.11.54*
Gmt 9 12 28 6 1954
51 31N 0 20W

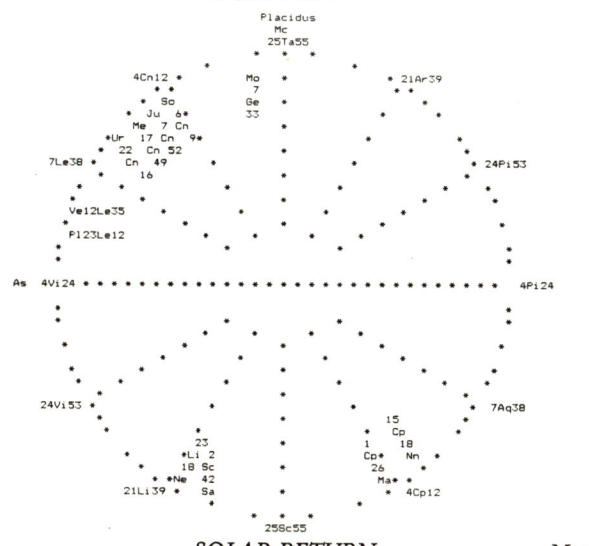

SOLAR RETURN

Ref:
Natal Chart No.27

Event: Birth of son, 15.5.57   ANN: S/R. 56/57   *No.30*
Gmt 20 47 27 6 1956
51 31N 0 20W

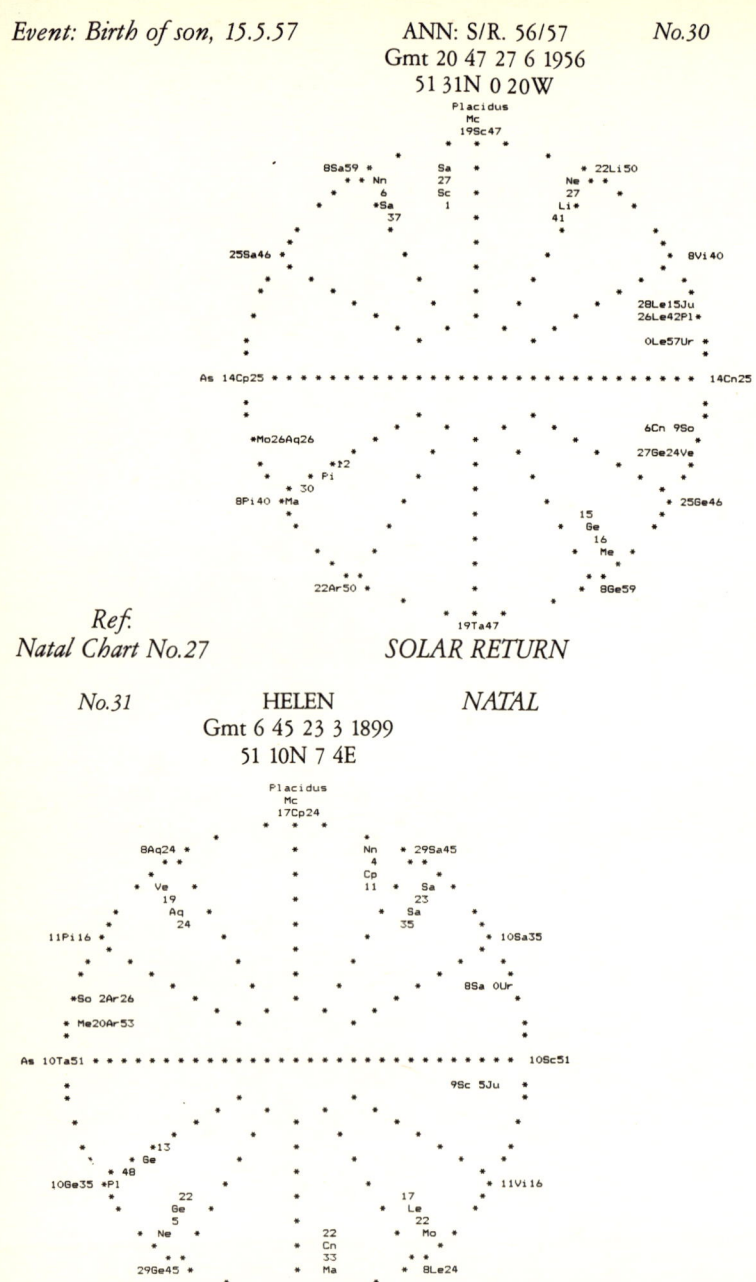

Ref:
Natal Chart No.27   SOLAR RETURN

No.31   HELEN   *NATAL*
Gmt 6 45 23 3 1899
51 10N 7 4E

Event: Marriage, 13.1.23   HELEN: S/R. 22/23   *No.32*
                                  Gmt 20 46 23 3 1922
                                  51 10N 7 4E

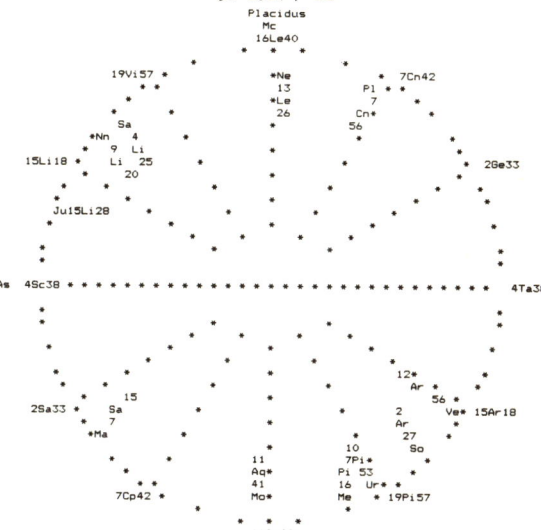

Ref:
Natal Chart No.31   **SOLAR RETURN**

No.33   HELEN: S/R. 25/26   *Event: Birth of daughter 28.6.25*
               Gmt 14 9 23 3 1925
               51 10N 7 4E

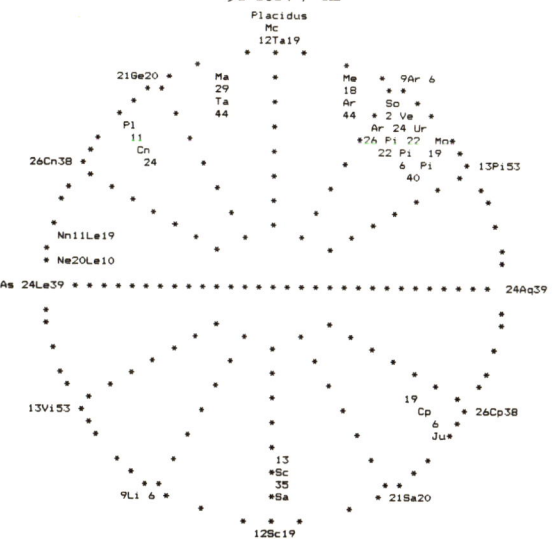

SOLAR RETURN   *Ref:*
                                              Natal Chart No.31

Event: Birth of daughter, 29.8.28   HELEN: S/R. 28/29   No.34
Gmt 7 41 23 3 1928
51 10N 7 4E

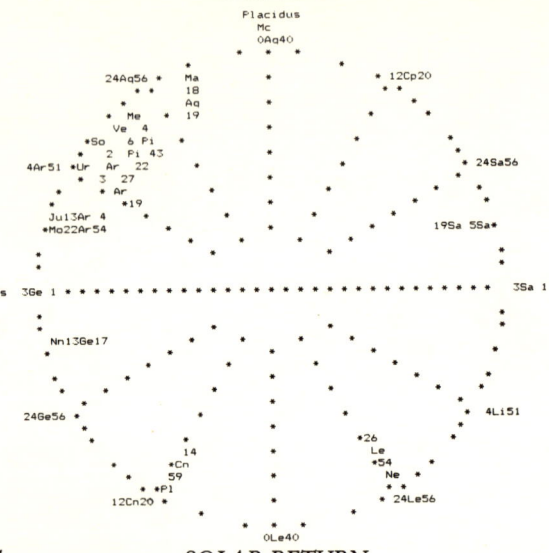

```
                              Placidus
                                Mc
                              0Aq40
          24Aq56  *   Ma                        * 12Cp20
              * *      18
                       Aq
              * Me  *  19
            Ve  4
          *So    6 Pi
              2  Pi 43
    4Ar51 *Ur  Ar  22                            * 24Sa56
          *  3  27
             * Ar
              *19
         Ju13Ar 4
         *Mo22Ar 54                              19Sa 5Sa*

As  3Ge 1 * * * * * * * * * * * * * * * * * * * * * * * 3Sa 1

         * Nn13Ge17

        24Ge56                                   * 4Li51
                                        *26
                                        Le
                             14         *54
                            *Cn         Ne *
                             59
                            * Pl             * 24Le56
        12Cn20 *
                              0Le40
```

                Ref:
        Natal Chart No.31   SOLAR RETURN

        No.35   SALLY   NATAL
                Gmt 9 0 11 5 1953
                51 37N 0 17W

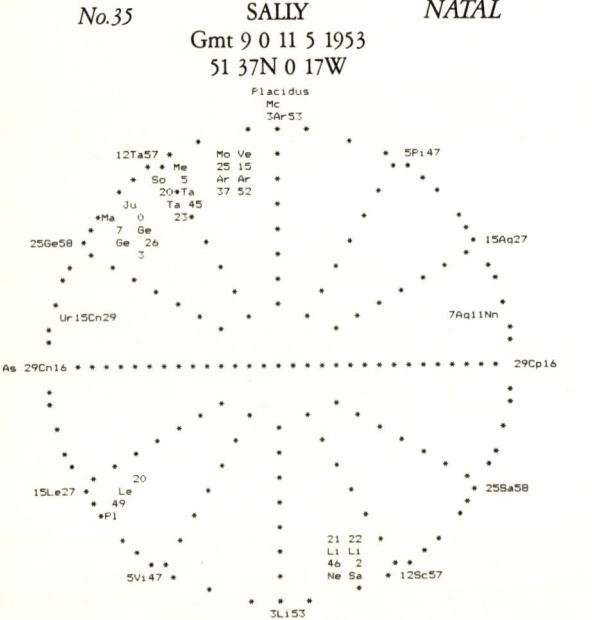

```
                          Placidus
                            Mc
                          3Ar53
        12Ta57 *     Mo Ve          * 5Pi47
            * * Me   25 15
          *  So  5   Ar Ar
             20*Ta   37 52
          Ju    Ta 45
       *Ma   0    23*
          7  Ge
25Ge58  * Ge  26
             3

        Ur15Cn29                      7Aq11Nn

As 29Cn16 * * * * * * * * * * * * * * * * * * * * 29Cp16

                                          * 25Sa58
            20
15Le27 *   Le
          49
         *Pl
                          21 22
                          Li Li
                          46 2    * * *
        5Vi47 *           Ne Sa  * 12Sc57
                        *
                      3Li53
```

Event: Birth of daughter, 17.10.80   SALLY: S/R. 80/81   *No.36*
Gmt 21 52 10 5 1980
51 37N 0 17W

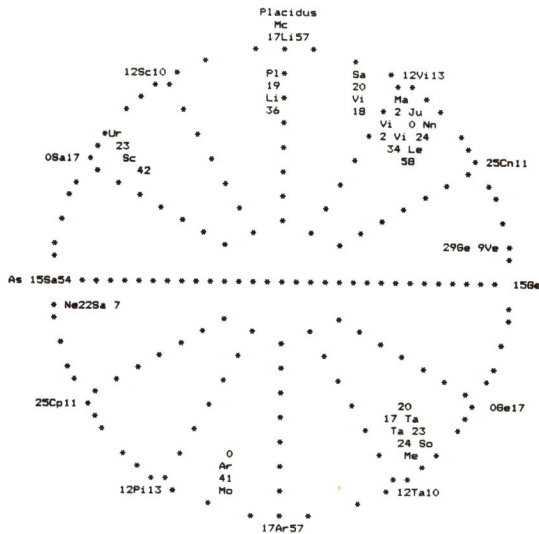

Placidus
Mc
17Li57

P1 19 Li 36

Sa 20 Vi 18   12Vi13
Ma   2 Ju
Vi 0 Nn
2 Vi 24
34 Le
58

12Sc10

Ur 23 Sc 42

0Sa17

25Cn11

29Ge 9Ve

As 15Sa54   15Ge54

Ne22Sa 7

25Cp11

20 17 Ta Ta 23 24 So Me

0Ge17

0 Ar 41 Mo

12Pi13

12Ta10

17Ar57

Ref:
Natal Chart No.35   **SOLAR RETURN**

No.37   SALLY S/R. 86/87   *Event: Birth of son, 8.10.86*
Gmt 8 35 11 5 1986
51 37N 0 17W

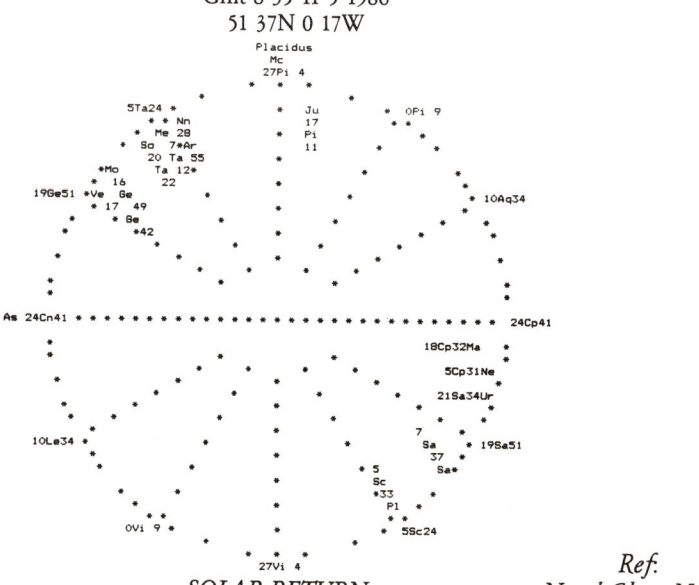

Placidus
Mc
27Pi 4

5Ta24
Nn
Me 28
So 7*Ar
20 Ta 55
Ta 12*
16
22

Ju 17 Pi 11

0Pi 9

Mo
19Ge51 *Ve Ge
17 49
Ge
*42

10Aq34

As 24Cn41   24Cp41

18Cp32Ma

5Cp31Ne

21Sa34Ur

10Le34

7 Sa 37 5 Sc *33 P1

19Sa51
Sa*

0Vi 9

5Sc24

27Vi 4

SOLAR RETURN   *Ref:*
Natal Chart No.35

NATAL   **MOLLY**   *No.38*

Gmt 23 10 4 3 1956
51 30N 0 8W

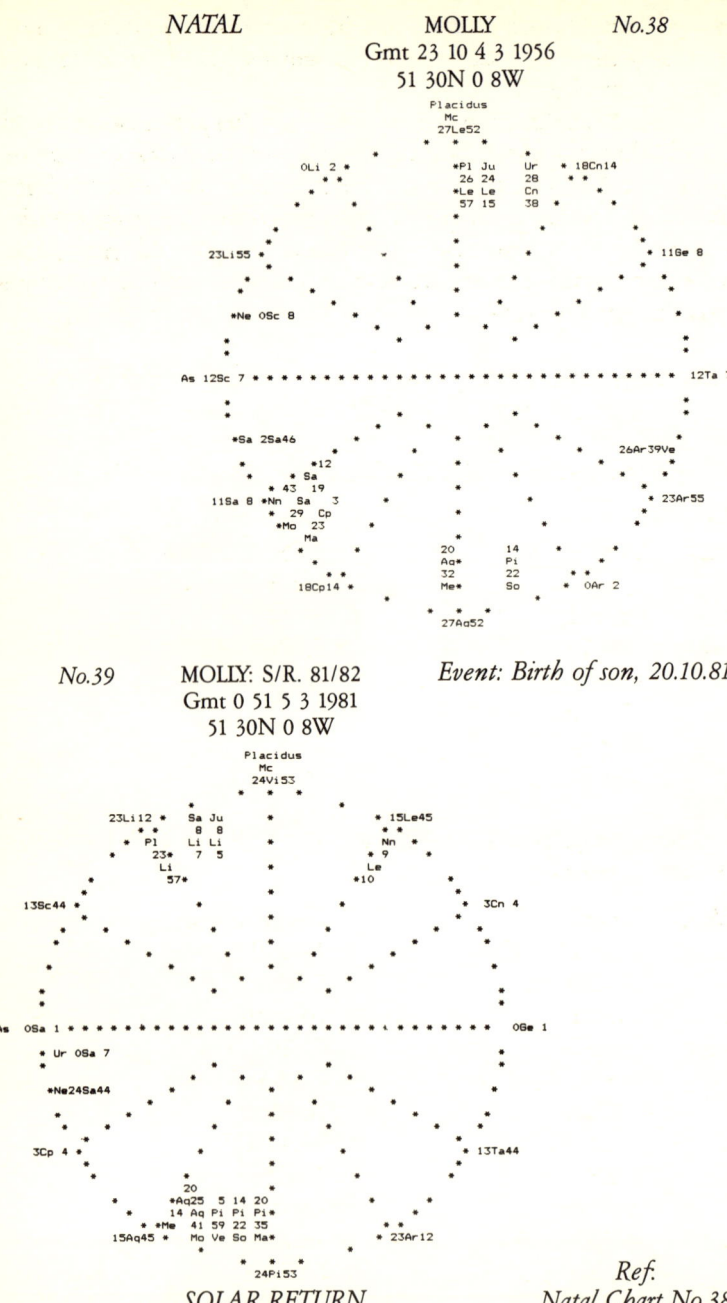

No.39   MOLLY: S/R. 81/82   *Event: Birth of son, 20.10.81*

Gmt 0 51 5 3 1981
51 30N 0 8W

SOLAR RETURN   *Ref:*
Natal Chart No.38

expect to find Saturn to the fore with probably an active Neptune indicating the flurry and fluster that normally attends weddings and similar functions.

The birth of a child, which is normally another joyous event, would probably have the Sun, Moon or Jupiter prominent in the appropriate returns. A child's natal positions are transits in the mother's chart, and much can be learned from this regarding the mother/child relationship. The few cases which have been listed may prove interesting in determining whether the return symbolism correlates with the type of event.

Lunar Returns covering the period preceding weddings (W) and the birth of children (C)

1. *Birth data: 9.05 UT 12.6.29 London. Natal Moon 27° 31' Leo*

Chart	Event:	Lunar Return:
No.40	24.6.50 (W)	16.56 UT 20.6.50
		London
No.41	05.30 UT (C)	19.49 UT
	12.9.53	6.9.53
	London	London
No.42	21.50 UT (C)	19.43 UT
	28.3.56	23.3.56
	London	London

2. *Birth data: 11.50 UT 29.8.28. 48° 47' N, 9° 11' E. Natal Moon 15° 40' Aquarius*

Chart	Event	Lunar return
No.43	14.30 UT (W)	18.46 UT
	13.5.50	8.5.50
	London	London
No.44	9.0 UT (C)	12.20 UT
	11.5.53	6.5.53
	London	London
No.45	23.10 UT (C)	08.54 UT
	4.3.56	11.2.56
	London	London
No.46	19.22 UT (C)	18.17 UT
	16.3.63	22.2.63
	London	London

3. Birth data: 9.08 UT 28.6.25. 51° 10′ N. 7° 04′ E. Natal Moon 24° 14′ Virgo

Chart	Event	Lunar return
No.47	13.30 UT (W)	12.44 UT
	1.9.51	6.8.51
	London	London
No.48	21.31 UT (C)	12.49 UT
	18.11.54	23.10.54
	London	London
No.49	21.19 UT (C)	18.16 UT
	15.5.57	9.5.57
	London	London

4. Birth data: 6.45 UT 23.3.1899. 51° 10′ N. 7° 04′ E. Natal Moon 17° 22′ Leo

Chart	Event	Lunar return
No.50	13.1.23 (W)	16.26 UT
	51° 10′ N	5.1.23
	7 04 E	51° 10′ N
		7 04 E
No.51	9.08 UT (C)	07.51 UT
	28.6.25	25.6.25
	51° 10′ N	51° 10′ N
	7 04 E	7 04 E
No.52	11.50 UT (C)	04.57 UT
	29.8.28	15.8.28
		Lat. 48.47N
		Long. 9.11E

5. Birth data: 9.0 UT 11.5.53. London. Natal Moon 25° 37′ Aries

Chart	Event	Lunar return
No.53	03.45 UT (C)	01.58 UT
	17.10.80	26.9.80
	London	London
No.54	15.07 UT (C)	14.03 UT
	8.10.86	20.9.86
	London	London

6. *Birth data: 23.10 UT 4.3.56. London. Natal Moon 19° 29' Sagittarius*

Chart	Event	Lunar return
No.55	22.20 UT (C)	08.33 UT
	20.10.81	4.10.81
	London	London

7. *Birth data: 01.40 UT 21.4.26. 51° 30' N. 00.08W. Natal Moon 12° 07' Leo*

Chart	Event	Lunar return
No.56	11.38 UT (W)	16.32 UT
	20.11.47	5.11.47
	London	London
No.57	21.14 UT (C)	06.50 UT
	14.11.48	26.10.48
	London	London

8. *Birth data: 09.03 UT 15.10.59. 51° 31' N. 00.09 W. Natal Moon 6° 38' Aries*

Chart	Event	Lunar return
No.58	10.50 UT (W)	00.12 UT
	23.7.86	29.6.86
	London	London

9. *Birth data: 15.30 UT 19.2.60. 51° 30' N. 00.08 W. Natal Moon 25° 29' Scorpio*

Chart	Event	Lunar return
No.59	10.50 UT (W)	05.06 UT
	23.7.86	17.7.86
	London	London

10. *Birth data: 23.07 UT 2.6.53. 34° 21' N. 119° 04' W. Natal Moon 18° 48' Aquarius*

Chart	Event	Lunar return
No.60	13.20 UT (W)	13.27 UT
	1.1.77	24.12.76
	50° 35' N	50° 35' N
	01° 05' W	01° 05' W

11. *Birth data: 04.00 UT 17.10.49. 34° 09′ N. 118° 09′ W. Natal*
Moon 18° 25′ Leo

Chart	Event	Lunar return
No.61	14.55 UT (W)	14.09 UT
	27.10.73	20.10.73
	50° 35′ N	50° 35′ N
	01° 05′ W	01° 05′ W

Examples No.10 and 11, are the data for two sisters born in
California but long resident in Britain. The object of including their
data is to see whether a return set for the birthplace is more indicative
of an event than one computed for the place of residence at the time
of the return.

Some researchers, whose views deserve every respect, state quite
clearly that lunar returns should be computed for the birthplace.
Others, that the return should always be for the place of residence
at the time of the return. The matter is by no means resolved and
like many other contentious factors in astrology the question of
birthplace or residence requires a considerable amount of detailed
research.

In deciding the 'effectiveness' of lunar returns or, for that matter,
any kind of return, the relationship of natal planets with the angles
of the return is important. This factor, among others, may assist in
showing whether the birthplace is the significant locality or whether
the place of residence for the date and time of the return should
be taken.

With the 'birth of aviation' and its Gemini/Sagittarius correlation,
time and space have a new significance. The mobility of the masses,
in contrast to previous generations, means that a child can be
conceived, born and nurtured in widely separated localities. Even
the most infrequent traveller can, at times, be far from their birthplace
either through choice or circumstances. All this has important
implications for the charting of returns. The planetary positions are,
of course, the same for a given time and date, but the mundane
framework (houses) of a chart will differ considerably depending
upon the locality for which the chart is erected. As the angles of
a chart are so important in return charts, the question of birthplace
or residence cannot be lightly dismissed.

There are two principal methods of progressing a solar return or
ingress chart, the quotidian measure of 3 minutes 57 seconds per
day and the progressed solar return based on the daily increase in

Event: Marriage, 24.6.50   MARY: LUNAR/RETURN   *No.40*
Gmt 16.56 20 6 1950
51 32N 0 20W

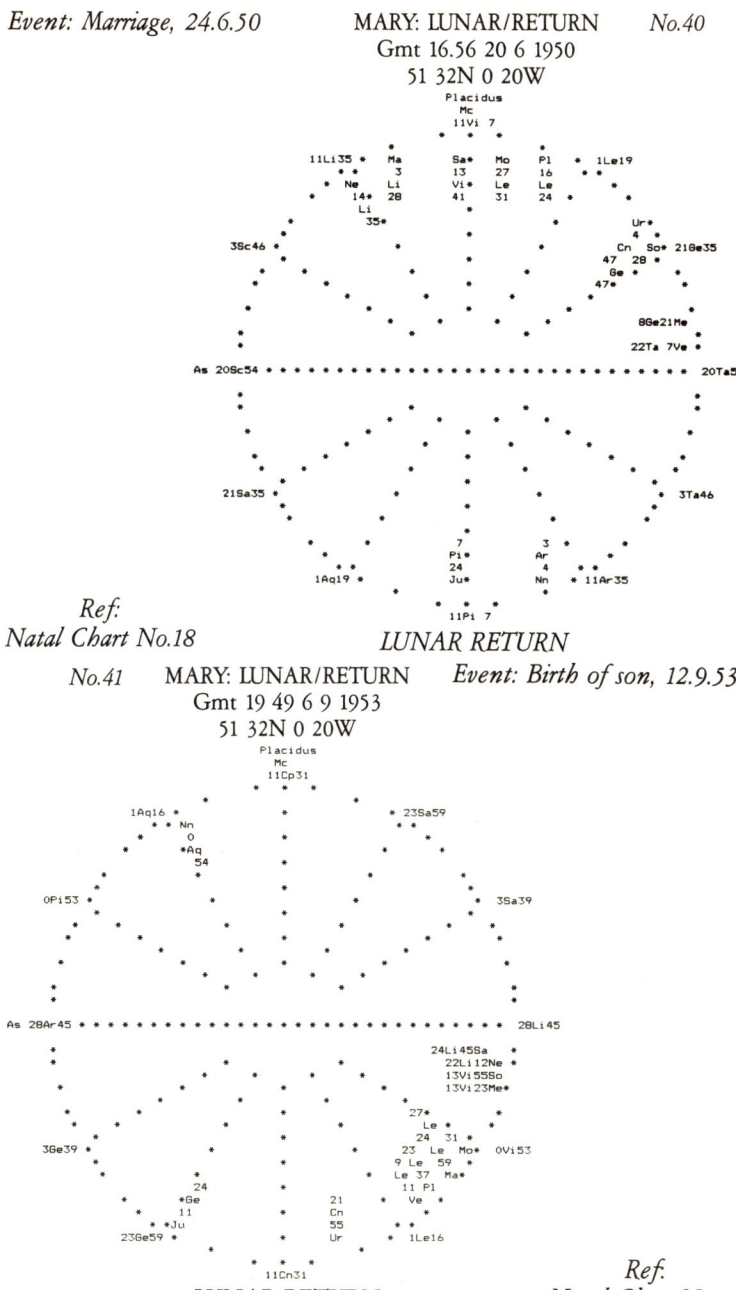

Ref:
Natal Chart No.18   *LUNAR RETURN*

No.41   MARY: LUNAR/RETURN   *Event: Birth of son, 12.9.53*
Gmt 19 49 6 9 1953
51 32N 0 20W

LUNAR RETURN   *Ref:*
Natal Chart No.18

Event: Birth of son, 28.3.56   MARY: LUNAR/RETURN   *No.42*
Gmt 19 43 23 3 1956
51 32N 0 20W

```
                        Placidus
                           Mc
                         24Cn45
                           •
                        •     •
              29Le34  •  Pl Ju   Ur•        • 17Ge 8
                   • •  Mo 26 22  28           • •
                       27 Le Le   Cn•
                      •Le33 25  17
                        31
                   •                              •
        27Vi20  •                                    •  Ve• 14Ta47
                                                          17 •
                                                          Ta •
                                                          48•
            •                                                  •
            •                                                  •
            •                                                  •
  As 18Li47 • • • • • • • • • • • • • • • • • • • • • • • • •  18Ar47
            •                                                  •
         Ne29Li44   •                    •   •       3Ar10So•
            •                                                  •
                                                      20
       14Sc47  •        2              •          Pi  •  27Pi20
                       Sa                              34
                    42   11•                           Me•
                  Sa   Sa
                   43•                      15
                   • Nn                     Co
                                            42
                17Sa 8 •                     Ma      • 29Aq34
                                    •  •  •
                                     24Co45
```

Ref:
Natal Chart No.18   **LUNAR RETURN**

    No.43   SUSI: LUNAR/RETURN   *Event: Marriage, 13.5.50*
Gmt 18 46 8 5 50
48 47N 9 11E

```
                         Placidus
                            Mc
                          3Vi39
                         •  •  •
          5Li12  •       Ma Sa   •    Pl    • 24Cn54
             • •         22 12        15       • •
                         Vi Vi        Le
                         10 37        47   •
             Ne                           •
             15                                Jr•
             Li                                 2
  28Li59 •    9        •            •      Cn  • 17Ge29
                                           26    •
             •                                  •
             •                                  •
             •                           26Ta28Me •
             •                           17Ta36So •
  As 17Sc31 • • • • • • • • • • • • • • • • • • •  17Ta31
             •                                 •
             •                                 •
             •                                 •
             •                                 •
      17Sa29 •                          • 28Ar59
             •                                 •
                •                   • 5
                                    3 Ar
                    15      3     Ar•21
                    Aq     •Pi    16 Nn •
                    40     49     Ve• •
               24Co54 •    Mo    •Ju   • 5Ar12
                    •   3Pi39
```

    LUNAR RETURN (Birthplace)   *Ref:*
                                         Natal Chart No.22

Event: Birth of daughter, 11.5.53 SUSI: LUNAR/RETURN   *No.44*
Gmt 12 20 6 5 1953
48 47N 9 11E

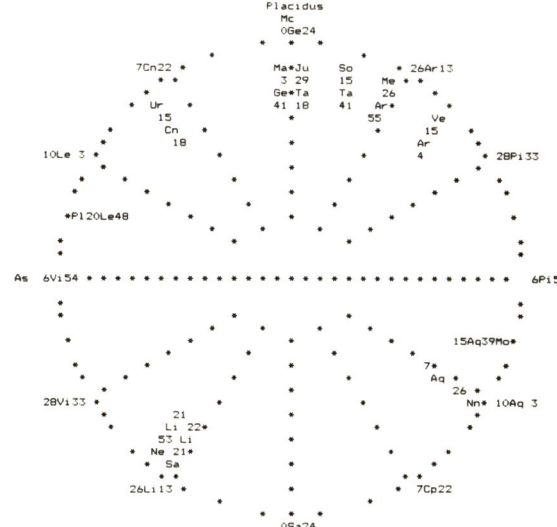

Ref:
Natal Chart No.22   *LUNAR RETURN* (Birthplace)

No.44(a)   SUSI: LUNAR/RETURN   *Event:*
Gmt 12 20 6 5 1953   *Birth of daughter, 11.5.53*
51 32N 0 20W

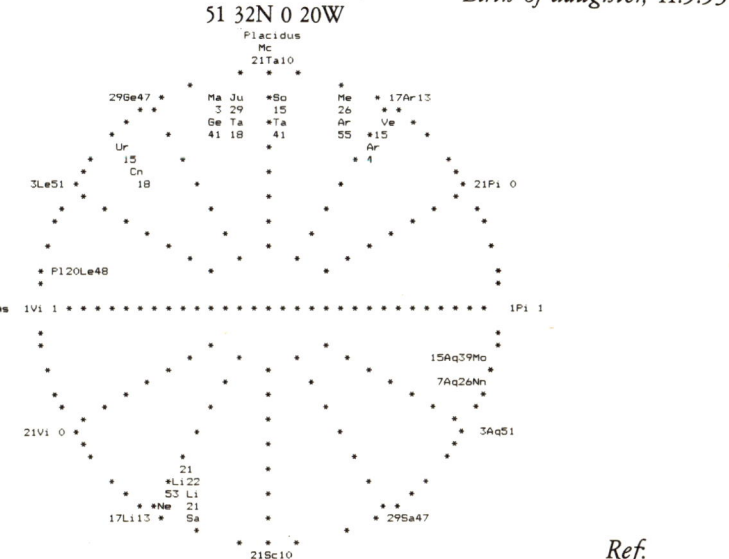

LUNAR RETURN (Residence)   *Ref:*
Natal Chart No.22

Event: Birth of daughter, 4.3.56 SUSI: LUNAR/RETURN   *No.45*
Gmt 8 54 11 2 1956
48 47N 9 11E

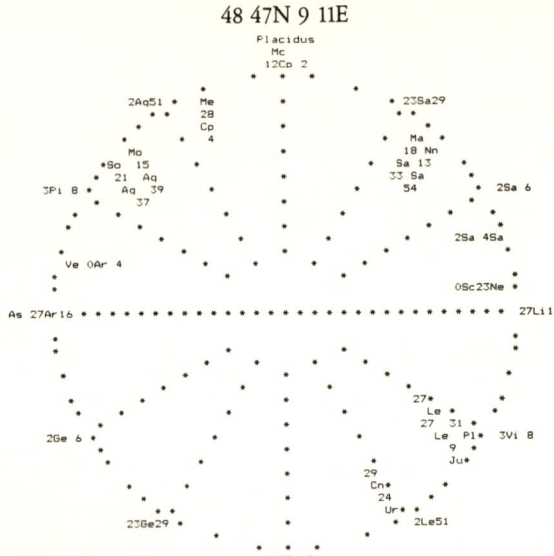

Ref:
Natal Chart No.22   LUNAR RETURN (Birthplace)

No.45(a)   SUSI: LUNAR/RETURN *Event: Birth of daughter, 4.3.56*
Gmt 8 54 11 2 1956

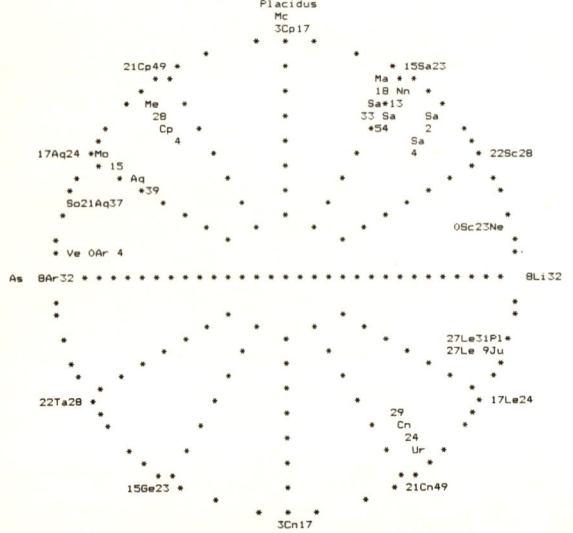

LUNAR RETURN (Residence)   *Ref:*
Natal Chart No.22

*Event: Birth of **daughter**, 16.3.63* SUSI: LUNAR/RETURN   *No.46*
Gmt 18 17 22 2 1963
48 47N 9 11E

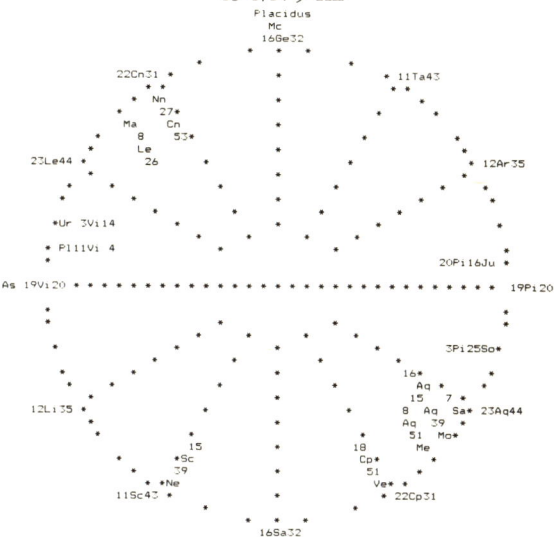

Ref:
Natal Chart No.22   *LUNAR RETURN* (Birthplace)

No.46(a)   SUSI: LUNAR/RETURN *Event: Birth of **daughter**, 16.3.63*
Gmt 18 17 22 2 1963

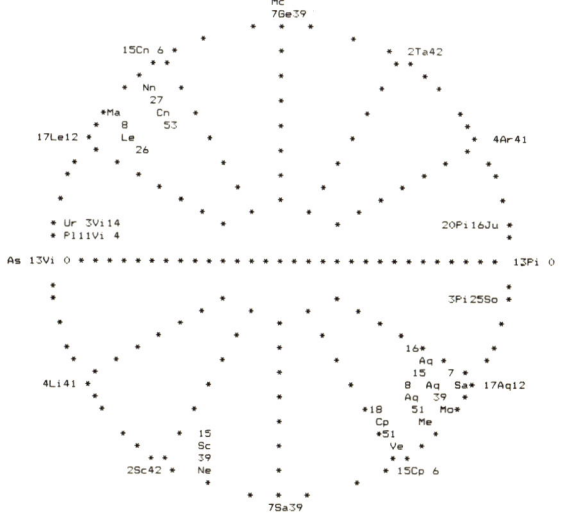

LUNAR RETURN (Residence)   *Ref:*
Natal Chart No.22

Event: Marriage, 1.9.51   ANN: LUNAR/RETURN   *No.47*
                                   Gmt 12 44 6 8 1951
                                   51 32N 0 20W

```
                              Placidus
                                Mc
                              22Le33
                            *   *   *   *
            25Vi19 *    Ve  Me         *Pl  So    Ma    * 13Cn 8
                 * *  Mo 17  10         19  13    22      * *
                   * Sa  24  Vi       *Le  Le    Cn    Ur  *
                   * 29*Vi29  19        18  15    16  *11   *
                     Vi  14                        Cn
                     16*                          *44

     19Li51 *Ne                    *                      6Ge58
          * 17                     *
            * Li                   *
            * 9                    *
               *                  *
                *                *
                 *              *
     As  8Sc31 * * * * * * * * * * * * * * * * * * * * * * *  8Ta31
                *              *
                 *           *
                  *        *                             14
     6Sa58 *       *      *                *            Ar  * 19Ar51
                    *    *            *                 11
                     *  *          11                   Ju*
                      **           Pi
            13Cp 8 *              16
                        *         Nn  * 25Pi19
                          *     *
                          22Aq33
```

                    Ref.
         Natal Chart No.27   **LUNAR RETURN**

            No.48   ANN: LUNAR/RETURN   *Event: Birth of son, 18.11.54*
                       Gmt 12 49 23 10 1954
                       51 32N 0 20W

```
                              Placidus
                                Mc
                              15Sc47
                            *   *   *
            5Sa29 *    Ve         *Me  Sa  So  Ne    * 17Li37
                 * *   29          12  10  29  25    * *
                   *   Sc         *Sc  Sc  Li  Li    *
                   *   59          54  34  35  57  *
                                             Mo
                                             24
     22Sa14 *                                Vi
                                             14        * 2Vi 9
                                                     *
                 *                                 *   26Le30Pl
                   *                             *
                     *                        *       28Cn59Ju
       * Nn 9Cp 6                                      27Cn39Ur
     As 10Cp 1 * * * * * * * * * * * * * * * * * * * *  10Cn 1
                *                            *
       * Ma 1Aq17      *                  *
                 *                       *
     2Pi 9 *        *                  *               * 22Ge14
                      *             *
                        *        *
            17Ar37 *       *    *       * 5Ge29
                          15Ta47
```

            LUNAR RETURN (Residence)   *Ref.*
                                         Natal Chart No.27

Event: Birth of son, 18.11.54   ANN: LUNAR/RETURN   *No.48(a)*
Gmt 12 49 23 10 1954
51 10N 7 4E

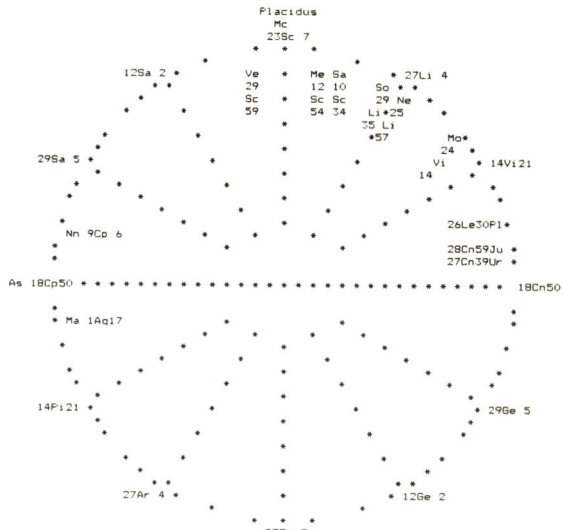

Ref:
Natal Chart No.27   LUNAR RETURN (Birthplace)

No.49   ANN: LUNAR/RETURN   *Event: Birth of son, 15.5.57*
Gmt 18 16 9 5 1957
51 32N 0 20W

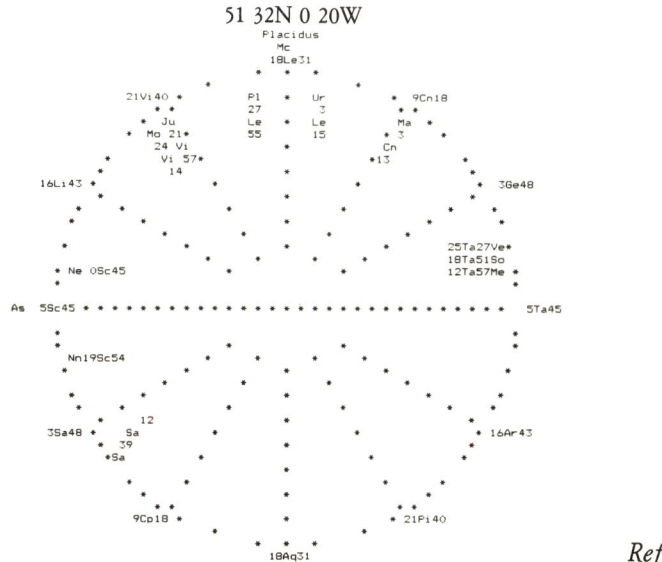

LUNAR RETURN (Residence)   *Ref:*
Natal Chart No.27

Event: Birth of son, 15.5.57   ANN: LUNAR/RETURN   *No.49(a)*
Gmt 18 16 9 5 1957
51 10N 7 4E

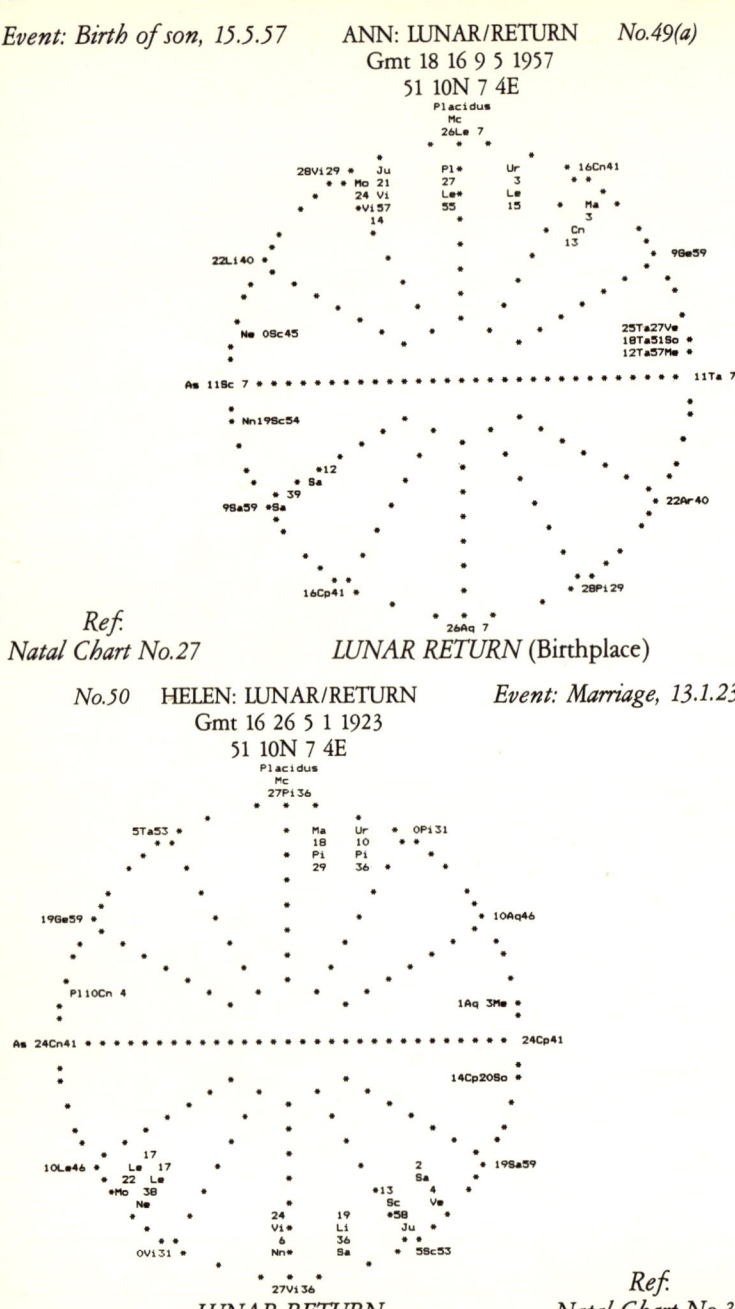

Ref:
Natal Chart No.27   *LUNAR RETURN* (Birthplace)

No.50   HELEN: LUNAR/RETURN   *Event: Marriage, 13.1.23*
Gmt 16 26 5 1 1923
51 10N 7 4E

LUNAR RETURN   *Ref:*
Natal Chart No.31

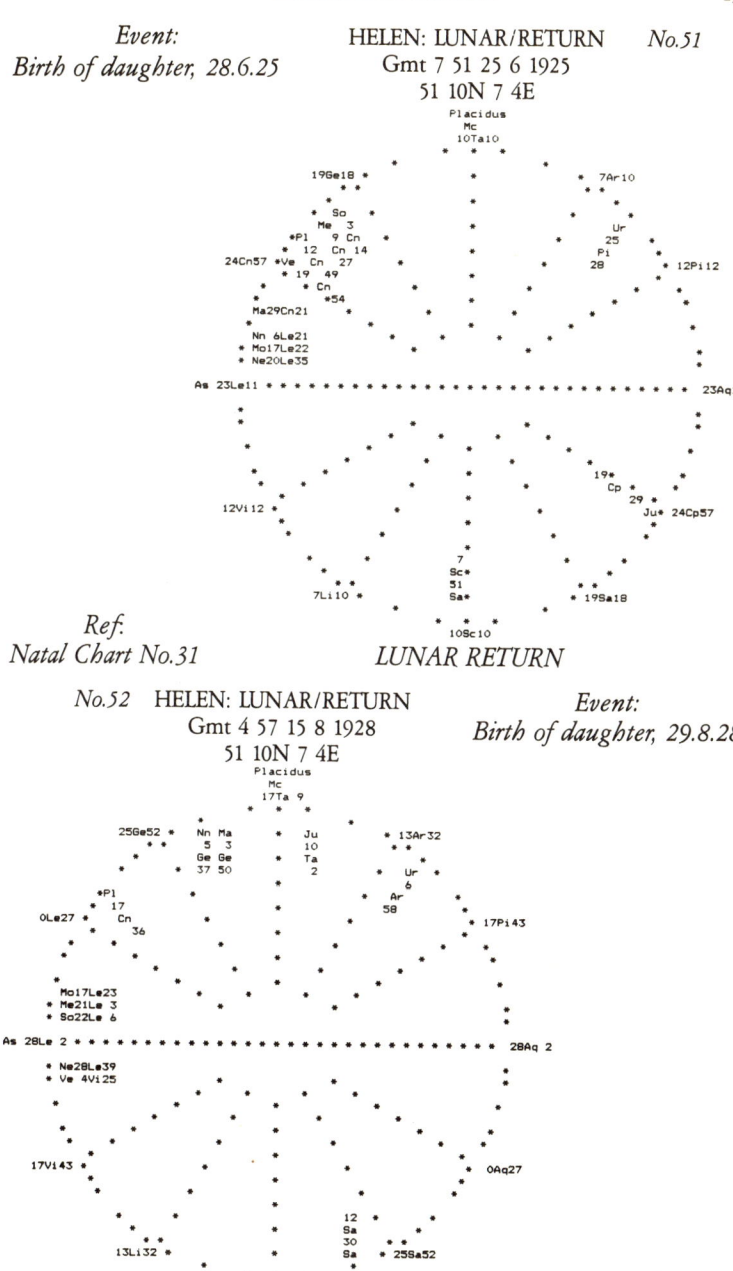

Event:
Birth of daughter, 28.6.25

HELEN: LUNAR/RETURN   *No.51*
Gmt 7 51 25 6 1925
51 10N 7 4E

Placidus
Mc
10Ta10

19Ge18

7Ar10

So
Me 3
*Pl   9 Cn
*   12 Cn 14
24Cn57 *Ve   Cn   27
* 19   49
* Cn
*54
Ma29Cn21

Ur
25
Pi
28

12Pi12

Nn 6Le21
* Mo17Le22
* Ne20Le35

As 23Le11 * 23Aq11

19*
Cp
29 *
Ju* 24Cp57

12Vi12

7
Sc*
51
Sa*

7Li10

19Sa18

10Sc10

Ref:
Natal Chart No.31   *LUNAR RETURN*

No.52   HELEN: LUNAR/RETURN   *Event:*
Gmt 4 57 15 8 1928   *Birth of daughter, 29.8.28*
51 10N 7 4E

Placidus
Mc
17Ta 9

25Ge52 *   Nn Ma   Ju   * 13Ar32
5 3   10
Ge Ge   Ta
37 50   2
Ur
6
*Pl   Ar
*   17   58
0Le27 *   Cn
36   17Pi43

Mo17Le23
* Me21Le 3
* So22Le 6

As 28Le 2 * 28Aq 2

* Ne28Le39
* Ve 4Vi25

17Vi43   0Aq27

12
Sa
30
13Li32   Sa   * 25Sa52

17Sc 9

LUNAR RETURN (Birthplace)   *Ref:*
Natal Chart No.31

Event:
Birth of daughter, 29.8.28

HELEN: LUNAR/RETURN   *No.52(a)*
Gmt 4 57 15 8 1928
48 47N 9 11E

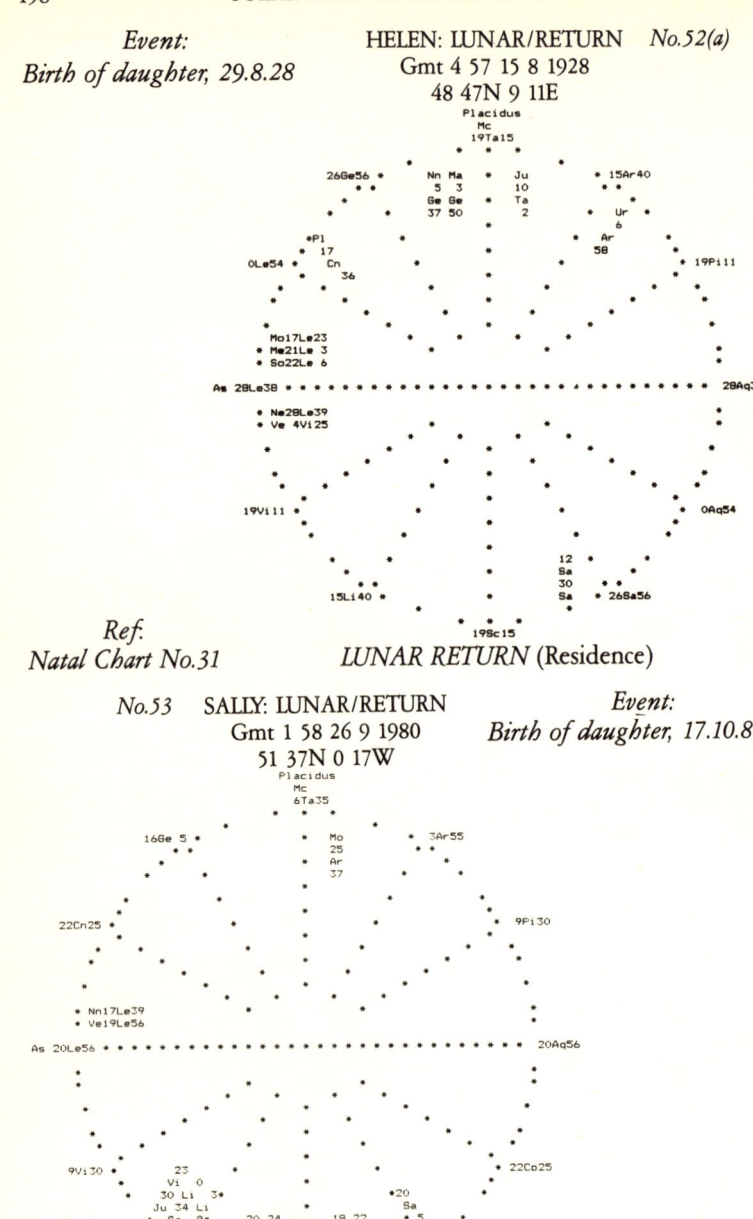

Ref:
Natal Chart No.31

LUNAR RETURN (Residence)

No.53   SALLY: LUNAR/RETURN
Gmt 1 58 26 9 1980
51 37N 0 17W

Event:
Birth of daughter, 17.10.80

LUNAR RETURN

Ref:
Natal Chart No.35

Event: Birth of son, 8.10.86   SALLY: LUNAR/RETURN   *No.54*
Gmt 14 3 20 9 1986
51 37N 0 17W

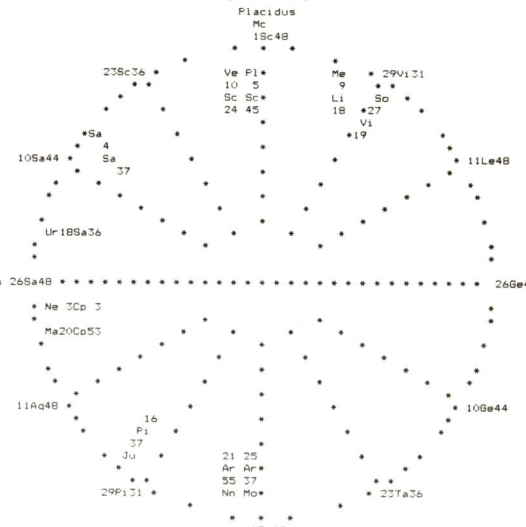

Ref:
Natal Chart No.35   *LUNAR RETURN*

No.55   MOLLY: LUNAR/RETURN   *Event: Birth of son, 20.10.81*
Gmt 8 33 4 10 1981
51 30N 0 8W

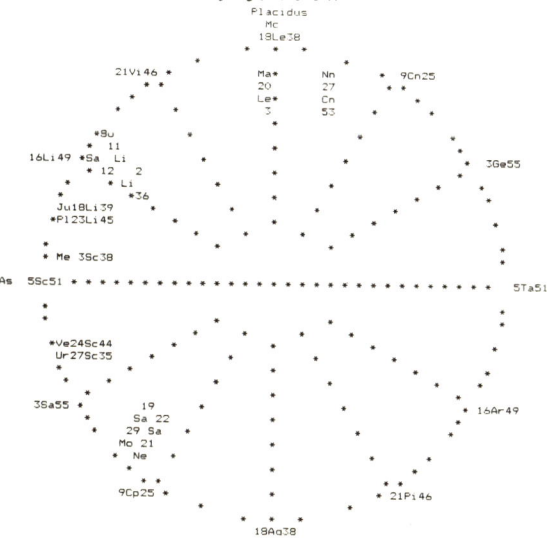

LUNAR RETURN   *Ref:*
Natal Chart No.38

Event: Marriage, 20.11.47   ELIZABETH II: LUNAR/RETURN   *No.56*

Gmt 16 32 5 11 1947
51 30N 0 8W

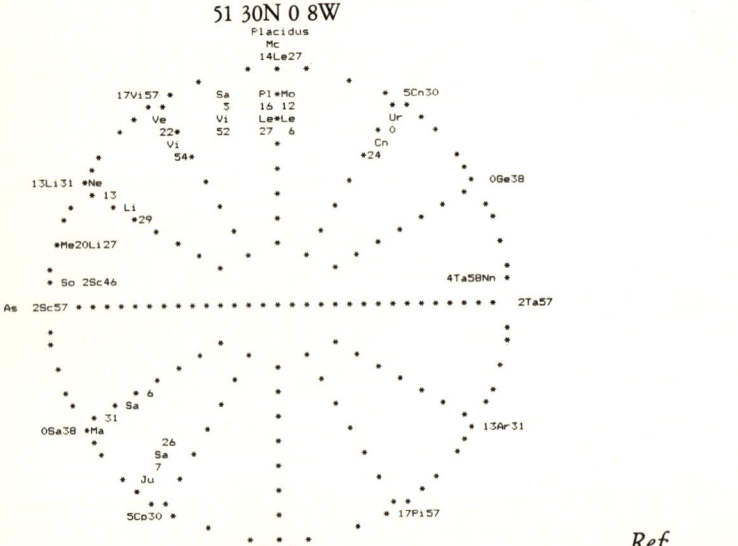

Ref:
Natal Chart No.5   *LUNAR RETURN*

No.57   ELIZABETH II: LUNAR/RETURN   *Event:*
Gmt 6 50 26 10 1948   *Birth of son, 14.11.48*
51 30N 0 8W

LUNAR RETURN   *Ref:*
Natal Chart No.5

Event: Marriage, 23.7.86 DUCHESS OF YORK: LUNAR/RETURN *No.58*

Gmt 0 12 29 6 1986

51 31N 0 9W

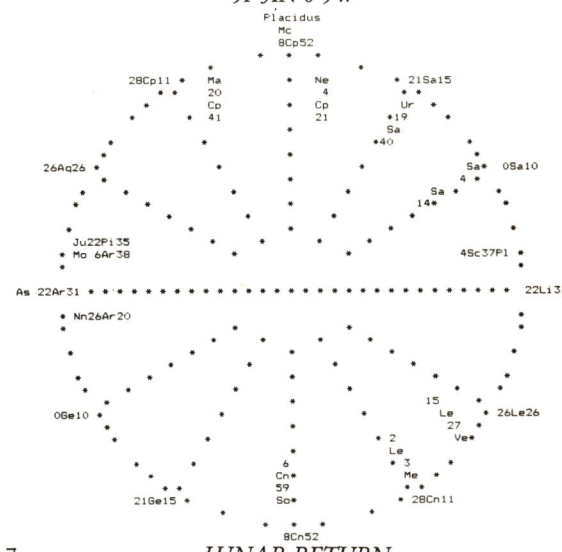

Ref:
Natal Chart No.7

LUNAR RETURN

No.59 DUKE OF YORK: LUNAR/RETURN *Event: Marriage, 23.7.86*

Gmt 5 6 17 7 1986

51 30N 0 8W

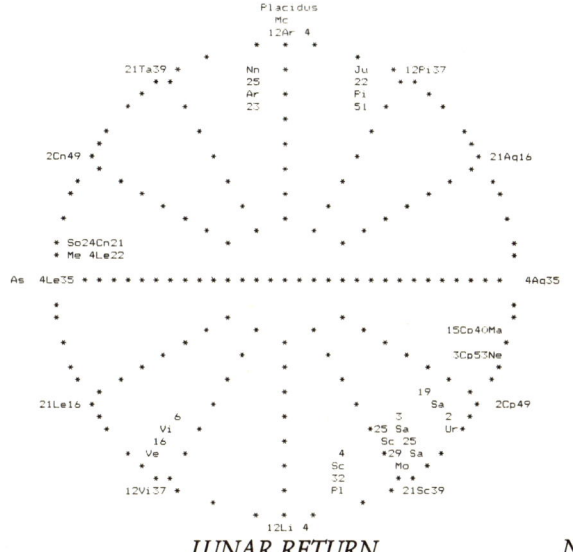

Ref:
Natal Chart No.6

LUNAR RETURN

Event: Marriage, 1.1.77   **MD: LUNAR/RETURN**   *No.60*
Gmt 13 27 24 12 1976
50 35N 1 5W

```
                        Placidus
                          Mc
                        22Cp 5
                      *   *   *
        14Aq20 *          Me*        *   4Cp 5
          * *             22          So   *
        * Ve              Cp*        * 2
        * Mo 17*          12         Cp     Ma
          18 Aq                      *53    24   *
          Aq 32*                           Sa
            48                             27      *  15Sa26
  19Pi44 *                                 *
     *                                          *
        *                                      *   14Sa24Ne
        *                                    *
        *                                  *
        *                              *
As 18Ta44 * * * * * * * * * * * * * * * * * * * *  18Sc44
     * Ju22Ta 0                            10Sc35Ur
        *                                  0Sc17Nn *
        *                                  14Li  3Pi
        *                              *
   15Ge25 *                              *   19Vi44
     *                            *16
        *                          Le
        *                         *15
        *                          Sa   *
           4Cn 5 *                * 14Le20
                      22Cn 5
```

Ref.
Natal Chart No.9   *LUNAR RETURN* (Residence)

No.60(a)   **MD: LUNAR/RETURN**   *Event: Marriage, 1.1.77*
Gmt 13 27 24 12 1976
34 21N 119 4W

```
                        Placidus
                          Mc
                        25Vi31
          *                   *
  25Li28 *    Pi       *        * 20Le 0
     * *      14                 * *
     * Nn     Li       *        Sa  *
     * O*  3            *       *16
     *Ur   Sc                   Le
       * 10 17*                *15
19Sc55 *  Sc          *              *
     *    35                         * 13Cn37
        *                          *
        *                        *
        *                      *
As 11Sa17 * * * * * * * * * * * * * * * * * * *  11Ge17
   * Ne14Sa24                              *
   Ma24Sa27                           *
   *So 2Cp53          *          *
     *            *          * 22Ta 0Ju
        *     22          *
13Cp37 *   Cp         *          *   19Ta55
     * 12    17
     *Me    Aq 18*
       32 Aq
     * Ve 48*
     * Mo
     20Aq 0 *              * 25Ar28
              25Pi31
```

LUNAR RETURN (Birthplace)   *Ref:*
Natal Chart No.9

Event: Marriage, 27.10.73 ND: LUNAR/RETURN *No.61*
Gmt 14 9 20 10 1973
50 35N 1 5W

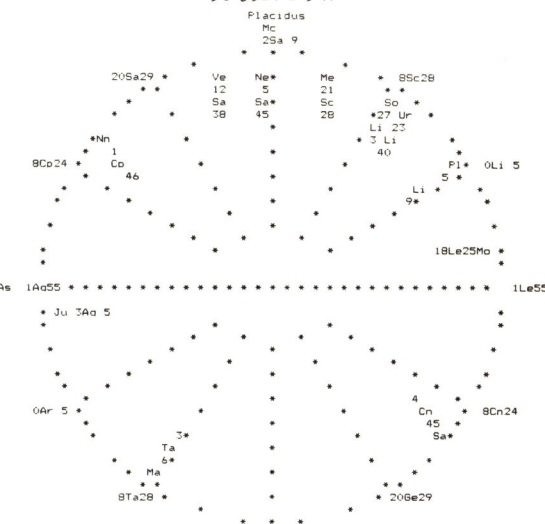

Ref:
Natal Chart No.10 LUNAR RETURN (Residence)

No.61(a) ND: LUNAR/RETURN *Event: Marriage, 27.10.73*
Gmt 14 9 20 10 1973
34 9N 118 9W

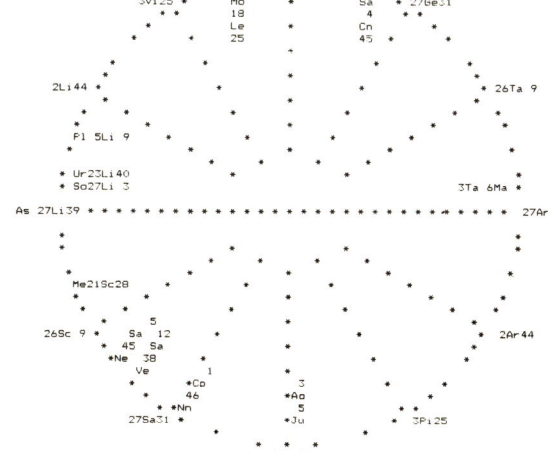

LUNAR RETURN (Birthplace) *Ref:*
Natal Chart No.10

sidereal time from one return to the next. The solar and lunar return charts can have several 'offshoots' in that returns can be computed for the position of the Moon in the solar return (solar Moon or kinetic return), for the opposition place of the Sun or Moon (demi-solar or lunar) or for the 'square' of the solar or lunar longitude (quarti-solar/lunar). All these types of returns and other similar techniques are discussed in Chapter 3. All these methods can be investigated by the enthusiast using well-attested data but obviously there is a limit to the amount of time and labour that can be devoted to any particular study. However, for this work we can take a few examples and process them through the 'calculating mill' and try to discover whether, in fact, some of these return techniques and the appropriate charts reflect the life experiences for the period for which they cover.

Example No.1 (Tropical): The Wedding of the Duchess of York (Sarah Ferguson)
Time: 10.50 UT as noted from TV broadcast
Date: 23.7.86: Westminster Abbey, Lat. 51.30N 0.07W.
Duchess of York
Birth data: 09.03 UT 15.10.59. 51.31N 0.09W
Natal Sun: 21° 15′ 38″ Libra: Natal Moon 6° 38′ Aries
RAMC 10.35.00: Mean Sun 13.32.36: Apparent Sun 13.18.35
Asc. 18° Scorpio: MC 7° Virgo:

Marriage data:		*Solar return* 1985/86	*Lunar return* (6° 38′ Aries)
Time UT	10.50	16.16	00.10
Date	23.7.86	14.10.85	29.6.86
Lat.	51.30N	51.30N	51.30N
Long.	00.07W	00.07W	00.07W
Sun	0.17.44 Leo	21.15.38 Libra	6.59 Cancer
Moon	27.33 Aquarius	28.09.00 Libra	6.38 Aries
RAMC	6.53.04	17.48.08	18.36.41
Mean Sun	8.03.32	13.32.36	6.27.09
App. Sun	8.09.58	13.18.35	6.30.24
Asc.	9 Libra	23 Pisces	22 Aries
MC	12 Cancer	27 Sagittarius	8 Capricorn

Solar moon return: 02.08 UT 16.7.86. London

Progressed solar return: 23.7.86. London

Solar quotidian: 23.7.86. London

All the foregoing charts have been computed in terms of the tropical zodiac and have been based on the given time of birth. No attempt has been made to 'rectify' or juggle the official time in order to accord with 'preconceived' ideas concerning the symbolism and angularity of the planets for an event such as this. For an event such as a marriage we should expect to find Venus prominent, either angular or closely configurated with appropriate planets. The Moon, signifying the emotional content and the mood of the time, along with Jupiter—joy and elation—with possibly Saturn—restructuring—and Pluto—new beginnings—would all be significant contacts. This is all traditional teaching and if we find that the return charts do in fact reflect the events and conditions of a given time by their apt symbolism, both in time and in nature, then we have a valuable technique for the investigation of serious astrology.

The Duchess of York's solar return for the year of her marriage has a cluster of planets in the seventh house which include a conjunction of the Sun and Moon in Libra. Sun/Moon contacts, particularly the conjunction, often indicate the start of a new phase. The conjunction of Mars/Venus on the seventh cusp and the culminating Neptune close to the MC mark out the year as highly significant with regard to partnerships and relationships. As an added testimony concerning dramatic changes, we have Pluto in close conjunction with Mercury and receiving the application of the Moon.

The solar return progressed to the date of marriage brings the natal Venus/Pluto to the seventh cusp. The solar return Ascendant (Pisces) has the exact opposition of the solar Mars/Venus and on the date of the wedding, the transiting Jupiter was conjunct the solar Ascendant. Uranus, the planet of thrill and delight, holds the Midheaven exactly, with transiting Venus in the seventh house opposed to the Ascendant.

The solar quotidian progression for this date has 5° Libra on the MC placing the natal Moon conjunct the fourth cusp, with the solar Mars/Venus close to the MC. The solar Moon return (lunar kinetic) occurred at 02.08 UT 16.7.86.

This return with 27° Gemini rising and the MC 22° Aquarius, has the natal Uranus conjunct the fourth cusp. Progressed to the date of the event it brings Neptune to the seventh and the transiting Moon on the Midheaven.

All the contacts operating in these various types of returns are appropriate to the event, especially a royal wedding which is conducted in a blaze of publicity and ceremonial.

Event: Marriage, 23.7.86   **DUCHESS OF YORK: S/R**   *No.62*

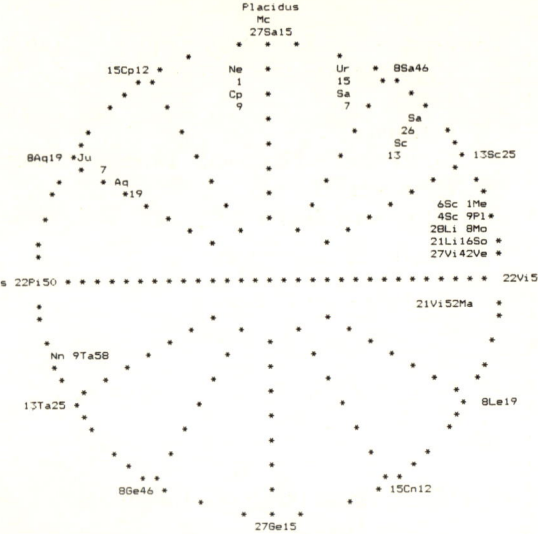

Ref:
Natal Chart No.7   *SOLAR RETURN*

No.63   **DUCHESS OF YORK**   *Event: Marriage, 23.7.86*

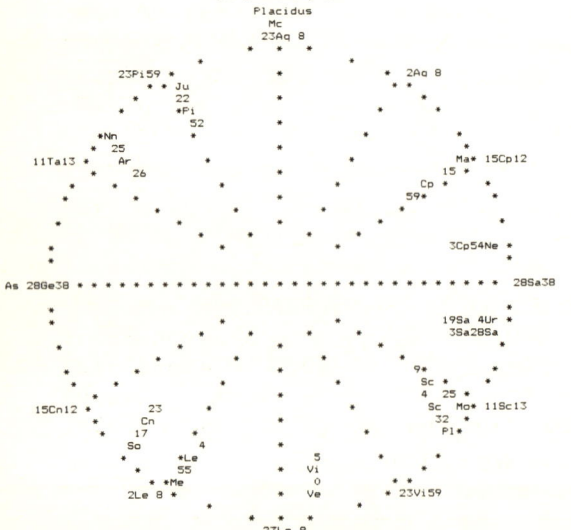

SOLAR MOON RETURN S/R. 1985/86   *Ref:*
                                      Natal Chart No.7

```
                    SOLAR MOON RETURN

                                                   H M S
(A) Date 15.7.86 Time 00.00 Required: Mean Sun    07 30 13
    Date 14.10.85 Time 16.16 Solar Return  – Mean
    Sun                                           13 32 36
    Difference                                    17 57 37
    Correction for Mean Solar Time      minus –  00 02 57
    Mean Solar Hours                              17 54 40
    UT of Solar Return                  Add +    16 16 00
    Progressed Solar Return                       10 10 40

    UT 10.11 Date 15.10.85
```

(B) Progressed Solar Return: Moon's Longitude: Sign Deg. Min.
    10.11 UT: 15.10.85 Date:

♏	9	25

(C) Moon Transits progressed Longitude: Date   UT
    = Solar Moon Return

16.7.86	02.08

```
                                                   H M S
(D) ST at 0 hr. UT on Transit date             * 19 34 09
    UT of Moon's Return              Add +       02 08 00
    Correction 9.86 sec. per hour   Add +  ** 00 00 20
    RAMC at Greenwich                           21 42 29

    Long. Equiv.                        – W: 00 00 28
    RAMC Solar Moon Return                      21 42 01

    Mean Sun = * + ** + 12 hours                07 34 29
```

```
(E) PROGRESSED SOLAR MOON RETURN
    Date 23.7.86 Time 10.50 Required:    Mean Sun 08 03 32
    Solar Moon Return           minus – Mean Sun 07 34 29
    Difference                                   00 29 03
    RAMC Solar Moon Return          Add +        21 42 01
    RAMC Progressed Solar Moon Return            22 11 04
```

The Astrology of Luck

A recent news item shown on British television concerned the presentation of a cheque for several hundreds of thousands of pounds to a couple who had been successful in winning the football pools. The 'pools' are a lottery whereby, from a coupon containing the listed names and numbers of football teams, an attempt is made to select the possible winners. The selection of numbers on a piece of paper has Mercury connotations combined with, in the case of the pools, risk-taking and gambling (Sun/Leo, fifth house). Football is a sport, so there is probably an element of Jupiter, not only from the sporting associations, but also because the 'luck factor' is strongly Jupiterian. As astrology should always be related to everyday life it may be interesting to study a few case of lottery and contest winners. The following examples have been compiled from the natal data as given in L. M. Rodden, *The American Book of Charts* (see Bibliography). The progressed solar return for the date of winning is based on the average advance of sidereal time per day, namely 4.9 minutes. The transiting planets on the day of the event are given in round degrees for 0 hours UT. All positions relate to the tropical zodiac.

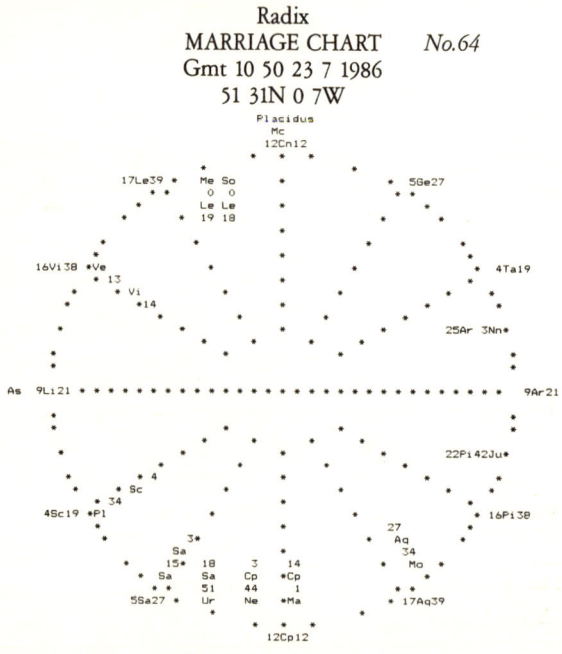

Radix
MARRIAGE CHART   *No.64*
Gmt 10 50 23 7 1986
51 31N 0 7W

Duke and Duchess of York

PROGRESSED SOLAR RETURN   No.65

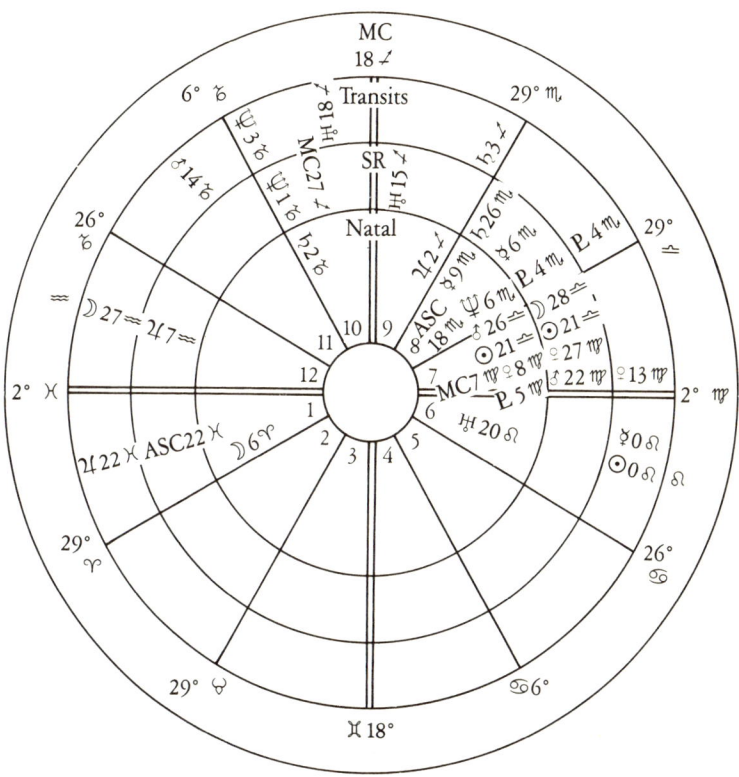

SOLAR RETURN				PROGRESSED RETURN			
Date 14.10.85 Time 16.16				Date 23.7.86 Time 10.50			
	H	M	S		H	M	S
RA Sun	13	18	35	RA Sun PSR	08	09	58
RAMC	17	48	08	RA Sun SR −	13	18	35
Constant	1.2395			= Difference	18	51	23
Duchess of York				× Constant =	23	22	21
(Tropical)				RAMC SR +	17	48	08
				RAMC PSR	17	10	29

Natal Data
Lottery and Contest Winners

	(1)		(2)		(3)	
Time UT	20.45		22.30		06.01	
Date	18.6.43		10.8.30		06.2.26	
Lat.	40.38N		41.52N		30.20N	
Long.	73.56W		87.39W		96.09W	
Natal Sun	26.43.20	♓	17.32.20	♌	16.42.19	♒
Natal Moon	05.46	♑	03.41	♓	20.02	♏
RAMC	09.34.07		13.54.05		08.38.52	
Mean Sun	05.44.51		09.14.41		21.02.28	
Apparent Sun	05.45.43		09.19.57		21.16.39	
Asc.	12	♏	5	♑	4	♏
MC	21	♌	0	♏	7	♌

	(4)		(5)		(6)	
Time UT	20.23		10.43		09.30	
Date	12.6.52		13.10.57		19.6.19	
Lat.	34.01N		40.45N		51.28N	
Long.	118.29W		73.47W		00.12W	
Natal Sun	21.46.19	♓	19.49.46	♎	27.02.32	♓
Natal Moon	25.25	♒	11.29	♓	03.51	♓
RAMC	05.53.28		07.14.46		03.15.26	
Mean Sun	05.24.23		13.26.55		05.46.11	
Apparent Sun	05.24.10		13.13.13		05.47.06	
Asc.	28	♍	15	♎	1	♍
MC	28	♓	17	♋	21	♉

Lottery and Contest Winners
Solar and lunar return data covering period of win.

SOLAR

	(1)		(2)		(3)	
Time UT	20.40		19.17		09.43	
Date	17.6.72		10.8.75		6.2.72	
Lat.	40.38N		41.52N		30.20N	
Long.	73.56W		87.37W		96.09W	
Sun	26.43.20	♓	17.32.20	♌	16.42.19	♒
Moon	17.45	♍	3.58	♎	5.10	♏
RAMC	09.33.21		10.45.35		12.22.25	
Mean Sun	05.44.51		09.14.41		21.02.28	

	(1)		(2)		(3)	
Apparent Sun	05.45.43		09.19.57		21.16.39	
Asc.	11	♏	25	♏	22	♐
MC	20	♌	9	♍	6	♎
Date of win	5.8.72		19.9.75		8.1.73	

SOLAR

	(4)		(5)		(6)	
Time UT	04.49		01.20		22.20	
Date	13.6.70		13.10.76		18.6.46	
Lat.	34.01N		40.45N		51.28N	
Long.	118.29W		73.47W		00.12W	
Sun	21.46.19	♓	19.49.46	♎	27.02.32	♓
Moon	03.12	♎	12.20	♓	13.26	♒
RAMC	14.18.20		21.42.40		16.05.23	
Mean Sun	05.24.23		13.26.55		05.46.11	
Apparent Sun	05.24.10		13.13.13		05.47.06	
Asc.	17	♑	18	♓	2	♒
MC	7	♏	23	♒	3	♐
Date of win	3.10.70		14.2.77		12.10.46	

Lottery and Contest Winners

Solar and lunar return data covering period of win.

LUNAR

	(1)		(2)		(3)	
Time UT	03.21		12.56		01.37	
Date	24.7.72		18.9.75		21.12.73	
Lat.	40.38N		41.52N		30.20N	
Long.	73.56W		87.39W		96.09W	
Moon	05.46	♑	03.41	♓	20.02	♏
RAMC	18.33.03		06.52.41		01.10.12	
Mean Sun	08.07.48		11.48.04		17.57.58	
Asc.	14	♈	10	♎	28	♋
MC	7	♑	12	♋	19	♈
Date of win	5.8.72		19.9.75		8.1.73	

	(4)	(5)	(6)
Time UT	16.38	02.46	18.08
Date	13.9.70	30.1.77	07.10.46
Lat.	34.01N	40.45N	51.28N

Long.	118.29W		73.47W		00.12W
Moon	25.25	≈	11.29	♓	03.51 ♓
RAMC	08.13.05		06.27.42		19.11.36
Mean Sun	11.29.00		20.36.55		13.03.07
Asc.	28	♎	5	♎	9 ♈
MC	1	♌	6	♋	16 ♑
Date of win	3.10.70		14.2.77		12.10.46

Case No.1: Date of win, 5.8.72.
This is 49 days from the date of the solar return which gives, roughly, an advance of 4 hours sidereal time ($\frac{49 \times 4.9}{60}$). Add to RAMC solar return 9.33.21 = 13.33 approximately = Asc. 1° Capricorn: MC 25° Libra. The solar Jupiter is 4° Capricorn, the natal Moon 6° Capricorn, so these two bodies were close to the progressed Ascendant of the return on the date in question. Transiting Venus and Jupiter were in 29° Gemini and Sagittarius respectively, contacting the Sun.

The lunar return preceding the event has the Moon conjunct Jupiter on the Midheaven with Uranus (surprise) opposing the Ascendant. For a thoroughly detailed analysis, the data requires to be studied and compared using the various return techniques. However, the above gives a broad outline showing the correlation of the event with the appropriate planetary contacts.

Case No.2: Date of win, 19.9.75.
40 days subsequent to the date of the solar return = 3 hr. 16 min. approx. plus RAMC solar return = 14 hour ST = RAMC progressed return. Ascendant 6° Capricorn: MC 2° Scorpio. This brings the natal Jupiter and Saturn to the Ascendant/Descendant.

The lunar return has the lunar Pluto on the Ascendant and the natal Jupiter and Saturn again on angles, only in this return they are on the tenth/fourth. The natal Uranus is, as in case 1, on the seventh angle. Using the lunar quotidian advance brings the natal Sun to the Midheaven. So again we have reasonable contacts which accord with the nature of the event.

Case No.3: Date of win, 8.1.73.
336 days after solar return date = 336 × 4.9 = 3 hr. 26 min. + SR RAMC = 15.48 = Asc. 14° Aquarius: MC 29° Scorpio: Prog. solar return. This brings the Sun conjunct the Ascendant; natal Moon close to the Midheaven; natal Venus and Jupiter within a few degrees

of the Ascendant; Saturn (natal) is conjunct the Midheaven, while Saturn (solar) is opposing the Midheaven. Perhaps Saturn signifies the continuous efforts that this person expended over two days of sustained playing to win thousands of dollars.

In the lunar return for this period, we have a Venus/Jupiter conjunction with the lunar Pluto close to the solar return MC. The lunar quotidian measure brings the Ascendant to about 13° Leo, which puts the lunar Jupiter and Venus in combination with the other Aquarius planets on or close to the seventh angle. The MC by this measure is about 8° Taurus, which brings the solar Moon to the fourth angle.

Case No.4: Date of win, 3.10.70.
112 days × 4.9 min. = 9 hr. 09 min. approx; add SR RAMC = 23.27 approx. = Asc. 8° Cancer: MC 21° Pisces. This brings the solar Mars to the Ascendant and the solar Pluto to the fourth angle (opposite MC). The natal Uranus in Cancer is also close to the progressed Ascendant. The quotidian measure applied to the lunar return brings the natal Pluto conjunct the MC, with the natal Jupiter opposite the quotidian Ascendant. The solar Saturn and the lunar Venus are also close to the Ascendant/Descendant axis.

Case No.5: Date of win, 14.2.77.
14.2 = 45 days + 365 = 410 − 286 (SR 13.10.76) = 124 × 4.9 min. = 10 hr. 07 min. approx., which added to the RAMC SR = 7.50 approx. RAMC progressed return. Asc. 21° Libra: MC 25° Cancer. All the natal planets in Libra are now clustered on or near the progressed Ascendant in combination with the solar Pluto. The lunar return has the natal Jupiter and the other Libra planets close to the Ascendant along with the solar and lunar Pluto. By the quotidian measure, the Sun, Mars, Jupiter and Pluto are all close to angles.

Case No.6: Date of win, 12.10.46.
This case, a football pools winner, won a fortune on the 12.10.46, the number of days elapsed from the date of the solar return being 116.
116 × 4.9 = 9.28 + SR RAMC 16.05 = 1.33 approx. Asc. 13° Leo: MC 25° Aries.

The natal Venus and Neptune in Leo are close to the progressed Ascendant. The solar Moon in Aquarius is conjunct the seventh angle with the solar Pluto close to the Leo Ascendant. The lunar return preceding the date of the win has Mars/Jupiter on the seventh cusp, the natal Jupiter opposite the lunar MC with Pluto nearby but rather wide to be classified as an opposition. The quotidian measure applied to the lunar return brings the natal Jupiter to the lower angle. On the day of the win, the transiting Moon (Taurus) was passing over the lunar Ascendant with the transiting Sun (Libra) conjunct the solar Jupiter.

The foregoing cases have been looked at very briefly and a rough approximation taken as to whether the event bears any relationship to the astrological factors operating at the time in question. Six cases on their own mean little or nothing, but if we find that an event such as winning a prize or acquiring vast sums of money correlate more often than not with certain significant astrological factors and patterns, then we may feel a little optimistic that our techniques have some validity. The test-checking of the above examples showed that the planets associated with sudden occurrences—Uranus and Pluto—were often involved in one way or another. Surprise and unexpectedness with feelings of joy and elation are Jupiter/Uranus expressions. Add to this the 'influence' of the dramatic Pluto, which is often observable at the times of major adjustments, and the whole planetary set-up is in conformity with the events and conditions relating to lottery winners.

Although the return techniques applied to the above cases were rough approximations, it may be interesting to do a more exact study on one of the cases to see whether, in fact, detailed calculations are in accordance with our original findings.

Case No.6: Pools winner.
Natal data: 9.30 UT 19.6.1919, 51.28N 0.12W.
Natal Sun 27° 02′ 32″ Gemini: natal Moon 3° 51′ Pisces:
RAMC 3.15.26: Mean Sun 5.46.11: Apparent Sun 5.47.06:
Asc. 1° Virgo: MC 21° Taurus.

Solar return 1947,	03. 57	UT 19.6.47 RAMC	21. 42. 21
Solar return 1946,	22. 20	UT 18.6.46 RAMC	16. 05. 23
	05. 37		05. 36. 58
			+ 24. 00. 00

$$\frac{29.37}{24} = 1.2340 \text{ Constant}$$

Solar return 1946: RAMC 16.05.23: Mean Sun 5.46.11.
Apparent Sun 5.47.06.

	H	M	S
Date of win, 12.10.46: Sun's Apparent RA (noon)	13	08	27
Solar return 18.6.46: Sun's Apparent RA	05	47	06 −
	07	21	21
Difference × 1.2340 =	09	04	37
Solar return RAMC add	16	05	23
RAMC prog. solar return at London	01	10	00

Asc. 9° Leo: MC 19° Aries.

This calculation now shows the solar Pluto right on the progressed Ascendant (ecliptically) with the solar Jupiter close to the lower angle. Neptune, that significator of nervous excitement and unreality, natally conjunct Venus in Leo, is also on the Ascendant. So we have Venus, Neptune, Jupiter and Pluto all prominent on the day that our pools winner gained a fortune (see prog. solar return chart No.1).

Joy and Sorrow

Elizabeth of Austria

One of the more interesting aspects of returns is the way in which events of a totally differing nature are often indicated. Elizabeth was the consort of Francis Joseph, whose Hapsburg Empire perished as the result of the First World War. Her life was tragic: her son Rudolph was found shot at Mayerling and she was assassinated at Geneva in 1898. She was married at sixteen (24.4.1854) and her solar return (24.12.1853) covering this period is as one would expect for marriage. Venus is conjunct the seventh cusp, Uranus/Pluto (excitement and change) hold the MC. The Sun is with Jupiter in the traditional house of love affairs (fifth). The solar Mars/Neptune are close to the natal Ascendant/Descendant with the solar Moon in opposition to the natal Pluto. Her lunar for this event has the natal Pluto conjunct the seventh cusp, and the lunar Neptune/Venus on her natal seventh cusp.

On the 10.9.1898, whilst boarding a steamer at Geneva, she was stabbed to death. Her solar return (1897), taken on its own does not look particularly violent, except for the Saturn/Uranus conjunction in the eighth house and the Mars/Venus/Neptune contacts. However, if we relate the natal to the return we have the natal Pluto conjunct the solar return Ascendant and the solar Pluto/Neptune on the natal

WINNERS: SUN/RETURN—1
Gmt 20 40 17 6 1972
40 38N 73 56W

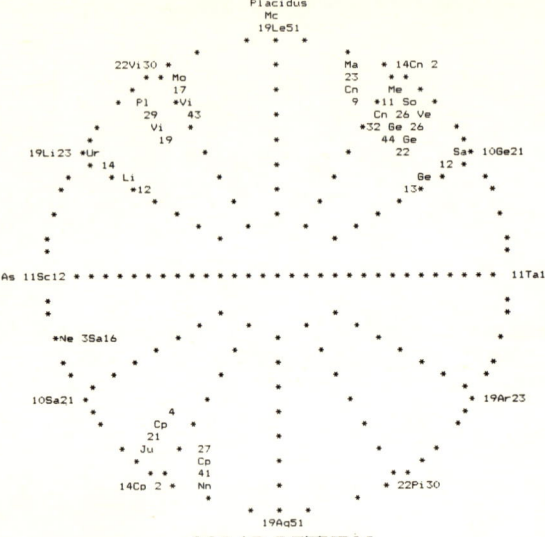

Ref:
Natal Chart 1

SOLAR RETURN

Radix
WINNERS—1
Gmt 20 45 18 6 1943
40 38N 73 56W

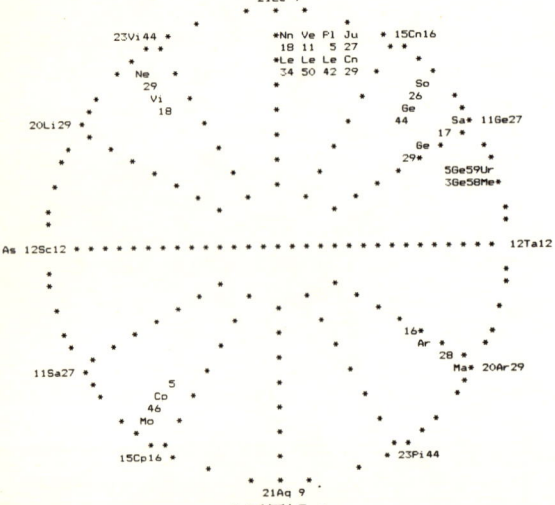

NATAL 1

WINNERS: LUNAR—1
Gmt 3 21 24 7 1972
40 38N 73 56W

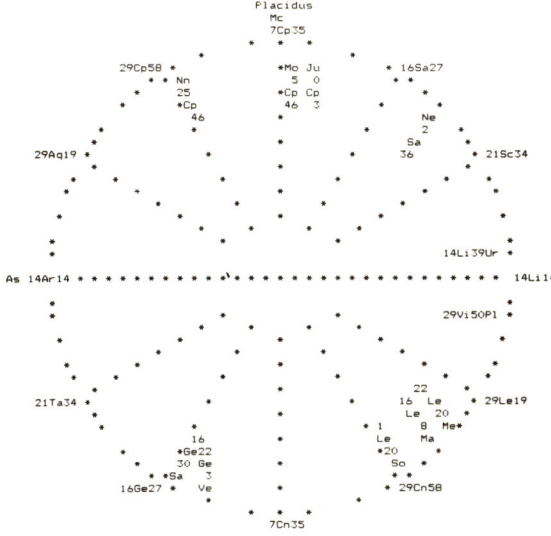

Ref:
Natal Chart 1

LUNAR RETURN

Radix
WINNERS—2
Gmt 22 30 10 8 1930
41 52N 87 39W

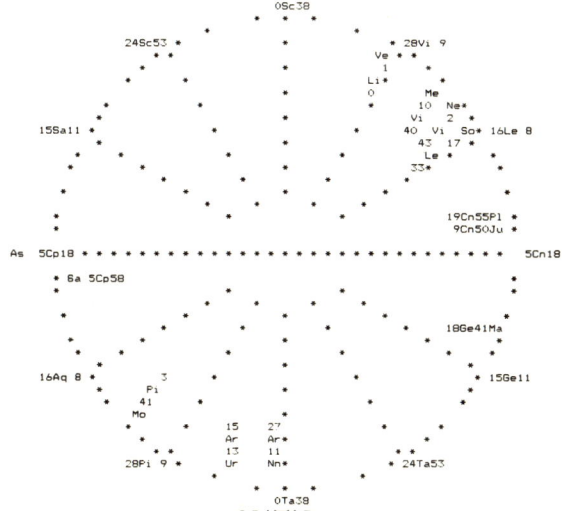

NATAL 2

WINNERS: SUN/RETURN—2
Gmt 19 17 10 8 1975
41 52N 87 37W

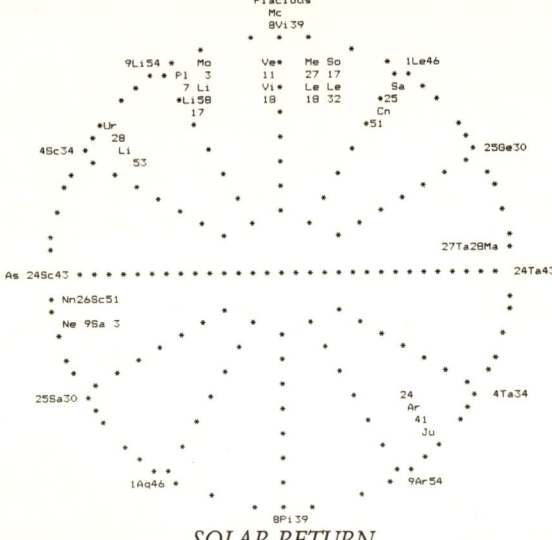

Ref:
Natal Chart 2

SOLAR RETURN

WINNERS: LUNAR—2
Gmt 12 56 18 9 1975
41 52N 87 39W

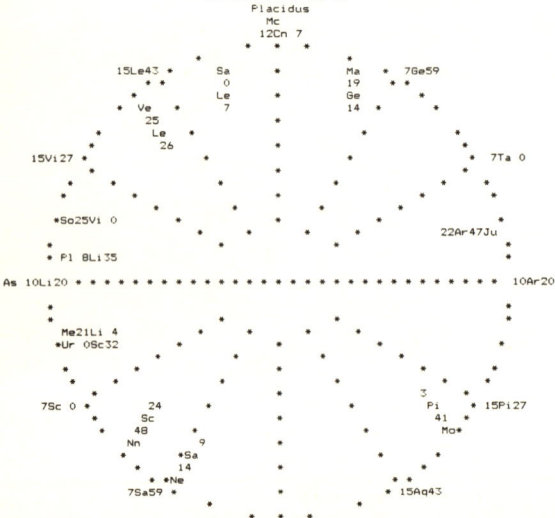

LUNAR RETURN

Ref:
Natal Chart 2

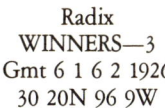

Radix
WINNERS—3
Gmt 6 1 6 2 1926
30 20N 96 9W

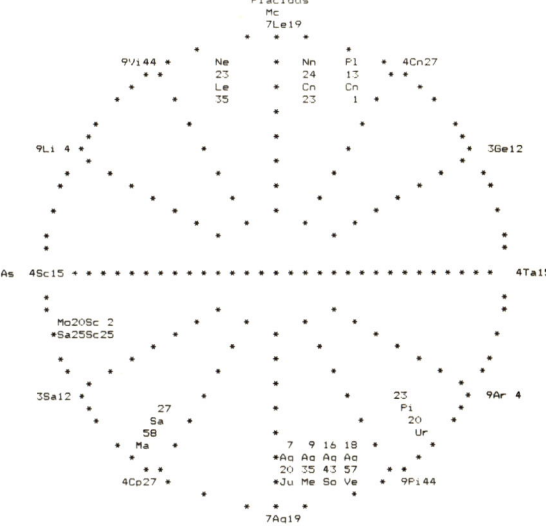

NATAL 3

WINNERS: SUN/RETURN—3
Gmt 9 43 6 2 1972
30 20N 96 9W

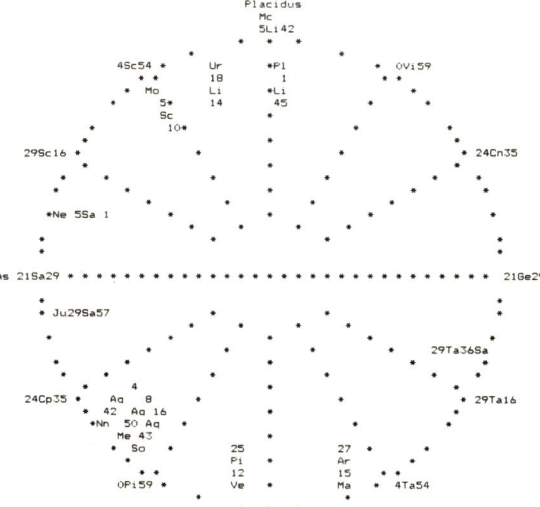

SOLAR RETURN

Ref:
Natal Chart 3

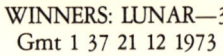

WINNERS: LUNAR—3
Gmt 1 37 21 12 1973
30 20N 96 9W

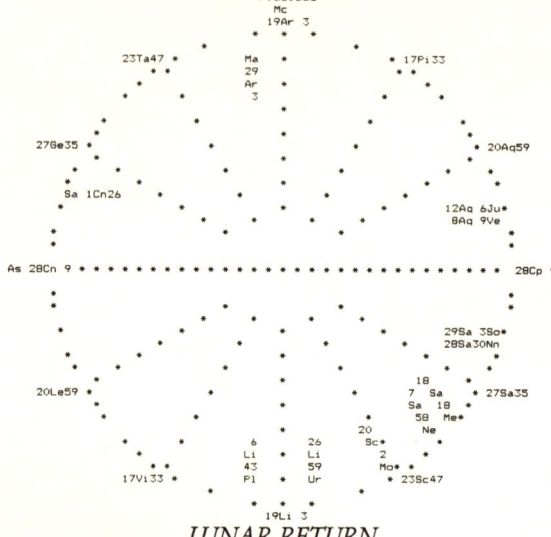

Ref.
Natal Chart 3   *LUNAR RETURN*

Radix
WINNERS—4
Gmt 20 23 12 6 1952
34 1N 118 29W

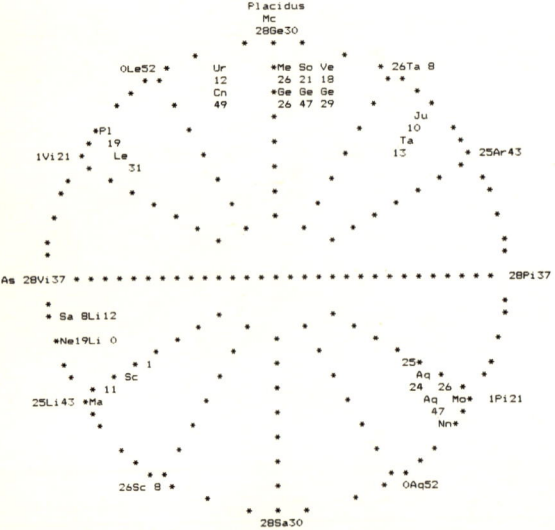

NATAL 4

WINNERS: SUN/RETURN—4
Gmt 4 49 13 6 1970
34 1N 118 29W

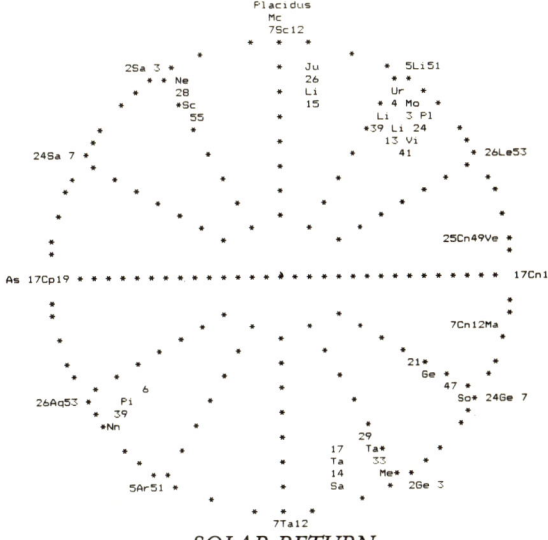

Ref:
Natal Chart 4

SOLAR RETURN

WINNERS: LUNAR—4
Gmt 16 38 13 9 1970
34 1N 118 29W

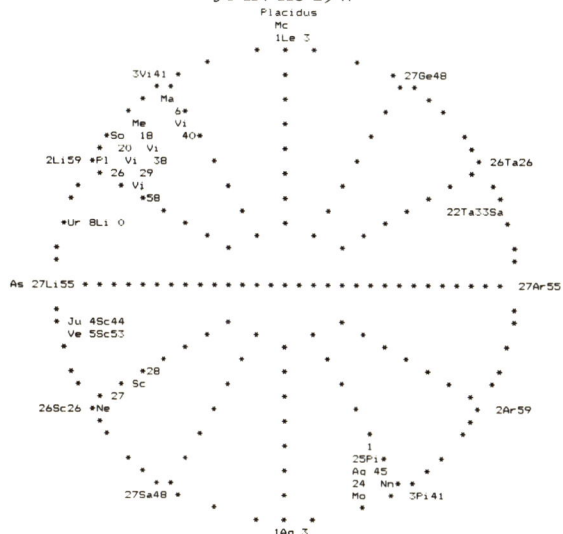

LUNAR RETURN

Ref:
Natal Chart 4

Radix
WINNERS—5
Gmt 10 43 13 10 1957
40 45N 73 47W

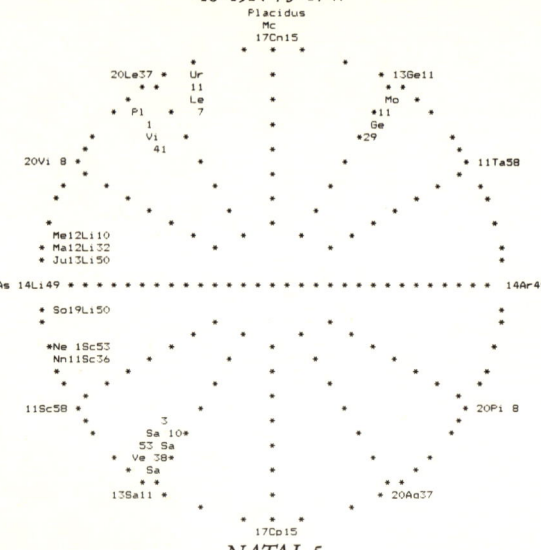

Placidus
Mc
17Cn15

20Le37 * Ur   * 13Ge11
            11
            Le   Mo
      * Pl   7   *11
      1   Ge
      Vi   *29
      41

20Vi 8 *   * 11Ta58

      Me12Li10
    * Ma12Li32
    * Ju13Li50

As 14Li49 * 14Ar49

    * So19Li50

   *Ne 1Sc53
    Nn11Sc36

11Sc58 *   * 20Pi 8

          3
         Sa 10*
         53 Sa
       * Ve 38*
         * Sa
       13Sa11 *

          17Cp15

NATAL 5

WINNERS: SUN/RETURN—5
Gmt 1 20 13 10 1976
40 45N 73 47W

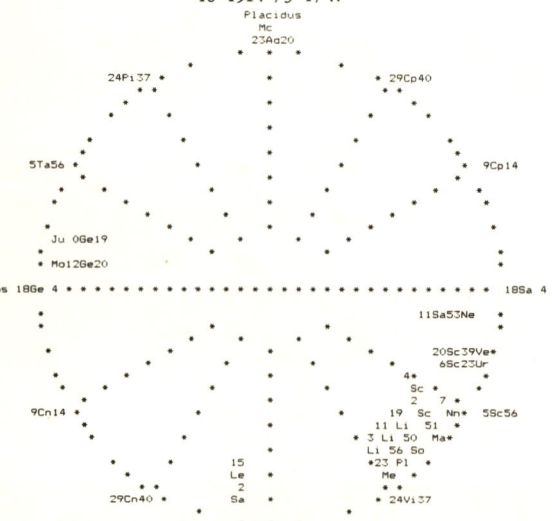

Placidus
Mc
23Aq20

24Pi37 *   * 29Cp40

5Ta56 *   * 9Cp14

Ju 0Ge19
* Mo12Ge20

As 18Ge 4 * 18Sa 4

                    11Sa53Ne *

                    20Sc39Ve*
                    6Sc23Ur
                  4*
                  Sc *
                  2   7
9Cn14 *   19   Sc Nn* 5Sc56
                  11 Li 51
                * 3 Li 50 Ma*
                  Li 56 So
       15   *23 Pi
       Le   Me *
       2   * *
29Cn40 *   Sa   * 24Vi37

       23Le20

SOLAR RETURN   *Ref:*
                            Natal Chart 5

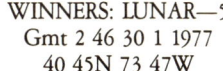

WINNERS: LUNAR—5
Gmt 2 46 30 1 1977
40 45N 73 47W

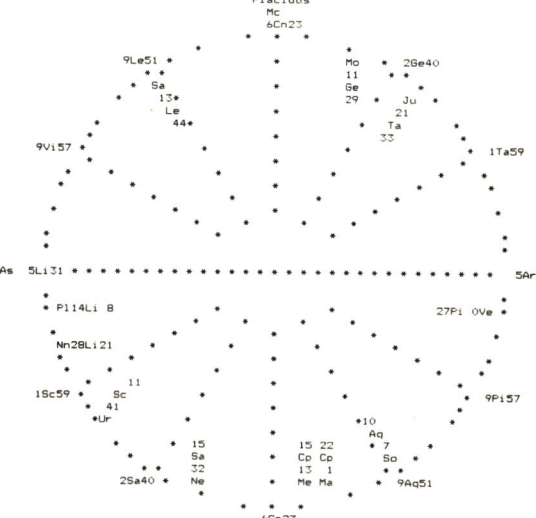

Ref.
Natal Chart 5

LUNAR RETURN

Radix
WINNERS—6
Gmt 9 30 19 6 1919
51 28N 0 12W

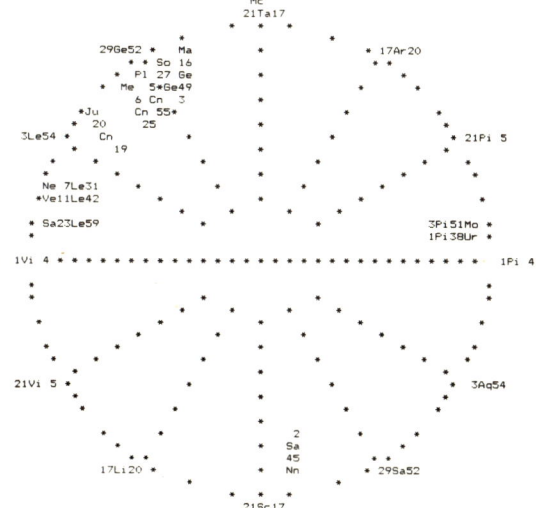

NATAL 6

WINNERS: SUN/RETURN—6
Gmt 22 20 18 6 1946
51 28N 0 12W

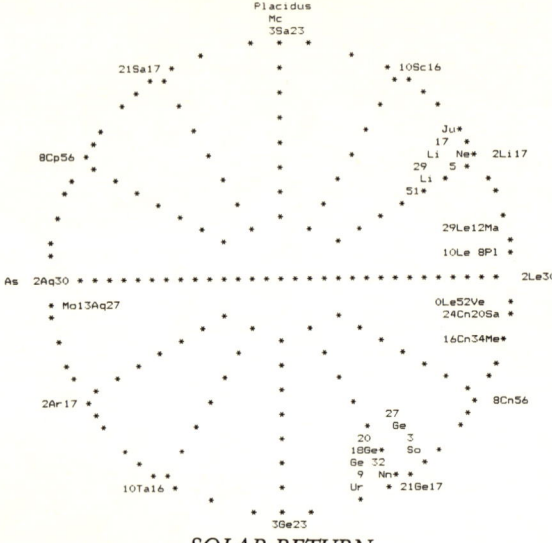

Ref:
Natal Chart 6

SOLAR RETURN

WINNERS: LUNAR—6
Gmt 18 8 7 10 1946
51 28N 0 12W

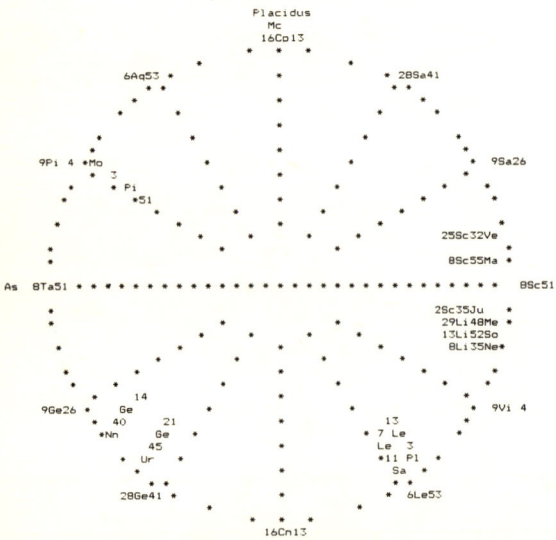

LUNAR RETURN

Ref:
Natal Chart 6

PROGRESSED SOLAR RETURN

Pools Winner

Ref:
Natal Chart 6

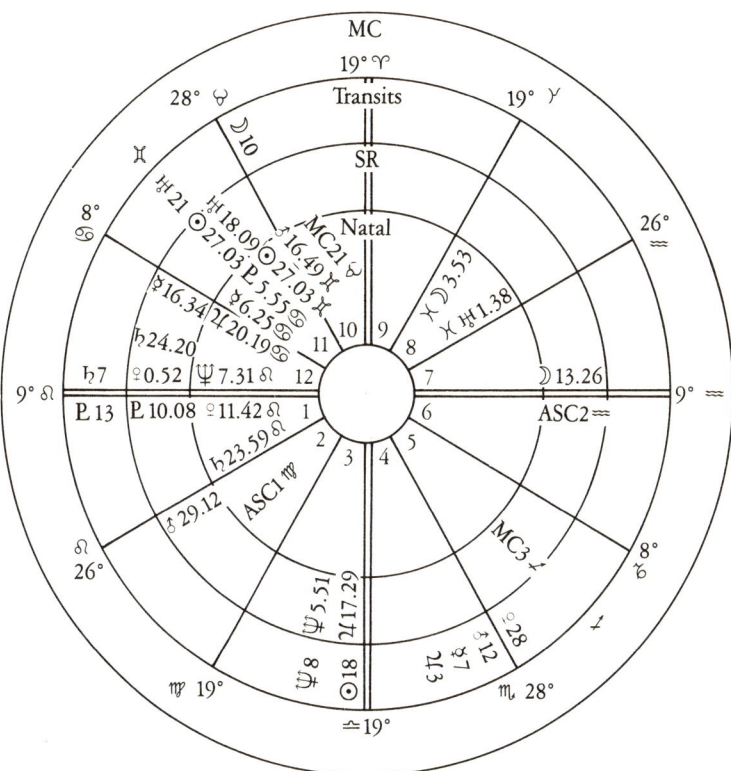

SOLAR RETURN				PROGRESSED RETURN			
Date 18.6.46 Time 22.20				Date 12.10.46 Time 12.0			
	H	M	S		H	M	S
RA Sun	5	47	06	RA Sun PSR	13	08	27
RAMC	16	05	23	RA Sun SR −	05	47	06
Constant 1.2340				= Difference	07	21	21
Pools Winner				× Constant =	09	04	37
(Tropical)				RAMC SR +	16	05	23
				RAMC PSR	01	10	00

MC. The solar Mars is close to the natal fourth house cusp.

The lunar return, despite the elevated Venus/Jupiter, has the natal Pluto on the lower angle with Mars/Neptune close to the lunar Descendant. Pluto in the lunar return is within a degree or so of the lunar Descendant. Progressing the solar return for 260 days gives an approximate arc of 21 hours which, added to the sidereal time of the return equals a sidereal time of 15.40 approximately. The Ascendant progressed is 29° Capricorn with a MC of 27° Scorpio. The natal Moon/Saturn conjunction is now on the progressed MC with the natal Neptune close to the progressed Ascendant. On the day of death the transiting Sun in Virgo was on the natal Ascendant and the transiting Moon in Cancer opposition the natal Mars and Mercury in Capricorn. The transiting Mars (4° Cancer) was on the lower angle of the solar return, opposite the Sun. There are other factors in these returns which are important and which could be dealt with at length, but the brief outline given above shows how return charts are interrelated one with another and with the natal chart.

The tragic death of Elizabeth should be reflected in the returns of her husband (Francis Joseph). His solar return prior to this event occurred on the 17.8.1898. This return has a grouping in the seventh house, but the chief contact is the angular Saturn with Pluto/Mars in the fourth house. The Sun/Moon conjunction appears in this chart, as in others, where there has been loss due to death. This may be coincidental or it may have some relevance.

The lunar return also occurred on the date of the solar return with the Sun/Moon conjunction close to the twelfth house and Neptune/Mars/Pluto on the MC. On the day in question (10.9.1898) the transiting Mars was on the natal MC opposite the natal Jupiter. Francis Joseph died on the 21.11.1916. The solar return (18.8.1916) has Neptune/Saturn rising with Mars on the lower angle. The Moon with Jupiter possibly shows an 'easy departure'. Comparing the natal with the solar return shows the solar Pluto on the natal MC, and the natal Mars/Pluto close to the solar MC. The solar Saturn is conjunct the natal Venus and in opposition to the natal Neptune.

Of course, many of the contacts of the outer planets will be in orb for many weeks or months, but when these contacts are brought into focus through their relationship with other return factors, then they assume importance. The lunar return covering his death has the Moon/Uranus on angles with Mars within a degree of the seventh cusp. On the day of death the transiting Moon was on the natal Ascendant (Libra) and close to the solar Mars on the lower angle.

ELIZABETH OF AUSTRIA   *No.1*
Gmt 22 0 24 12 1837
47 59N 11 20E

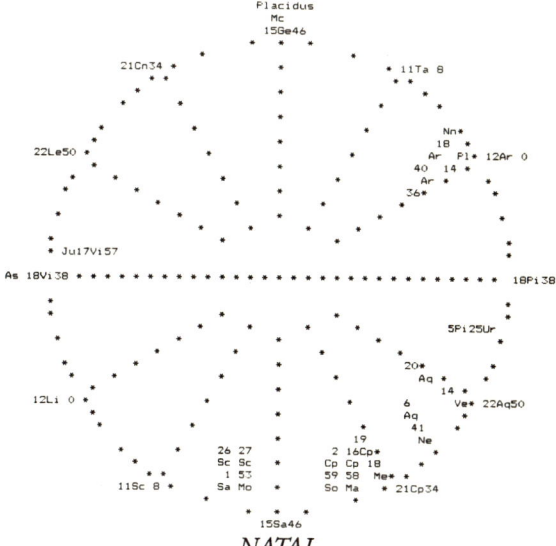

NATAL

No.1(a)   ELIZABETH OF AUSTRIA   *Event: Marriage, 24.4.1854*
Gmt 19 18 24 12 1853
47 59N 11 20E

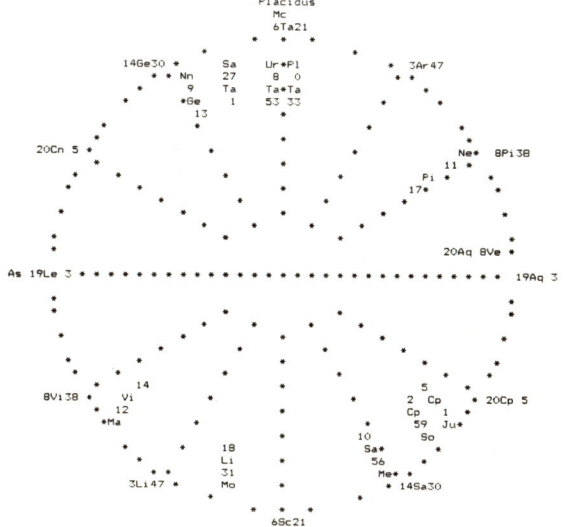

SOLAR RETURN

Ref:
Natal Chart No.1

Event: Marriage, 24.4.1854   ELIZABETH OF AUSTRIA   *No.1(b)*
Gmt 16 46 15 4 1854
47 59N 11 20E

```
                          Placidus
                            Mc
                          15Cn10
                        *   *   *
        19Le46 *            *              *  9Ge20
            *  *  *         *              *  *
        *  Ma  *            *            *  Nn  *
           28                            *  3  Sa
           Le                            Ge  1
           17                            *17 Ge
                                           7
    18Vi50 *                                    *
       *                                     Ur*  7Ta59
       *                                     11 *
       *                                     Ta  *
                                             38*    *
                                           1Ta46Pl*
                                           25Ar23So
       *
  As 12Li 6 * * * * * * * * * * * * * * * * * * * * * 12Ar 6
       *                                     *
       *                                     28Pi49Me
       *                                     *
                                           14*   *
                                           Pi  *
                                           12  58  *
    7Sc59 *                                Pi  Ne* 18Pi50
       *        27         *                3  *
                Sc                          Ve*
                53
          *  Mo         *    25
            *  *             Cp
          9Sa20 *           53
                            Ju      * 19Aq46
                        *  *  *
                          15Cp10
```

Ref:
Natal Chart No.1   *LUNAR RETURN*

No.1(c)   ELIZABETH OF AUSTRIA   *Event: Assassination at*
Gmt 11 26 24 12 1897   *Geneva, 10.9.1898*
47 59N 11 20E

```
                          Placidus
                            Mc
                           5Cp38
                         *  *  *
     25Cp45 *       Mo  *So     Ma  * 16Sa33
        * * Me      12   2      23  Ve * *
      *  Nn 22      Cp  *Cp     Sa  20  *
        28*Cp        5  59      31Sa*   *
        Cp 24                   11      Sa
        13*                          6  Ur*
                                       Sa  1
    23Aq18 *                     *   42  Sa  * 23Sc 7
       *                              18
       *
       *
       *
  As 12Ar48 * * * * * * * * * * * * * * * * * * * * 12Li48
       *
       *                              8Li49Ju  *
       *                                    *
       *                                    *
       *                                    *
    23Ta 7 *                         *  23Le18
       *        13*
                Ge
          *  21*  20
          * Pl   Ge
          *  *   49
        16Ge33 *  Ne        * 25Cn45
                  *  *  *
                   5Cn38
```

SOLAR RETURN   *Ref:*
Natal Chart No.1

Event: Death, 10.9.98   ELIZABETH OF AUSTRIA   *No.1(d)*
                                               Gmt 14 01 24 8 1898
                                                 47 59N 11 20E

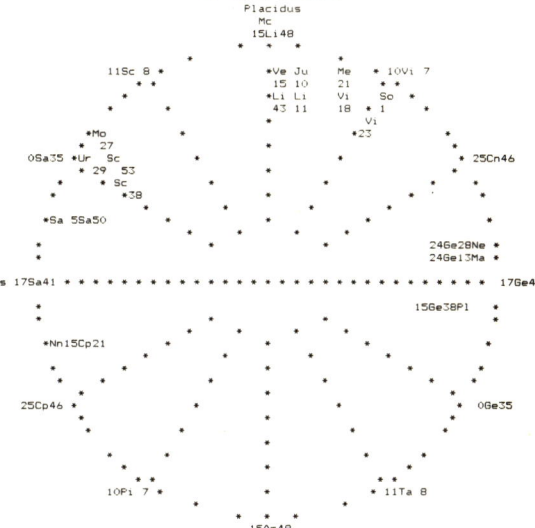

Ref:
Natal Chart No.1   **LUNAR RETURN**

No.2   FRANCIS JOSEPH
            Gmt 7 17 18 8 1830
              48 12N 16 23E

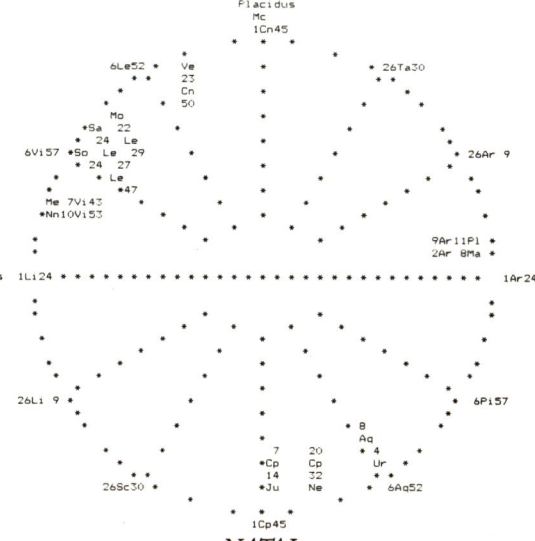

                        NATAL

Event: Death of wife, 10.9.1898   FRANCIS JOSEPH   *No.2(a)*
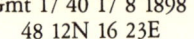

Gmt 17 40 17 8 1898
48 12N 16 23E

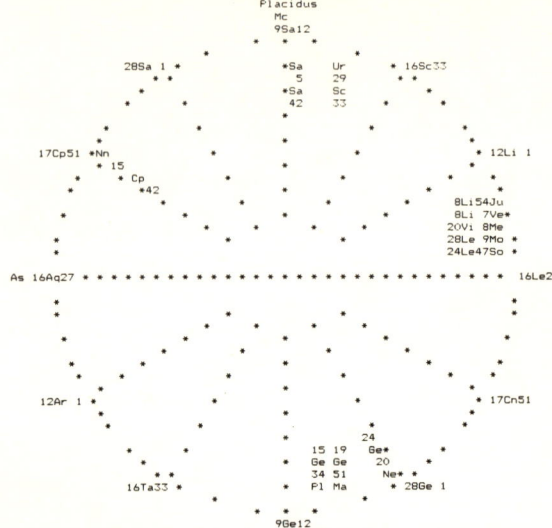

Placidus
Mc
9Sa12

28Sa 1   •Sa   Ur   • 16Sc33
                 5   29
                •Sa   Sc
                42   33

17Cp51 •Nn   • 12Li 1
     • 15
       • Cp
       •42
                                    8Li54Ju
                                    8Li 7Ve•
                                    20Vi 8Me
                                    28Le 9Mo •
                                    24Le47So

As 16Aq27 • 16Le27

12Ar 1   • 17Cn51

                          24
                    15 19 6e•
                    Ge Ge 20
                    34 51 Ne• •
16Ta33   Pl Ma   • 28Ge 1

                     9Ge12

Ref:
Natal Chart No.2   SOLAR RETURN

No.2(b)   FRANCIS JOSEPH   *Event: Death of wife, 10.9.1898*

Gmt 6 39 17 8 1898
48 12N 16 23E

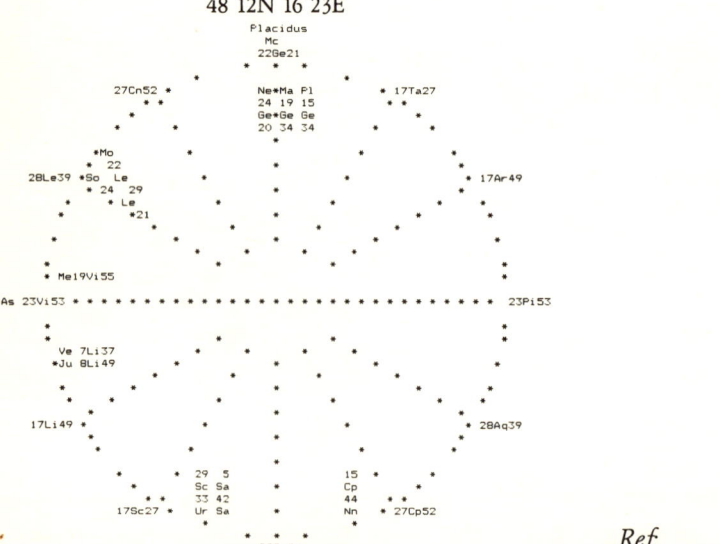

Placidus
Mc
22Ge21

27Cn52 •   Ne•Ma Pl   • 17Ta27
                 24 19 15
                 Ge•Ge Ge
                 20 34 34

     •Mo
     • 22
28Le39 •So Le   • 17Ar49
     • 24   29
       • Le
       •21

 • Me19Vi55

As 23Vi53 • 23Pi53

Ve 7Li37
•Ju 8Li49

17Li49 •   • 28Aq39

          29 5   15
          Sc Sa   Cp
          33 42   44
17Sc27 • Ur Sa   Nn • 27Cp52

               22Sa21
          LUNAR RETURN   *Ref:*
                                    Natal Chart No.2

Event: Death, 21.11.1916   FRANCIS JOSEPH   *No.2(c)*
                                    Gmt 02 06 18 8 1916
                                      48 12N 16 23E

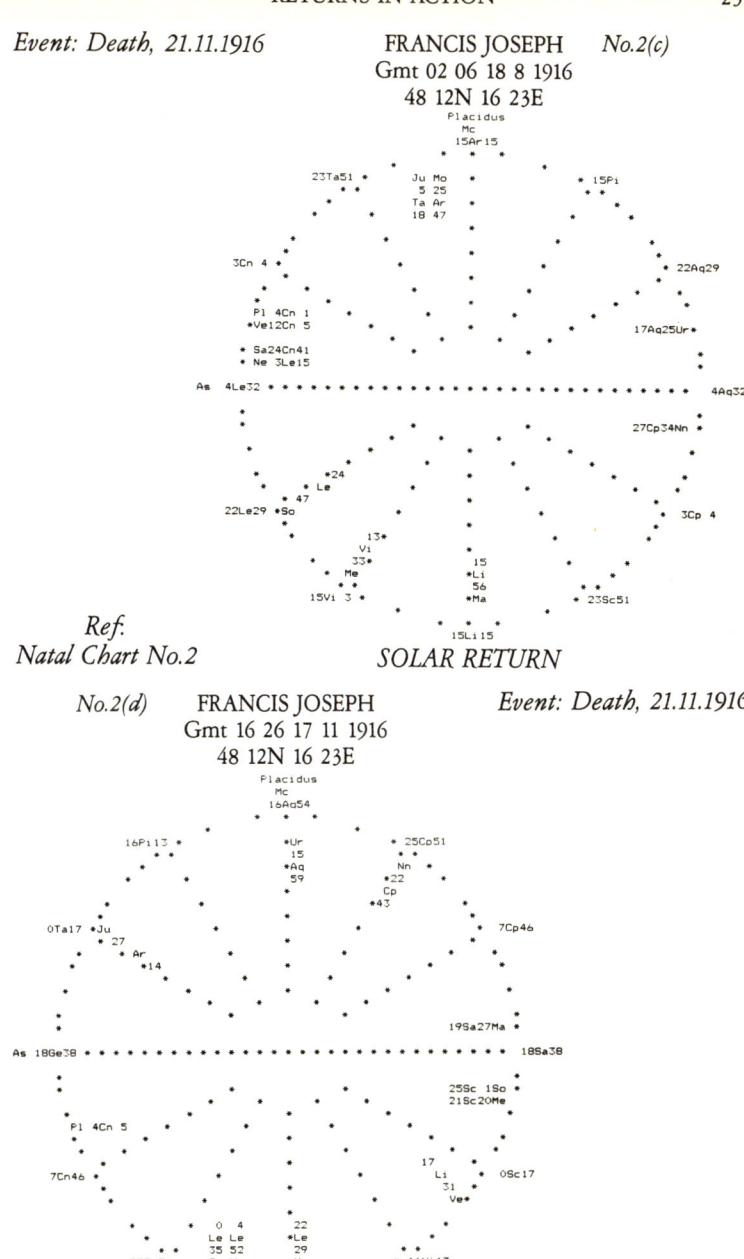

Ref:
Natal Chart No.2   **SOLAR RETURN**

No.2(d)   FRANCIS JOSEPH   *Event: Death, 21.11.1916*
             Gmt 16 26 17 11 1916
               48 12N 16 23E

LUNAR RETURN   *Ref:*
                                   Natal Chart No.2

In the lunar chart, the transiting Moon was with Venus.

Bullfighter

Manuel Garcia was killed in the Plaza de Toros, Madrid, on 27 May 1894, probably in the late afternoon. If we study his solar return prior to his death the first thing, and the most impressive, is the remarkable conjunction of the Gemini planets precisely on the MC with Mars in exact opposition from the lower angle. The lunar return (25.5.1894) has Saturn on the MC opposed to Venus. The natal Neptune in Aries is on the lower angle of the return. In most return charts there are many subtle contacts which, although not always apparent, have some importance. In the lunar (25.5.1894) the Sun in Gemini is precisely conjunct the Moon in the solar return. Another interesting fact which may be important is that the Gemini planets fall close to the natal eighth house. On the day of death the transiting Sun was exactly on the solar MC and conjunction the natal eighth house cusp. The Moon on this day was passing over the natal Descendant in conjunction with the transiting Mars. If death occurred in the late afternoon, the natal Pluto would be setting with the natal Moon close to the lower angle.

BULLFIGHTER   *No.3*
Gmt 1 39 18 1 1866
37 23N 6 0W

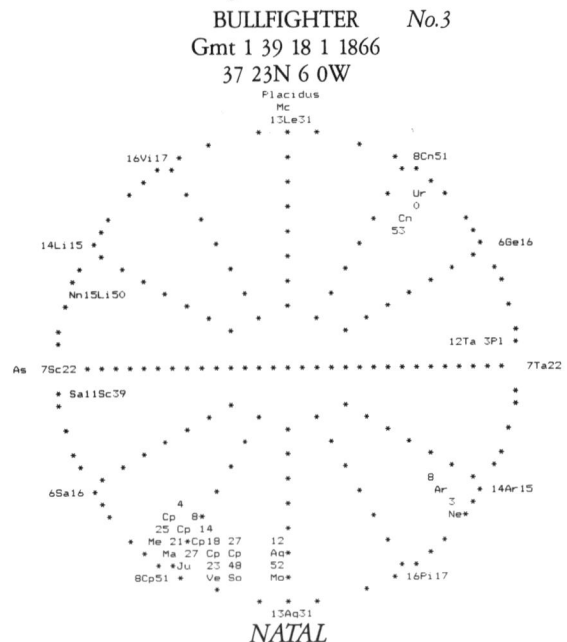

NATAL

Event: Death in the ring,   **BULLFIGHTER**   *No.3(a)*
27.5.1894, Madrid   Gmt 20 51 17 1 1894
                                      37 23N 6 0W

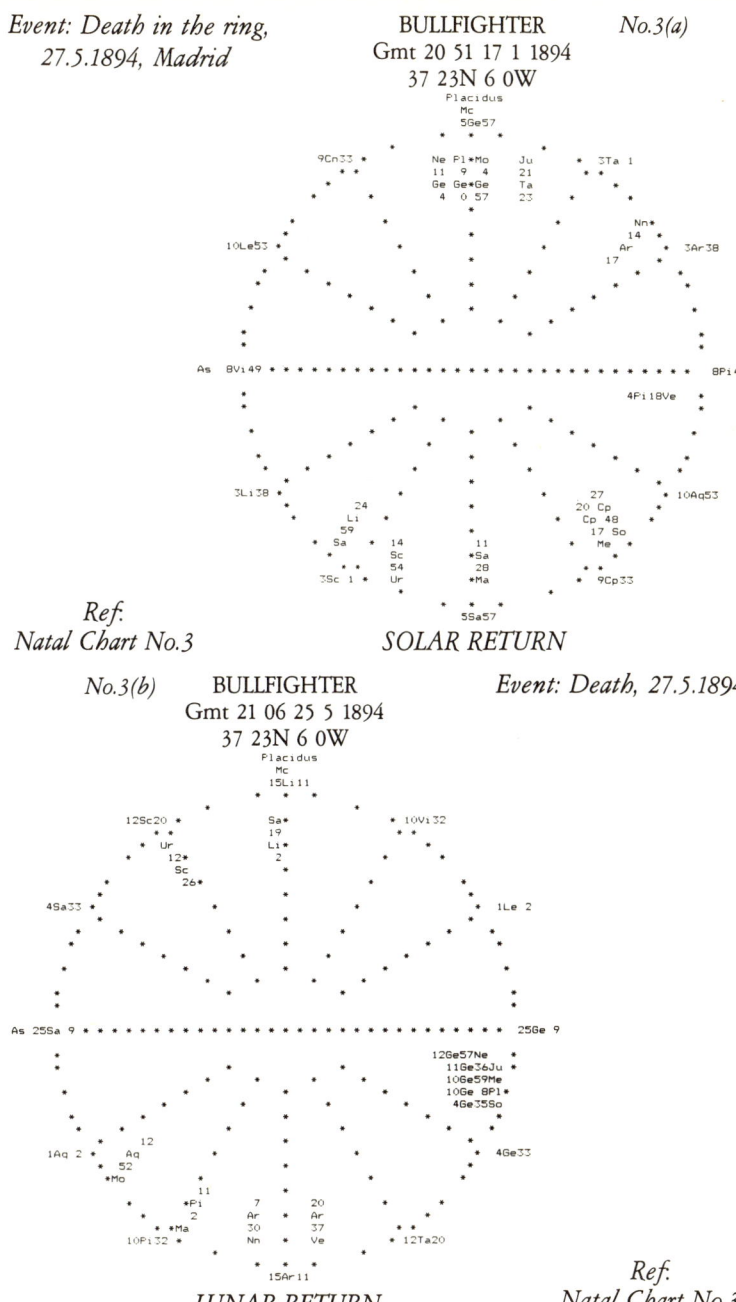

Ref:
Natal Chart No.3   **SOLAR RETURN**

No.3(b)   **BULLFIGHTER**   *Event: Death, 27.5.1894*
            Gmt 21 06 25 5 1894
              37 23N 6 0W

LUNAR RETURN   *Ref:*
                                    Natal Chart No.3

Air raid victims

No.1. The solar return for this victim (15.6.44) has Libra rising, the Sun with Saturn and Venus and the Moon setting in Aries. Not a very favourable return, especially as the natal Saturn is rising in the return. The lunar return has the Moon with Saturn and Sun/Mars opposed to Uranus. On the day of death, the transiting Moon (Aquarius) was precisely opposed to the natal Neptune. This transit occurs each month, but taken in relation to the other indications, it appears to have acted as 'marker'. The Mercury/Saturn contact at the time of death, aspects the natal Cancer planets. The number of days elapsed from the date of the solar return to the day of death is 187, which gives an approximate progressed Ascendant of about 10° Cancer, which brings the natal Mars/Pluto/Moon to the Ascendant. The transiting Saturn/Mercury are also to the fore.

No.2. The solar return (9.12.40) has the natal Mars exactly rising, Pluto conjunct the MC and the Moon setting in Aries. The natal Moon in Libra rises in the solar return but is conjunct the fourth angle in the lunar return. The significance of Neptune at the time of death is again shown in this lunar return where it receives the opposition of the applying Sun (Pisces/Virgo). The approximate progressed solar return Ascendant for the day of death is about 10° Pisces, which brings the natal Neptune/Saturn to the angles.

No.3. This solar return has the solar Pluto conjunct the fourth angle with the solar Uranus close to the Ascendant. The lunar return has Pluto within a couple of degrees of the Ascendant and the Moon is with Neptune, rather wide of the fourth angle. A rough progression of the solar return (139 days) brings the Ascendant to about 15° Libra and the MC 20° Cancer. Pluto is now on the upper angle, somewhat wide. Using the lunar quotidian rate of progression, brings the lunar Saturn/Jupiter conjunct the progressed MC. By this measure the natal Neptune is on the quotidian Ascendant and the natal Saturn on the fourth angle.

No.4. In the solar return for this case, the natal Uranus is precisely conjunct the fourth angle with the natal Mars on the MC. The natal Moon is setting in Gemini and the return Sun is exactly conjunct the solar Mars in Virgo. The natal Jupiter/Saturn opposition falls across the solar return's first/seventh angles. In the lunar return the natal Mercury/Mars is precisely on the MC conjunct the lunar Neptune. The lunar Mars is opposed to Pluto and the lunar Sun is separating from a conjunction with the natal Uranus. Progressing the solar return for 224 days gives, as a rough approximation, an Ascendant of 10° Libra and a MC of 13° Cancer. This brings the natal Mars and Uranus to Ascendant/Descendant with the natal Pluto on the MC.

These types of returns which precede tragedy will often show appropriate contacts involving the 'heavy' planets, particularly Saturn or Neptune which seem to 'hug' the angles prior to disasters or personal misfortune. Forecasting precisely is not of this world, but we can anticipate the times when life will test us to the limits of our endurance. In more normal times it is possible that the four victims who died as the result of enemy action would have survived and that the indications in their return charts would have been experienced less violently.

Although the returns connected with these four cases have only been very briefly studied, it is highly probable that a detailed study using many of the other return techniques, would reveal a complex and intricate pattern of relationships in conformity with the tragic nature of their deaths.

Mary

Natal Data: 09.05 UT 12.6.29. 51.32N 0.20W.
Natal Moon: 27.31 Leo (see natal chart No.18)

As an example of Neptune's influence at the time of death or loss we can study the three lunar returns preceding the loss of a husband, father and mother. In the lunar chart (21.12.67) covering the loss of the father, Neptune is on the fourth angle and the lunar Sun/Mercury are opposed to their natal positions. In the lunar chart, Jupiter is with the Moon and the natal Jupiter is on the lunar Midheaven opposed to the lunar Neptune. The prominence of Jupiter in this case is not clear; perhaps it has some other significance during the return period.

The return for the death of the husband also has an angular Neptune combined with a Sun/Saturn conjunction in Gemini and Venus/Mercury close by in Cancer. The natal Jupiter is again on the lunar MC with the natal Moon/Neptune conjunction close to the lunar Ascendant. The Jupiter and Neptune contacts also appear in the return preceding the death of the mother. The natal Jupiter is

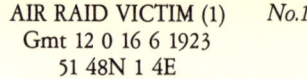

AIR RAID VICTIM (1)   *No.1*
Gmt 12 0 16 6 1923
51 48N 1 4E

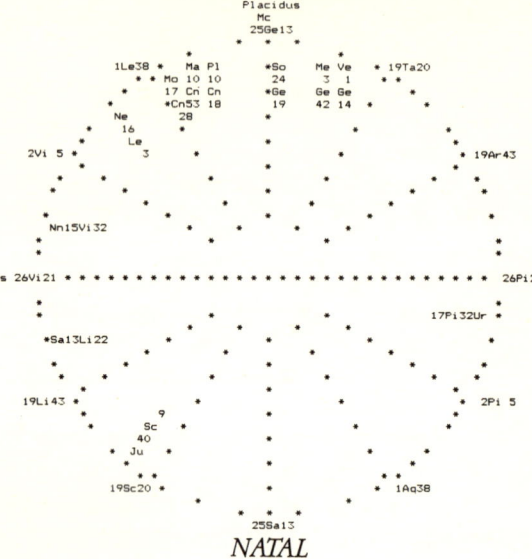

NATAL

No.1(a)   AIR RAID VICTIM (1)   *Event: Death, noon, 19.12.44*
Gmt 13 52 15 6 1944
51 48N 1 4E

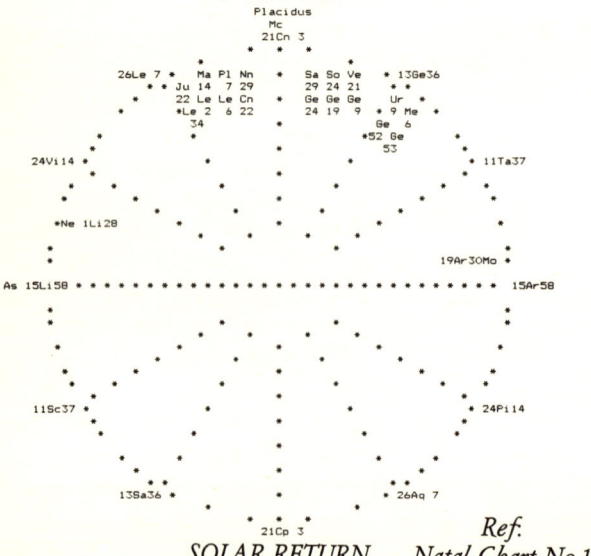

SOLAR RETURN   *Ref:*
Natal Chart No.1

Event: Death, noon, 19.12.44   AIR RAID VICTIM (1)   *No.1(b)*
Gmt 22 36 2 12 1944
51 48N 1 4E

```
                        Placidus
                          Mc
                        23Ta59
                       *   *   *
      2Cn31 *          Ur      *        * 19Ar49
         * *           11    *            * *
       * Sa            Ge  *
        Mo  9          7 *
     *Nn  17 Cn  *
      * 20  Cn 20 *
  6Le14 *  Cn  28  *                          * 23Pi18
          *   20    *
   P110Le10    *          *

   As  3Vi 7 * * * * * * * * * * * * * * * * * * * * * * *   3Pi

                      *25
                    * Vi
                   3
   23Vi18 *Ju      6    *          20         6Aq14
        *  Li                      Cp
        5                           7   *
        Ne            *      1      Ve
                   *   5 10  Cp*
                     Sa Sa  32  *
                     13 39  Me* *
        19Li49 *     Ma So    * 2Cp31
                    *   *   *
                     23Sc59
```
Ref.
Natal Chart No.1   **LUNAR RETURN**

No.1(c)   FLYING BOMB VICTIM
Gmt 12 0 19 12 1944
51 44N 0 28E

```
                       Placidus
                         Mc
                       28Sa33
                      *   *   *
   16Cp31 *        Me    *So    Ma  * 10Sa19
      * *          5     27     17    * *
     *  Cp         *Sa    Sa
        46         29     14  *

10Aq 3 *Ve                            * 15Sc36
     *  9
     * Aq
     *  *52
  Mo16Aq15                        6Li20Ne *
                                  26Vi38Ju
  As 26Pi12 * * * * * * * * * * * * * * * * * *  26Vi12

                                   9*
                                   Le
                                   57 *
  15Ta36 *                         P1* 10Le 3
                              *19
                   10         Cn
                 *Ge     8    *28
                 26      Cn   Nn *
              *  *Ur     6    * *
              10Ge19 *   Sa   * 16Cn31
                    *   *   *
                     28Ge33
```
Death chart   *Ref.*
Natal Chart No.1

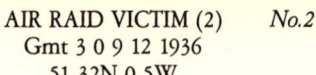

AIR RAID VICTIM (2)   *No.2*

Gmt 3 0 9 12 1936

51 32N 0 5W

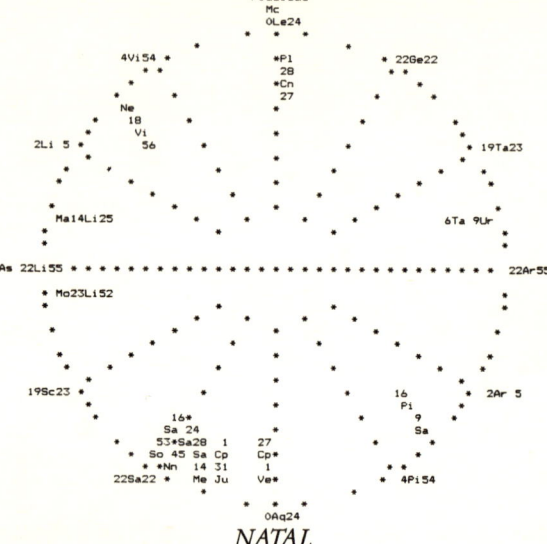

NATAL

No.2(a)   AIR RAID VICTIM (2)

Gmt 2 24 9 12 1940

51 32N 0 5W

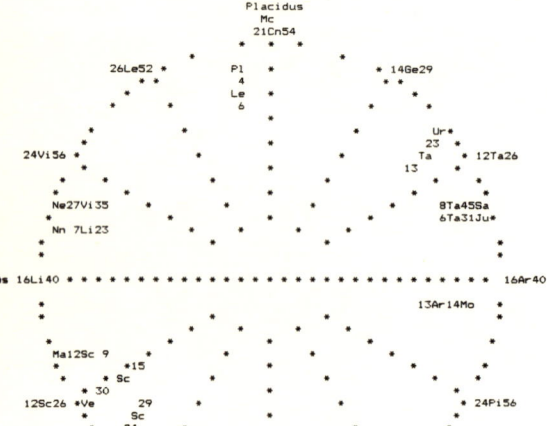

SOLAR RETURN   *Ref:*
Natal Chart No.2

AIR RAID VICTIM   *No.2(b)*
Gmt 14 11 15 3 1941
51 32N 0 5W

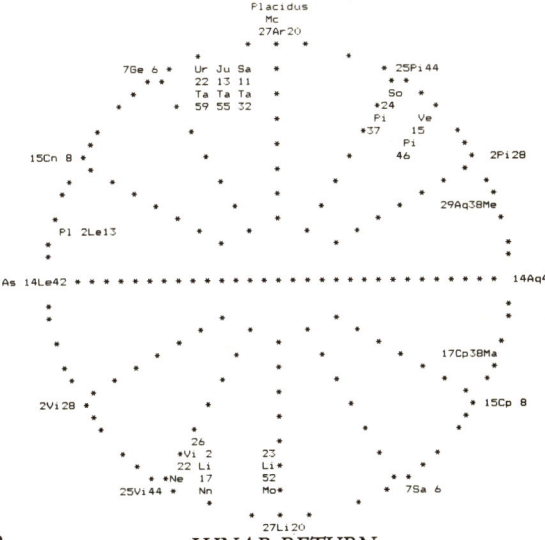

Ref:
Natal Chart No.2

LUNAR RETURN

No.3   AIR RAID VICTIM (3)
Gmt 19 0 21 11 1924
51 32N 0 5W

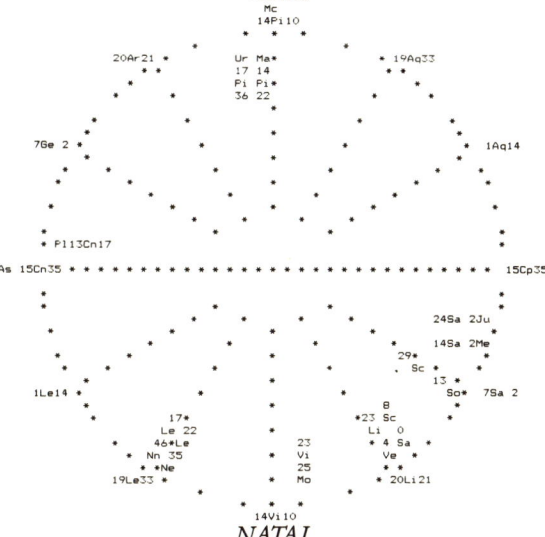

NATAL

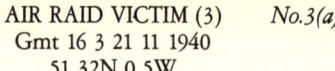

AIR RAID VICTIM (3)   No.3(a)
Gmt 16 3 21 11 1940
51 32N 0 5W

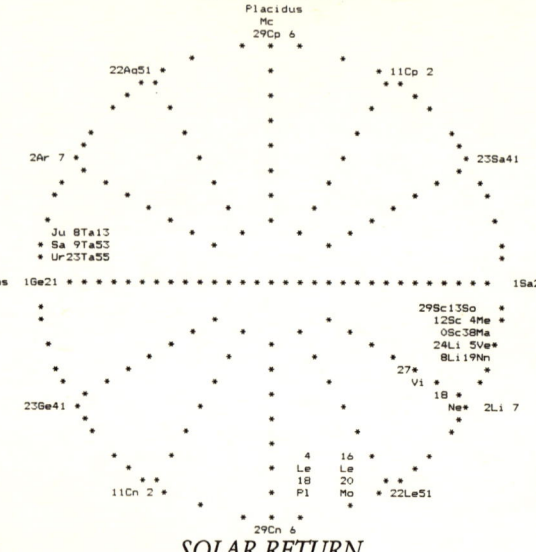

Ref:
Natal Chart No.3   **SOLAR RETURN**

No.3(b)   AIR RAID VICTIM (3)
Gmt 13 15 13 3 1941
51 32N 0 5W

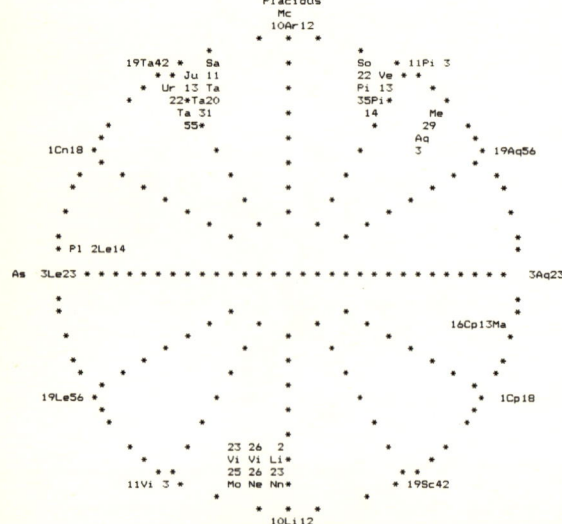

LUNAR RETURN   *Ref:*
Natal Chart No.3

AIR RAID VICTIM (4)   *No.4*
Gmt 22 30 28 8 1929
51 32N 0 5W

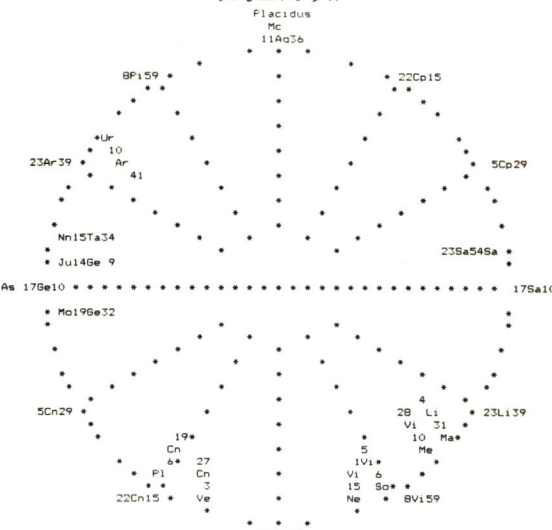

NATAL

No.4(a)   AIR RAID VICTIM (4)
Gmt 14 13 28 8 1940
51 32N 0 5W

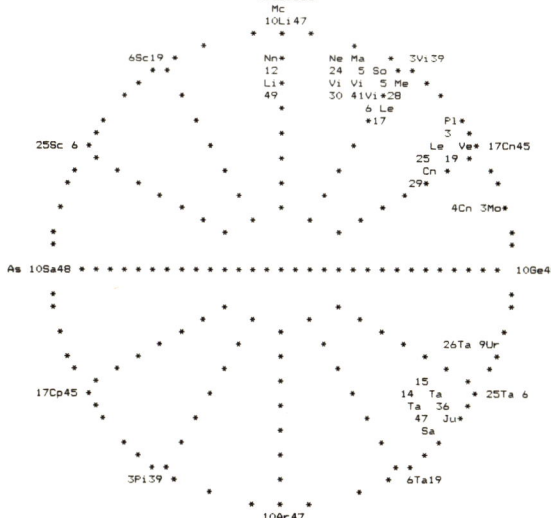

SOLAR RETURN

Ref:
Natal Chart No.4

AIR RAID VICTIM (4)   *No.4(b)*

Gmt 23 11 2 4 1941
51 32N 0 5W

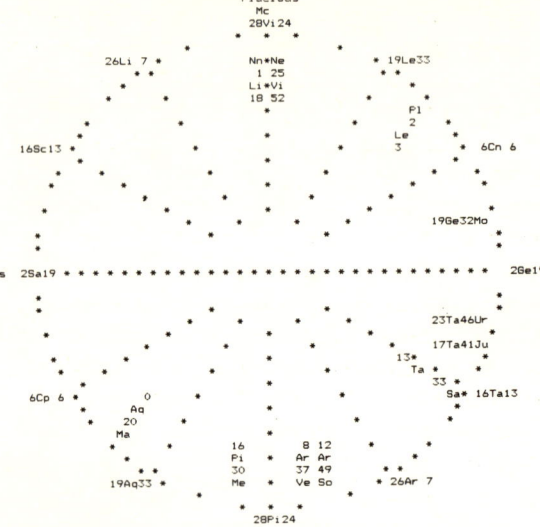

Ref:
Natal Chart No.4

LUNAR RETURN

No.5   AIR RAID VICTIMS

Gmt 12 0 9 4 1941
51 32N 0 5W

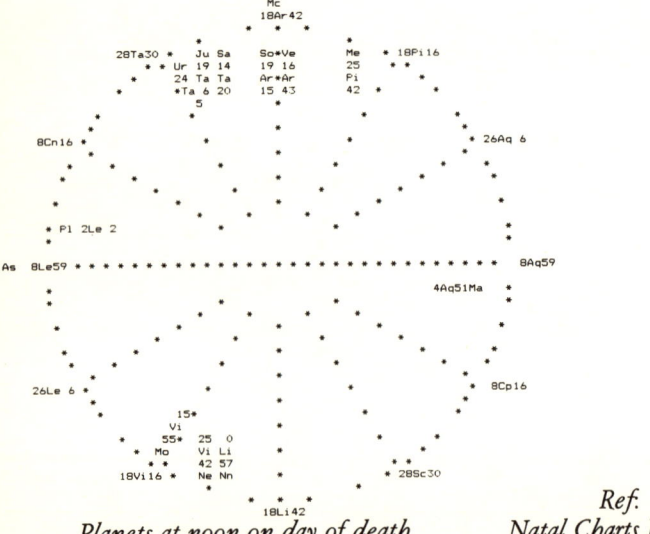

Planets at noon on day of death

Ref:
Natal Charts Nos.2–4

close to the lunar MC and the lunar Neptune is about ten degrees from the lower angle.

On the day the father died the transiting Moon was in Sagittarius applying to a conjunction of the natal Saturn and an opposition of the natal Sun/Mercury. The transiting Mars in 22° Aquarius was on the natal Descendant applying to an opposition of the natal Moon/Neptune. When the husband died (29.6.73) the transiting Moon in Gemini was conjunct the natal Sun/Mercury, opposite the natal Saturn. On 6.11.79, the transiting Moon was again in Gemini applying to a conjunction of the natal Sun and Mercury, opposite the natal Saturn. The transiting Mars in Leo was on the natal Ascendant applying to the conjunction of the natal Moon/Neptune.

All this may seem to be coincidental but it is these similarities which often open up the field for more intensive research which may uncover some fundamental laws concerning the operation of returns and the timing of events and conditions.

As has been stated elsewhere in this work, a few cases will not prove very much but if we have a repetition of contacts and patterns which coincide with events of a similar nature, then we may be able to assess future returns with some confidence.

Event: Death of father,   MARY   *No.1*
       29.12.1967   Gmt 21 52 21 12 1967
                       51 32N 0 20W

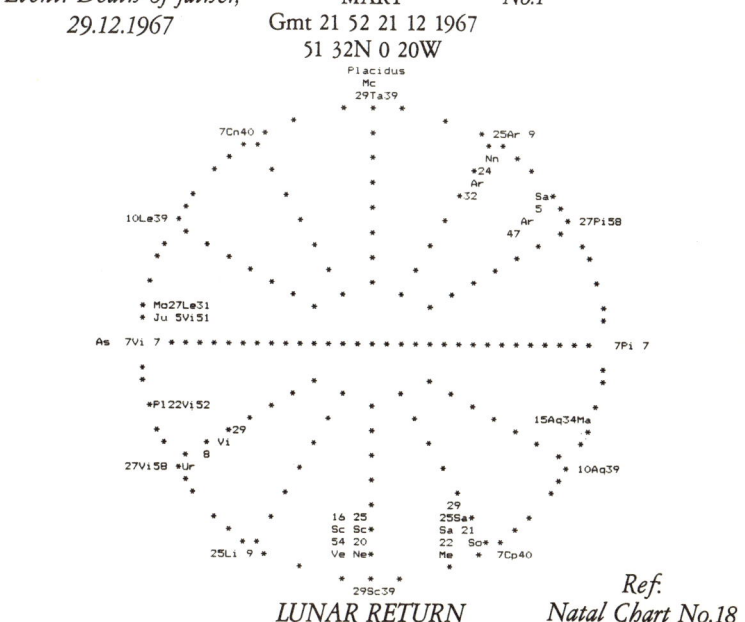

LUNAR RETURN   *Ref:*
                                Natal Chart No.18

Event: Death of husband, 29.6.73   MARY: S/R. 73/74   *No.2*

Gmt 0 4 12 6 1973

51 32N 0 20W

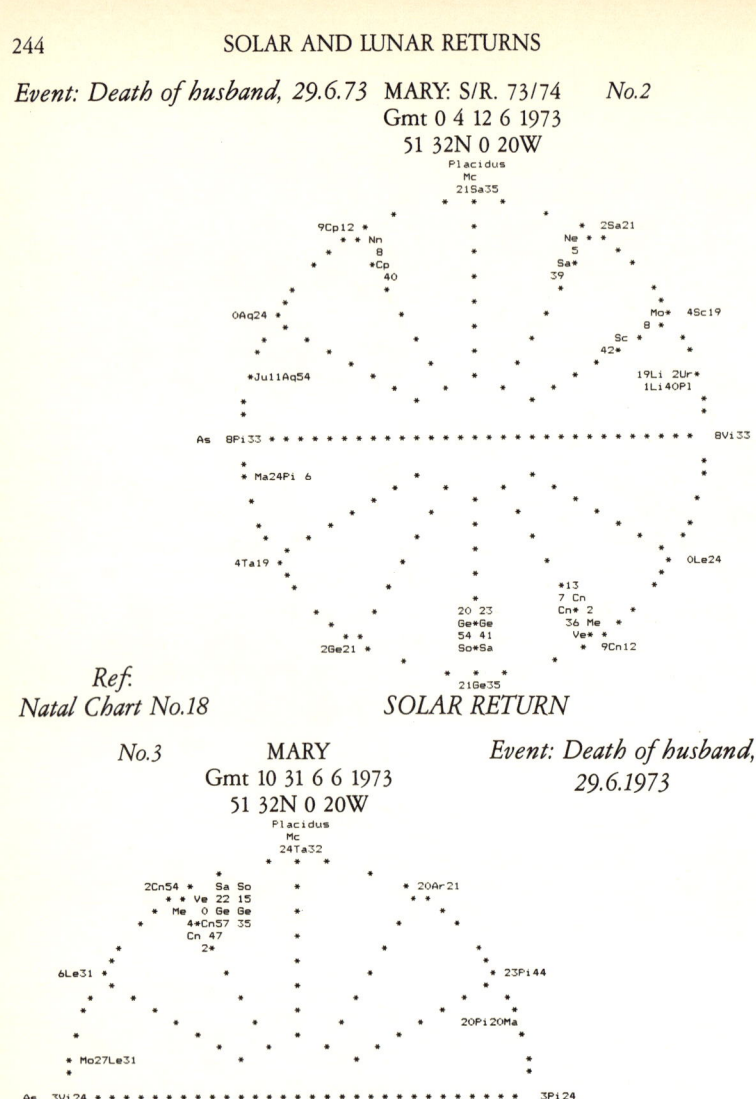

Ref:
Natal Chart No.18   SOLAR RETURN

No.3   MARY   *Event: Death of husband,*

Gmt 10 31 6 6 1973   *29.6.1973*

51 32N 0 20W

LUNAR RETURN   *Ref:*
Natal Chart No.18

PROGRESSED SOLAR RETURN   No.4

Ref:
Natal Chart No.18

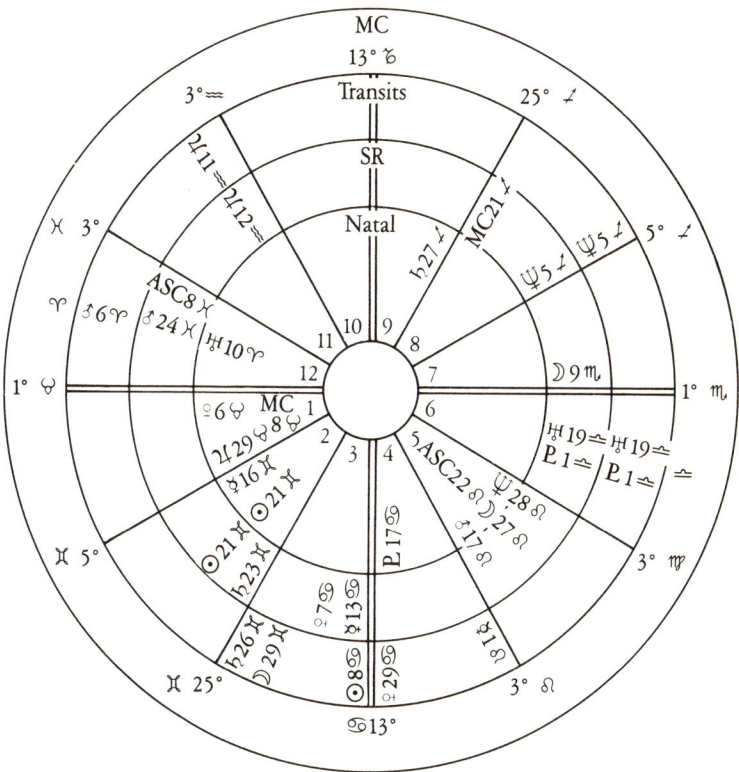

SOLAR RETURN				PROGRESSED RETURN			
Date 12.6.73 Time 00.04				Date 29. 6.73 Time 21.00			
	H	M	S		H	M	S
RA Sun	05	20	21	RA Sun PSR	06	34	37
RAMC	17	23	23	RA Sun SR −	05	20	21
Constant 1.2402				= Difference	01	14	16
Death of husband				× Constant =	01	32	06
(Tropical)				RAMC SR +	17	23	23
				RAMC PSR	18	55	29

Event: Death of
mother, 6.11.1979

MARY   No.5
Gmt 02 48 16 10 1979
51 32N 0 20W

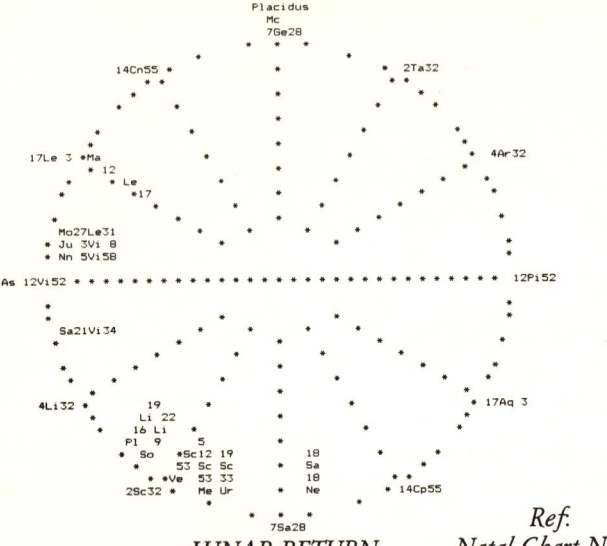

LUNAR RETURN   *Ref:*
Natal Chart No.18

10.

MUNDANE CHARTS

Ingress Charts

One question that must occur is that if the revolutions should be worked for the sidereal zodiac, so ought ingresses. That is to say, one should take the time that the Sun enters the cardinal constellations, instead of its entry into the signs. But the usual ingresses have proved themselves, time and again, to be valid, and it must remain for the advocates of the sidereal zodiac to demonstrate that theirs are better. Such a demonstration would, to my mind, be more conclusive than many personal returns, because the times of the ingresses and the subsequent events are on record. If these new ingresses are better, then the sooner this is proved and acknowledged, the happier it will be for all of us.

Charles E.O. Carter, Editorial, *Astrology*, Vol.23. No.3 1949

The editorial quoted above shows the fair-mindedness of Carter, whose approach to the then 'new-fangled' sidereal techniques showed a commendable tolerance often found lacking in some of his contemporaries.

The entry of the Sun into the four cardinal signs (Aries, Cancer, Libra and Capricorn) marks the commencement of what has been termed the Spring, Summer, Autumn and Winter Ingresses. Irrespective of their astrological significance the tropical ingresses are important astronomical phenomena and have always been regarded as significant. Likewise, the researches into sidereal techniques have demonstrated the importance of the Sun's entry into the cardinal constellations, particularly Capricorn, which occurs around about mid-January each year in contrast to the tropical entry which occurs about 21 December.

The traditional teaching regarding tropical ingresses was that their 'influence and indications' extended for the ensuing three months until the commencement of the following ingress. Additional research in relation to both the tropical and sidereal ingresses suggests that although the Aries, Cancer and Libra ingresses are significant, in some cases remarkably so, it is the Capricorn ingress which holds pride of place as the 'master chart of the year'. This is particularly true of the Sun's entry into sidereal Capricorn whose symbolism is often indicative of mundane events and conditions for periods and localities for which it is calculated.

The two types of solar ingresses are entirely different as there is now about twenty-four days difference between their dates. For example the Sun's entry into tropical Capricorn occurs at 04.02 UT 22.12.86 but its entry into sidereal Capricorn is 06.24 ET 15.1.87. ET = Ephemeris Time, which is usually quoted in ephemerides as Delta T. The value which is listed in seconds has to be added to the UT if using an ephemeris based on ET before interpolating to find the planetary positions. The sidereal time of a chart is found by using UT (GMT). For normal charting the difference between ET and UT can be disregarded, but for exact work such as the times of ingresses which may be listed in ET, the adjustment should be made.

The calculation of an ingress chart is in no way different from that of a solar return. The date and time of the entry is usually shown in most ephemerides, so it is comparatively simple to erect the ingress chart for the locality required. Sidereal ephemerides are now available which again saves a great amount of time and labour regarding calculations.

As with the usual solar and lunar returns, ingress charts can be progressed for a definite time and period but their indications have to be related to the conditions and nature of the particular area. Charts of countries, states, leaders and monarchs often reflect the cosmic patterns operating at certain times. All charts respond in one way or another to the law of subsumption and therefore much can be learned from comparing an ingress chart for a definite period with the charts of those politically prominent in a country's affairs and with the chart of the nation if available. It is not always easy to distinguish whether a particular contact in a leader's or monarch's chart will be expressed publically or privately. Some charts 'speak louder than others' but generally some indication can be obtained provided the data are reliable and an assessment is made which incorporates all known factors relative to the period and place under review.

The astrology of disasters illustrates vividly the cosmic connection which exists throughout existence. At the times of catastrophes and disasters, either natural or man-made, invariably the appropriate astrological pattern(s) will signify the event. The ingress chart for the locality may or may not show the potential for danger, although quite often it does, but when the chart 'comes alive', i.e. is progressed for the date and time of the disaster, the astrological correlation is all-apparent. The ideal to strive for in all studies such as these is to be able to pinpoint time and places in advance when a disaster is likely to occur. Much progress in this direction is being made but astrology is a complex combination of many factors some of which we do not, as yet, fully understand.

In the same way that the entry of the Sun into cardinal signs and constellations is important, so also is the entry of the Moon. These lunar ingresses occur each month and are said to be indicative of the period to which they relate. As with the sidereal solar ingress, that for the entry into Capricorn is considered the most important.

For the review of any given period the solar ingress chart in conjunction with the lunar ingress chart is useful and these along with the Capricorn ingress charts often indicate in broad outline the pattern of the period. One can, of course, calculate other types of charts such as the demi-solar return, etc., but unless there is a need to do an 'in-depth' study of a particular period or condition with as many relevant return charts as possible, it is better to concentrate on the most important return charts rather than be overwhelmed by a 'sea of charting, figures and symbols' which, for a beginner using these techniques, will cause endless confusion and desperation.

The procedure for charting and progressing mundane return charts is not difficult and follows the practice adopted in calculating the usual solar and lunar returns. There is a slight technicality regarding sidereal charts when a tropical ephemeris has to be used because of the lack of a sidereal one, but the examples should make the procedure clear.

Calculation of Ingress Charts (Tropical)
The time and date of the Sun's entry into the signs is given in most ephemerides so the calculation of the chart is quite straightforward. With the older ephemerides this information is not listed so we have no alternative but to calculate the time of entry ourselves. Fortunately, Neil Michelsen's *American Ephemeris for the Twentieth Century*

has all the information that is required.

Example No.1:
Required the tropical Capricorn ingress for 1913/14 at London.

From Ephemeris:	H	M	S
Dec. 1913, Sun enters Capricorn 22 Dec.	10	35	00 UT
ST at 0 hr. UT	+ 05	59	47
Correction 9.86 sec. per hour (10.35)	+ 00	01	44
ST at Greenwich	16	36	31
Long. Equiv.	—	—	—
RAMC 1913 Capricorn ingress	16	36	31

Asc. 15° Aquarius: MC 10° Sagittarius.

Example No.2:
Same data, at New York:

ST at Greenwich	16	36	31
New York slow on Greenwich (73° 57′W)	− 04	55	48
RAMC 1913 Capricorn ingress	11	40	43

Asc. 7° Sagittarius: MC 24° Virgo.

Example No.3:
Same data. at Berlin:

	H	M	S
ST at Greenwich	16	36	31
Berlin fast on Greenwich (13° 23′ E)	+ 00	53	32
RAMC 1913 Capricorn ingress	17	30	03

Asc. 11° Pisces: MC 23° Sagittarius.

If the time and date of the ingress had not been tabulated in the ephemeris the following calculation would have been needed:

	Deg.	Min.	Sec.	
Sun's long. 22.12.13 Noon. UT				
Capricorn	00	03	37	
Sun's long. required Capricorn	00	00	00	
Difference	00	03	37	(0.060)
Sun's daily motion 21/22 Dec.	01	01	08	(1.020)

Calculator:

$$\frac{0.060 \times 24}{1.020} = 1 \text{ hr. } 25 \text{ min. before noon } 22.12.13$$

Sun enters Capricorn: 10.35 UT 22.12.1913

The planets' positions are calculated for the UT of the return with the Ascendant, MC and cusps extracted for the sidereal time (RAMC) of the return. The 1913/14 Capricorn ingress can be studied in relation to the outbreak of the First World War—23.00 UT 4.8.14, London. The 1917/18 Capricorn ingress can, in the same manner, be analysed in relation to the Armistice, 05.00 UT 11.11.18, 49° 25′ N 2° 29′ E. In addition to the Capricorn ingress, the Sun's entry into Aries and Cancer during 1914 may also provide supplementary information concerning the calamity which engulfed so many nations during the period 1914/18.

Aries ingress 1914:	H	M	S	
Sun enters Aries 21 March	11	11	00	UT
ST 0 hr. UT 21.3.14	+ 11	50	40	
Correction	+ 00	01	50	
RAMC at London	23	03	30	

Asc. 16° Cancer: MC 15° Pisces.

Cancer ingress 1914:			
Sun enters Cancer 22 June	06	55	00
ST 0 hr. UT 22 June	+ 17	57	19
Correction	+ 00	01	08
RAMC at London	00	53	27

Asc. 6° Leo: MC 14° Aries.

Aries ingress at Berlin:			
RAMC at Berlin	23	57	02

Asc. 27° Cancer: MC 29° Pisces.

Cancer ingress at Berlin:	H	M	S
RAMC at Berlin	01	46	59

Asc. 16° Leo: MC 28° Aries.

The ceasefire sounded on the Western Front at 11.00 UT 11.11.18.
The Capricorn ingress chart 1917 covers this period in conjunction
with the other three ingress charts (Aries, Cancer and Libra).

At London:	*Berlin*	*Western Front*
		*49° 25'N 2° 29'E
Capricorn ingress 1917		
09.46 UT 22.12.17.		
RAMC 15.47.31	16.41.03	15.57.27
Asc. 26° Capricorn	16° Aquarius	3° Aquarius
MC 29° Scorpio	12° Sagittarius	1° Sagittarius
Aries ingress 1918		
10.26 UT 21.3.18		
RAMC 22.18.31	23.12.03	22.28.27
Asc. 6° Cancer	18° Cancer	6° Cancer
MC 2° Pisces	17° Pisces	5° Pisces
At London:	*Berlin*	*Western Front*
Cancer ingress 1918		
05.59 UT 22.6.18		
RAMC 23.57.26	00.50.58	00.07.02
Asc. 26° Cancer	6° Leo	26° Cancer
MC 29° Pisces	13° Aries	2° Aries
Libra ingress 1918		
20.46 UT 23.9.18		
RAMC 20.53.32	21.47.04	21.03.28
Asc. 16° Gemini	1° Cancer	15° Gemini
MC 11° Aquarius	24° Aquarius	13° Aquarius
Armistice signed		
05.00 UT 11.11.18		
RAMC 08.18.08	09.11.40	08.28.04
Asc. 24° Libra	3° Scorpio	26° Libra
MC 2° Leo	15° Leo	4° Leo

As the lunar ingresses are also important it may be interesting
to see how the four ingresses preceding the Armistice relate to the
overall pattern of the solar ingresses.

Lunar Ingress

At London	Berlin	Western Front
Aries		
05.14 UT 18.10.18		
RAMC 06.57.32	07.51.04	07.07.28
Asc. 10° Libra	19° Libra	12° Libra
MC 13° Cancer	26° Cancer	15° Cancer
Cancer		
06.40 UT 24.10.18		
RAMC 08.47.27	09.40.59	08.57.23
Asc. 29° Libra	8° Scorpio	2° Scorpio
MC 9° Leo	22° Leo	11° Leo
Libra		
10.45 UT 31.10.18		
RAMC 13.20.43	14.14.15	13.30.39
Asc. 19° Sagittarius	29° Sagittarius	23° Sagittarius
MC 22° Libra	6° Scorpio	24° Libra
Capricorn		
22.50 UT 7.11.18		
RAMC 01.55.17	02.48.49	02.05.13
Asc. 17° Leo	26° Leo	17° Leo
MC 1° Taurus	14° Taurus	3° Taurus

The following charts summarize all the planetary positions for the ingress data. These may prove useful for studying with other forms of return techniques. Similar data for the Second World War are also listed.

Progressing the Ingress Charts

These charts can be progressed for any day in the return year, using either the Mean Sun rate or the Apparent Sun.

The 1913 Capricorn Ingress with its Mercury/Saturn opposition exactly on the angles and the Mars/Neptune conjunction in Cancer opposite Jupiter, is not a particularly favourable chart. When the chart is progressed using the Apparent Sun we have the transit Mars/Venus in Virgo close to the progressed MC. The day war was declared (4.8.14) the transiting Moon in 28° Capricorn was opposed to the ingress Mars/Neptune and opposed the Mercury/Neptune conjunction in Cancer.

Radix
DECEMBER SOLSTICE: 1913   *No.1*
Gmt 10 35 22 12 1913 (London)
51 32N 0 0E

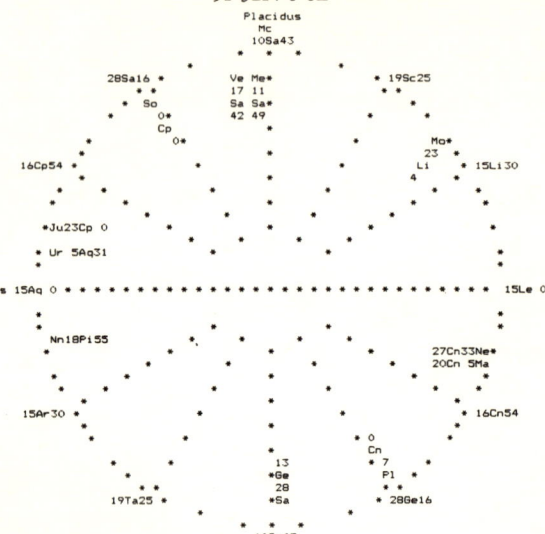

```
                    Placidus
                       Mc
                     10Sa43
                  *       *
   28Sa16 *         Ve Me*        * 19Sc25
      * *           17 11
      * So          Sa Sa*            *
         O*         42 49          *
         Cp           *         *
         O*           *       Mo*
                      *        23
 16Cp54               *       Li     * 15Li30
                      *        4
                      *       *   *
     *Ju23Cp 0        *    *        *
      * Ur 5Aq31      *           *
 As 15Aq 0 * * * * * * * * * * * * * * * * * * 15Le 0
     Nn18Pi55        *    *       27Cn33Ne*
                   *   *        20Cn 5Ma
       *                          *
  15Ar30                          * 16Cn54
      *             *        * O
                             Cn
         *        *      * 7
         *       13      Pl
         *      *Ge      * *
   19Ta25 *      28      * 28Ge16
                *Sa
                10Ge43
```

Radix
No.2   DECEMBER SOLSTICE: 1913
Gmt 10 35 22 12 1913 (Berlin)
52 30N 13 23E

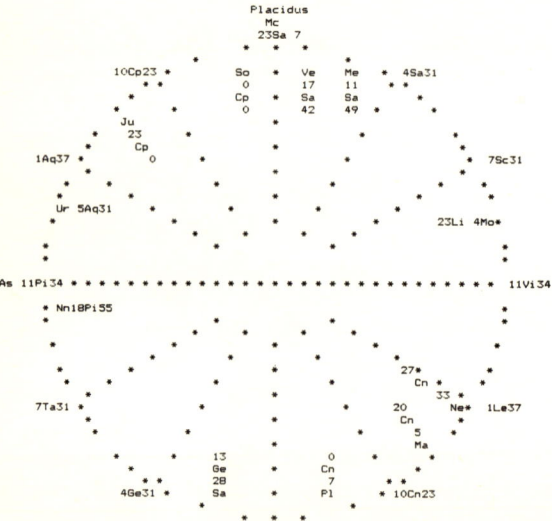

```
                    Placidus
                       Mc
                     23Sa 7
                 *     *
   10Cp23 *       So   * Ve   Me  * 4Sa31
      * *          O     17   11  * *
      *   *        Cp  * Sa   Sa  *
      Ju           O     42   49 *
      23
      Cp                        *
 1Aq37 *    O                    * 7Sc31
      *                        *
   Ur 5Aq31                  * 23Li 4Mo*
     *                      *
 As 11Pi34 * * * * * * * * * * * * * * * * * 11Vi34
   * Nn18Pi55                     *
       *                        *
       *                      *
       *          *        27*
       *                   Cn
                      *      33 *
  7Ta31              *     20  Ne* 1Le37
                          Cn   *
                     *    5  *
                          Ma
     *      *   13     *  O   *
                Ge     *  Cn  * *
    4Ge31 *     28        7   * 10Cn23
                Sa      Pl
                * *   *
                23Ge 7
```

Radix
WW1: DECLARATION   *No.3*
Gmt 23 0 4 8 1914 (London)
51 32N 0 8W

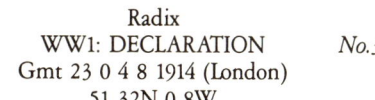

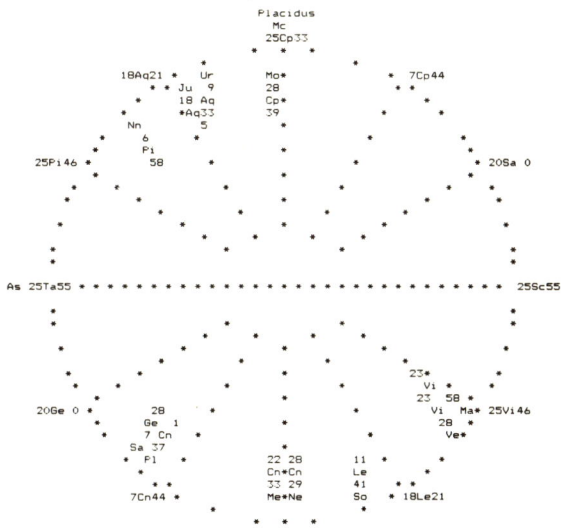

```
                        Placidus
                          Mc
                        25Cp33
                       *   *    *
  18Aq21  *    Ur        Mo*        *   7Cp44
      * * Ju   9         28            * *
    *    18 Aq           Cp*
    *    *Aq33           39        *         *
     Nn        5                *
      6     *                  *
      Pi                      *
25Pi46  *    58       *       *                  *  20Sa 0
     *                 *       *
    *                   *       *
   *                     *       *
  *                       *       *
  *                        *       *
As 25Ta55 * * * * * * * * * * * * * * * * * * * * * *  25Sc55
  *                        *       *
  *                       *       *
   *                     *       *
    *                   *       *        23*
     *                 *       *         Vi
      *               *       *       23  58  *
20Ge 0  *       28      *       *      Vi Ma* 25Vi46
     *        Ge  1     *       *       28   *
    *         7 Cn   *         *        Ve*
              Sa 37           *
     *        P1    *      22 28    11  *       *
      *      *  *          Cn*Cn    Le
        * *              33 29    41   * *
     7Cn44 *  *           Me*Ne    So  *  18Le21
              *       *                 *
                   *    *    *
                     25Cn33
```

Radix
No. 4   WW1: DECLARATION
Gmt 23 0 4 8 1914 (Berlin)
52 30N 13 23E

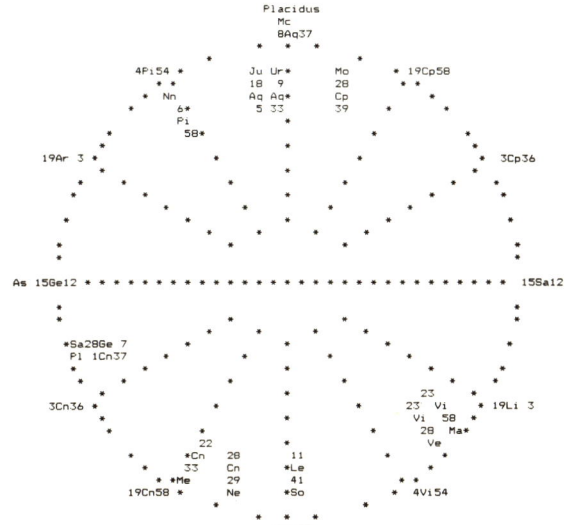

```
                        Placidus
                          Mc
                        8Aq37
                       *   *    *
  4Pi54  *       Ju Ur*      Mo    *  19Cp58
      * *        18   9      28      * *
    *   Nn       Aq Aq*      Cp    *    *
    *            5  33       39   *
      6*                   *
      Pi                  *
      58*               *                *
19Ar 3  *             *       *          *  3Cp36
     *              *       *       *   *
    *              *       *       *   *
   *              *       *       *
  *              *       *       *
  *             *       *       *
As 15Ge12 * * * * * * * * * * * * * * * * * * * *  15Sa12
  *             *       *       *
   *             *       *       *
  *Sa28Ge 7      *       *       *
   P1 1Cn37   *         *       *
     *   *           *       *       *
    *   *           *       *     23
3Cn36 *            *       *     23  Vi   *  19Li 3
     *            *       *      Vi  58  *
        *       22      *       28  Ma*
       *      *Cn   28    11     Ve
        *     33   Cn   *Le         *
        * *Me     29   41      * *
   19Cn58 *      Ne   *So      *  4Vi54
              *       *       *  *
                   *   *   *
                   8Le37
```

Radix
ARIES INGRESS 1914   No.5
Gmt 11 11 21 3 1914
51 32N 0 0E

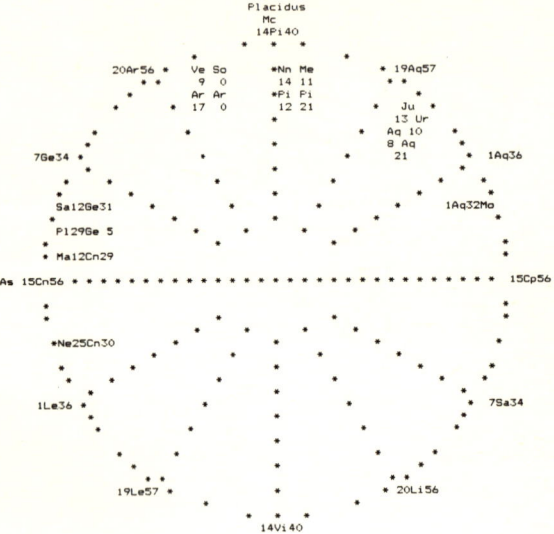

Radix
No.6   CANCER INGRESS 1914
Gmt 6 55 22 6 1914
51 32N 0 0E

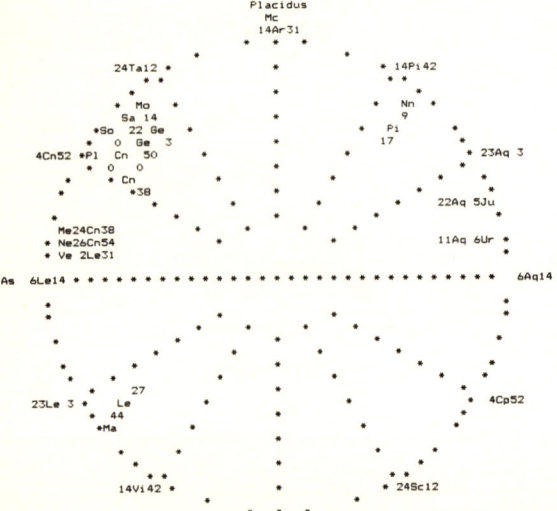

Radix
DECEMBER SOLSTICE: 1917   *No.7*
Gmt 9 46 22 12 1917
51 32N 0 0E

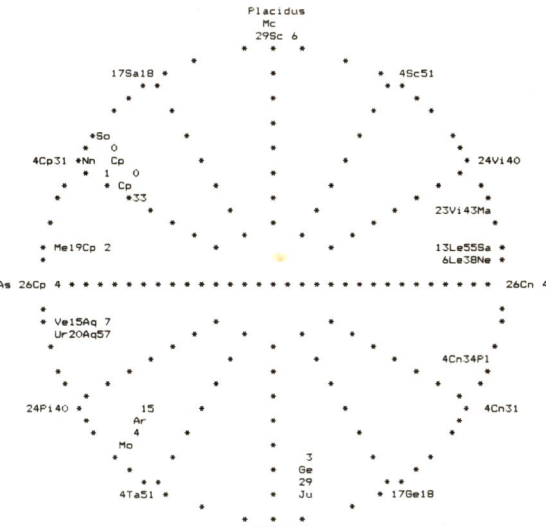

Radix
No.8   ### ARIES INGRESS 1918
Gmt 10 26 21 3 1918
51 32N 0 0E

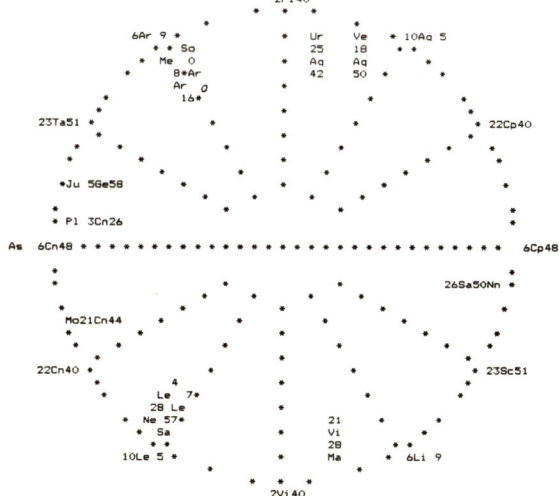

Radix
CANCER INGRESS 1918   *No.9*
Gmt 5 59 22 6 1918
51 32N 0 0E

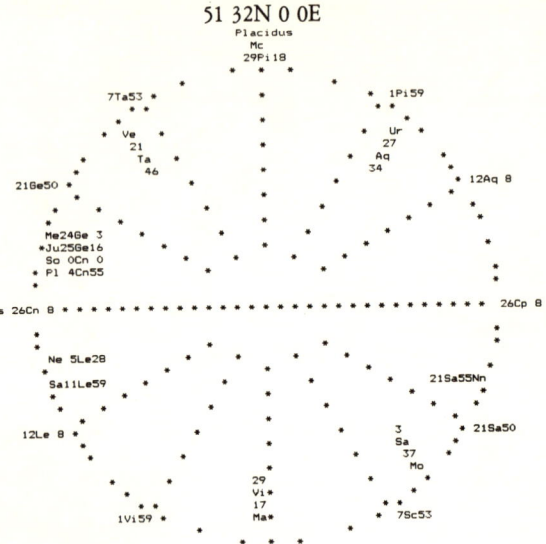

Radix
No.10   LIBRA INGRESS 1918
Gmt 20 46 23 9 1918
51 32N 0 0E

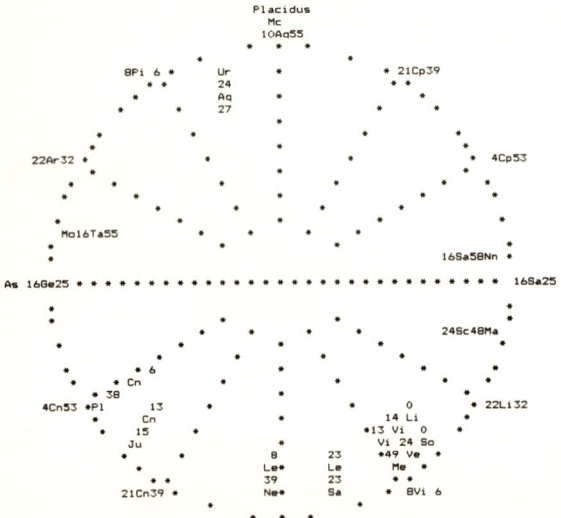

Radix
LUNAR INGRESS: ARIES   *No.11*
Gmt 5 14 18 10 1918
51 32N 0 0E

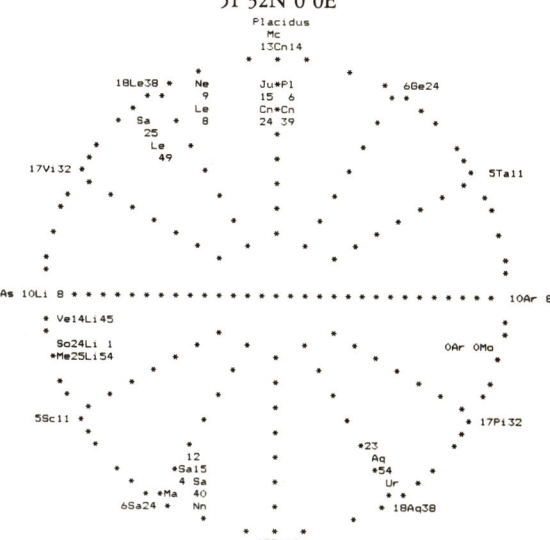

Radix
No.12   LUNAR INGRESS: CANCER
Gmt 6 40 24 10 1918
51 32N 0 0E

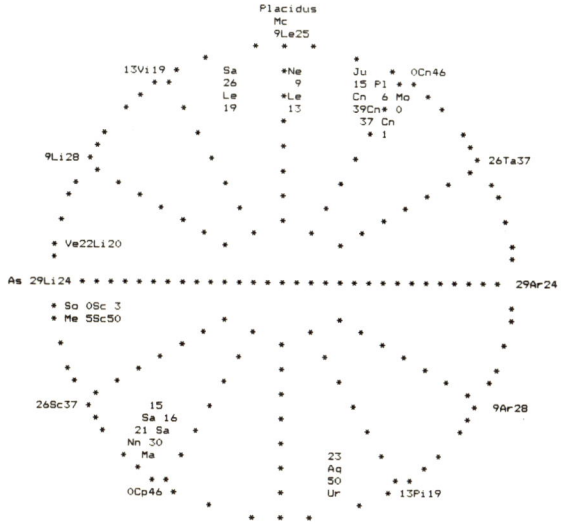

Radix
WW1: ARMISTICE   *No.13*
Gmt 5 0 11 11 1918
49 25N 2 29E

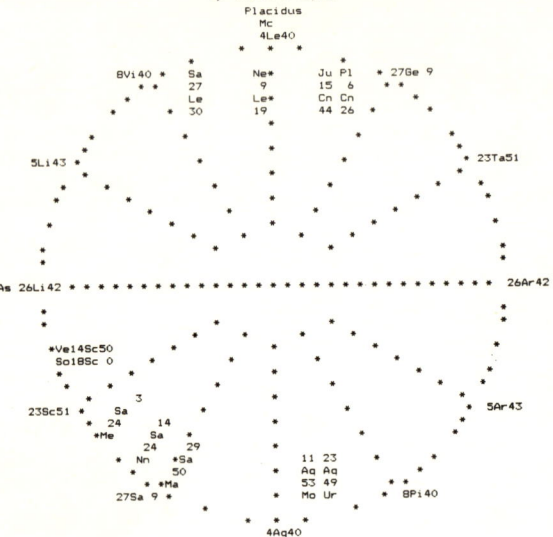

```
                    Placidus
                      Mc
                    4Le40
                *   *   *   *
          BVi40 *  Sa    Ne*     Ju Pl  * 27Ge 9
             * *   27     9      15  6   * *
                   Le    Le*     Cn Cn
                *      30   19    44 26  *     *
           *                    *             *
     5Li43 *                  *                    * 23Ta51
       *                                         *
          *                                     *
             *                               *
          *                                  *
          *
  As 26Li42 * * * * * * * * * * * * * * * * * * * 26Ar42
          *                                     *
     *Ve14Sc50                               *
      So18Sc 0                              *
          *                               *
    23Sc51 *    Sa   3                  *         * 5Ar43
             *  24   14                *
           *Me   Sa   *               *
                 24   29             *
           *   Nn  *Sa              *  11 23
                    50            *   Aq Aq    *
             * *Ma               *   53 49   * *
          27Sa 9 *              *    Mo Ur  * 8Pi40
                    *         *
                       4Aq40
```

Radix
No.14   ## LUNAR INGRESS: LIBRA
Gmt 10 45 31 10 1918
51 32N 0 0E

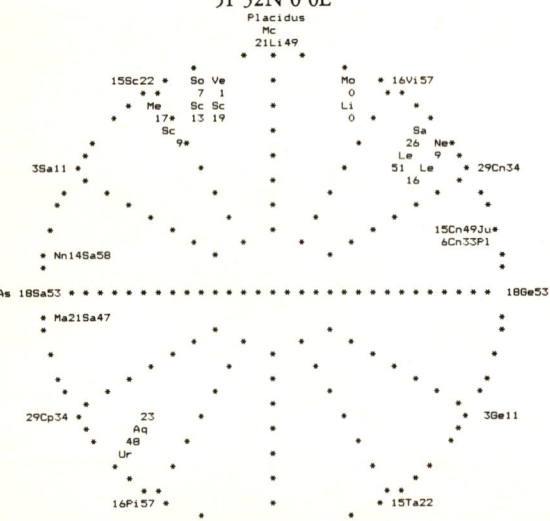

```
                    Placidus
                      Mc
                    21Li49
                *   *   *   *
     15Sc22 *   So Ve    *      Mo  * 16Vi57
         * *    7  1            0   * *
     *    Me   Sc Sc   *        Li
          17*  13 19            0   *      Sa
          Sc                            *  26  Ne*
          9*               *            Le  9  *
    3Sa11 *                  *       51  Le   * 29Cn34
       *                           *    16   *
          *                             *
             *                       *    15Cn49Ju*
          *                          *    6Cn33P1
     * Nn14Sa58              *        *
  As 18Sa53 * * * * * * * * * * * * * * * * * * 18Ge53
     * Ma21Sa47                      *
          *                        *
       *                         *
          *                     *
    29Cp34 *    23            *               * 3Ge11
             *  Aq           *
                48          *
                Ur         *
             *           *
          16Pi57 *      *      * 15Ta22
                    *   *
                    21Ar49
```

Radix
LUNAR INGRESS: CAPRICORN   *No.15*
Gmt 22 50 7 11 1918
51 32N 0 0E

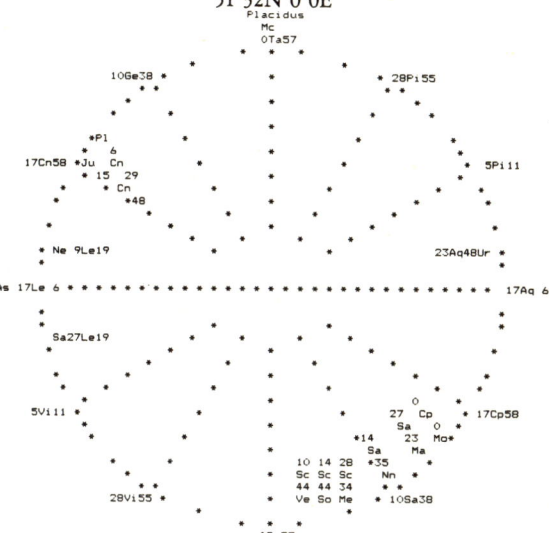

Radix
No.16   WW2: DECLARATION
Gmt 10 0 3 9 1939
51 30N 0 7W

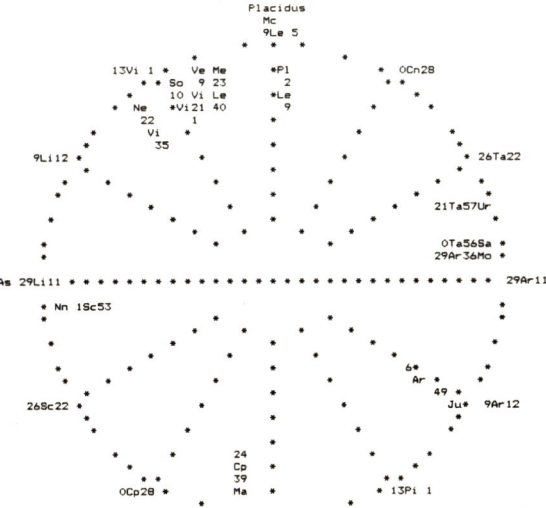

Radix
ARIES INGRESS: 1939   *No.17*
Gmt 12 28 21 3 1939
51 30N 0 7W

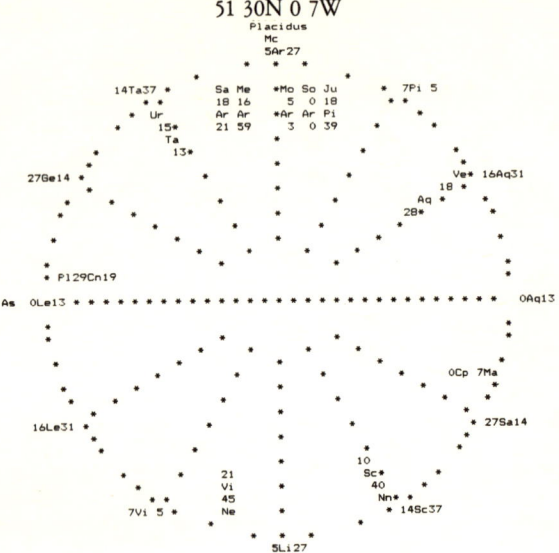

Radix
No.18   CANCER INGRESS: 1939
Gmt 7 39 22 6 1939
51 30N 0 7W

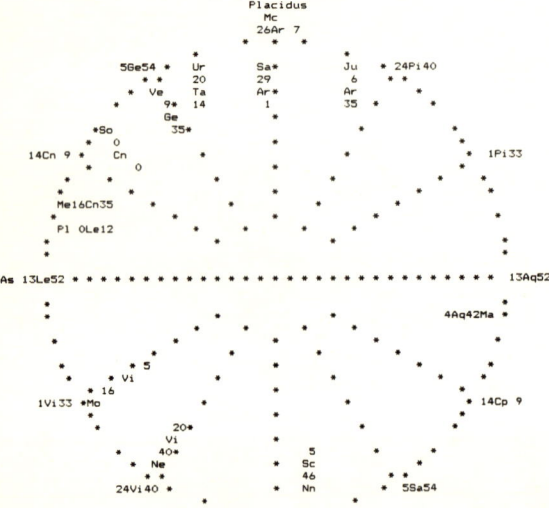

Radix
DECEMBER SOLSTICE: 1938   *No.19*
Gmt 12 14 22 12 1938
51 30N 0 7W

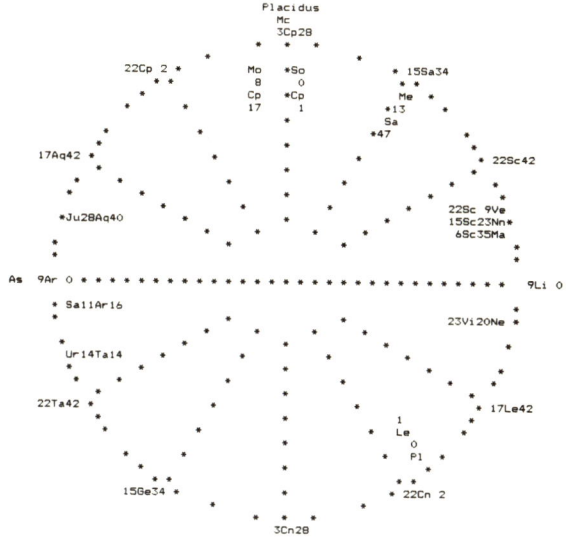

```
                            Placidus
                              Mc
                             3Cp28
                           *   *   *
          22Cp 2 *             Mo  *So           * 15Sa34
                  * *          B    O              * *
                               Cp  *Cp             Me  *
                               17   1             *13   *
                                                   Sa
                                                  *47
     17Aq42 *                                             * 22Sc42
                                                      *
        *Ju28Aq40                                    228c 9Ve
                                                    15Sc23Nn*
                                                    6Sc35Ma
  As  9Ar 0 * * * * * * * * * * * * * * * * * * * * * * * 9Li 0
        * Sa11Ar16                                 23Vi20Ne *
       Ur14Ta14                                        *
     22Ta42 *                                        * 17Le42
                                            1
                                            Le
                                            O
                                            P1  *
        15Ge34 *                        * 22Cn 2
                             3Cn28
```

Using the Mean Sun rate, we have:

4.8.14 Mean Sun	8	50	38
Ingress Mean Sun	18	01	30 −
Arc	14	49	08
Ingress RAMC	16	36	31 +
RAMC prog.	07	25	39

At London: Asc. 15° Libra: MC 20° Cancer.

This brings the ingress Mars/Jupiter to the fourth/tenth angles with Neptune also within orbs. The ingress Moon (23° Libra) is close to the Ascendant. The transiting Moon (28° Capricorn) is close to the fourth angle. When the Armistice was signed in 1918, the transiting Moon in 12° Aquarius was precisely opposed to the Sun (12° Leo) in the war declaration chart. This contact is, of course, repeated each month, but it is interesting to see it close to the angles at this particular time.

The lunar ingress into Aries prior to the Armistice has Libra rising with Venus, planet of peace and victory, exactly rising. Jupiter and Pluto hold the Midheaven. Progressed by the Mean Sun rate brings the Ascendant to 27° Libra and the MC 6° Leo. The lunar Mercury is now conjunct the Ascendant with Neptune close to the MC.

The lunar ingress into Cancer prior to 11.11.18 has Neptune exactly on the MC with Venus, Sun and Mercury on the Ascendant. The Moon's entry into Libra and Capricorn has Venus within about ten degrees of the angles conjunct the Sun. The rising Mars seems strange in a chart indicative of peace overtures; perhaps it shows the efforts being expended to reach an agreement.

The December Solstice prior to the outbreak of the Second World War has a conjunction of the Sun and Moon in Capricorn on the Midheaven. Saturn, the 'heavy one', is conjunct the Ascendant and in close aspect with the Moon. The war declaration chart (3.9.39) has Pluto on the Midheaven with the Moon exactly setting in Aries. Mars aspects the Moon and Ascendant although it is widely conjunct the fourth cusp. Progressing the ingress chart (1938) by the Mean Sun rate brings the ingress Neptune to the progressed Midheaven and the transiting Mars to the Ascendant. The Aries ingress prior to the war has the Sun/Moon conjunction exactly on the MC with Pluto close to the Ascendant. At the Cancer ingress, Saturn is exactly on the MC with Mars and Pluto in opposition close to the Asc./Desc.

The foregoing is an outline of what can be extracted from this type of return provided that the indications in the relevant charts are all related one to another. Many of these mundane charts show 'collective responses' and prove very informative particularly when they are compared with the national chart (if known) and the charts of individuals who are prominent in the affairs of the nation.

The various types of progressions which are applicable to personal charts can be used with these ingress charts when a particular month or period requires to be reviewed.

Calculation of Ingress Charts (Sidereal)

If a sidereal ephemeris for the period required is available, the chart calculations present no difficulties. However, when no sidereal ephemeris is available the tropical longitude corresponding to 0° of the sidereal Sun must be calculated.

Example:
Required the time and date of the Capricorn sidereal solar ingress for 1918.

From tropical ephemeris 14 January 1918
SVP 6° 23′ 57″ deducted from 30° = 23° 36′ 03″ Ayanamsa =

tropical longitude of the sidereal Sun which is used to calculate the time of the return.

Tropical Sun Noon UT	Deg.	Min.	Sec.	
14.1.1918	23	32	01	Capricorn
Sid. Sun tropical long.	23	36	03	Capricorn
Difference	00	04	02	(0.067)
Sun's motion 14/15 Jan.	01	01	09	(1.02)

$$\frac{0.067 \times 24}{1.02} = 1.58 = 1 \text{ hr. } 35 \text{ min. after noon}$$

= 13.35 UT 14.1.1918 = time and date of sidereal Capricorn solar ingress.

The planets' positions are calculated for 13.35 UT and transposed to the sidereal longitudes (+ SVP − 30°), likewise the Ascendant, MC, and house cusps.

The lunar ingresses are dealt with in a similar manner to that of the solar ingresses.

The Asc. and MC are found in the usual manner:

	H	M	S
ST 0 hr. UT 14.1.18	07	30	36
Time elapsed	+ 13	35	00
Correction	+ 00	02	14
RAMC at London	21	07	50

Asc. 26° Taurus: MC 20° Capricorn (sidereal)

At Berlin:

RAMC	22	01	22

Asc. 10° Gemini: MC 4° Aquarius: (sidereal)

Western Front

RAMC	21	17	46

Asc. 25° Taurus: MC 23° Capricorn (sidereal)

The sidereal Capricorn lunar ingress immediately preceding the Armistice occurred at: 19.33 UT 9.11.18

SVP 6° 23′ 19″ 10 Nov. 1918 deducted from 30° = 23° 36′ 41″

	Deg.	Min.	Sec.	
Tropical Moon Noon UT 10.11.18	02	29	53	Aquarius
Sid. Moon tropical long.	23	36	41	Capricorn
Difference	08	53	12	(8.88)
Moon's motion 9/10 Nov.	12	58	00	(12.96)

$$\frac{8.88 \times 24}{12.96} = 16.448 = 16 \text{ hr. } 27 \text{ min. before noon}$$

$$= \underline{19.33 \text{ UT } 9.11.18} = \text{time and date of lunar ingress.}$$

	H	M	S
ST 0 hr. 9.11.18	03	09	26
Time elapsed	+ 19	33	00
Correction	+ 00	03	13
RAMC at London	22	45	39

Asc. 17° Gemini: MC 15° Aquarius: (sidereal).

The sidereal Capricorn lunar ingress for January 1986 occurred at
19.57 UT 10 January:
Check using a tropical ephemeris:
SVP 5° 27' 26" (10.1.86) from 30°   = 24° 32' 34"

	D	M	S	
Tropical Moon midnight 10/11th	26	59	25	Capricorn
Sidereal Moon's tropical long.	24	32	34	Capricorn
Difference	02	26	51	(2.447)
Moon's 12-hour motion 10th	07	14	37	(7.244)

$$\frac{2.447 \times 12}{7.244} = 4.05 = 4 \text{ hr. } 03 \text{ min. before}$$

midnight (0 hr.) = $\underline{7.57 = 19.57 \text{ UT } 10.1.86}$

	H	M	S
ST 0 hr. UT 10.1.86	07	16	53
Time elapsed	+ 19	57	00
Correction	+ 00	03	17
ST at Greenwich	03	17	10
Longitude Equiv. (80° 50'W)	− 05	23	20
RAMC	21	53	50

Asc. 19° Taurus: MC 1° Aquarius: (sidereal).

The tropical Capricorn lunar ingress occurred at 03.42 UT 9.1.86.

		H	M	S
ST 0 hr. UT 9.1.86		07	12	57
Time elapsed	+	03	42	00
Correction	+	00	00	36
ST at Greenwich		10	55	33
Longitude Equiv. (80° 50′W)	−	05	23	20
RAMC		05	32	13

Asc. 24° Virgo: MC 24° Gemini: (tropical) at Latitude 28° 28′ North.

The Sun's entry into sidereal Capricorn occurred at 0.10 ET 15.1.86 (*American Sidereal Ephemeris*)

SVP 5° 27′ 25″		H	M	S
ST 0 hr. UT		07	36	36
Time elapsed UT	+	00	09	00
Correction	+	00	00	01
ST at Greenwich		07	45	37
Longitude Equiv. (80° 50′W)	−	05	23	20
RAMC		02	22	17

Asc. 18° Cancer: MC 13° Aries: (sidereal) at Latitude 28° 28′ North.

Tropical solar Capricorn ingress occurred at 22.08 UT 21.12.85.

		H	M	S
ST 0 hr. UT 21.12.85		05	58	02
Time elapsed	+	22	08	00
Correction	+	00	03	38
ST at Greenwich		04	09	40
Longitude Equiv. (80° 50′W)	−	05	23	20
RAMC		22	46	20

Asc. 25° Gemini: MC 10° Pisces: (tropical) at Latitude 28° 28′ North.

The foregoing Capricorn ingresses, both sidereal and tropical, cover the period of the American Shuttle disaster which occurred at 16.39 UT (nearest minute) 28 January 1986 at the above latitude and longitude. The data are from current TV and press reports.

Event Chart Calculations:
Tropical

		H	M	S
ST 0 hr. UT 28.1.86		08	27	51
Time elapsed	+	16	39	00
Correction	+	00	02	44
ST at Greenwich		01	09	35
Longitude Equiv. (80° 50′W)	−	05	23	20
RAMC		19	46	15

Asc. 7° Taurus: MC 25° Capricorn: (tropical) at Latitude 28° 28′ North.

11.

MUNDANE CHARTS AND EVENTS

Event Chart: Shuttle explosion.
Sidereal   28.1.86 SVP 5° 27′ 23″
Calculations as for tropical and convert by + 5° 27′ less 30°.
Asc. 12° Aries: MC 0° Capricorn.

The explosion of the American Space Shuttle was a disastrous event, not only for American space technology but also for the unfortunate astronauts who perished in this calamity. In studying the astrological indications of an event such as this there are many techniques which can be employed. We could, for example, study the eclipses positions for the months preceding the disaster and note any correspondences with the 'disaster chart'. We could also consider how the United States foundation chart was affected at this particular time. This national chart with Gemini rising has been questioned not only regarding the time—early morning 4 July 1776, Philadelphia—but also regarding the actual day. For a work devoted solely to this question, Helen Boyd's book is very worthwhile (see references).

So far as return charts are concerned, these should show appropriate indications at the time of the disaster. The personal charts of those that perished will, if related to the event, also show appropriate correspondences. The only civilian among the seven killed in the Shuttle disaster was Christa McAuliffe, a teacher, whose birth data are given as: 10.13 p.m. EDT 2.9.1948. Boston, Mass., which is equivalent to 02.13 UT 3.9.1948 (see data references).

Christa: *Natal chart* (tropical)
Sun. 10° 28′ 39″ Virgo: Moon. 5° 01′ Virgo:
RAMC Boston. 42° 22′N 71° 04′W 20.17.15

Solar return 1985/86: 00.56 UT 3.9.85. RAMC 19.00.10
Asc. 26° Aries: MC 14° Capricorn: (birthplace).

Natal Sidereal

Sun's tropical long.		10° 28′ 39″ Virgo
SVP	+	5 58 45
		16 27 24
Less 1 sign		30 00 00
Sun's sidereal long.		16 27 24 Leo

Moon's sidereal long. =	10 59 45 (say 11° Leo)

The tropical lunar return preceding death occurred on the day of
the disaster at 05.53 UT 28.1.86.

RAMC at birthplace: 9.37.09 Asc. 12° Scorpio: MC 22° Leo.

RAMC at site: 8.58.29 Asc. 9° Scorpio: MC 12° Leo.

Interestingly enough, the natal Saturn is conjunct the lunar
Midheaven at the birthplace and the natal Pluto close to the
Midheaven when the return is relocated to the site. When the solar
return is progressed for the date of the disaster her natal Neptune
is on the progressed Ascendant. Her lunar, preceding death, has

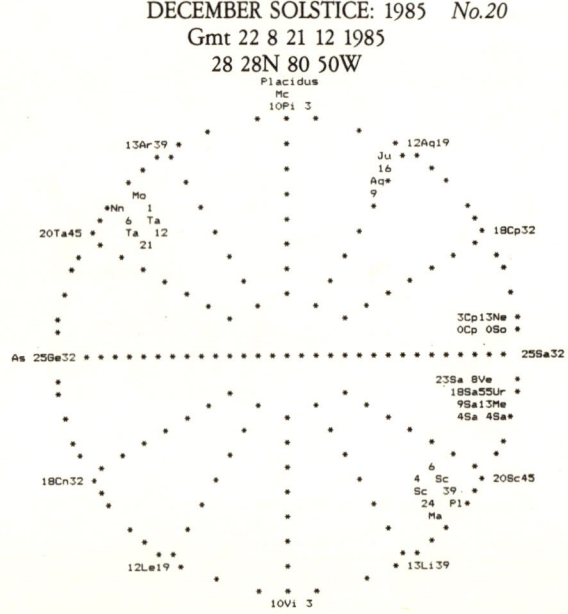

Radix
DECEMBER SOLSTICE: 1985   *No.20*
Gmt 22 8 21 12 1985
28 28N 80 50W

Radix
SHUTTLE DISASTER   *No.21*
Gmt 16 39 28 1 1986
28 28N 80 50W

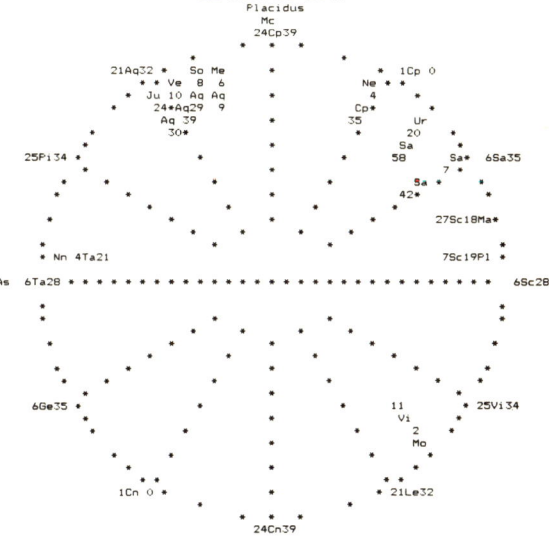

EVENT CHART

No.22   CHRISTA:
Gmt 2 13 3 9 1948
42 22N 71 4W

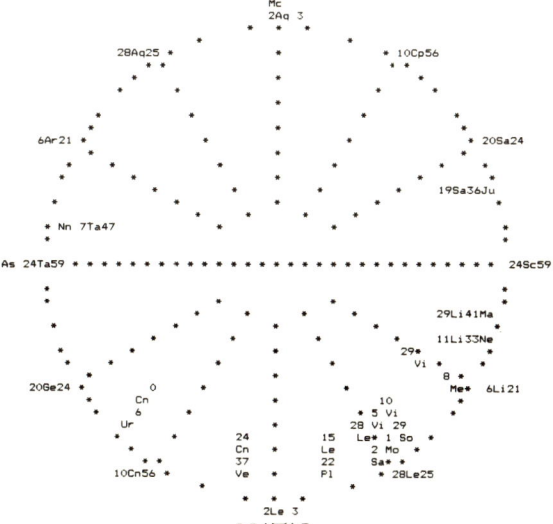

NATAL

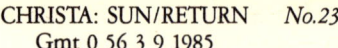

CHRISTA: SUN/RETURN   *No.23*

Gmt 0 56 3 9 1985

42 22N 71 4W

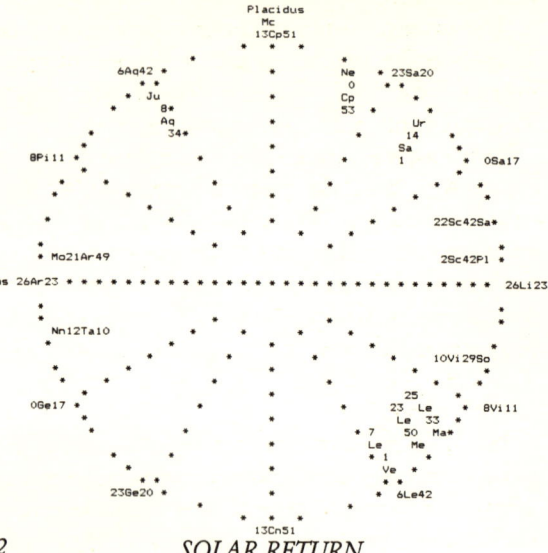

Ref:
Natal Chart No.22   **SOLAR RETURN**

No.24   CHRISTA: LUNAR/RETURN

Gmt 5 53 28 1 1986

42 22N 71 4W

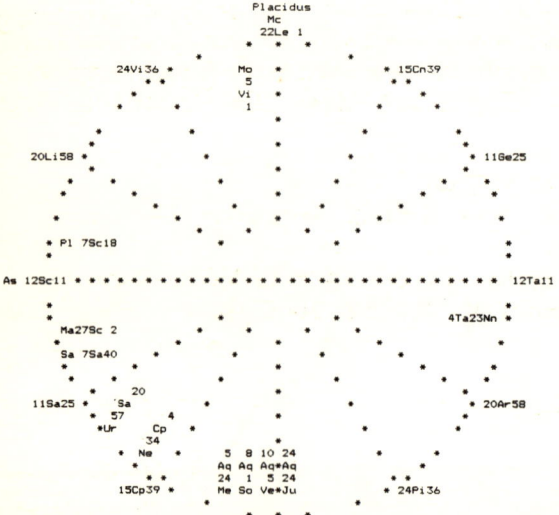

LUNAR RETURN   *Ref:*
Natal Chart No.22

Pluto close to the Ascendant and the natal Pluto close to the lunar MC. Jupiter in the lunar return is on the fourth cusp, which seems rather unusual.

The quotidian rate of progression brings the natal planets in Leo/Virgo close to the quotidian Ascendant with the natal Jupiter opposite the MC. On the day of the disaster the transiting Saturn/Uranus was opposed to this MC.

Judy's solar return for 1985/86 has the Moon precisely on the MC opposed to the Aries planets in the fourth. Uranus rises within a degree or so of the Ascendant. When we compare her natal chart with the solar return we see her cluster of Aries planets exactly on the fourth angle of the return, with Mars precisely on the angle. The natal Neptune is on the return MC conjunct the solar Moon opposed to the Aries planets; the natal Uranus is on the solar Descendant. This is an imposing array of contacts, marking out the year as one of fateful significance.

Her lunar return has Saturn and Uranus on the Ascendant, which again illustrates the importance of studying more than one chart when endeavouring to estimate the potentials of any particular period. An approximate calculation of the solar return progressions (298 days) shows the return has completed one full cycle, bringing the solar Uranus once again to the Ascendant and the solar Moon elevated near the MC. All the foregoing comments have been based on the tropical version of the returns, but no doubt, the sidereal equivalent would show similar and appropriate contacts.

Judy Resnik, an astronaut who died in the disaster, was born at: 06.52 EST (11.52 UT) 5.4.1949, Akron, Ohio, 41° 05′N 81° 31′W (see references).

Judy: Natal chart (tropical)
Sun. 15° 22′ 08″ Aries: Moon. 2° 33′ Cancer.
RAMC 19.19.44.
Solar return 1985/86: 05.14 UT 5.4.85 RAMC 12.41.45.
Asc. 19° Sagittarius: MC 11° Libra: (birthplace).

Natal Sidereal

Sun's tropical long.		15°	22′	08″ Aries
SVP	+	5	58	18
Less		30	00	00
Sun's sidereal long.		21	20	26 Pisces
Moon's sidereal long.	=	8	31	18 Gemini

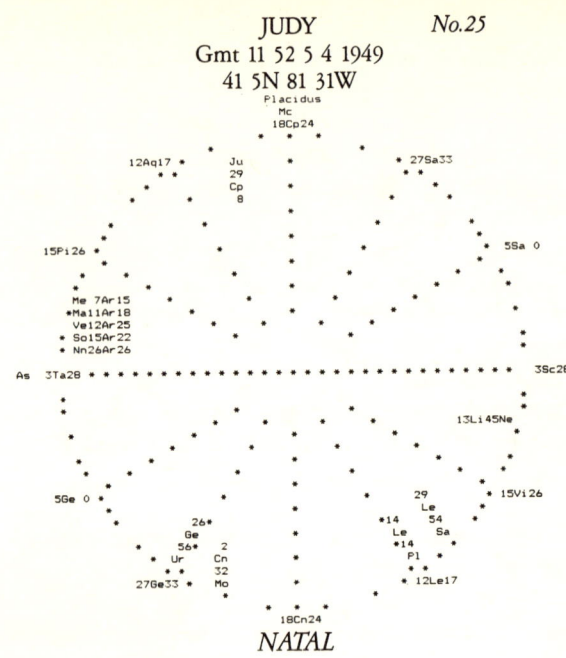

JUDY   No.25
Gmt 11 52 5 4 1949
41 5N 81 31W

Placidus
Mc
18Cp24

12Aq17   Ju
29
Cp
8

27Sa33

15Pi26

5Sa 0

Me 7Ar15
•Ma11Ar18
Ve12Ar25
• So15Ar22
• Nn26Ar26

As 3Ta28

3Sc28

13Li45Ne

5Ge 0

29   15Vi26
Le
•14   54
Le   Sa
•14
Pl
• 12Le17

26•
Ge
56•   2
• Ur   Cn
32
27Ge33 • Mo

18Cn24

NATAL

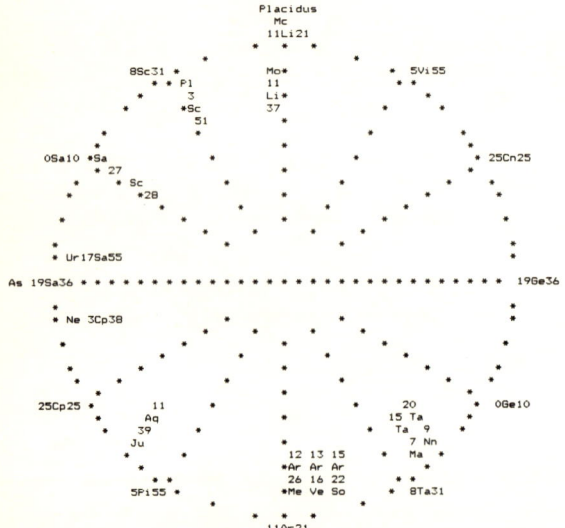

No.26   JUDY—SUN/RETURN
Gmt 5 14 5 4 1985
41 5N 81 31W

Placidus
Mc
11Li21

8Sc31   Mo•   5Vi55
•• Pl   11
3   Li •
•Sc   37
51

0Sa10 •Sa
• 27
• Sc
•28

25Cn25

• Ur17Sa55

As 19Sa36

19Ge36

• Ne 3Cp38

25Cp25   11   20   0Ge10
Aq   15 Ta
39   Ta   9
Ju   7 Nn
12 13 15   Ma
•Ar Ar Ar
26 16 22
5Pi55 •   •Me Ve So   • 8Ta31

11Ar21

SOLAR RETURN

Ref:
Natal Chart No.25

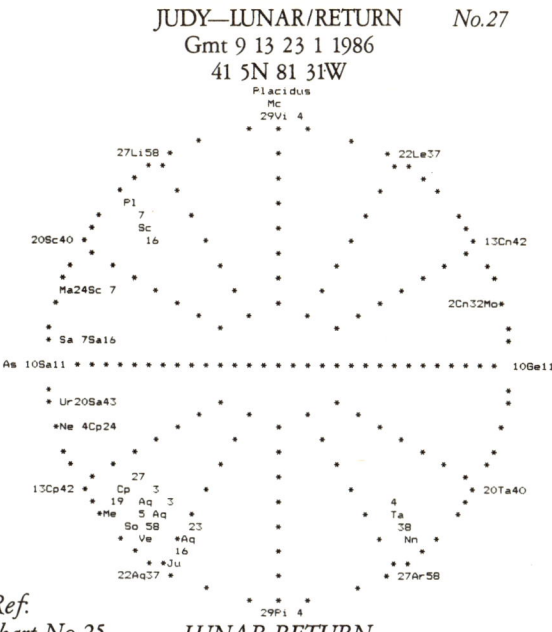

JUDY—LUNAR/RETURN *No.27*
Gmt 9 13 23 1 1986
41 5N 81 31W

Ref:
Natal Chart No.25   *LUNAR RETURN*

The tropical lunar return preceding death occurred at:
09.13 UT 23.1.86.

RAMC at birthplace: 11.56.36 Asc. 10° Sagittarius
                                    MC 29° Virgo.
RAMC at site   11.59.20 Asc. 18° Sagittarius
                                    MC 29° Virgo.

Shuttle victims Sidereal returns 1985/86

Christa:

Sidereal Sun	16°	27′	24″	Leo
Tropical Sun	10	28	39	Virgo
SVP	5	58	45	

Accrued precession:

SVP 3.9.48	5°	58′	45″	
SVP 3.9.85	5	27	46	
	0	30	59	
Sun's long.	+ 10	28	39	Virgo
	10	59	38	Virgo

The Sun's return to this tropical longitude will give the date and time of the sidereal return.

	D	M	S	
Sun's long. required	10	59	38	Virgo
Sun's long. 3.9.85	10	55	26	
Difference	00	04	12	(0.07)
Sun's daily motion 2/3 Sept.	00	58	06	(0.97)

$$\frac{0.07 \times 24}{0.97} = 1.735 = 1 \text{ hr. } 44 \text{ min. after noon} =$$

13.44 UT 3.9.85 = time and date of sidereal solar return

		H	M	S
ST 0 hr. UT 3.9.85		22	48	17
Time elapsed	+	13	44	00
Correction	+	00	02	15
ST at Greenwich		12	34	32
Longitude Equiv. (71° 04′W)	−	04	44	16
RAMC at birthplace		07	50	16

Asc. 26° Virgo: MC 0° Cancer.

Transposed to the site location the Ascendant is 20° Virgo: MC 21° Gemini: RAMC 7.11.12.

Sidereal Lunar Return preceding death:

Sidereal Moon	10° 59′ 45″ Leo
Tropical Moon	5 01 00 Virgo
SVP	5 58 45

Accrued precession:

SVP 3.9.48		5° 58′ 45″
SVP 1.1.86		5 27 28
		0 31 17
Moon's long.	+	5 01 00 Virgo
		5 32 17 Virgo

The Moon's return to this tropical longitude will give the date and time of the sidereal lunar return.

	D	M	S	
Moon's long. required	5	32	17	Virgo
Moon's long. 28.1.86 noon UT	8	26	38	
Difference	2	54	21	(2.906)
Moon's motion 27/28 Jan.	13	20	31	(13.342)

$$\frac{2.906 \times 24}{13.342} = 5.227 = 5 \text{ hr. } 14 \text{ min. before noon}$$

= 06.46 UT 28.1.86 = time and date of lunar return.

		H	M	S
ST 0 hr. UT 28.1.86		8	27	51
Time elapsed	+	6	46	00
Correction	+	0	01	07
ST at Greenwich		15	14	58
Longitude Equiv. (71° 04′W)	−	04	44	16
		10	30	42

Asc. 27° Libra: MC 10° Leo; at birthplace.
Asc. 26° Libra: MC 0° Leo; at site.

Judy:

Sidereal Sun	21° 20′ 26″ Pisces
Tropical Sun	15 22 08 Aries
SVP	5 58 18

Accrued precession:

SVP 5.4.49	5° 58′ 18″
SVP 5.4.85	5 28 10
	0 30 08
Sun's long.	+ 15 22 08 Aries
	15 52 16 Aries

	D	M	S	
Sun's long. required	15	52	16	Aries
Sun's long. 5.4.85	15	38	48	
Difference	00	13	28	(0.224)
Sun's daily motion	00	59	01	(0.984)

$$\frac{0.224 \times 24}{0.984} = 5.476 = 5 \text{ hr. } 29 \text{ min. after noon}$$

= $\underline{17.29 \text{ UT } 5.4.85}$ = time and date of sidereal solar return.

		H	M	S
ST 0 hr. UT 5.4.85		12	52	57
Time elapsed	+	17	29	00
Correction	+	00	02	52
ST at Greenwich		06	24	49
Longitude Equiv. (81° 31'W)	−	05	26	04
RAMC at birthplace		00	58	45

Asc. 6° Cancer: MC 21° Pisces: at birthplace.
Asc. 0° Cancer: MC 21° Pisces: at site.

Sidereal lunar return preceding death:

Sidereal Moon	8° 31' 18" Gemini
Tropical Moon	2 33 00 Cancer
SVP	5 58 18

Accrued precession:

SVP 5.4.49		5° 58' 18"
SVP 23.1.86		5 27 24
		0 30 54
Moon's long.	+	2 33 00 Cancer
		3 03 54 Cancer

	D	M	S	
Moon's long. required	3	03	54	Cancer
Moon's long. 23.1.86 noon UT	3	57	46	Cancer
Difference	0	53	52	(0.898)
Moon's motion 22/23 Jan.	12	11	07	(12.185)

$$\frac{0.898 \times 24}{12.185} = 1.768 = 1 \text{ hr. } 46 \text{ min. before noon}$$

= $\underline{10.14 \text{ UT } 23.1.86}$ = time and date of lunar return.

	H	M	S
ST 0 hr. UT 23.1.86	08	08	08
Time elapsed +	10	14	00
Correction +	00	01	41
ST at Greenwich	18	23	49
Longitude Equiv. (81° 31'W) −	05	26	04
RAMC at birthplace	12	57	45

Asc. 28° Scorpio: MC 21° Virgo: at birthplace.
Asc. 6° Sagittarius: MC 21° Virgo: at site.

The calculations of the solar and lunar returns in relation to the Space Shuttle disaster and two of its victims have been listed in some detail in order that the method for dealing with these types of returns may prove helpful for those new to the return techniques.

Mundane events studied in relation to astrological symbolism are always interesting not only for the wide implications they may have for individuals and society at large, but also because the data are generally well-documented, particularly for major events. The chart for an event will usually show the appropriate symbolism but even if its indications are not in complete accord with what one would expect, comparison with relevant ingress charts and progressions will confirm that the event or condition materialized at the specific time and place according to cosmic law. Success may depend on being in the right place at the right time but failure and even disaster can also be related, among other things, to being in the wrong place at the wrong time. Natural disasters which occur with sickening regularity destroying thousands and wreaking untold havoc can be related to the cosmic patterns operating at the time and place in question.

Earthquakes
Several major earthquakes have occurred during this century and it may be useful to see how the actual event was 'triggered off' in terms of astrological symbolism. The following examples are given with all the relevant data for those wishing to investigate using the various return methods.

(Tropical)	No.1	No.2
Time UT	13.13	02.59 (nearest min.)
Date	18.4.06	1.9.23

(Tropical)	No.1	No.2
Place	San Francisco	Tokyo
Lat.	37.47N	35.41N
Long.	122.26W	139.45E
Sun	27.34.55 Aries	7.38.55 Virgo
Moon	00.01.00 Pisces	11.15.00 Taurus
RAMC	18.46.14	10.54.37
Mean Sun	01.42.58	10.37.01
App. Sun	01.42.25	10.37.20
Asc.	18 Aries	0 Sagittarius
MC	10 Capricorn	12 Virgo

Capricorn Solar Ingress

12.03 UT 22.12.1905   14.57 UT 22.12.22

Capricorn Lunar Ingress
prior to event

01.23 UT 14.4.1906   17.49.UT 21.8.23

(Tropical)	No.3	No.4
Time UT	23.40.14	01.55
Date	29.2.60	11.3.33
Place	Agadir	Long Beach. California
Lat.	30.27N	33.46N
Long.	9.37W	118.11W
Sun	10.24.28 Pisces	20.03.17 Pisces
Moon	20.10.00 Aries	6.51.00 Virgo
RAMC	9.36.54	5.15.23
Mean Sun	22.35.08	23.13.07
App. Sun	22.47.40	23.23.27
Asc.	16 Scorpio	20 Virgo
MC	22 Leo	20 Gemini

Capricorn Solar Ingress

14.35 UT 22.12.59   01.15. UT 22.12.32

Capricorn Lunar Ingress
prior to event

01.39 UT 22.2.60   19.22 UT 19.2.33

(Tropical)	No.5	No.6
Time UT	13.22	17.55
Date	19.9.85	10.10.86
Place	Mexico City	San Salvador

(Tropical)	No.5	No.6
Lat.	19.26N	13.42N
Long.	99.09W	89.12W
Sun	26.32.46 Virgo	17.07.57 Libra
Moon	1.37.00 Sagittarius	19.33.00 Capricorn
RAMC	6.38.58	13.14.23
Mean Sun	11.53.35	13.16.11
App. Sun	11.47.19	13.03.10
Asc.	9 Libra	11 Capricorn
MC	9 Cancer	20 Libra

Capricorn Solar Ingress

16.23 UT 21.12.84   22.08 UT 21.12.85

Capricorn Lunar Ingress
prior to event

08.24 UT 25.8.85   08.52 UT 9.10.86

The December Solstice (1905) prior to the earthquake which devastated San Franciso (1906) has Mars and Saturn precisely on the lower angle. These two planets when acting in concert are the significators of destruction and violence, and their position in this chart is appropriate, particularly when related to the Sun/Uranus conjunction which is in wide opposition to Pluto. On the day of the earthquake, the Moon in the heavens was applying to a conjunction of Saturn with the transiting Uranus and Neptune exactly on the upper and lower angles respectively. This is a classic example of returns in action.

The entry of the Moon into Capricorn prior to the day of the disaster has Uranus again exactly on an angle, conjunct the Moon, in opposition to the upper angle Neptune. Whereas at the time of the earthquake Uranus was conjunct the upper meridian, in the lunar return it is on the lower angle, Neptune's mundane position is also reversed.

The Tokyo earthquake (1.9.23) also has Uranus on the lower angle opposite the Sun. At the Solstice (1922) Pluto culminated with a wide opposition to Sun/Mercury across the upper and lower angles. On the day of the disaster, the ingress Mars and Uranus (8/10° Pisces) were exactly on the lower angle at the time of the disaster.

The Capricorn lunar ingress (21.8.23) has Saturn precisely on the lower angle with a cluster of planets in the second house.

The Agadir earthquake has Uranus on the upper meridian at the time of the city's destruction. At the time of the December Solstice (1959) the Sun was conjunct Saturn, and at the time of the disaster the ingress Uranus was within a degree of the Midheaven. Although ingress Venus rose at the time of the disaster (16° Scorpio) the more powerful contacts of Uranus, Pluto and Saturn prevailed. The Capricorn lunar return has Sun opposition Pluto, rather wide of the fourth/tenth angles but still significant of the event to come.

All the other earthquake examples have very appropriate contacts, either in the chart for the event, or in the ingress charts preceding it. In the Long Beach disaster (1933), the event chart has an opposition of Sun/Jupiter, which is not particularly bad, but when we relate the ingress positions to the day of the event, the Mars/Jupiter conjunction is on the Ascendant and the transiting Moon is conjunct Mars and Neptune and applying to the ingress grouping in Virgo on the lower meridian.

In the Mexico City earthquake, the Moon is separating from a conjunction with Saturn and applying to a conjunction with Uranus. At the December ingress prior to the disaster, Saturn was conjunct the Midheaven with Mars rising in Aquarius. Venus, although close to the Ascendant has a wide contact with Saturn and, if we take midpoint positions, with Pluto also. The Moon/Neptune conjunction in the lunar ingress chart (25.8.85) falls close to the lower angle in the event chart.

Saturn is again prominent in the lunar ingress into Capricorn prior to the San Salvador earthquake. In the December ingress it was close to the seventh cusp, while in the lunar return it holds the lower angle within a couple of degrees.

When we study some of the mine disasters such as the Gresford (1934) we see Uranus exactly on the Midheaven at the time of the disaster. The rising Mars in opposition to Saturn across the horizon is a further testimony of violence and destruction. The angular Jupiter aspecting Saturn and Pluto is not, in this case, particularly beneficial. The lunar ingress into Capricorn has Pluto rising, while on the day of the disaster the transiting Moon (13° Pisces) was in opposition to Neptune.

The Capricorn ingress Moon (the Moon in the December Solstice chart) is in 10.49 Pisces. If we compute a return for the date and time the Moon transits this longitude, we have an anlunar return. Referring to the Gresford disaster we find Saturn precisely on the Midheaven at the time of this return, with Mars close to the lower angle. The symbolism is apt for the event and shows how there is

Radix
EARTHQUAKE: (1) *No.1*
Gmt 13 13 18 4 1906
37 47N 122 26W

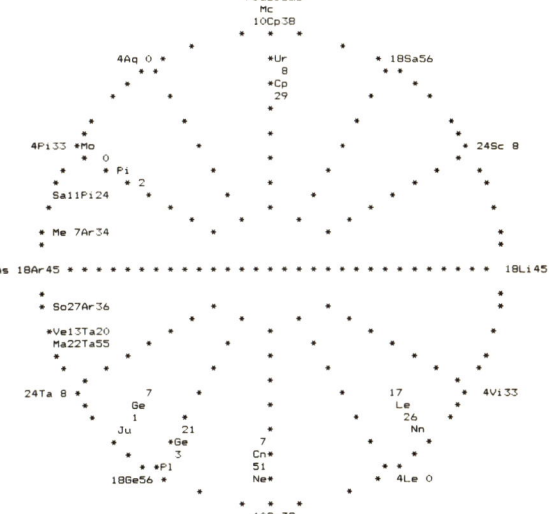

Radix *EVENT CHART*
DECEMBER SOLSTICE: 1905
Gmt 12 3 22 12 1905
37 47N 122 26W

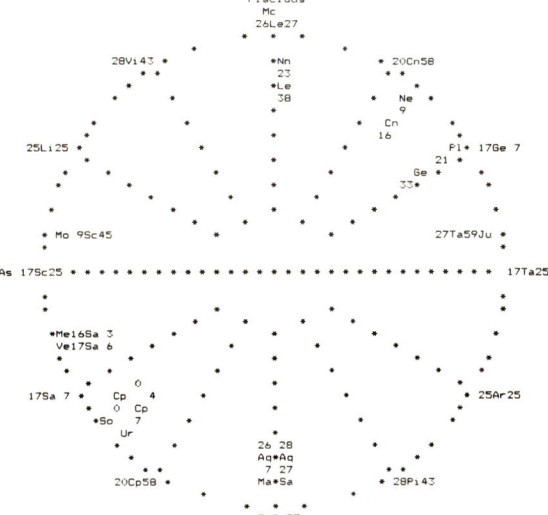

Capricorn ingress prior to event

Radix
LUNAR/RETURN: CAPRICORN
Gmt 1 23 14 4 1906 (1)
37 47N 122 26W

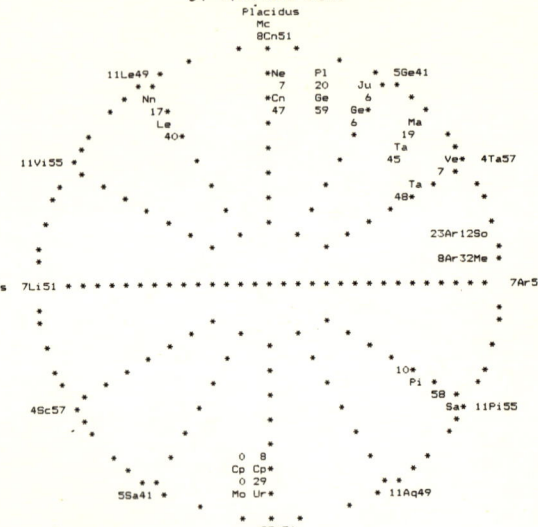

Radix   *Capricorn lunar ingress*

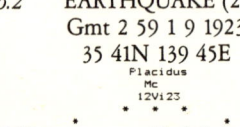

No.2   EARTHQUAKE (2)
Gmt 2 59 1 9 1923
35 41N 139 45E

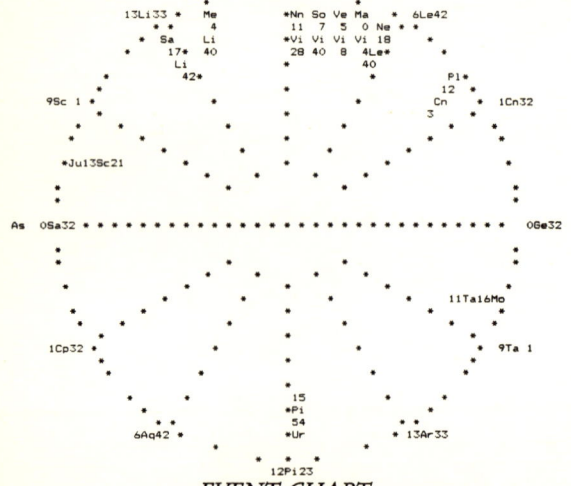

EVENT CHART

Radix
DECEMBER SOLSTICE: 1922
Gmt 14 57 22 12 1922 (2)
35 41N 139 45E

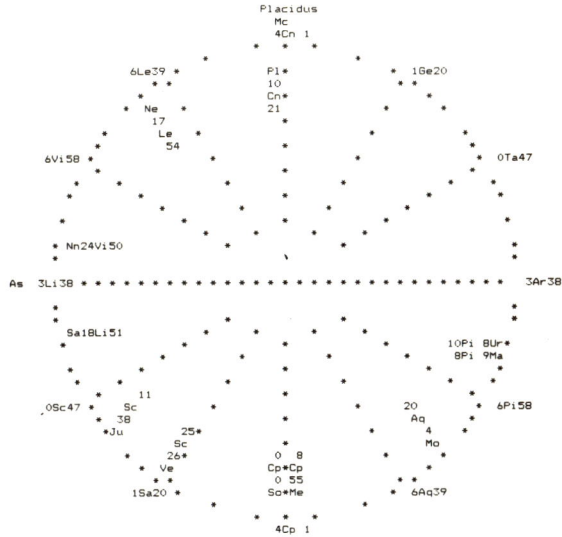

Capricorn ingress prior to event

Radix
LUNAR/RETURN: CAPRICORN
Gmt 17 49 21 8 1923 (2)
35 41N 139 45E

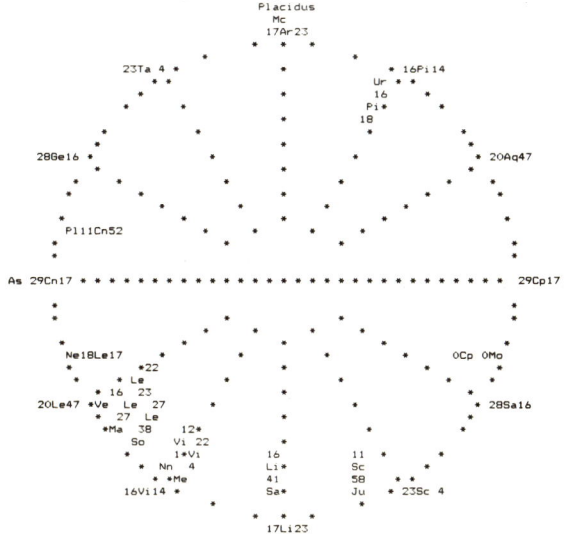

Capricorn lunar ingress

Radix
EARTHQUAKE (3)   *No.3*
Gmt 23 40 29 2 1960
30 27N 9 37W

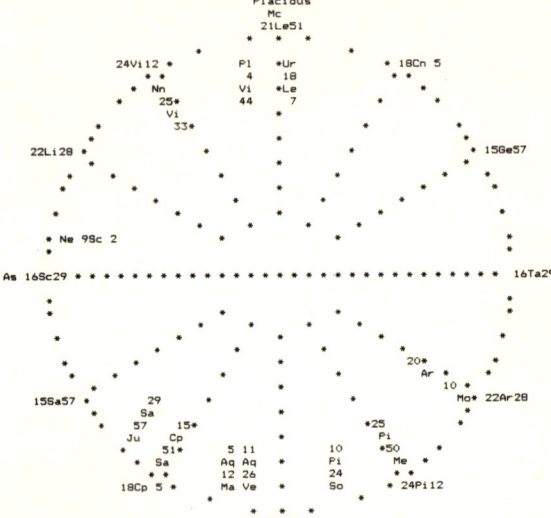

Radix   *EVENT CHART*
DECEMBER SOLSTICE: 1959
Gmt 14 35 22 12 1959 (3)
30 27N 9 37W

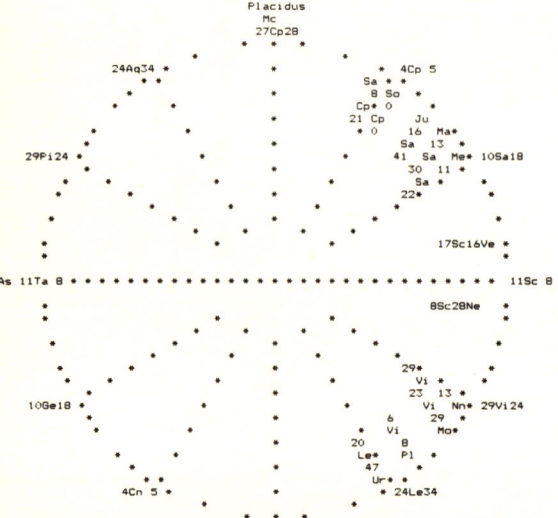

Capricorn ingress prior to event

Radix
LUNAR/RETURN: CAPRICORN
Gmt 1 39 22 2 1960 (3)
30 27N 9 37W

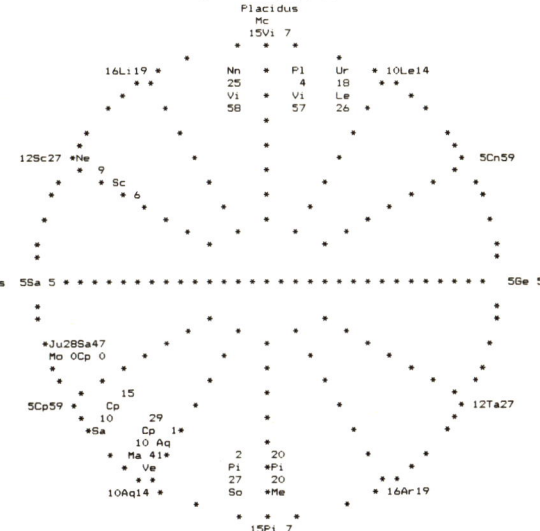

Radix *Capricorn lunar ingress*

No.4 EARTHQUAKE (4)
Gmt 1 55 11 3 1933
33 46N 118 11W

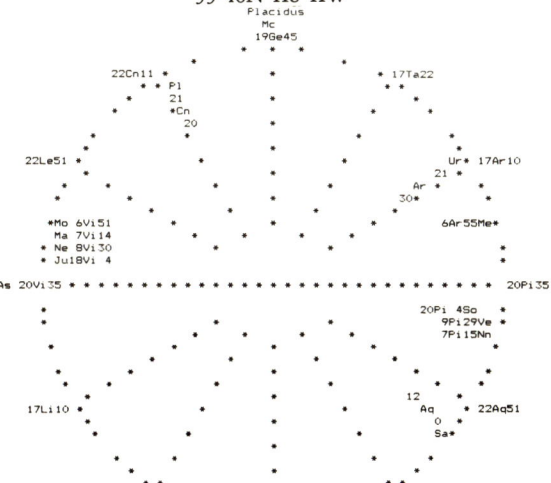

EVENT CHART

Radix
DECEMBER SOLSTICE: 1932
Gmt 1 15 22 12 1932 (4)
33 46N 118 11W

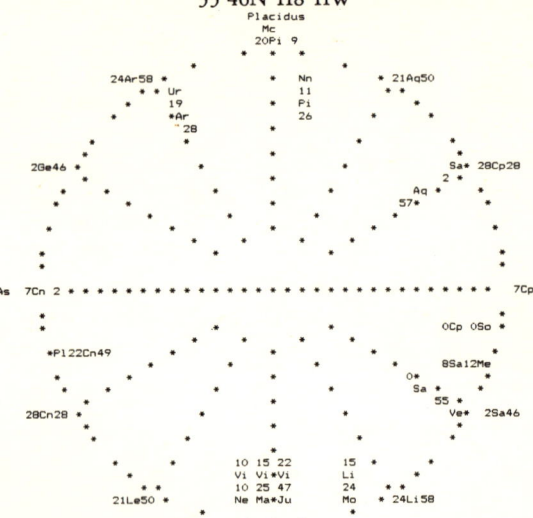

Capricorn ingress prior to event

Radix
LUNAR/RETURN: CAPRICORN
Gmt 19 22 19 2 1933 (4)
33 46N 118 11W

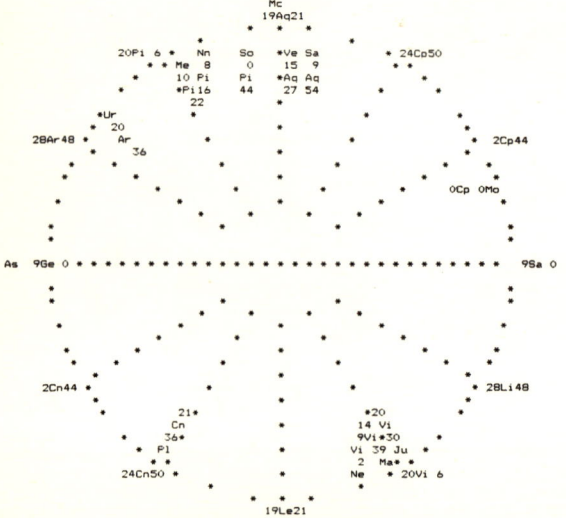

Capricorn lunar ingress

Radix
EARTHQUAKE (5) *No.5*
Gmt 13 22 19 9 1985
19 26N 99 9W

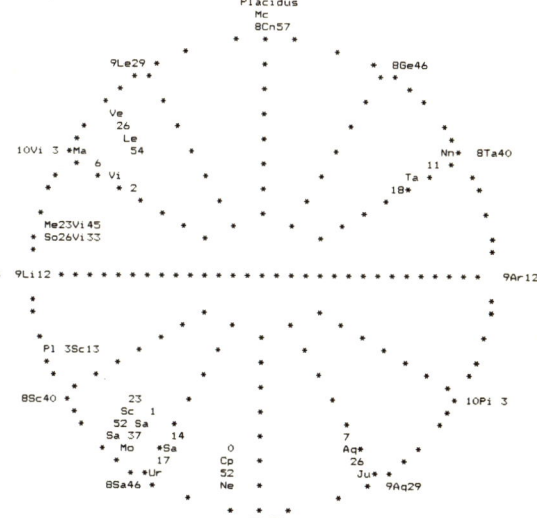

EVENT CHART

Radix
DECEMBER SOLSTICE: 1984
Gmt 16 23 21 12 1984 (5)
19 26N 99 9w

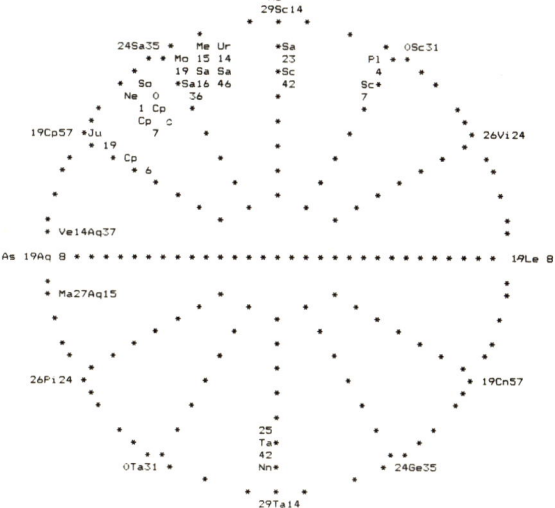

Capricorn ingress prior to event

Radix
LUNAR/RETURN: CAPRICORN
Gmt 8 24 25 8 1985 (5)
19 26N 99 9W

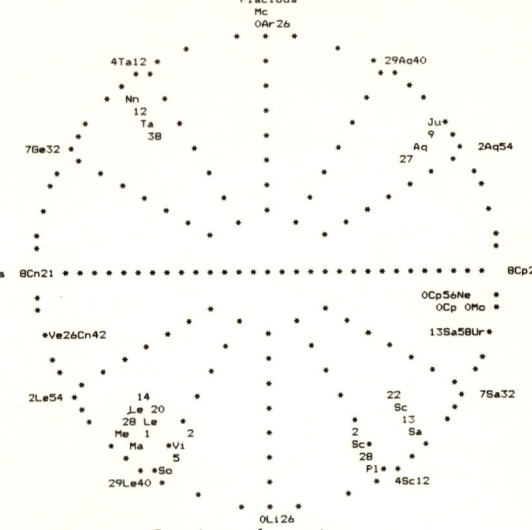

Capricorn lunar ingress

Radix
No.6   EARTHQUAKE (6)
Gmt 17 55 10 10 1986
13 42N 89 12W

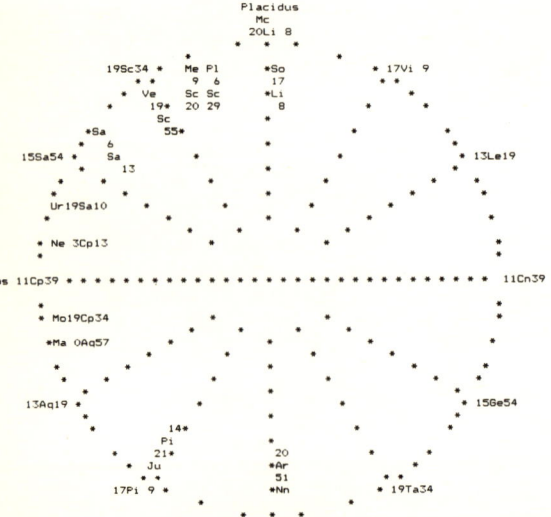

EVENT CHART

Radix
DECEMBER SOLSTICE: 1985
Gmt 22 8 21 12 1985 (6)
13 42N 89 12W

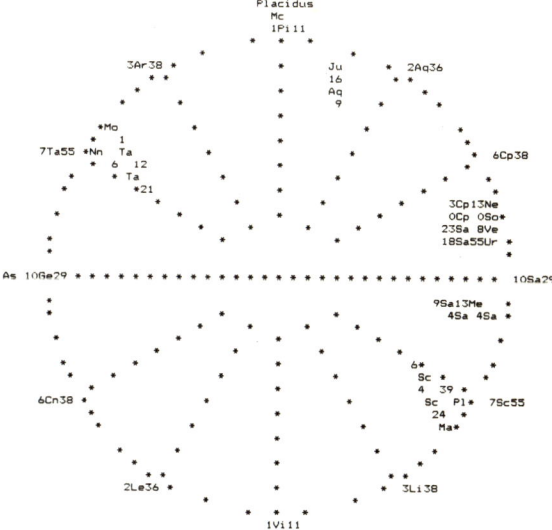

Capricorn ingress prior to event

Radix
LUNAR/RETURN: CAPRICORN
Gmt 8 52 9 10 1986 (6)
13 42N 89 12W

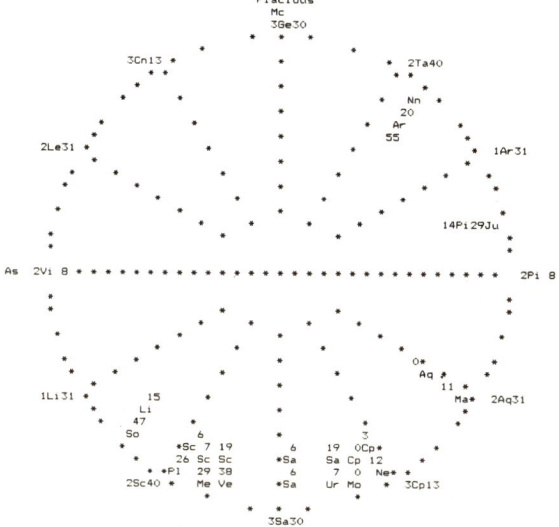

Capricorn lunar ingress

a remarkable interrelatedness of the various kinds of returns. Naturally, a detailed study is required to see whether this technique stands up when applied to a variety of cases, but initially it looks promising.

The explosion chart (6.12.17) shows a setting Pluto opposed to a rising Mercury. The Moon is with Mars in Virgo. The December Solstice prior to the event has Pluto again prominent, this time on the Midheaven. The Capricorn ingress Moon return shows Uranus close to the upper angle with Neptune/Saturn in opposition on the lower angle.

The chemical planet explosion (1.6.74) has Uranus and the Moon rising at the time of the event with Mars close to the upper angle. The December Solstice prior to the event has Saturn precisely on the upper angle and Pluto rising. The lunar ingress into Capricorn (9.5.74) has Uranus conjunct the upper angle with Neptune fairly close to the Ascendant. The Capricorn ingress Moon return has Mars/Saturn on the upper angle with Pluto close to the Ascendant. All these contacts and, more importantly, the bodies involved are highly appropriate for the events and the timing which they portray.

The atomic bomb on Hiroshima fell at precisely the time when Uranus culminated. As with other disaster charts, we see the transiting Moon conjunct Saturn. At the 1944 December Solstice the Sun/Mercury opposed Saturn and at the date of the event the transiting Moon/Saturn in Cancer were passing over the seventh angle. The lunar ingress into Capricorn (22.7.45) has Mars rising and an exact conjunction of Uranus/Venus close to the Ascendant. Pluto is close to the lower angle. At Nagasaki, Saturn is close to the Midheaven at the time of the event. The other return charts are almost identical except for the slight adjustment for longitude.

The air-raid victims' returns, prior to their deaths are in accordance with what might be expected considering the conditions existing at the time. No doubt all victims of disasters have stressful contacts operating at the crucial time; whether they live or die will depend on the severity of the contacts and, in a wider context, the time and place of the disaster.

Mine Disasters

(Tropical)	No.1	No.2
Time UT	02.00 approx.	08.20 approx.
Date	22.9.34	14.10.13

(Tropical)	No.1	No.2
Place	Gresford (Wrexham)	Nr. Cardiff
Lat.	53.03N	51.28N
Long.	3.00W	3.10W
Sun	28.22.45 Virgo	20.23.02 Libra
Moon	13.22.00 Pisces	10.28.00 Aries
RAMC	1.49.00	9.36.26
Mean Sun	12.01.00	13.29.06
App. Sun	11.54.03	13.15.18
Asc.	17 Leo	7 Scorpio
MC	29 Aries	21 Leo

Capricorn Solar Ingress

06.58 UT 22.12.33   04.45 UT 22.12.12

Capricorn Lunar Ingress
prior to event

0.36 UT 17.9.34   01.10 UT 6.10.13

Explosions

(Tropical)	No.1	No.2
Time UT	13.06	15.53
Date	6.12.17	1.6.74
Place	Halifax, Nova Scotia	Flixborough
Lat.	44.38N	53.35N
Long.	63.35W	00.40W
Sun	13.51.39 Sagittarius	10.46.22 Gemini
Moon	13.22.00 Virgo	2.33.00 Scorpio
RAMC	13.50.39	8.29.20
Mean Sun	16.58.59	4.39.00
App. Sun	16.49.58	4.36.44
Asc.	2 Capricorn	25 Libra
MC	29 Libra	5 Leo

Capricorn Solar Ingress

03.58 UT 22.12.16   00.08 UT 22.12.73

Capricorn Lunar Ingress
prior to event

15.55 UT 17.11.17   22.15 UT 9.5.74

Radix
GRESFORD MINE   *No.1*
Gmt 2 0 22 9 1934
53 3N 3 0W

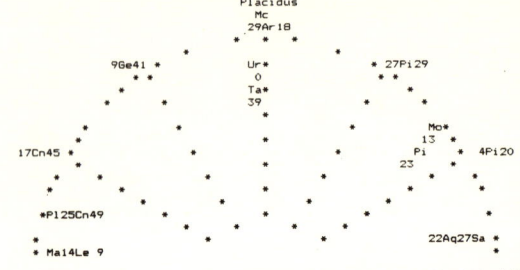

Event chart

Radix
DECEMBER SOLSTICE: 1933
Gmt 6 58 22 12 1933 (1)
53 3N 3 0W

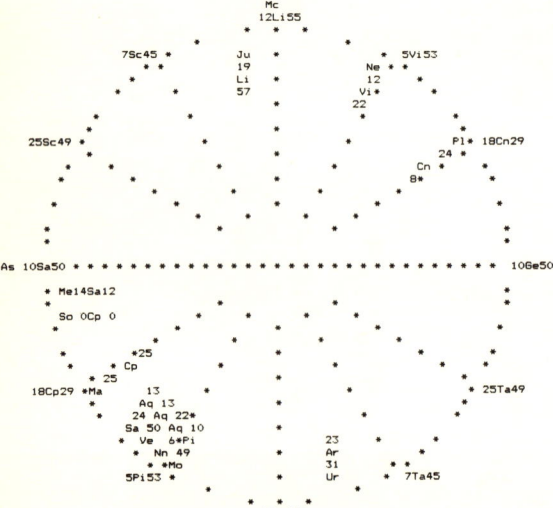

Capricorn ingress prior to event

Radix
LUNAR/RETURN: CAPRICORN
Gmt 0 36 17 9 1934 (1)
53 3N 3 0W

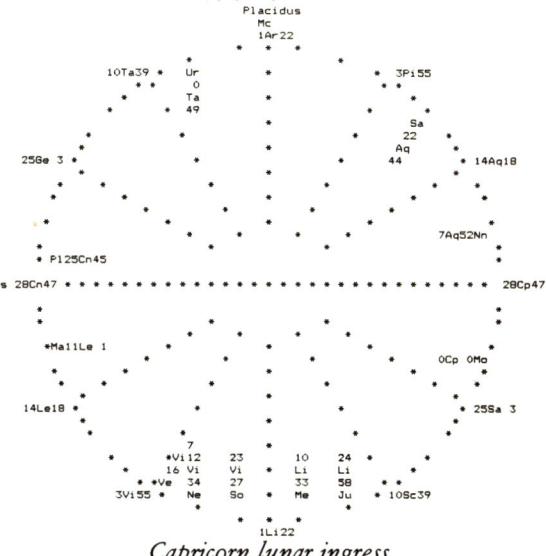

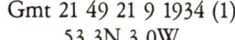

Capricorn lunar ingress

Gmt 21 49 21 9 1934 (1)
53 3N 3 0W

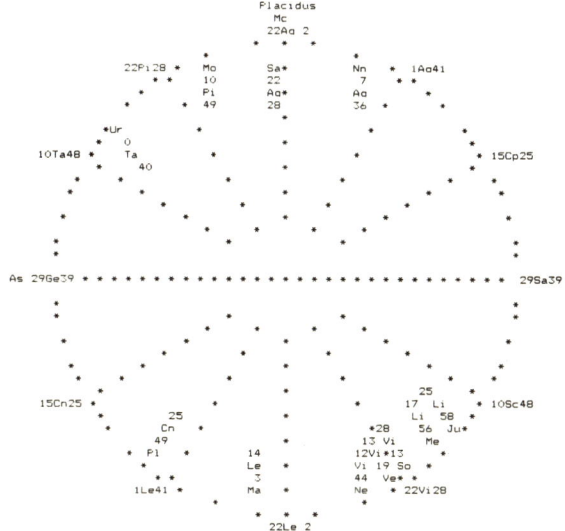

Capricorn ingress Moon return prior to event

Radix
MINE: NEAR CARDIFF (2) *No.2*
Gmt 8 20 14 10 1913
51 28N 3 10W

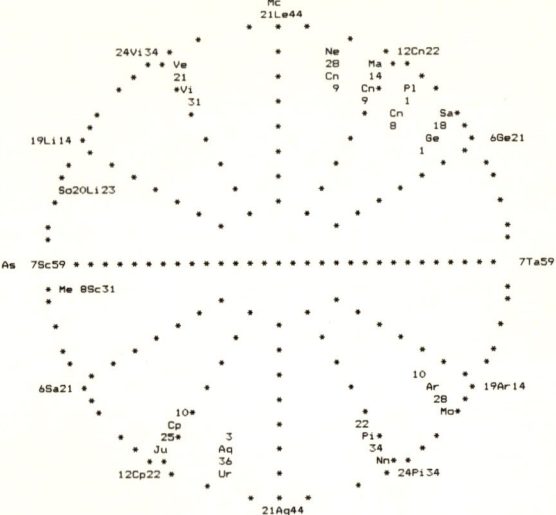

Event chart

Radix
DECEMBER SOLSTICE: 1912
Gmt 4 45 22 12 1912 (2)
51 28N 3 10W

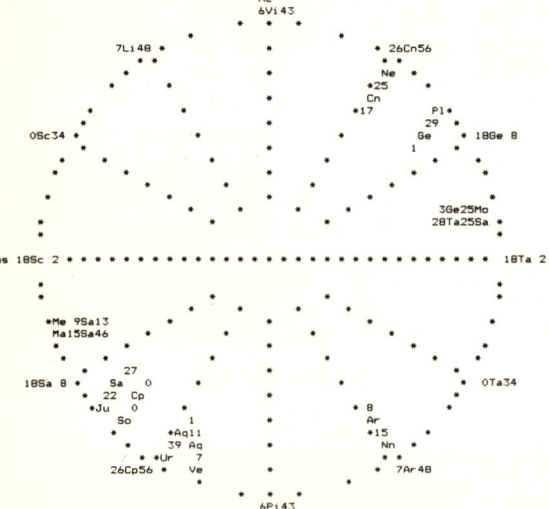

Capricorn ingress prior to event

Gmt 11 10 21 9 1913 (2)
51 28N 3 10W

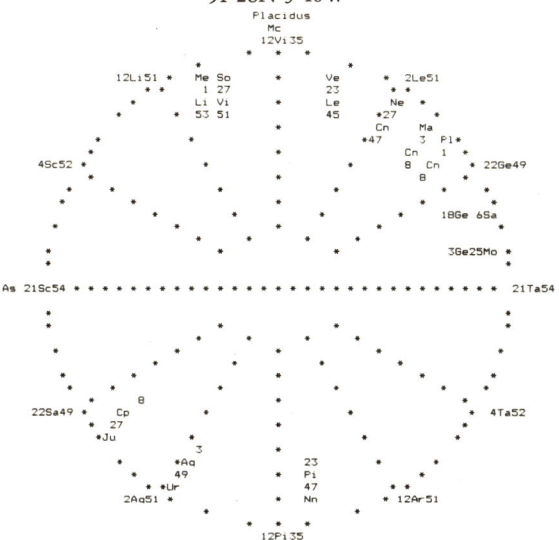

Capricorn ingress Moon return prior to event

Atomic Bombs

(Tropical)	*No.1*	*No.2*
Time UT	23.16	02.02
Date	5.8.45	9.8.45
Place	Hiroshima	Nagasaki
Lat.	34.24N	32.43N
Long.	132.25E	129.52E
Sun	13.07.47 Leo	16.07.01 Leo
Moon	17.58.00 Cancer	28.43.00 Leo
RAMC	5.02.12	7.50.17
Mean Sun	8.56.32	9.08.50
App. Sun	9.02.23	9.14.18
Asc.	17 Virgo	23 Libra
MC	16 Gemini	25 Cancer

Capricorn Solar Ingress

23.15 UT 21.12.44 ....

Capricorn Lunar Ingress
prior to event

16.29 UT 22.7.45 ....

Radix
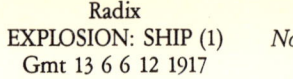
EXPLOSION: SHIP (1)   No.1
Gmt 13 6 6 12 1917
44 38N 63 35W

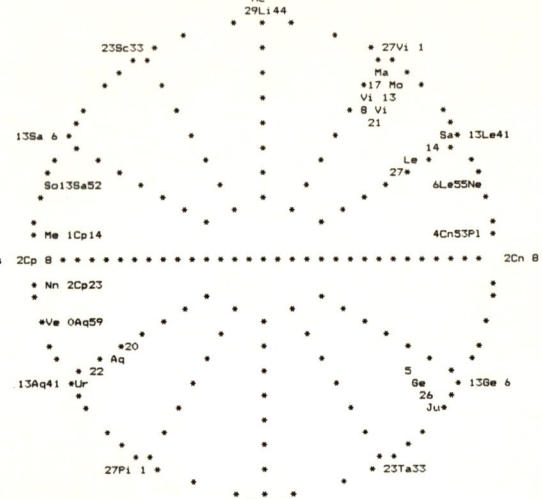

Event chart

Radix
DECEMBER SOLSTICE: 1916
Gmt 3 58 22 12 1916 (1)
44 38N 63 35W

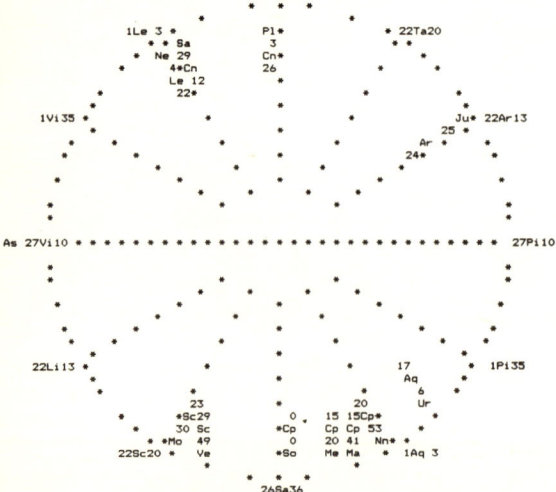

Capricorn ingress prior to event

Radix
LUNAR/RETURN: CAPRICORN
Gmt 15 55 17 11 1917 (1)
44 38N 63 35W

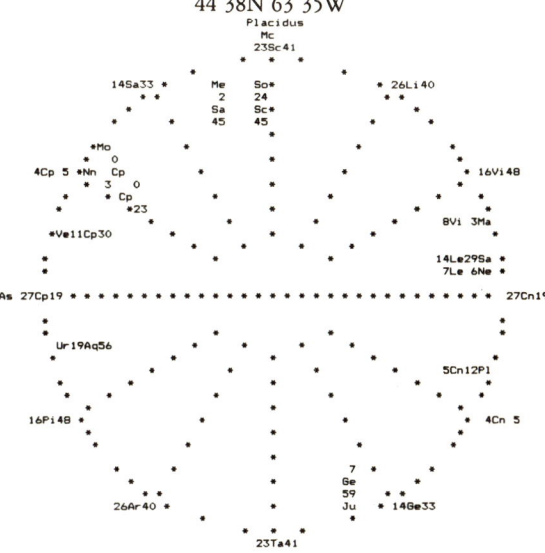

Capricorn lunar ingress

Gmt 21 34 14 11 1917 (1)
44 38N 63 35W

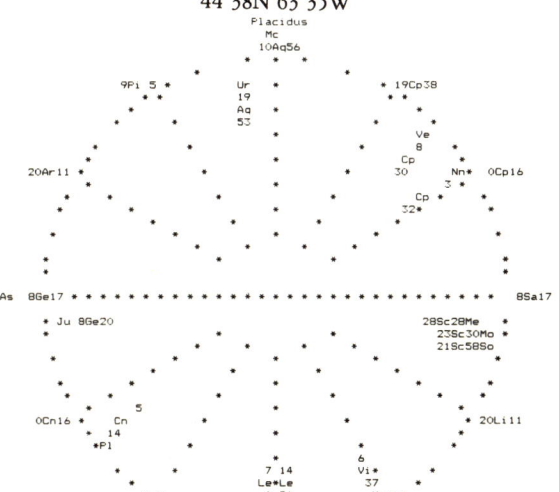

Capricorn ingress Moon return prior to event

Radix
EXPLOSION: PLANT (2)   *No.2*
Gmt 15 53 1 6 1974
53 35N 0 40W

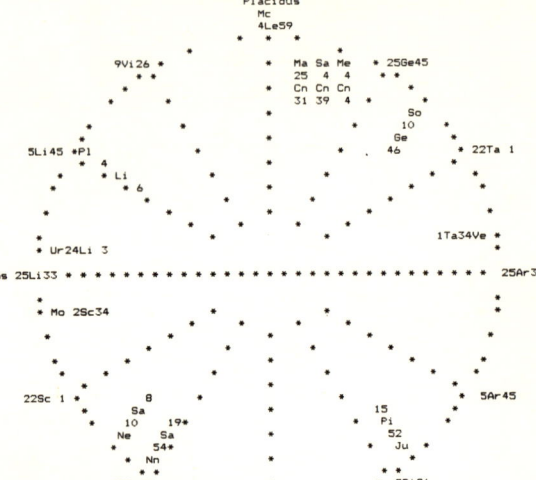

Event chart

Radix
DECEMBER SOLSTICE: 1973
Gmt 0 8 22 12 1973 (2)
53 35N 0 40W

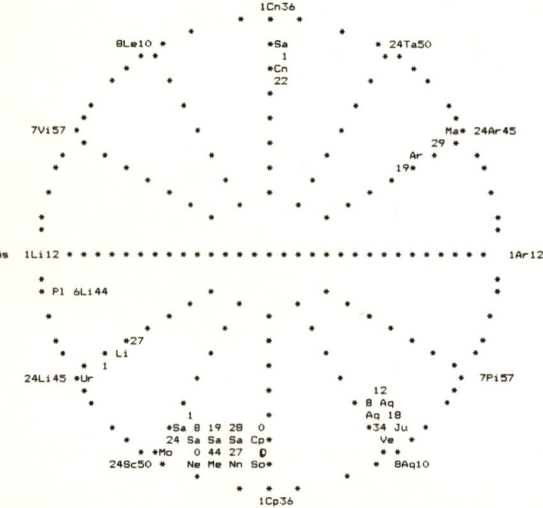

Capricorn ingress prior to event

Radix
LUNAR/RETURN: CAPRICORN
Gmt 22 15 9 5 1974 (2)
53 35N 0 40W

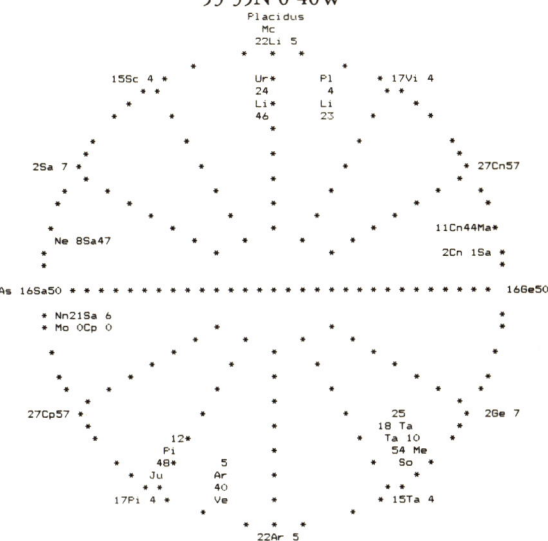

Capricorn lunar ingress

Gmt 14 45 7 5 1974 (2)
53 35N 0 40W

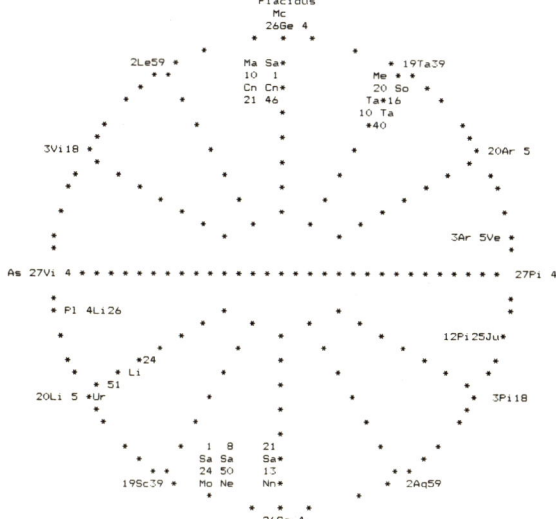

Capricorn ingress Moon return prior to event

Radix
HIROSHIMA: (1)   *No.1*
Gmt 23 16 5 8 1945
34 24N 132 25E

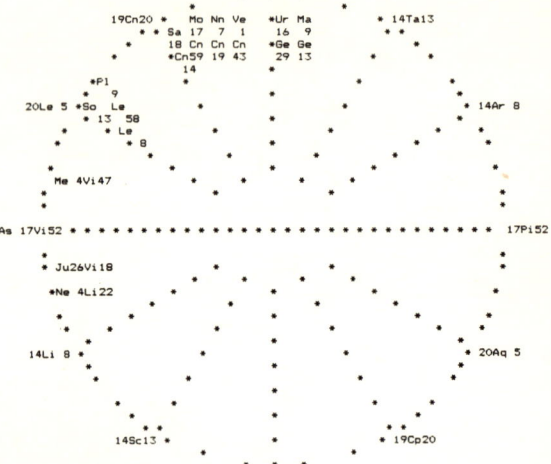

Event chart

Radix
DECEMBER SOLSTICE: 1944
Gmt 23 15 21 12 1944 (1)
34 24N 132 25E

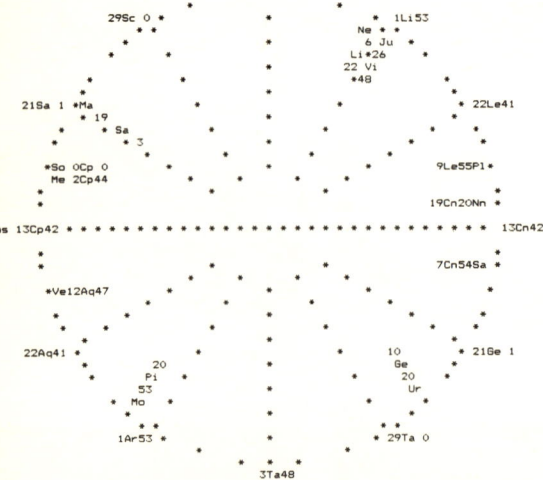

Capricorn ingress 1944

Radix
LUNAR/RETURN: CAPRICORN
Gmt 16 29 22 7 1945 (1)
34 24N 132 25E

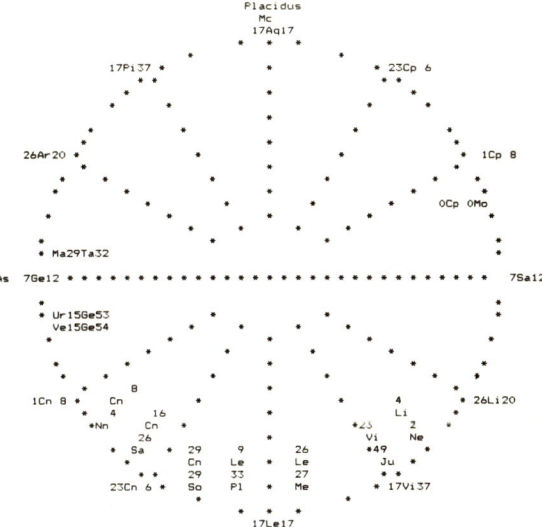

Capricorn lunar ingress prior to event

Gmt 14 49 28 7 1945 (1)
34 24N 132 25E

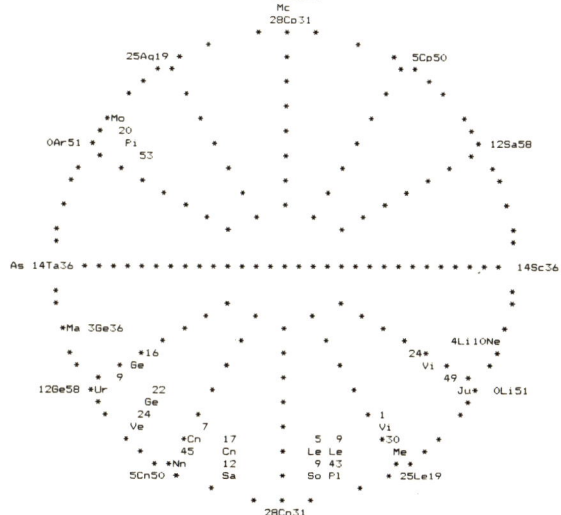

Capricorn ingress Moon return prior to event

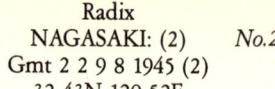

Radix
NAGASAKI: (2)   *No.2*
Gmt 2 2 9 8 1945 (2)
32 43N 129 52E

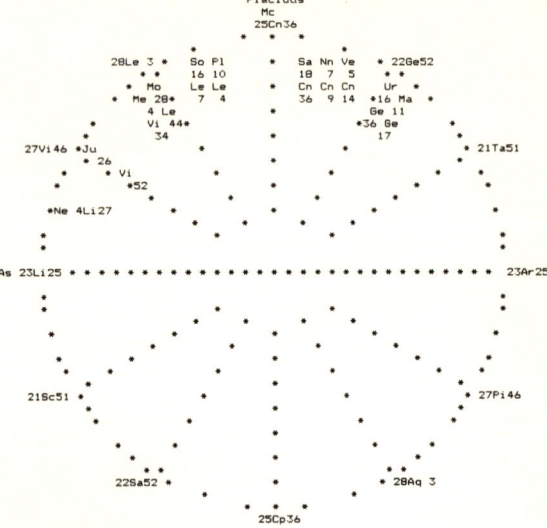

Event chart

Radix
DECEMBER SOLSTICE: 1944
Gmt 23 15 21 12 1944 (2)
32 43N 129 52E

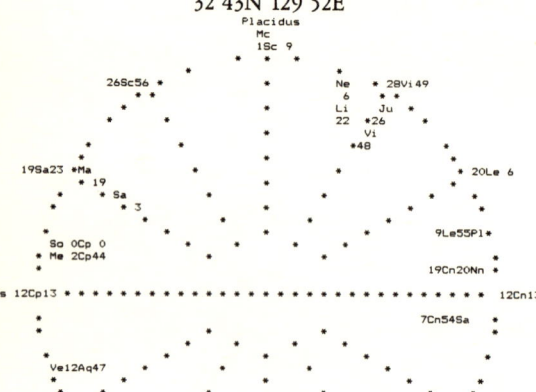

Capricorn ingress prior to event

Radix
LUNAR/RETURN: CAPRICORN
Gmt 16 29 22 7 1945 (2)
32 43N 129 52E

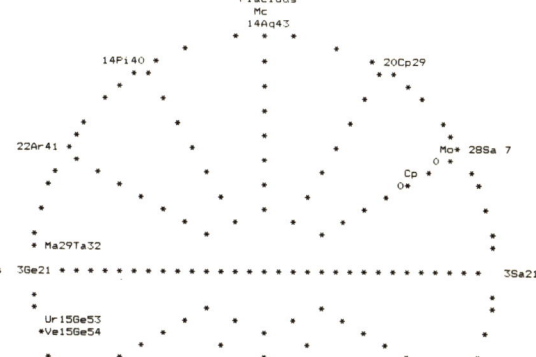

Capricorn lunar ingress prior to event

Gmt 14 49 28 7 1945 (2)
32 43N 129 52E

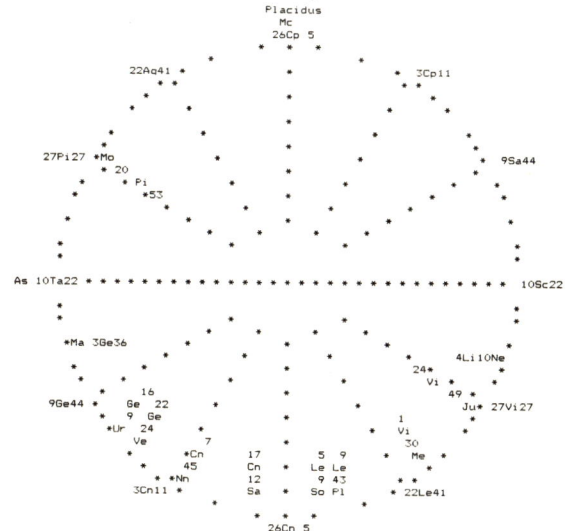

Capricorn ingress Moon return prior to event

12.

CONCLUSION

Evaluation of Return charts

The interest generated in solar returns and the various subsidiary charts is due, in no small measure, to the pioneering work of those who favoured the sidereal zodiac. Whatever arguments exist regarding the sidereal zodiac, the net result has, in the main, been beneficial for astrology in general. The investigation of any technique or theory is always stimulating and, in the case of returns, often enlightening as to the real significance of astrological concepts.

The sidereal approach has been demonstrated to be a valid method for dealing with returns, and the evidence in support of it is incontestable. However, it does not follow that because one system 'works', other systems must be wrong. The tropical return has never been accorded its full value because it was always considered, in most cases, to be a static instrument. Like other factors in astrology the approach to its interpretation was either faulty or simplistic. The research into the tropical returns, using techniques initiated by the sidereal advocates shows that these returns are as valuable, in their own right, as their sidereal counterparts.

The value of any system depends upon how well it performs when related to life, either personally or collectively. If, by using a few test examples, we find the astrological symbolism appropriate for the event or condition, we are justified in assuming that there may be something of value which warrants further investigation. If we seek to 'prove', in so far as proof is possible, the truth of some astrological concepts, we should be prepared to examine different approaches, which in the case of returns, entails comparison with both 'zodiacs'. An unbiased attitude—no easy matter—has to be adopted if we wish to achieve useful results.

The beauty of astrological symbolism, which is observable at all levels of existence, enables us to appreciate the subtle relationship which exists between 'heaven and earth'. Our perceptions and experiences reflect the cosmic inheritance which we acquired at birth. We bear the imprint of our natal chart from birth to death, but this 'foundation' chart is subject to kinetic processes which are in continual motion all the days of our life. These processes synchronize with our experiences. How and in what manner we express the planetary correlation will be governed, in a greater or lesser degree, according to our natal make-up.

The various techniques used in astrology to assess future trends vary from the complex to the simple. However, it is not the complexity or simplicity which is important, but whether the technique has validity and produces results which conform both in time and nature with the astrological factors. Experience with return charts, particularly the solar and lunar returns, suggest that these charts do reflect the conditions and the events likely to be encountered during the period of their operation.

One of the chief advantages of using solar or lunar return charts, supplemented by subsidiary charts if the circumstances warrant it, is that they indicate the nature of the developments which will be significant or affect the person during the period of the return. Of course, if we spend all our time poring over sheaves of charts, there is no time for living. Discretion concerning the type and number of charts to be studied or consulted is essential if a realistic analysis is to be obtained. Initially, it is sufficient to give priority to the annual solar return in conjunction with lunars for each month. Often the lunar return will highlight a significant period, particularly if natal planets are also involved.

The prominence of a planet, either close to an angle or forming part of some major pattern, will be indicative that the period will be coloured by the nature of the planet and those matters traditionally associated with it. Naturally, the chart has to be assessed in relation to the chart as a whole and in conjunction with the natal chart.

The sombre Saturn or aggressive Mars prominent in a return chart may indicate demanding conditions, not necessarily inimical to the person, but requiring responsible attitudes or energetic action. At the time of marriage, Saturn is sometimes to the fore which is not so irrelevant as it may seem. Marriage, one can say without being too cynical, is a curbing influence in that bonding ties are accepted and a sense of responsibility demanded. The Sun or Moon angular is associated with 'exposure' in that attention is directed towards the person or their interests. Sometimes the publicity is welcome, sometimes not. It all depends on the charts as a whole. When the Sun and Moon are together, i.e., conjunct, a new phase of life often commences. Plutonian contacts are notable for the dramatic changes which always mark the end of the 'old' and the beginning of the 'new'. Whether the Plutonian action is beneficial or not, the result is a feeling of finality and that things will never be the same again. Venus denotes ease and compliance so its prominence at the time of weddings is in accord with its nature of harmonious togetherness. The same reasoning applies to all the other planets in that the basic attributes of the planet will be experienced or expressed in conformity with the chart in its entirety.

The approach to astrology has to be undertaken in a realistic manner and its concepts related to real life. The profusion of subjects 'ruled' by any given house requires overhauling in the light of practical research. Admittedly, some of the houses and the matters traditionally associated with them have stood the test of time; others have not. Some of the examples in this book have shown the prominence of the fifth/eleventh houses in relation to the birth of children. Obviously, no firm conclusions can be drawn from a few cases, but at least we may have some confirmation, however slight, that the traditional teaching concerning the fifth and eleventh and their association with children (fifth) and hopes, wishes and expectations (eleventh) has some foundation. If we see Pluto prominent, as in the Shuttle disaster, or Uranus angular at the time when Hiroshima was destroyed, we realize how much we need to discover concerning planetary action and its effects at a particular time or place.

The timing of the return charts using the various methods of progression will often 'mirror' the developments affecting the individual during a certain period. Some of these will be psychological, others will be the result of events. In endeavouring to relate the indications as portrayed in the return charts to actual life we can obtain a better understanding of astrology which in turn will lead us to a greater awareness of ourselves and others.

APPENDIX 1.
CALCULATION TABLES

(i) Conversion of Mean Solar into Mean Sidereal Time (9.86 seconds per hour)

Mean Time Hours	Amount '	Amount "
1	0	9.86
2	0	19.71
3	0	29.57
4	0	39.43
5	0	49.28
6	0	59.14
7	1	09.00
8	1	18.85
9	1	28.71
10	1	38.56
11	1	48.42
12	1	58.28
13	2	08.13
14	2	17.99
15	2	27.85
16	2	37.70
17	2	47.56
18	2	57.42
19	3	07.27
20	3	17.13
21	3	26.99
22	3	36.84
23	3	46.70
24	3	56.56

Mean Time '	Amount "	Mean Time '	Amount "
1	0.16	31	5.09
2	0.33	32	5.26
3	0.49	33	5.42
4	0.66	34	5.59
5	0.82	35	5.75
6	0.99	36	5.92
7	1.15	37	6.08
8	1.31	38	6.24
9	1.48	39	6.41
10	1.64	40	6.57
11	1.81	41	6.74
12	1.97	42	6.90
13	2.14	43	7.07
14	2.30	44	7.23
15	2.46	45	7.39
16	2.63	46	7.56
17	2.79	47	7.72
18	2.96	48	7.89
19	3.12	49	8.05
20	3.29	50	8.22
21	3.45	51	8.38
22	3.61	52	8.54
23	3.78	53	8.71
24	3.94	54	8.87
25	4.11	55	9.04
26	4.27	56	9.20
27	4.44	57	9.37
28	4.60	58	9.53
29	4.76	59	9.69
30	4.93		

(ii) Hours and Minutes as a Decimal of a Day

	HOURS					
	0	1	2	3	4	5
M	Decimal of a Day					
0	0.000 000	0.041 667	0.083 333	0.125 000	0.166 667	0.208 333
1	.000 694	.042 361	.084 028	.125 694	.167 361	.209 028
2	.001 389	.043 056	.084 722	.126 389	.168 056	.209 722
3	.002 083	.043 750	.085 417	.127 083	.168 750	.210 417
4	.002 778	.044 444	.086 111	.127 778	.169 444	.211 111
5	0.003 472	0.045 139	0.086 806	0.128 472	0.170 139	0.211 806
6	.004 167	.045 833	.087 500	.129 167	.170 833	.212 500
7	.004 861	.046 528	.088 194	.129 861	.171 528	.213 194
8	.005 556	.047 222	.088 889	.130 556	.172 222	.213 889
9	.006 250	.047 917	.089 583	.131 250	.172 917	.214 583
10	0.006 944	0.048 611	0.090 278	0.131 944	0.173 611	0.215 278
11	.007 639	.049 306	.090 972	.132 639	.174 306	.215 972
12	.008 333	.050 000	.091 667	.133 333	.175 000	.216 667
13	.009 028	.050 694	.092 361	.134 028	.175 694	.217 361
14	.009 722	.051 389	.093 056	.134 722	.176 389	.218 056
15	0.010 417	0.052 083	0.093 750	0.135 417	0.177 083	0.218 750
16	.011 111	.052 778	.094 444	.136 111	.177 778	.219 444
17	.011 806	.053 472	.095 139	.136 806	.178 472	.220 139
18	.012 500	.054 167	.095 833	.137 500	.179 167	.220 833
19	.013 194	.054 861	.096 528	.138 194	.179 861	.221 528
20	0.013 889	0.055 556	0.097 222	0.138 889	0.180 556	0.222 222
21	.014 583	.056 250	.097 917	.139 583	.181 250	.222 917
22	.015 278	.056 944	.098 611	.140 278	.181 944	.223 611
23	.015 972	.057 639	.099 306	.140 972	.182 639	.224 306
24	.016 667	.058 333	.100 000	.141 667	.183 333	.225 000
25	0.017 361	0.059 028	0.100 694	0.142 361	0.184 028	0.225 694
26	.018 056	.059 722	.101 389	.143 056	.184 722	.226 389
27	.018 750	.060 417	.102 083	.143 750	.185 417	.227 083
28	.019 444	.061 111	.102 778	.144 444	.186 111	.227 778
29	.020 139	.061 806	.103 472	.145 139	.186 806	.228 472
30	0.020 833	0.062 500	0.104 167	0.145 833	0.187 500	0.229 167
31	.021 528	.063 194	.104 861	.146 528	.188 194	.229 861
32	.022 222	.063 889	.105 556	.147 222	.188 889	.230 556
33	.022 917	.064 583	.106 250	.147 917	.189 583	.231 250
34	.023 611	.065 278	.106 944	.148 611	.190 278	.231 944
35	0.024 306	0.065 972	0.107 639	0.149 306	0.190 972	0.232 639
36	.025 000	.066 667	.108 333	.150 000	.191 667	.233 333
37	.025 694	.067 361	.109 028	.150 694	.192 361	.234 028
38	.026 389	.068 056	.109 722	.151 389	.193 056	.234 722
39	.027 083	.068 750	.110 417	.152 083	.193 750	.235 417
40	0.027 778	0.069 444	0.111 111	0.152 778	0.194 444	0.236 111
41	.028 472	.070 139	.111 806	.153 472	.195 139	.236 806
42	.029 167	.070 833	.112 500	.154 167	.195 833	.237 500
43	.029 861	.071 528	.113 194	.154 861	.196 528	.238 194
44	.030 556	.072 222	.113 889	.155 556	.197 222	.238 889
45	0.031 250	0.072 917	0.114 583	0.156 250	0.197 917	0.239 583
46	.031 944	.073 611	.115 278	.156 944	.198 611	.240 278
47	.032 639	.074 306	.115 972	.157 639	.199 306	.240 972
48	.033 333	.075 000	.116 667	.158 333	.200 000	.241 667
49	.034 028	.075 694	.117 361	.159 028	.200 694	.242 361
50	0.034 722	0.076 389	0.118 056	0.159 722	0.201 389	0.243 056
51	.035 417	.077 083	.118 750	.160 417	.202 083	.243 750
52	.036 111	.077 778	.119 444	.161 111	.202 778	.244 444
53	.036 806	.078 472	.120 139	.161 806	.203 472	.245 139
54	.037 500	.079 167	.120 833	.162 500	.204 167	.245 833
55	0.038 194	0.079 861	0.121 528	0.163 194	0.204 861	0.246 528
56	.038 889	.080 556	.122 222	.163 889	.205 556	.247 222
57	.039 583	.081 250	.122 917	.164 583	.206 250	.247 917
58	.040 278	.081 944	.123 611	.165 278	.206 944	.248 611
59	0.040 972	0.082 639	0.124 306	0.165 972	0.207 639	0.249 306

(ii) Continued

	HOURS					
	6	7	8	9	10	11
M	Decimal of a Day					
0	0.250 000	0.291 667	0.333 333	0.375 000	0.416 667	0.458 333
1	.250 694	.292 361	.334 028	.375 694	.417 361	.459 028
2	.251 389	.293 056	.334 722	.376 389	.418 056	.459 722
3	.252 083	.293 750	.335 417	.377 083	.418 750	.460 417
4	.252 778	.294 444	.336 111	.377 778	.419 444	.461 111
5	0.253 472	0.295 139	0.336 806	0.378 472	0.420 139	0.461 806
6	.254 167	.295 833	.337 500	.379 167	.420 833	.462 500
7	.254 861	.296 528	.338 194	.379 861	.421 528	.463 194
8	.255 556	.297 222	.338 889	.380 556	.422 222	.463 889
9	.256 250	.297 917	.339 583	.381 250	.422 917	.464 583
10	0.256 944	0.298 611	0.340 278	0.381 944	0.423 611	0.465 278
11	.257 639	.299 306	.340 972	.382 639	.424 306	.465 972
12	.258 333	.300 000	.341 667	.383 333	.425 000	.466 667
13	.259 028	.300 694	.342 361	.384 028	.425 694	.467 361
14	.259 722	.301 389	.343 056	.384 722	.426 389	.468 056
15	0.260 417	0.302 083	0.343 750	0.385 417	0.427 083	0.468 750
16	.261 111	.302 778	.344 444	.386 111	.427 778	.469 444
17	.261 806	.303 472	.345 139	.386 806	.428 472	.470 139
18	.262 500	.304 167	.345 833	.387 500	.429 167	.470 833
19	.263 194	.304 861	.346 528	.388 194	.429 861	.471 528
20	0.263 889	0.305 556	0.347 222	0.388 889	0.430 556	0.472 222
21	.264 583	.306 250	.347 917	.389 583	.431 250	.472 917
22	.265 278	.306 944	.348 611	.390 278	.431 944	.473 611
23	.265 972	.307 639	.349 306	.390 972	.432 639	.474 306
24	.266 667	.308 333	.350 000	.391 667	.433 333	.475 000
25	0.267 361	0.309 028	0.350 694	0.392 361	0.434 028	0.475 694
26	.268 056	.309 722	.351 389	.393 056	.434 722	.476 389
27	.268 750	.310 417	.352 083	.393 750	.435 417	.477 083
28	.269 444	.311 111	.352 778	.394 444	.436 111	.477 778
29	.270 139	.311 806	.353 472	.395 139	.436 806	.478 472
30	0.270 833	0.312 500	0.354 167	0.395 833	0.437 500	0.479 167
31	.271 528	.313 194	.354 861	.396 528	.438 194	.479 861
32	.272 222	.313 889	.355 556	.397 222	.438 889	.480 556
33	.272 917	.314 583	.356 250	.397 917	.439 583	.481 250
34	.273 611	.315 278	.356 944	.398 611	.440 278	.481 944
35	0.274 306	0.315 972	0.357 639	0.399 306	0.440 972	0.482 639
36	.275 000	.316 667	.358 333	.400 000	.441 667	.483 333
37	.275 694	.317 361	.359 028	.400 694	.442 361	.484 028
38	.276 389	.318 056	.359 722	.401 389	.443 056	.484 722
39	.277 083	.318 750	.360 417	.402 083	.443 750	.485 417
40	0.277 778	0.319 444	0.361 111	0.402 778	0.444 444	0.486 111
41	.278 472	.320 139	.361 806	.403 472	.445 139	.486 806
42	.279 167	.320 833	.362 500	.404 167	.445 833	.487 500
43	.279 861	.321 528	.363 194	.404 861	.446 528	.488 194
44	.280 556	.322 222	.363 889	.405 556	.447 222	.488 889
45	0.281 250	0.322 917	0.364 583	0.406 250	0.447 917	0.489 583
46	.281 944	.323 611	.365 278	.406 944	.448 611	.490 278
47	.282 639	.324 306	.365 972	.407 639	.449 306	.490 972
48	.283 333	.325 000	.366 667	.408 333	.450 000	.491 667
49	.284 028	.325 694	.367 361	.409 028	.450 694	.492 361
50	0.284 722	0.326 389	0.368 056	0.409 722	0.451 389	0.493 056
51	.285 417	.327 083	.368 750	.410 417	.452 083	.493 750
52	.286 111	.327 778	.369 444	.411 111	.452 778	.494 444
53	.286 806	.328 472	.370 139	.411 806	.453 472	.495 139
54	.287 500	.329 167	.370 833	.412 500	.454 167	.495 833
55	0.288 194	0.329 861	0.371 528	0.413 194	0.454 861	0.496 528
56	.288 889	.330 556	.372 222	.413 889	.455 556	.497 222
57	.289 583	.331 250	.372 917	.414 583	.456 250	.497 917
58	.290 278	.331 944	.373 611	.415 278	.456 944	.498 611
59	0.290 972	0.332 639	0.374 306	0.415 972	0.457 639	0.499 306

(iii) Minutes as a decimal of a Degree or Hour; Seconds as a decimal of a Minute

′ ″	Decimal	′ ″	Decimal
1	0.0166	31	0.5166
2	.0333	32	.5333
3	.0500	33	.5500
4	.0666	34	.5666
5	.0833	35	.5833
6	.1000	36	.6000
7	.1166	37	.6166
8	.1333	38	.6333
9	.1500	39	.6500
10	.1666	40	.6666
11	.1833	41	.6833
12	.2000	42	.7000
13	.2166	43	.7166
14	.2333	44	.7333
15	.2500	45	.7500
16	.2666	46	.7666
17	.2833	47	.7833
18	.3000	48	.8000
19	.3166	49	.8166
20	.3333	50	.8333
21	.3500	51	.8500
22	.3666	52	.8666
23	.3833	53	.8833
24	.4000	54	.9000
25	.4166	55	.9166
26	.4333	56	.9333
27	.4500	57	.9500
28	.4666	58	.9666
29	.4833	59	.9833
30	.5000		

(iv) Longitude Equivalent in Time

Long. °	Equiv. Hours	Mins		Long. °	Equiv. Hours	Mins
1	0	04		39	2	36
2	0	08		40	2	40
3	0	12		41	2	44
4	0	16		42	2	48
5	0	20		43	2	52
6	0	24		44	2	56
7	0	28		45	3	00
8	0	32		46	3	04
9	0	36		47	3	08
10	0	40		48	3	12
11	0	44		49	3	16
12	0	48		50	3	20
13	0	52		51	3	24
14	0	56		52	3	28
15	1	00		53	3	32
				54	3	36
16	1	04		55	3	40
17	1	08		56	3	44
18	1	12		57	3	48
19	1	16		58	3	52
20	1	20		59	3	56
21	1	24		60	4	00
22	1	28				
23	1	32		61	4	04
24	1	36		62	4	08
25	1	40		63	4	12
26	1	44		64	4	16
27	1	48		65	4	20
28	1	52		66	4	24
29	1	56		67	4	28
30	2	00		68	4	32
				69	4	36
31	2	04		70	4	40
32	2	08		71	4	44
33	2	12		72	4	48
34	2	16		73	4	52
35	2	20		74	4	56
36	2	24		75	5	00
37	2	28		76	5	04
38	2	32				

(iv)

Long. °	Equiv. Hours	Mins		Long. °	Equiv. Hours	Mins
77	5	08		114	7	36
78	5	12		115	7	40
79	5	16		116	7	44
80	5	20		117	7	48
81	5	24		118	7	52
82	5	28		119	7	56
83	5	32		120	8	00
84	5	36				
85	5	40		121	8	04
86	5	44		122	8	08
87	5	48		123	8	12
88	5	52		124	8	16
89	5	56		125	8	20
90	6	00		126	8	24
				127	8	28
91	6	04		128	8	32
92	6	08		129	8	36
93	6	12		130	8	40
94	6	16		131	8	44
95	6	20		132	8	48
96	6	24		133	8	52
97	6	28		134	8	56
98	6	32		135	9	00
99	6	36				
100	6	40		136	9	04
101	6	44		137	9	08
102	6	48		138	9	12
103	6	52		139	9	16
104	6	56		140	9	20
105	7	00		141	9	24
				142	9	28
106	7	04		143	9	32
107	7	08		144	9	36
108	7	12		145	9	40
109	7	16		146	9	44
110	7	20		147	9	48
111	7	24		148	9	52
112	7	28		149	9	56
113	7	32		150	10	00

| Long. | Equiv. | | Long. | Equiv. | |
°	Hours	Mins	°	Hours	Mins
151	10	04	166	11	04
152	10	08	167	11	08
153	10	12	168	11	12
154	10	16	169	11	16
155	10	20	170	11	20
156	10	24	171	11	24
157	10	28	172	11	28
158	10	32	173	11	32
159	10	36	174	11	36
160	10	40	175	11	40
161	10	44	176	11	44
162	10	48	177	11	48
163	10	52	178	11	52
164	10	56	179	11	56
165	11	00	180	12	00

| Long. | Equiv. | | Long. | Equiv. | |
′	′	″	′	′	″
1	0	04	16	1	04
2	0	08	17	1	08
3	0	12	18	1	12
4	0	16	19	1	16
5	0	20	20	1	20
6	0	24	21	1	24
7	0	28	22	1	28
8	0	32	23	1	32
9	0	36	24	1	36
10	0	40	25	1	40
11	0	44	26	1	44
12	0	48	27	1	48
13	0	52	28	1	52
14	0	56	29	1	56
15	1	00	30	2	00

(iv)

Long. ′	Equiv. ′	Equiv. ″
31	2	04
32	2	08
33	2	12
34	2	16
35	2	20
36	2	24
37	2	28
38	2	32
39	2	36
40	2	40
41	2	44
42	2	48
43	2	52
44	2	56
45	3	00

Long. ′	Equiv. ′	Equiv. ″
46	3	04
47	3	08
48	3	12
49	3	16
50	3	20
51	3	24
52	3	28
53	3	32
54	3	36
55	3	40
56	3	44
57	3	48
58	3	52
59	3	56
60	4	00

Example:

What is the longitude equivalent in time of 145° 18′ ?

		H	M	S
From Tables: 145°	=	9	40	00
18′	=	0	01	12 +
		9	41	12

Or using calculator:

$$145° \ 18′ \ = \ \frac{145.3°}{15} \ = \ 9.6866 \qquad = \quad 9 \quad 41 \quad 12$$

(v) Day of the year

	Jan.	Feb.	Mar.	Apr.	May	June
1	1	32	60	91	121	152
2	2	33	61	92	122	153
3	3	34	62	93	123	154
4	4	35	63	94	124	155
5	5	36	64	95	125	156
6	6	37	65	96	126	157
7	7	38	66	97	127	158
8	8	39	67	98	128	159
9	9	40	68	99	129	160
10	10	41	69	100	130	161
11	11	42	70	101	131	162
12	12	43	71	102	132	163
13	13	44	72	103	133	164
14	14	45	73	104	134	165
15	15	46	74	105	135	166
16	16	47	75	106	136	167
17	17	48	76	107	137	168
18	18	49	77	108	138	169
19	19	50	78	109	139	170
20	20	51	79	110	140	171
21	21	52	80	111	141	172
22	22	53	81	112	142	173
23	23	54	82	113	143	174
24	24	55	83	114	144	175
25	25	56	84	115	145	176
26	26	57	85	116	146	177
27	27	58	86	117	147	178
28	28	59	87	118	148	179
29	29	—	88	119	149	180
30	30	—	89	120	150	181
31	31	—	90	—	151	—

	July	*Aug.*	*Sept.*	*Oct.*	*Nov.*	*Dec.*
1	182	213	244	274	305	335
2	183	214	245	275	306	336
3	184	215	246	276	307	337
4	185	216	247	277	308	338
5	186	217	248	278	309	339
6	187	218	249	279	310	340
7	188	219	250	280	311	341
8	189	220	251	281	312	342
9	190	221	252	282	313	343
10	191	222	253	283	314	344
11	192	223	254	284	315	345
12	193	224	255	285	316	346
13	194	225	256	286	317	347
14	195	226	257	287	318	348
15	196	227	258	288	319	349
16	197	228	259	289	320	350
17	198	229	260	290	321	351
18	199	230	261	291	322	352
19	200	231	262	292	323	353
20	201	232	263	293	324	354
21	202	233	264	294	325	355
22	203	234	265	295	326	356
23	204	235	266	296	327	357
24	205	236	267	297	328	358
25	206	237	268	298	329	359
26	207	238	269	299	330	360
27	208	239	270	300	331	361
28	209	240	271	301	332	362
29	210	241	272	302	333	363
30	211	242	273	303	334	364
31	212	243	—	304	—	365

(vi) SOLAR RETURN

Increments of *mean solar time* to be added to the Universal Time (UT) or GMT of the *tropical solar return* to obtain the UT or GMT of the progressed tropical solar return for any subsequent day of the solar return year.

Day	Day	Hour	Min.	Sec.
1	1	00	00	57
2	2	00	01	55
3	3	00	02	52
4	4	00	03	49
5	5	00	04	47
6	6	00	05	44
7	7	00	06	41
8	8	00	07	39
9	9	00	08	36
10	10	00	09	33
15	15	00	14	20
20	20	00	19	07
25	25	00	23	53
30	30	00	28	40
35	35	00	33	27
40	40	00	38	13
45	45	00	43	00
50	50	00	47	47
60	60	00	57	20
70	70	01	06	53
80	80	01	16	27
90	90	01	26	00
100	100	01	35	33
200	200	03	11	06
300	300	04	46	39
365	365	05	48	46

(vii) SOLAR RETURN

Increments of *sidereal time* to be added to the RAMC (or sidereal time) of the *tropical solar return* to obtain the RAMC (or sidereal time) of the progressed tropical solar return for any subsequent day in the solar return year.

Day	Hour	Min.	Sec.	Day	Hour	Min.	Sec.
1 =	0	04	54	25 =	2	02	31
2 =	0	09	48	30 =	2	27	01
3 =	0	14	42	35 =	2	51	32
4 =	0	19	36	40 =	3	16	02
5 =	0	24	30	45 =	3	40	32
6 =	0	29	24	50 =	4	05	02
7 =	0	34	18	55 =	4	29	32
8 =	0	39	12	60 =	4	54	03
9 =	0	44	06	70 =	5	43	03
10 =	0	49	00	80 =	6	32	03
11 =	0	53	54	90 =	7	21	04
12 =	0	58	48	100 =	8	10	04
13 =	1	03	42	150 =	12	15	06
14 =	1	08	37	200 =	16	20	09
15 =	1	13	31	250 =	20	25	11
16 =	1	18	25	300 =	00	30	13
17 =	1	23	19				
18 =	1	28	13				
19 =	1	33	07				
20 =	1	38	01				

Hours

	Hour	Min.	Sec.
6 =	0	01	13
12 =	0	02	27
18 =	0	03	41
24 =	0	04	54

(viii) RIGHT ASCENSION OF THE APPARENT SUN

(For Libra to Pisces ADD 12 hours)

Deg.	Aries			Taurus			Gemini			Cancer			Leo			Virgo		
	H	M	S	H	M	S	H	M	S	H	M	S	H	M	S	H	M	S
0	0	00	00	1	51	37	3	51	15	6	00	00	8	08	45	10	08	23
1	0	03	40	1	55	27	3	55	25	6	04	22	8	12	54	10	12	12
2	0	07	20	1	59	17	3	59	36	6	08	43	8	17	03	10	16	00
3	0	11	00	2	03	08	4	03	48	6	13	05	8	21	11	10	19	48
4	0	14	41	2	06	59	4	08	00	6	17	26	8	25	19	10	23	35
5	0	18	21	2	10	51	4	12	13	6	21	48	8	29	26	10	27	22
6	0	22	02	2	14	44	4	16	26	6	26	09	8	33	31	10	31	08
7	0	25	42	2	18	37	4	20	40	6	30	30	8	37	37	10	34	54
8	0	29	23	2	22	31	4	24	55	6	34	51	8	41	41	10	38	40
9	0	33	04	2	26	25	4	29	10	6	39	11	8	45	45	10	42	25
10	0	36	45	2	30	20	4	33	26	6	43	31	8	49	48	10	46	09
11	0	40	26	2	34	16	4	37	42	6	47	51	8	53	51	10	49	53
12	0	44	08	2	38	13	4	41	59	6	52	11	8	57	52	10	53	37
13	0	47	50	2	42	10	4	46	16	6	56	31	9	01	53	10	57	20
14	0	51	32	2	46	08	4	50	34	7	00	50	9	05	53	11	01	03
15	0	55	14	2	50	07	4	54	52	7	05	08	9	09	53	11	04	46
16	0	58	57	2	54	07	4	59	10	7	09	26	9	13	52	11	08	28
17	1	02	40	2	58	07	5	03	29	7	13	44	9	17	50	11	12	10
18	1	06	23	3	02	08	5	07	49	7	18	01	9	21	47	11	15	52
19	1	10	07	3	06	09	5	12	09	7	22	18	9	25	44	11	19	34
20	1	13	51	3	10	12	5	16	29	7	26	34	9	29	40	11	23	15
21	1	17	35	3	14	15	5	20	49	7	30	50	9	33	35	11	26	56
22	1	21	20	3	18	19	5	25	09	7	35	05	9	37	29	11	30	37
23	1	25	06	3	22	23	5	29	30	7	39	20	9	41	23	11	34	18
24	1	28	52	3	26	29	5	33	51	7	43	34	9	45	16	11	37	58
25	1	32	38	3	30	35	5	38	12	7	47	47	9	49	09	11	41	39
26	1	36	25	3	34	41	5	42	34	7	52	00	9	53	01	11	45	19
27	1	40	12	3	38	49	5	46	55	7	56	12	9	56	52	11	49	00
28	1	44	00	3	42	57	5	51	17	8	00	24	10	00	43	11	52	40
29	1	47	48	3	47	06	5	55	38	8	04	35	10	04	33	11	56	20
	Libra			Scorpio			Sagitt.			Capricorn			Aquarius			Pisces		

Intermediate values found by interpolation:
Example Sun's longitude 16°54′ Scorpio = from tables

	H	M	S
17° Scorpio	14	58	07 (Taurus table + 12 hours)
16 Scorpio	– 14	54	07
1 (60′)	0	04	00 Difference

There if 60 min. = 4 min. difference

$$54 \text{ min.} = \frac{54 \times 4}{60} = 3 \text{ min. } 36 \text{ sec. which}$$

added to 14.54.07 = 14.57.43 = Right Ascension of the Apparent Sun as required.

Trigonometrical formulae:
tan A = cos E, tan L where A is the required RA, E the obliquity of the Ecliptic and L the Sun's tropical longitude.

16°54′ Scorpio = 46°54′ from Libra:
46°54′ tan 1.06862 × 23°27′ (E) cos 0.9174 = tan 44.4318 plus 180° = 224.43 (224°26′) divided by 15 = 14.57.43 as required.

(ix) SOLAR QUOTIDIAN INCREMENT
$$\frac{(\ \ 24\ \ )}{365.25}$$

Days	Increment			Days	Increment		
	H	M	S		H	M	S
1	0	03	57	25	1	38	34
2	0	07	53	30	1	58	17
3	0	11	50	35	2	17	59
4	0	15	46	40	2	37	42
5	0	19	43	45	2	57	25
6	0	23	39	50	3	17	08
7	0	27	36	55	3	36	51
8	0	31	32	60	3	56	33
9	0	35	29	65	4	16	16
10	0	39	26	70	4	35	59
11	0	43	22	75	4	55	42
12	0	47	19	80	5	15	24
13	0	51	15	85	5	35	07

Days	Increment			Days	Increment		
	H	M	S		H	M	S
14	0	55	12	90	5	54	50
15	0	59	08	100	6	34	16
16	1	03	05	150	9	51	23
17	1	07	01	200	13	08	31
18	1	10	58	250	16	25	39
19	1	14	55	300	19	42	47
20	1	18	51	350	22	59	53

HOURS

H		M	S	H		M	S	H		M	S
1	=	0	10	8	=	01	19	18	=	02	57
4	=	0	39	12	=	01	58	21	=	03	27
6	=	0	59	15	=	02	28	24	=	03	57

(x) SYNETIC VERNAL POINT (SVP)

The SVP is the sidereal longitude of the Vernal Equinox—0° Aries Tropical—as determined by Fagan and Bradley. The 'two zodiacs' coincided in AD 221 but as the tropical zodiac's starting-point is in retrograde motion due to precession there is a divergence between the tropical and sidereal zodiacs of approximately one degree every 71½ years. At the present time the difference is approximately 24½°. From 221 until 2376 the SVP will be in Pisces. To convert tropical positions to sidereal, add the degree, minutes and seconds of the SVP to the tropical longitudes and deduct one sign (30°).

Sidereal Longitude in Pisces of the SVP for 1 January (* indicates leap year)

	Year	°	′	″		Year	°	′	″
*	1900	6	39	04		1910	6	31	14
	1901	6	38	16		1911	6	30	21
	1902	6	37	29	*	1912	6	29	26
	1903	6	36	44		1913	6	28	30
*	1904	6	36	00		1914	6	27	34
	1905	6	35	15		1915	6	26	39
	1906	6	34	30	*	1916	6	25	44
	1907	6	33	44		1917	6	24	51
*	1908	6	32	56		1918	6	23	59
	1909	6	32	06		1919	6	23	10

		°	′	″			°	′	″
*	1920	6	22	23		1961	5	48	21
	1921	6	21	36		1962	5	47	36
	1922	6	20	51		1963	5	46	50
	1923	6	20	07	*	1964	5	46	01
*	1924	6	19	23		1965	5	45	11
	1925	6	18	37		1966	5	44	19
	1926	6	17	50		1967	5	43	25
	1927	6	17	02	*	1968	5	42	30
*	1928	6	16	11		1969	5	41	34
	1929	6	15	18		1970	5	40	39
	1930	6	14	24		1971	5	39	43
	1931	6	13	29	*	1972	5	38	48
*	1932	6	12	33		1973	5	37	56
	1933	6	11	37		1974	5	37	05
	1934	6	10	42		1975	5	36	15
	1935	6	09	48	*	1976	5	35	28
*	1936	6	08	55		1977	5	34	42
	1937	6	08	04		1978	5	33	57
	1938	6	07	16		1979	5	33	13
	1939	6	06	29	*	1980	5	32	28
*	1940	6	05	43		1981	5	31	43
	1941	6	04	58		1982	5	30	55
	1942	6	04	14		1983	5	30	06
	1943	6	03	30	*	1984	5	29	16
*	1944	6	02	43		1985	5	28	23
	1945	6	01	56		1986	5	27	28
	1946	6	01	07		1987	5	26	33
	1947	6	00	15	*	1988	5	25	37
*	1948	5	59	22		1989	5	24	41
	1949	5	58	27		1990	5	23	46
	1950	5	57	32		1991	5	22	52
	1951	5	56	36	*	1992	5	22	00
*	1952	5	55	40		1993	5	21	09
	1953	5	54	45		1994	5	20	21
	1954	5	53	52		1995	5	19	34
	1955	5	53	00	*	1996	5	18	49
*	1956	5	52	10		1997	5	18	04
	1957	5	51	21		1998	5	17	20
	1958	5	50	36		1999	5	16	35
	1959	5	49	50	*	2000	5	15	49
*	1960	5	49	06					

(xi) *SOLAR RETURN*

Increments of *mean solar time* to be added to the UT or GMT of the *sidereal solar return* to obtain the UT or GMT of the progressed sidereal solar return for any subsequent day of the solar return year.

MEAN SOLAR TIME

Day		Day	Hour	Min.	Sec.	Day		Day	Hour	Min.	Sec.
1	=	1	00	01	01	25	=	25	00	25	17
2	=	2	00	02	01	30	=	30	00	30	20
3	=	3	00	03	02	35	=	35	00	35	24
4	=	4	00	04	03	40	=	40	00	40	27
5	=	5	00	05	03	45	=	45	00	45	31
6	=	6	00	06	04	50	=	50	00	50	34
7	=	7	00	07	05	60	=	60	01	00	41
8	=	8	00	08	05	70	=	70	01	10	48
9	=	9	00	09	06	80	=	80	01	20	55
10	=	10	00	10	07	90	=	90	01	31	01
11	=	11	00	11	08	100	=	100	01	41	08
12	=	12	00	12	08	150	=	150	02	31	42
13	=	13	00	13	09	200	=	200	03	22	16
14	=	14	00	14	10	250	=	250	04	12	51
15	=	15	00	15	10	300	=	300	05	03	25
16	=	16	00	16	11	365	=	365	06	09	09
17	=	17	00	17	12						
18	=	18	00	18	12						
19	=	19	00	19	13						
20	=	20	00	20	14						

(xii) SOLAR RETURN

Increments of *sidereal time* to be added to the RAMC (or sidereal time) of the *sidereal solar return* to obtain the RAMC (or sidereal time) of the progressed sidereal solar return for any subsequent day in the solar return year.

SIDEREAL TIME

Day		Hour	Min.	Sec.	Day		Hour	Min.	Sec.
1	=	0	04	57	25	=	2	03	55
2	=	0	09	54	30	=	2	28	42
3	=	0	14	52	35	=	2	53	29
4	=	0	19	50	40	=	3	18	16
5	=	0	24	47	45	=	3	43	03
6	=	0	29	44	50	=	4	07	50
7	=	0	34	42	60	=	4	57	24
8	=	0	39	39	70	=	5	46	58
9	=	0	44	37	80	=	6	36	32
10	=	0	49	34	90	=	7	26	06
11	=	0	54	31	100	=	8	15	40
12	=	0	59	29	150	=	12	23	29
13	=	1	04	26	200	=	16	31	19
14	=	1	09	24	250	=	20	39	09
15	=	1	14	21	300	=	00	46	59
16	=	1	19	18	365	=	06	09	09
17	=	1	24	16					
18	=	1	29	13					
19	=	1	34	11					
20	=	1	39	08					

(xiii) *EQUATION OF TIME*

		M			M			M			M
Jan.	1	− 3	Apr.	19	+ 1	Sept.	22	+ 7	Dec.	27	− 1
	2	− 4		23	+ 2		24	+ 8		29	− 2
	4	− 5		29	+ 3		27	+ 9		31	− 3
	6	− 6	May	9	+ 4		30	+ 10			
	8	− 7		23	+ 3	Oct.	3	+ 11			
	11	− 8	Jun.	1	+ 2		6	+ 12			
	13	− 9		7	+ 1		9	+ 13			
	16	− 10		13	0		14	+ 14			
	19	− 11		17	− 1		19	+ 15			
	23	− 12		22	− 2		24	+ 16			
	27	− 13		27	− 3	Nov.	15	+ 15			
Feb.	2	− 14	Jul.	1	− 4		20	+ 14			
	24	− 13		7	− 5		24	+ 13			
Mar.	2	− 12		14	− 6		28	+ 12			
	7	− 11	Aug.	10	− 5	Dec.	1	+ 11			
	11	− 10		16	− 4		4	+ 10			
	14	− 9		21	− 3		6	+ 9			
	18	− 8		25	− 2		8	+ 8			
	22	− 7		29	− 1		11	+ 7			
	25	− 6	Sept.	1	0		13	+ 6			
	28	− 5		4	+ 1		15	+ 5			
Apr.	1	− 4		8	+ 2		17	+ 4			
	4	− 3		10	+ 3		19	+ 3			
	7	− 2		13	+ 4		21	+ 2			
	11	− 1		15	+ 5		23	+ 1			
	15	− 0		18	+ 6		25	0			

(xiv) *TROPICAL INGRESSES*
SUN'S ENTRY INTO TROPICAL ARIES, CANCER, LIBRA

YEAR	ARIES UT	MARCH	CANCER UT	JUNE	LIBRA UT	SEPT.
1900	01.39	21	21.40	21	12.20	23
1901	07.23	21	03.28	22	18.09	23
1902	13.16	21	09.15	22	23.55	23
1903	19.15	21	15.05	22	05.44	24
1904	00.58	21	20.51	21	11.40	23
1905	06.57	21	02.51	22	17.30	23
1906	12.52	21	08.42	22	23.15	23
1907	18.33	21	14.23	22	05.09	24
1908	00.27	21	20.19	21	10.58	23
1909	06.13	21	02.06	22	16.44	23
1910	12.03	21	07.48	22	22.31	23
1911	17.55	21	13.35	22	04.18	24
1912	23.29	20	19.17	21	10.08	23
1913	05.17	21	01.09	22	15.53	23
1914	11.11	21	06.55	22	21.34	23
1915	16.52	21	12.29	22	03.24	24
1916	22.46	20	18.24	21	09.15	23
1917	04.37	21	00.14	22	15.00	23
1918	10.26	21	05.59	22	20.46	23
1919	16.19	21	11.53	22	02.35	24
1920	21.59	20	17.40	21	08.28	23
1921	03.51	21	23.35	21	14.20	23
1922	09.48	21	05.27	22	20.09	23
1923	15.28	21	11.03	22	02.04	24
1924	21.20	20	16.59	21	07.58	23
1925	03.12	21	22.50	21	13.43	23
1926	09.02	21	04.30	22	19.27	23
1927	14.59	21	10.22	22	01.17	24
1928	20.44	20	16.06	21	07.05	23
1929	02.35	21	22.01	21	12.52	23
1930	08.30	21	03.53	22	18.36	23
1931	14.06	21	09.28	22	00.23	24
1932	19.54	20	15.22	21	06.16	23
1933	01.42	21	21.12	21	12.01	23
1934	07.27	21	02.48	22	17.45	23
1935	13.18	21	08.38	22	23.38	23

YEAR	ARIES UT	ARIES MARCH	CANCER UT	CANCER JUNE	LIBRA UT	LIBRA SEPT.
1936	18.58	20	14.21	21	05.26	23
1937	00.45	21	20.12	21	11.13	23
1938	06.43	21	02.03	22	16.59	23
1939	12.28	21	07.39	22	22.49	23
1940	18.24	20	13.36	21	04.46	23
1941	00.20	21	19.33	21	10.33	23
1942	06.11	21	01.16	22	16.16	23
1943	12.03	21	07.12	22	22.12	23
1944	17.49	20	13.02	21	04.02	23
1945	23.37	20	18.52	21	09.50	23
1946	05.32	21	00.44	22	15.41	23
1947	11.13	21	06.19	22	21.29	23
1948	16.57	20	12.11	21	03.22	23
1949	22.48	20	18.03	21	09.06	23
1950	04.35	21	23.36	21	14.44	23
1951	10.26	21	05.25	22	20.37	23
1952	16.13	20	11.12	21	02.24	23
1953	22.00	20	17.00	21	08.06	23
1954	03.53	21	22.54	21	13.55	23
1955	09.35	21	04.31	22	19.41	23
1956	15.20	20	10.24	21	01.35	23
1957	21.16	20	16.20	21	07.26	23
1958	03.06	21	21.57	21	13.09	23
1959	08.55	21	03.50	22	19.09	23
1960	14.42	20	09.42	21	00.59	23
1961	20.32	20	15.30	21	06.43	23
1962	02.29	21	21.24	21	12.35	23
1963	08.20	21	03.04	22	18.23	23
1964	14.10	20	08.57	21	00.17	23
1965	20.05	20	14.56	21	06.06	23
1966	01.53	21	20.33	21	11.43	23
1967	07.37	21	02.23	22	17.38	23
1968	13.22	20	08.13	21	23.26	22
1969	19.08	20	13.55	21	05.07	23
1970	00.56	21	19.43	21	10.59	23
1971	06.38	21	01.19	22	16.45	23
1972	12.21	20	07.06	21	22.33	22
1973	18.13	20	13.01	21	04.21	23
1974	00.07	21	18.38	21	09.59	23

YEAR	ARIES UT	MARCH	CANCER UT	JUNE	LIBRA UT	SEPT.
1975	05.56	21	00.26	22	15.55	23
1976	11.50	20	06.24	21	21.48	22
1977	17.43	20	12.14	21	03.29	23
1978	23.34	20	18.09	21	09.26	23
1979	05.21	21	23.56	21	15.17	23
1980	11.10	20	05.47	21	21.09	22
1981	17.03	20	11.45	21	03.05	23
1982	22.56	20	17.23	21	08.46	23
1983	04.39	21	23.09	21	14.42	23
1984	10.25	20	05.02	21	20.33	22
1985	16.14	20	10.44	21	02.08	23
1986	22.03	20	16.30	21	07.59	23
1987	03.52	21	22.11	21	13.45	23
1988	09.39	20	03.57	21	19.29	22
1989	15.29	20	09.53	21	01.20	23
1990	21.20	20	15.33	21	06.56	23
1991	03.02	21	21.19	21	12.48	23
1992	08.48	20	03.14	21	18.43	22
1993	14.41	20	09.00	21	00.23	23
1994	20.28	20	14.48	21	06.19	23
1995	02.15	21	20.34	21	12.13	23
1996	08.03	20	02.24	21	18.00	22
1997	13.55	20	08.20	21	23.56	22
1998	19.55	20	14.03	21	05.38	23
1999	01.46	21	19.49	21	11.32	23
2000	07.36	20	01.48	21	17.28	22

(xv) *Sun's Entry into Capricorn (December Solstice)*

Tropical

Year	Dec.	Time	Year	Dec.	Time	Year	Dec.	Time
1900	22	06.42	1940	21	23.54	1980	21	16.57
1901	22	12.37	1941	22	05.44	1981	21	22.51
1902	22	18.36	1942	22	11.39	1982	22	04.39
1903	23	00.20	1943	22	17.29	1983	22	10.30
1904	22	06.14	1944	21	23.15	1984	21	16.23
1905	22	12.03	1945	22	05.03	1985	21	22.08
1906	22	17.54	1946	22	10.54	1986	22	04.02
1907	22	23.51	1947	22	16.43	1987	22	09.46
1908	22	05.33	1948	21	22.33	1988	21	15.28
1909	22	11.20	1949	22	04.24	1989	21	21.22
1910	22	17.12	1950	22	10.14	1990	22	03.07
1911	22	22.53	1951	22	16.00	1991	22	08.54
1912	22	04.45	1952	21	21.43	1992	21	14.43
1913	22	10.35	1953	22	03.32	1993	21	20.26
1914	22	16.23	1954	22	09.25	1994	22	02.23
1915	22	22.16	1955	22	15.11	1995	22	08.17
1916	22	03.58	1956	21	20.59	1996	21	14.06
1917	22	09.46	1957	22	02.49	1997	21	20.07
1918	22	15.42	1958	22	08.40	1998	22	01.57
1919	22	21.27	1959	22	14.35	1999	22	07.44
1920	22	03.17	1960	21	20.26	2000	21	13.38
1921	22	09.07	1961	22	02.19			
1922	22	14.57	1962	22	08.16			
1923	22	20.53	1963	22	14.02			
1924	22	02.45	1964	21	19.50			
1925	22	08.37	1965	22	01.40			
1926	22	14.34	1966	22	07.28			
1927	22	20.18	1967	22	13.17			
1928	22	02.04	1968	21	19.00			
1929	22	07.53	1969	22	00.44			
1930	22	13.39	1970	22	06.36			
1931	22	19.30	1971	22	12.24			
1932	22	01.15	1972	21	18.13			
1933	22	06.58	1973	22	00.08			
1934	22	12.49	1974	22	05.57			
1935	22	18.37	1975	22	11.46			
1936	22	00.27	1976	21	17.36			
1937	22	06.21	1977	21	23.24			
1938	22	12.14	1978	22	05.21			
1939	22	18.06	1979	22	11.10			

(xvi) DIURNAL PROPORTIONAL LOGARITHMS

Min. or Sec.	Hour or Min.	Hour or Min.	Hour or Min.	Hour or Min.	Hour or Min.	Hour or Min.	Hour or Min.	Hour or Min.	Hour or Min.	Hour or Min.	Hour or Min.	Hour or Min.
	0	1	2	3	4	5	6	7	8	9	10	11
0	Infinite	1.38021	1.07918	90309	77815	68124	60206	53511	47712	42597	38021	33882
1	3.15836	1.37303	1.07558	90069	77635	67980	60086	53408	47622	42517	37949	33816
2	2.85733	1.36597	1.07200	89829	77455	67836	59966	53305	47532	42436	37877	33751
3	2.68124	1.35902	1.06846	89591	77276	67692	59846	53202	47442	42356	37805	33685
4	2.55630	1.35218	1.06494	89355	77097	67549	59726	53100	47352	42276	37733	33620
5	2.45939	1.34545	1.06145	89119	76920	67406	59607	52997	47262	42197	37661	33554
6	2.38021	1.33882	1.05799	88885	76743	67264	59488	52895	47173	42117	37589	33489
7	2.31327	1.33229	1.05456	88652	76567	67123	59370	52794	47083	42038	37518	33424
8	2.25527	1.32585	1.05115	88421	76391	66981	59252	52692	46994	41958	37446	33359
9	2.20412	1.31951	1.04777	88190	76216	66841	59134	52591	46905	41879	37375	33294
10	2.15836	1.31327	1.04442	87961	76042	66700	59016	52490	46817	41800	37303	33229
11	2.11697	1.30711	1.04109	87733	75869	66560	58899	52389	46728	41721	37232	33164
12	2.07918	1.30103	1.03779	87506	75696	66421	58782	52288	46640	41642	37161	33099
13	2.04442	1.29504	1.03451	87281	75524	66282	58665	52188	46552	41564	37090	33035
14	2.01224	1.28913	1.03126	87056	75353	66143	58549	52087	46464	41485	37020	32970
15	1.98227	1.28330	1.02803	86833	75182	66005	58433	51987	46376	41407	36949	32906
16	1.95424	1.27755	1.02482	86611	75012	65868	58318	51888	46288	41329	36878	32842
17	1.92791	1.27187	1.02164	86390	74843	65730	58202	51788	46201	41251	36808	32778
18	1.90309	1.26627	1.01848	86170	74674	65594	58087	51689	46113	41173	36738	32713
19	1.87961	1.26074	1.01535	85951	74506	65457	57972	51590	46026	41095	36667	32649
20	1.85733	1.25527	1.01224	85733	74339	65321	57858	51491	45939	41018	36597	32585
21	1.83614	1.24988	1.00914	85517	74172	65186	57744	51393	45853	40940	36527	32522
22	1.81594	1.24455	1.00608	85301	74006	65051	57630	51294	45766	40863	36457	32458
23	1.79664	1.23929	1.00303	85087	73841	64916	57516	51196	45680	40786	36388	32394
24	1.77815	1.23408	1.00000	84873	73676	64782	57403	51098	45593	40709	36318	32331
25	1.76042	1.22894	0.99700	84661	73512	64648	57290	51000	45507	40632	36248	32267
26	1.74339	1.22387	0.99401	84450	73348	64514	57178	50903	45421	40555	36179	32204
27	1.72700	1.21884	0.99105	84239	73185	64382	57065	50806	45336	40478	36110	32141
28	1.71121	1.21388	0.98810	84030	73023	64249	56953	50709	45250	40402	36040	32078
29	1.69597	1.20897	0.98518	83822	72861	64117	56841	50612	45165	40325	35971	32014
30	1.68124	1.20412	0.98227	83614	72700	63985	56730	50515	45079	40249	35902	31951
31	1.66700	1.19932	0.97939	83408	72539	63854	56619	50419	44994	40173	35833	31889
32	1.65321	1.19458	0.97652	83203	72379	63723	56508	50323	44909	40097	35765	31826
33	1.63985	1.18988	0.97367	82998	72220	63592	56397	50227	44825	40021	35696	31763
34	1.62688	1.18524	0.97084	82795	72061	63462	56287	50131	44740	39945	35627	31700
35	1.61430	1.18064	0.96803	82593	71903	63332	56177	50035	44656	39870	35559	31638
36	1.60206	1.17609	0.96524	82391	71745	63202	56067	49940	44571	39794	35491	31575
37	1.59016	1.17159	0.96246	82190	71588	63073	55957	49845	44487	39719	35422	31513
38	1.57858	1.16714	0.95971	81991	71432	62945	55848	49750	44403	39644	35354	31451
39	1.56730	1.16273	0.95697	81792	71276	62816	55739	49655	44320	39569	35286	31389
40	1.55630	1.15836	0.95424	81594	71121	62688	55630	49560	44236	39494	35218	31327
41	1.54558	1.15404	0.95154	81397	70966	62561	55522	49466	44153	39419	35151	31265
42	1.53511	1.14976	0.94885	81201	70811	62434	55414	49372	44069	39344	35083	31203
43	1.52490	1.14554	0.94618	81006	70658	62307	55306	49278	43986	39270	35015	31141
44	1.51491	1.14133	0.94352	80812	70505	62181	55198	49185	43903	39195	34948	31079
45	1.50515	1.13717	0.94088	80618	70352	62054	55091	49091	43820	39121	34880	31017
46	1.49561	1.13306	0.93826	80426	70200	61929	54984	48998	43738	39047	34813	30956
47	1.48627	1.12898	0.93565	80234	70048	61803	54877	48905	43655	38973	34746	30894
48	1.47712	1.12494	0.93305	80043	69897	61678	54770	48812	43573	38899	34679	30833
49	1.46817	1.12094	0.93048	79853	69747	61554	54664	48719	43491	38825	34612	30772
50	1.45939	1.11697	0.92791	79664	69597	61430	54558	48627	43409	38751	34545	30710
51	1.45079	1.11304	0.92537	79475	69447	61306	54452	48534	43327	38678	34478	30649
52	1.44236	1.10915	0.92284	79288	69298	61182	54347	48442	43245	38604	34412	30588
53	1.43409	1.10529	0.92032	79101	69150	61059	54241	48350	43164	38531	34345	30527
54	1.42597	1.10146	0.91781	78915	69002	60936	54136	48259	43082	38458	34279	30467
55	1.41800	1.09767	0.91533	78730	68854	60814	54031	48167	43001	38385	34212	30406
56	1.41018	1.09391	0.91285	78545	68707	60691	53927	48076	42920	38312	34146	30345
57	1.40249	1.09018	0.91039	78362	68561	60570	53823	47985	42839	38239	34080	30284
58	1.39494	1.08648	0.90794	78179	68415	60448	53719	47894	42758	38166	34014	30224
59	1.38751	1.08282	0.90551	77997	68269	60327	53615	47803	42677	38094	33948	30163

(xvi) DIURNAL PROPORTIONAL LOGARITHMS

Min. or Sec.	Hour or Min. 12	Hour or Min. 13	Hour or Min. 14	Hour or Min. 15	Hour or Min. 16	Hour or Min. 17	Hour or Min. 18	Hour or Min. 19	Hour or Min. 20	Hour or Min. 21	Hour or Min. 22	Hour or Min. 23
0	30103	26627	23408	20412	17609	14976	12494	10146	07918	05799	03779	01848
1	30043	26571	23357	20364	17564	14934	12454	10108	7882	5765	3746	1817
2	29983	26516	23305	20316	17519	14891	12414	10070	7846	5730	3713	1786
3	29923	26460	23254	20268	17474	14849	12374	10032	7810	5696	3680	1754
4	29863	26405	23202	20220	17429	14806	12333	9994	7774	5662	3648	1723
5	29803	26349	23151	20172	17384	14764	12293	9956	7738	5627	3615	1691
6	29743	26294	23099	20124	17339	14722	12253	9918	7702	5593	3582	1660
7	29683	26239	23048	20076	17294	14679	12213	9880	7666	5559	3549	1629
8	29623	26184	22997	20028	17249	14637	12173	9842	7630	5524	3517	1597
9	29564	26129	22946	19980	17204	14595	12134	9804	7594	5490	3484	1566
10	29504	26074	22894	19932	17159	14553	12094	9767	7558	5456	3451	1535
11	29445	26019	22843	19885	17114	14511	12054	9729	7522	5422	3419	1504
12	29385	25964	22792	19837	17070	14468	12014	9691	7486	5388	3386	1472
13	29326	25909	22741	19789	17025	14426	11974	9653	7450	5354	3353	1441
14	29267	25854	22691	19742	16980	14384	11935	9616	7415	5319	3321	1410
15	29208	25800	22640	19694	16936	14342	11895	9578	7379	5285	3288	1379
16	29149	25745	22589	19647	16891	14300	11855	9541	7343	5251	3256	1348
17	29090	25691	22538	19599	16847	14258	11816	9503	7307	5217	3223	1317
18	29031	25636	22488	19552	16802	14217	11776	9466	7272	5183	3191	1286
19	28972	25582	22437	19505	16758	14175	11737	9428	7236	5149	3158	1255
20	28913	25527	22387	19458	16714	14133	11697	9391	7200	5115	3126	1224
21	28855	25473	22336	19410	16669	14091	11658	9353	7165	5081	3093	1193
22	28796	25419	22286	19363	16625	14050	11618	9316	7129	5048	3061	1162
23	28737	25365	22235	19316	16581	14008	11579	9278	7094	5014	3029	1131
24	28679	25311	22185	19269	16537	13966	11539	9241	7058	4980	2996	1100
25	28621	25257	22135	19222	16493	13925	11500	9204	7023	4946	2964	1069
26	28562	25203	22085	19175	16449	13883	11461	9167	6987	4912	2932	1038
27	28504	25149	22034	19128	16405	13842	11422	9129	6952	4879	2900	1007
28	28446	25095	21984	19082	16361	13800	11382	9092	6917	4845	2867	976
29	28388	25042	21934	19035	16317	13759	11343	9055	6881	4811	2835	945
30	28330	24988	21884	18988	16273	13717	11304	9018	6846	4777	2803	914
31	28272	24934	21835	18941	16229	13676	11265	8981	6811	4744	2771	884
32	28215	24881	21785	18895	16185	13635	11226	8944	6775	4710	2739	853
33	28157	24827	21735	18848	16141	13594	11187	8907	6740	4677	2707	822
34	28099	24774	21685	18802	16098	13552	11148	8870	6705	4643	2675	791
35	28042	24721	21636	18755	16054	13511	11109	8833	6670	4609	2642	761
36	27984	24667	21586	18709	16010	13470	11070	8796	6634	4576	2610	730
37	27927	24614	21536	18662	15967	13429	11031	8759	6599	4542	2578	699
38	27869	24561	21487	18616	15923	13388	10992	8722	6564	4509	2546	669
39	27812	24508	21437	18570	15880	13347	10953	8685	6529	4475	2514	638
40	27755	24455	21388	18524	15836	13306	10915	8648	6494	4442	2482	608
41	27698	24402	21339	18477	15793	13265	10876	8611	6459	4409	2451	577
42	27641	24349	21290	18431	15750	13224	10837	8575	6424	4375	2419	546
43	27584	24296	21240	18385	15706	13183	10798	8538	6389	4342	2387	516
44	27527	24244	21191	18339	15663	13142	10760	8501	6354	4309	2355	485
45	27470	24191	21142	18293	15620	13101	10721	8465	6319	4275	2323	455
46	27413	24138	21093	18247	15577	13061	10683	8428	6285	4242	2291	424
47	27357	24086	21044	18201	15533	13020	10644	8391	6250	4209	2260	394
48	27300	24033	20995	18156	15490	12979	10605	8355	6215	4176	2228	364
49	27244	23981	20946	18110	15447	12939	10567	8318	6180	4142	2196	333
50	27187	23929	20897	18064	15404	12898	10529	8282	6145	4109	2164	303
51	27132	23876	20849	18018	15361	12857	10490	8245	6111	4076	2133	272
52	27075	23824	20800	17973	15318	12817	10452	8209	6076	4043	2101	242
53	27018	23772	20751	17927	15275	12776	10413	8172	6041	4010	2069	212
54	26962	23720	20703	17882	15233	12736	10375	8136	6007	3977	2038	181
55	26906	23668	20654	17836	15190	12696	10337	8100	5972	3944	2006	151
56	26850	23616	20606	17791	15147	12655	10299	8063	5937	3911	1975	121
57	26794	23564	20557	17745	15104	12615	10260	8027	5903	3878	1943	91
58	26738	23512	20509	17700	15062	12574	10222	7991	5868	3845	1911	60
59	26683	23460	20460	17655	15019	12534	10184	7954	5834	3812	1880	30

SOLAR AND LUNAR RETURNS

(xvii) TERNARY PROPORTIONAL LOGARITHMS

					0 DEGREE, OR 0 HOUR					
″	0′	1′	2′	3′	4′	5′	6′	7′	8′	9′
0	Infinite	2.25527	1.95424	1.77815	1.65321	1.55630	1.47712	1.41017	1.35218	1.30103
1	4.03342	2.24809	1.95064	1.77575	1.65141	1.55486	1.47592	1.40914	1.35128	1.30023
2	3.73239	2.24103	1.94706	1.77335	1.64961	1.55342	1.47472	1.40811	1.35038	1.29942
3	3.55630	2.23408	1.94352	1.77097	1.64782	1.55198	1.47352	1.40708	1.34948	1.29862
4	3.43136	2.22724	1.94000	1.76861	1.64603	1.55055	1.47232	1.40606	1.34858	1.29782
5	3.33445	2.22051	1.93651	1.76625	1.64426	1.54912	1.47113	1.40503	1.34768	1.29703
6	3.25527	2.21388	1.93305	1.76391	1.64249	1.54770	1.46994	1.40401	1.34679	1.29623
7	3.18833	2.20735	1.92962	1.76158	1.64073	1.54629	1.46876	1.40300	1.34589	1.29544
8	3.13033	2.20091	1.92621	1.75927	1.63897	1.54487	1.46758	1.40198	1.34500	1.29464
9	3.07918	2.19457	1.92283	1.75696	1.63722	1.54347	1.46640	1.40097	1.34411	1.29385
10	3.03342	2.18833	1.91948	1.75467	1.63548	1.54206	1.46522	1.39996	1.34323	1.29306
11	2.99203	2.18217	1.91615	1.75239	1.63375	1.54066	1.46405	1.39895	1.34234	1.29227
12	2.95424	2.17609	1.91285	1.75012	1.63202	1.53927	1.46288	1.39794	1.34146	1.29148
13	2.91948	2.17010	1.90957	1.74787	1.63030	1.53788	1.46171	1.39694	1.34058	1.29070
14	2.88730	2.16419	1.90632	1.74562	1.62859	1.53649	1.46055	1.39593	1.33970	1.28991
15	2.85733	2.15836	1.90309	1.74339	1.62688	1.53511	1.45939	1.39493	1.33882	1.28913
16	2.82930	2.15261	1.89988	1.74117	1.62518	1.53374	1.45824	1.39394	1.33794	1.28835
17	2.80297	2.14693	1.89670	1.73896	1.62349	1.53236	1.45708	1.39294	1.33707	1.28757
18	2.77815	2.14133	1.89354	1.73676	1.62180	1.53100	1.45593	1.39195	1.33619	1.28679
19	2.75467	2.13580	1.89041	1.73457	1.62012	1.52963	1.45478	1.39096	1.33532	1.28601
20	2.73239	2.13033	1.88730	1.73239	1.61845	1.52827	1.45364	1.38997	1.33445	1.28524
21	2.71120	2.12494	1.88420	1.73023	1.61678	1.52692	1.45250	1.38899	1.33359	1.28446
22	2.69100	2.11961	1.88114	1.72807	1.61512	1.52557	1.45136	1.38800	1.33272	1.28369
23	2.67170	2.11435	1.87809	1.72593	1.61347	1.52422	1.45022	1.38702	1.33186	1.28292
24	2.65321	2.10914	1.87506	1.72379	1.61182	1.52288	1.44909	1.38604	1.33099	1.28215
25	2.63548	2.10400	1.87206	1.72167	1.61018	1.52154	1.44796	1.38506	1.33013	1.28138
26	2.61845	2.09893	1.86907	1.71956	1.60854	1.52021	1.44684	1.38409	1.32927	1.28061
27	2.60206	2.09390	1.86611	1.71745	1.60691	1.51888	1.44571	1.38312	1.32842	1.27984
28	2.58627	2.08894	1.86316	1.71536	1.60529	1.51755	1.44459	1.38215	1.32756	1.27908
29	2.57103	2.08403	1.86024	1.71328	1.60367	1.51623	1.44347	1.38118	1.32671	1.27831
30	2.55630	2.07918	1.85733	1.71120	1.60206	1.51491	1.44236	1.38021	1.32585	1.27755
31	2.54206	2.07438	1.85445	1.70914	1.60045	1.51360	1.44125	1.37925	1.32500	1.27679
32	2.52827	2.06964	1.85158	1.70709	1.59885	1.51229	1.44014	1.37829	1.32415	1.27603
33	2.51491	2.06494	1.84873	1.70504	1.59726	1.51098	1.43903	1.37733	1.32331	1.27527
34	2.50194	2.06030	1.84590	1.70301	1.59567	1.50968	1.43793	1.37637	1.32246	1.27451
35	2.48936	2.05570	1.84309	1.70099	1.59409	1.50838	1.43683	1.37541	1.32162	1.27376
36	2.47712	2.05115	1.84030	1.69897	1.59251	1.50708	1.43573	1.37446	1.32077	1.27300
37	2.46522	2.04665	1.83752	1.69696	1.59094	1.50579	1.43463	1.37351	1.31993	1.27225
38	2.45364	2.04220	1.83477	1.69497	1.58938	1.50451	1.43354	1.37256	1.31909	1.27150
39	2.44236	2.03779	1.83203	1.69298	1.58782	1.50322	1.43245	1.37161	1.31826	1.27075
40	2.43136	2.03342	1.82930	1.69100	1.58627	1.50194	1.43136	1.37067	1.31742	1.27000
41	2.42064	2.02910	1.82660	1.68903	1.58472	1.50067	1.43028	1.36972	1.31659	1.26925
42	2.41017	2.02482	1.82391	1.68707	1.58317	1.49940	1.42920	1.36878	1.31575	1.26850
43	2.39996	2.02060	1.82124	1.68512	1.58164	1.49813	1.42812	1.36784	1.31492	1.26776
44	2.38997	2.01639	1.81858	1.68318	1.58011	1.49687	1.42704	1.36691	1.31409	1.26701
45	2.38021	2.01223	1.81594	1.68124	1.57858	1.49560	1.42597	1.36597	1.31326	1.26627
46	2.37067	2.00812	1.81332	1.67932	1.57706	1.49435	1.42490	1.36504	1.31244	1.26553
47	2.36133	2.00404	1.81071	1.67740	1.57554	1.49309	1.42383	1.36411	1.31161	1.26479
48	2.35218	2.00000	1.80811	1.67549	1.57403	1.49184	1.42276	1.36318	1.31079	1.26405
49	2.34323	1.99600	1.80554	1.67359	1.57253	1.49060	1.42170	1.36225	1.30997	1.26331
50	2.33445	1.99203	1.80297	1.67170	1.57103	1.48936	1.42064	1.36133	1.30915	1.26257
51	2.32585	1.98810	1.80043	1.66981	1.56953	1.48812	1.41958	1.36040	1.30833	1.26184
52	2.31742	1.98421	1.79790	1.66794	1.56804	1.48688	1.41853	1.35948	1.30751	1.26110
53	2.30915	1.98035	1.79538	1.66607	1.56656	1.48565	1.41747	1.35856	1.30670	1.26037
54	2.30103	1.97652	1.79287	1.66421	1.56508	1.48442	1.41642	1.35765	1.30588	1.25964
55	2.29306	1.97273	1.79039	1.66236	1.56360	1.48320	1.41538	1.35673	1.30507	1.25891
56	2.28524	1.96897	1.78791	1.66051	1.56213	1.48197	1.41433	1.35582	1.30426	1.25818
57	2.27755	1.96524	1.78545	1.65868	1.56067	1.48076	1.41329	1.35491	1.30345	1.25745
58	2.27000	1.96154	1.78300	1.65685	1.55921	1.47954	1.41225	1.35400	1.30264	1.25672
59	2.26257	1.95788	1.78057	1.65503	1.55775	1.47833	1.41121	1.35309	1.30183	1.25600
60	2.25527	1.95424	1.77815	1.65321	1.55630	1.47712	1.41017	1.35218	1.30103	1.25527

′	10′	11′	12′	13′	14′	15′	16′	17′	18′	19′
				0 DEGREE, OR 0 HOUR						
0	1.25527	1.21388	1.17609	1.14133	1.10914	1.07918	1.05115	1.02482	1.00000	0.97652
1	1.25455	1.21322	1.17549	1.14077	1.10863	1.07870	1.05070	1.02440	0.99960	0.97614
2	1.25383	1.21257	1.17489	1.14022	1.10811	1.07822	1.05025	1.02397	0.99920	0.97576
3	1.25311	1.21191	1.17429	1.13966	1.10760	1.07774	1.04980	1.02355	0.99880	0.97538
4	1.25239	1.21126	1.17369	1.13911	1.10708	1.07726	1.04935	1.02312	0.99839	0.97500
5	1.25167	1.21060	1.17309	1.13855	1.10657	1.07678	1.04890	1.02270	0.99799	0.97462
6	1.25095	1.20995	1.17249	1.13800	1.10605	1.07630	1.04845	1.02228	0.99759	0.97424
7	1.25024	1.20930	1.17189	1.13745	1.10554	1.07582	1.04800	1.02185	0.99719	0.97386
8	1.24952	1.20865	1.17129	1.13690	1.10503	1.07534	1.04755	1.02143	0.99679	0.97348
9	1.24881	1.20800	1.17070	1.13635	1.10452	1.07486	1.04710	1.02101	0.99640	0.97310
10	1.24809	1.20735	1.17010	1.13580	1.10400	1.07438	1.04665	1.02059	0.99600	0.97273
11	1.24738	1.20670	1.16951	1.13525	1.10349	1.07391	1.04620	1.02017	0.99560	0.97235
12	1.24667	1.20605	1.16891	1.13470	1.10298	1.07343	1.04576	1.01974	0.99520	0.97197
13	1.24596	1.20541	1.16832	1.13415	1.10247	1.07295	1.04531	1.01932	0.99480	0.97159
14	1.24526	1.20476	1.16773	1.13360	1.10197	1.07248	1.04486	1.01890	0.99441	0.97122
15	1.24455	1.20412	1.16714	1.13306	1.10146	1.07200	1.04442	1.01848	0.99401	0.97084
16	1.24384	1.20348	1.16655	1.13251	1.10095	1.07153	1.04397	1.01806	0.99361	0.97047
17	1.24314	1.20284	1.16596	1.13197	1.10044	1.07105	1.04353	1.01764	0.99322	0.97009
18	1.24244	1.20219	1.16537	1.13142	1.09994	1.07058	1.04308	1.01723	0.99282	0.96972
19	1.24173	1.20155	1.16478	1.13088	1.09943	1.07011	1.04264	1.01681	0.99243	0.96934
20	1.24103	1.20091	1.16419	1.13033	1.09893	1.06964	1.04220	1.01639	0.99203	0.96897
21	1.24033	1.20028	1.16361	1.12979	1.09842	1.06916	1.04175	1.01597	0.99164	0.96859
22	1.23963	1.19964	1.16302	1.12925	1.09792	1.06869	1.04131	1.01556	0.99124	0.96822
23	1.23894	1.19900	1.16243	1.12871	1.09741	1.06822	1.04087	1.01514	0.99085	0.96784
24	1.23824	1.19837	1.16185	1.12817	1.09691	1.06775	1.04043	1.01472	0.99045	0.96747
25	1.23754	1.19773	1.16127	1.12763	1.09641	1.06728	1.03999	1.01431	0.99006	0.96710
26	1.23685	1.19710	1.16068	1.12709	1.09591	1.06681	1.03955	1.01389	0.98967	0.96673
27	1.23616	1.19647	1.16010	1.12655	1.09540	1.06634	1.03911	1.01348	0.98928	0.96635
28	1.23546	1.19584	1.15952	1.12601	1.09490	1.06588	1.03867	1.01306	0.98888	0.96598
29	1.23477	1.19520	1.15894	1.12548	1.09440	1.06541	1.03823	1.01265	0.98849	0.96561
30	1.23408	1.19457	1.15836	1.12494	1.09390	1.06494	1.03779	1.01223	0.98810	0.96524
31	1.23339	1.19395	1.15778	1.12440	1.09341	1.06447	1.03735	1.01182	0.98771	0.96487
32	1.23271	1.19332	1.15721	1.12387	1.09291	1.06401	1.03691	1.01141	0.98732	0.96450
33	1.23202	1.19269	1.15663	1.12333	1.09241	1.06354	1.03647	1.01100	0.98693	0.96413
34	1.23133	1.19206	1.15605	1.12280	1.09191	1.06308	1.03604	1.01058	0.98654	0.96376
35	1.23065	1.19144	1.15548	1.12227	1.09142	1.06261	1.03560	1.01017	0.98615	0.96339
36	1.22997	1.19081	1.15490	1.12173	1.09092	1.06215	1.03516	1.00976	0.98576	0.96302
37	1.22928	1.19019	1.15433	1.12120	1.09042	1.06168	1.03473	1.00935	0.98537	0.96265
38	1.22860	1.18957	1.15375	1.12067	1.08993	1.06122	1.03429	1.00894	0.98498	0.96228
39	1.22792	1.18895	1.15318	1.12014	1.08943	1.06076	1.03386	1.00853	0.98459	0.96191
40	1.22724	1.18833	1.15261	1.11961	1.08894	1.06030	1.03342	1.00812	0.98421	0.96154
41	1.22657	1.18771	1.15204	1.11908	1.08845	1.05983	1.03299	1.00771	0.98382	0.96117
42	1.22589	1.18709	1.15147	1.11855	1.08796	1.05937	1.03256	1.00730	0.98343	0.96081
43	1.22521	1.18647	1.15090	1.11802	1.08746	1.05891	1.03212	1.00689	0.98304	0.96044
44	1.22454	1.18585	1.15033	1.11750	1.08697	1.05845	1.03169	1.00648	0.98266	0.96007
45	1.22386	1.18523	1.14976	1.11697	1.08648	1.05799	1.03126	1.00607	0.98227	0.95971
46	1.22319	1.18462	1.14919	1.11644	1.08599	1.05753	1.03083	1.00567	0.98189	0.95934
47	1.22252	1.18400	1.14863	1.11592	1.08550	1.05707	1.03039	1.00526	0.98150	0.95897
48	1.22185	1.18339	1.14806	1.11539	1.08501	1.05662	1.02996	1.00485	0.98111	0.95861
49	1.22118	1.18278	1.14750	1.11487	1.08452	1.05616	1.02953	1.00445	0.98073	0.95824
50	1.22051	1.18217	1.14693	1.11435	1.08403	1.05570	1.02910	1.00404	0.98035	0.95788
51	1.21984	1.18155	1.14637	1.11382	1.08355	1.05524	1.02867	1.00363	0.97996	0.95751
52	1.21918	1.18094	1.14581	1.11330	1.08306	1.05479	1.02824	1.00323	0.97958	0.95715
53	1.21851	1.18033	1.14524	1.11278	1.08257	1.05433	1.02781	1.00282	0.97919	0.95678
54	1.21785	1.17973	1.14468	1.11226	1.08209	1.05388	1.02739	1.00242	0.97881	0.95642
55	1.21718	1.17912	1.14412	1.11174	1.08160	1.05342	1.02696	1.00202	0.97843	0.95606
56	1.21652	1.17851	1.14356	1.11122	1.08112	1.05297	1.02653	1.00161	0.97805	0.95569
57	1.21586	1.17790	1.14300	1.11070	1.08063	1.05251	1.02610	1.00121	0.97766	0.95533
58	1.21520	1.17730	1.14244	1.11018	1.08015	1.05206	1.02568	1.00080	0.97728	0.95497
59	1.21454	1.17669	1.14189	1.10966	1.07966	1.05161	1.02525	1.00040	0.97690	0.95460
60	1.21388	1.17609	1.14133	1.10914	1.07918	1.05115	1.02482	1.00000	0.97652	0.95424

"	0 DEGREE, OR 0 HOUR									
	20'	21'	22'	23'	24'	25'	26'	27'	28'	29'
0	95424	93305	91285	89354	87506	85733	84030	82391	80811	79287
1	95388	93271	91252	89323	87476	85704	84002	82364	80786	79262
2	95352	93236	91219	89292	87446	85675	83974	82337	80760	79238
3	95316	93202	91186	89260	87416	85646	83946	82311	80734	79213
4	95280	93168	91154	89229	87386	85618	83919	82284	80708	79188
5	95244	93133	91121	89197	87356	85589	83891	82257	80682	79163
6	95208	93099	91088	89166	87326	85560	83863	82230	80657	79138
7	95172	93065	91055	89135	87296	85531	83835	82204	80631	79113
8	95136	93030	91023	89103	87266	85502	83808	82177	80605	79088
9	95100	92996	90990	89072	87236	85473	83780	82150	80579	79063
10	95064	92962	90957	89041	87206	85445	83752	82124	80554	79039
11	95028	92928	90925	89010	87176	85416	83725	82097	80528	79014
12	94992	92894	90892	88978	87146	85387	83697	82070	80502	78989
13	94956	92860	90859	88947	87116	85358	83670	82044	80477	78964
14	94921	92825	90827	88916	87086	85330	83642	82017	80451	78939
15	94885	92791	90794	88885	87056	85301	83614	81991	80425	78915
16	94849	92757	90762	88854	87026	85272	83587	81964	80400	78890
17	94813	92723	90729	88823	86996	85244	83559	81938	80374	78865
18	94778	92689	90697	88792	86967	85215	83532	81911	80349	78840
19	94742	92655	90664	88761	86937	85187	83504	81884	80323	78816
20	94706	92621	90632	88730	86907	85158	83477	81858	80297	78791
21	94671	92587	90599	88699	86877	85129	83449	81832	80272	78766
22	94635	92554	90567	88668	86848	85101	83422	81805	80246	78742
23	94600	92520	90535	88637	86818	85072	83394	81779	80221	78717
24	94564	92486	90502	88606	86788	85044	83367	81752	80195	78693
25	94529	92452	90470	88575	86759	85015	83339	81726	80170	78668
26	94493	92418	90438	88544	86729	84987	83312	81699	80144	78643
27	94458	92385	90406	88513	86699	84958	83285	81673	80119	78619
28	94423	92351	90373	88482	86670	84930	83257	81647	80094	78594
29	94387	92317	90341	88451	86640	84902	83230	81620	80068	78570
30	94352	92283	90309	88420	86611	84873	83203	81594	80043	78545
31	94317	92250	90277	88390	86581	84845	83175	81568	80017	78521
32	94281	92216	90245	88359	86552	84816	83148	81541	79992	78496
33	94246	92183	90213	88328	86522	84788	83121	81515	79967	78472
34	94211	92149	90181	88297	86493	84760	83094	81489	79941	78447
35	94176	92115	90148	88267	86463	84732	83066	81463	79916	78423
36	94141	92082	90116	88236	86434	84703	83039	81436	79891	78398
37	94105	92048	90084	88205	86404	84675	83012	81410	79865	78374
38	94070	92015	90052	88175	86375	84647	82985	81384	79840	78349
39	94035	91981	90020	88144	86346	84619	82958	81358	79815	78325
40	94000	91948	89988	88114	86316	84590	82930	81332	79790	78300
41	93965	91915	89957	88083	86287	84562	82903	81305	79764	78276
42	93930	91881	89925	88052	86258	84534	82876	81279	79739	78252
43	93895	91848	89893	88022	86228	84506	82849	81253	79714	78227
44	93860	91815	89861	87991	86199	84478	82822	81227	79689	78203
45	93825	91781	89829	87961	86170	84450	82795	81201	79663	78179
46	93791	91748	89797	87930	86140	84421	82768	81175	79638	78154
47	93756	91715	89766	87900	86111	84393	82741	81149	79613	78130
48	93721	91682	89734	87870	86082	84365	82714	81123	79588	78106
49	93686	91648	89702	87839	86053	84337	82687	81097	79563	78081
50	93651	91615	89670	87809	86024	84309	82660	81071	79538	78057
51	93617	91582	89639	87778	85995	84281	82633	81045	79513	78033
52	93582	91549	89607	87748	85965	84253	82606	81019	79488	78009
53	93547	91516	89575	87718	85936	84225	82579	80993	79463	77984
54	93513	91483	89544	87687	85907	84197	82552	80967	79437	77960
55	93478	91450	89512	87657	85878	84169	82525	80941	79412	77936
56	93443	91417	89481	87627	85849	84141	82498	80915	79387	77912
57	93409	91384	89449	87597	85820	84114	82471	80889	79362	77888
58	93374	91351	89417	87566	85791	84086	82445	80863	79337	77863
59	93340	91318	89386	87536	85762	84058	82418	80837	79312	77839
60	93305	91285	89354	87506	85733	84030	82391	80811	79287	77815

	30′	31′	32′	33′	34′	35′	36′	37′	38′	39′
					0 DEGREE, OR 0 HOUR					
0	77815	76391	75012	73676	72379	71120	69897	68707	67549	66421
1	77791	76368	74990	73654	72358	71100	69877	68688	67530	66402
2	77767	76344	74967	73632	72337	71079	69857	68668	67511	66384
3	77743	76321	74944	73610	72316	71058	69837	68648	67492	66365
4	77719	76298	74922	73588	72294	71038	69817	68629	67473	66347
5	77695	76274	74899	73566	72273	71017	69797	68609	67454	66328
6	77671	76251	74877	73544	72252	70997	69777	68590	67435	66310
7	77647	76228	74854	73523	72231	70976	69756	68570	67416	66291
8	77623	76205	74832	73501	72209	70955	69736	68551	67397	66273
9	77599	76181	74809	73479	72188	70935	69716	68531	67378	66254
10	77575	76158	74787	73457	72167	70914	69696	68512	67359	66236
11	77551	76135	74764	73435	72146	70894	69676	68492	67340	66217
12	77527	76112	74742	73413	72125	70873	69656	68473	67321	66199
13	77503	76089	74719	73392	72103	70852	69636	68454	67302	66180
14	77479	76065	74697	73370	72082	70832	69616	68434	67283	66162
15	77455	76042	74674	73348	72061	70811	69596	68415	67264	66143
16	77431	76019	74652	73326	72040	70791	69576	68395	67245	66125
17	77407	75996	74629	73305	72019	70770	69557	68376	67226	66106
18	77383	75973	74607	73283	71998	70750	69537	68356	67207	66088
19	77359	75950	74585	73261	71977	70729	69517	68337	67188	66070
20	77335	75927	74562	73239	71956	70709	69497	68318	67170	66051
21	77311	75903	74540	73218	71935	70688	69477	68298	67151	66033
22	77288	75880	74517	73196	71914	70668	69457	68279	67132	66014
23	77264	75857	74495	73174	71892	70647	69437	68259	67113	65996
24	77240	75834	74473	73153	71871	70627	69417	68240	67094	65978
25	77216	75811	74450	73131	71850	70606	69397	68221	67075	65959
26	77192	75788	74428	73109	71829	70586	69377	68201	67056	65941
27	77169	75765	74406	73088	71808	70566	69358	68182	67038	65923
28	77145	75742	74383	73066	71787	70545	69338	68163	67019	65904
29	77121	75719	74361	73044	71766	70525	69318	68143	67000	65886
30	77097	75696	74339	73023	71745	70504	69298	68124	66981	65868
31	77074	75673	74317	73001	71724	70484	69278	68105	66962	65849
32	77050	75650	74294	72980	71703	70464	69258	68086	66944	65831
33	77026	75627	74272	72958	71682	70443	69239	68066	66925	65813
34	77002	75604	74250	72936	71662	70423	69219	68047	66906	65794
35	76979	75581	74228	72915	71641	70403	69199	68028	66887	65776
36	76955	75559	74205	72893	71620	70382	69179	68008	66869	65758
37	76931	75536	74183	72872	71599	70362	69159	67989	66850	65739
38	76908	75513	74161	72850	71578	70342	69140	67970	66831	65721
39	76884	75490	74139	72829	71557	70321	69120	67951	66812	65703
40	76861	75467	74117	72807	71536	70301	69100	67932	66794	65685
41	76837	75444	74095	72786	71515	70281	69080	67912	66775	65666
42	76813	75421	74072	72764	71494	70260	69061	67893	66756	65648
43	76790	75398	74050	72743	71473	70240	69041	67874	66737	65630
44	76766	75376	74028	72721	71453	70220	69021	67855	66719	65612
45	76743	75353	74006	72700	71432	70200	69002	67836	66700	65594
46	76719	75330	73984	72678	71411	70179	68982	67816	66681	65575
47	76696	75307	73962	72657	71390	70159	68962	67797	66663	65557
48	76672	75285	73940	72636	71369	70139	68942	67778	66644	65539
49	76649	75262	73918	72614	71349	70119	68923	67759	66625	65521
50	76625	75239	73896	72593	71328	70099	68903	67740	66607	65503
51	76602	75216	73874	72571	71307	70078	68884	67721	66588	65484
52	76578	75194	73852	72550	71286	70058	68864	67702	66570	65466
53	76555	75171	73830	72529	71265	70038	68844	67682	66551	65448
54	76531	75148	73808	72507	71245	70018	68825	6/663	66532	65430
55	76508	75126	73786	72486	71224	69998	68805	67644	66514	65412
56	76485	75103	73764	72465	71203	69977	68785	67625	66495	65394
57	76461	75080	73742	72443	71183	69957	68766	67606	66477	65376
58	76438	75058	73720	72422	71162	69937	68746	67587	66458	65357
59	76414	75035	73698	72401	71141	69917	68727	67568	66439	65339
60	76391	75012	73676	72379	71120	69897	68707	67549	66421	65321

SOLAR AND LUNAR RETURNS

"	0 DEGREE, OR 0 HOUR									
	40'	41'	42'	43'	44'	45'	46'	47'	48'	49'
0	65321	64249	63202	62180	61182	60206	59251	58317	57403	56508
1	65303	64231	63185	62164	61166	60190	59236	58302	57388	56493
2	65285	64214	63168	62147	61149	60174	59220	58287	57373	56478
3	65267	64196	63151	62130	61133	60158	59204	58271	57358	56463
4	65249	64178	63133	62113	61116	60142	59189	58256	57343	56449
5	65231	64161	63116	62096	61100	60126	59173	58241	57328	56434
6	65213	64143	63099	62080	61083	60110	59157	58225	57313	56419
7	65195	64125	63082	62063	61067	60094	59141	58210	57298	56404
8	65177	64108	63065	62046	61051	60078	59126	58194	57283	56390
9	65159	64090	63047	62029	61034	60061	59110	58179	57268	56375
10	65141	64073	63030	62012	61018	60045	59094	58164	57253	56360
11	65123	64055	63013	61996	61001	60029	59079	58148	57238	56345
12	65105	64038	62996	61979	60985	60013	59063	58133	57223	56331
13	65087	64020	62979	61962	60969	59997	59047	58118	57208	56316
14	65069	64002	62962	61945	60952	59981	59032	58102	57193	56301
15	65051	63985	62945	61929	60936	59965	59016	58087	57178	56287
16	65033	63967	62927	61912	60920	59949	59000	58072	57163	56272
17	65015	63950	62910	61895	60903	59933	58985	58056	57148	56257
18	64997	63932	62893	61878	60887	59917	58969	58041	57133	56243
19	64979	63915	62876	61862	60871	59901	58954	58026	57118	56228
20	64961	63897	62859	61845	60854	59885	58938	58011	57103	56213
21	64943	63880	62842	61828	60838	59870	58922	57995	57088	56199
22	64925	63862	62825	61812	60822	59854	58907	57980	57073	56184
23	64907	63845	62808	61795	60805	59838	58891	57965	57058	56169
24	64889	63827	62791	61778	60789	59822	58875	57949	57043	56155
25	64871	63810	62774	61762	60773	59806	58860	57934	57028	56140
26	64853	63792	62757	61745	60756	59790	58844	57919	57013	56125
27	64835	63775	62739	61728	60740	59774	58829	57904	56998	56111
28	64818	63757	62722	61712	60724	59758	58813	57888	56983	56096
29	64800	63740	62705	61695	60708	59742	58798	57873	56968	56081
30	64782	63722	62688	61678	60691	59726	58782	57858	56953	56067
31	64764	63705	62671	61662	60675	59710	58766	57843	56938	56052
32	64746	63688	62654	61645	60659	59694	58751	57827	56923	56037
33	64728	63670	62637	61628	60642	59678	58735	57812	56908	56023
34	64710	63653	62620	61612	60626	59663	58720	57797	56893	56008
35	64692	63635	62603	61595	60610	59647	58704	57782	56879	55994
36	64675	63618	62586	61579	60594	59631	58689	57767	56864	55979
37	64657	63601	62569	61562	60578	59615	58673	57751	56849	55964
38	64639	63583	62552	61545	60561	59599	58658	57736	56834	55950
39	64621	63566	62535	61529	60545	59583	58642	57721	56819	55935
40	64603	63548	62518	61512	60529	59567	58627	57706	56804	55921
41	64586	63531	62501	61496	60513	59551	58611	57691	56789	55906
42	64568	63514	62484	61479	60496	59536	58596	57675	56774	55892
43	64550	63496	62468	61463	60480	59520	58580	57660	56759	55877
44	64532	63479	62451	61446	60464	59504	58565	57645	56745	55862
45	64514	63462	62434	61429	60448	59488	58549	57630	56730	55848
46	64497	63444	62417	61413	60432	59472	58534	57615	56715	55833
47	64479	63427	62400	61396	60416	59457	58518	57600	56700	55819
48	64461	63410	62383	61380	60399	59441	58503	57584	56685	55804
49	64443	63392	62366	61363	60383	59425	58487	57569	56670	55790
50	64426	63375	62349	61347	60367	59409	58472	57554	56656	55775
51	64408	63358	62332	61330	60351	59393	58456	57539	56641	55761
52	64390	63340	62315	61314	60335	59378	58441	57524	56626	55746
53	64373	63323	62298	61297	60319	59362	58425	57509	56611	55732
54	64355	63306	62282	61281	60303	59346	58410	57494	56596	55717
55	64337	63289	62265	61264	60286	59330	58395	57479	56582	55703
56	64320	63271	62248	61248	60270	59314	58379	57463	56567	55688
57	64302	63254	62231	61231	60254	59299	58364	57448	56552	55674
58	64284	63237	62214	61215	60238	59283	58348	57433	56537	55659
59	64267	63220	62197	61198	60222	59267	58333	57418	56522	55645
60	64249	63202	62180	61182	60206	59251	58317	57403	56508	55630

°	0 DEGREE, OR 0 HOUR									
	50′	51′	52′	53′	54′	55′	56′	57′	58′	59′
0	55630	54770	53927	53100	52288	51491	50708	49940	49184	48442
1	55616	54756	53913	53086	52274	51478	50696	49927	49172	48430
2	55601	54742	53899	53072	52261	51465	50683	49914	49159	48418
3	55587	54728	53885	53059	52248	51452	50670	49902	49147	48405
4	55572	54714	53871	53045	52234	51438	50657	49889	49135	48393
5	55558	54699	53857	53031	52221	51425	50644	49876	49122	48381
6	55543	54685	53843	53018	52208	51412	50631	49864	49110	48369
7	55529	54671	53830	53004	52194	51399	50618	49851	49097	48356
8	55515	54657	53816	52991	52181	51386	50605	49838	49085	48344
9	55500	54643	53802	52977	52167	51373	50592	49826	49072	48332
10	55486	54629	53788	52963	52154	51360	50579	49813	49060	48320
11	55471	54614	53774	52950	52141	51346	50566	49800	49047	48307
12	55457	54600	53760	52936	52127	51333	50554	49788	49035	48295
13	55442	54586	53746	52922	52114	51320	50541	49775	49023	48283
14	55428	54572	53732	52909	52101	51307	50528	49762	49010	48271
15	55414	54558	53719	52895	52087	51294	50515	49750	48998	48258
16	55399	54544	53705	52882	52074	51281	50502	49737	48985	48246
17	55385	54530	53691	52868	52061	51268	50489	49724	48973	48234
18	55370	54516	53677	52855	52047	51255	50476	49712	48960	48222
19	55356	54501	53663	52841	52034	51242	50464	49699	48948	48210
20	55342	54487	53649	52827	52021	51229	50451	49687	48936	48197
21	55327	54473	53636	52814	52007	51215	50438	49674	48923	48185
22	55313	54459	53622	52800	51994	51202	50425	49661	48911	48173
23	55299	54445	53608	52787	51981	51189	50412	49649	48898	48161
24	55284	54431	53594	52773	51967	51176	50399	49636	48886	48149
25	55270	54417	53580	52760	51954	51163	50387	49623	48874	48136
26	55255	54403	53567	52746	51941	51150	50374	49611	48861	48124
27	55241	54389	53553	52732	51927	51137	50361	49598	48849	48112
28	55227	54375	53539	52719	51914	51124	50348	49586	48836	48100
29	55212	54361	53525	52705	51901	51111	50335	49573	48824	48088
30	55198	54347	53511	52692	51888	51098	50322	49560	48812	48076
31	55184	54332	53498	52678	51874	51085	50310	49548	48799	48063
32	55169	54318	53484	52665	51861	51072	50297	49535	48787	48051
33	55155	54304	53470	52651	51848	51059	50284	49523	48775	48039
34	55141	54290	53456	52638	51835	51046	50271	49510	48762	48027
35	55127	54276	53442	52624	51821	51033	50258	49498	48750	48015
36	55112	54262	53429	52611	51808	51020	50246	49485	48737	48003
37	55098	54248	53415	52597	51795	51007	50233	49472	48725	47990
38	55084	54234	53401	52584	51781	50994	50220	49460	48713	47978
39	55069	54220	53387	52570	51768	50981	50207	49447	48700	47966
40	55055	54206	53374	52557	51755	50968	50194	49435	48688	47954
41	55041	54192	53360	52543	51742	50955	50182	49422	48676	47942
42	55026	54178	53346	52530	51729	50942	50169	49410	48663	47930
43	55012	54164	53332	52516	51715	50929	50156	49397	48651	47918
44	54998	54150	53319	52503	51702	50916	50143	49385	48639	47906
45	54984	54136	53305	52489	51689	50903	50131	49372	48626	47893
46	54969	54122	53291	52476	51676	50890	50118	49360	48614	47881
47	54955	54108	53278	52462	51662	50877	50105	49347	48602	47869
48	54941	54094	53264	52449	51649	50864	50092	49334	48590	47857
49	54927	54080	53250	52436	51636	50851	50080	49322	48577	47845
50	54912	54066	53236	52422	51623	50838	50067	49309	48565	47833
51	54898	54052	53223	52409	51610	50825	50054	49297	48553	47821
52	54884	54038	53209	52395	51596	50812	50041	49284	48540	47809
53	54870	54024	53195	52382	51583	50799	50029	49272	48528	47797
54	54855	54011	53182	52368	51570	50786	50016	49259	48516	47785
55	54841	53997	53168	52355	51557	50773	50003	49247	48503	47772
56	54827	53983	53154	52342	51544	50760	49991	49234	48491	47760
57	54813	53969	53141	52328	51530	50747	49978	49222	48479	47748
58	54799	53955	53127	52315	51517	50734	49965	49209	48467	47736
59	54784	53941	53113	52301	51504	50721	49952	49197	48454	47724
60	54770	53927	53100	52288	51491	50708	49940	49184	48442	47712

	0′	1′	2′	3′	4′	5′	6′	7′	8′	9′	10′	11′
1 DEGREE, OR 1 HOUR												
0	47712	46994	46288	45593	44909	44236	43573	42920	42276	41642	41017	40401
1	47700	46982	46276	45582	44898	44225	43562	42909	42266	41632	41007	40391
2	47688	46971	46265	45570	44887	44214	43551	42898	42255	41621	40997	40381
3	47676	46959	46253	45559	44875	44203	43540	42887	42244	41611	40986	40371
4	47664	46947	46241	45547	44864	44191	43529	42877	42234	41600	40976	40361
5	47652	46935	46230	45536	44853	44180	43518	42866	42223	41590	40966	40350
6	47640	46923	46218	45524	44841	44169	43507	42855	42213	41579	40955	40340
7	47628	46911	46206	45513	44830	44158	43496	42844	42202	41569	40945	40330
8	47616	46899	46195	45501	44819	44147	43485	42833	42191	41559	40935	40320
9	47604	46888	46183	45490	44808	44136	43474	42823	42181	41548	40924	40310
10	47592	46876	46171	45478	44796	44125	43463	42812	42170	41538	40914	40300
11	47580	46864	46160	45467	44785	44114	43452	42801	42159	41527	40904	40289
12	47568	46852	46148	45456	44774	44102	43441	42790	42149	41517	40894	40279
13	47556	46840	46137	45444	44762	44091	43431	42780	42138	41506	40883	40269
14	47544	46828	46125	45433	44751	44080	43420	42769	42128	41496	40873	40259
15	47532	46817	46113	45421	44740	44069	43409	42758	42117	41485	40863	40249
16	47520	46805	46102	45410	44729	44058	43398	42747	42106	41475	40852	40239
17	47508	46793	46090	45398	44717	44047	43387	42737	42096	41464	40842	40228
18	47496	46781	46078	45387	44706	44036	43376	42726	42085	41454	40832	40218
19	47484	46769	46067	45375	44695	44025	43365	42715	42075	41443	40821	40208
20	47472	46758	46055	45364	44684	44014	43354	42704	42064	41433	40811	40198
21	47460	46746	46044	45353	44672	44003	43343	42693	42053	41423	40801	40188
22	47448	46734	46032	45341	44661	43992	43332	42683	42043	41412	40791	40178
23	47436	46722	46020	45330	44650	43981	43321	42672	42032	41402	40780	40168
24	47424	46710	46009	45318	44639	43969	43310	42661	42022	41391	40770	40157
25	47412	46699	45997	45307	44627	43958	43300	42651	42011	41381	40760	40147
26	47400	46687	45986	45295	44616	43947	43289	42640	42000	41370	40749	40137
27	47388	46675	45974	45284	44605	43936	43278	42629	41990	41360	40739	40127
28	47376	46663	45962	45273	44594	43925	43267	42618	41979	41350	40729	40117
29	47364	46652	45951	45261	44583	43914	43256	42608	41969	41339	40719	40107
30	47352	46640	45939	45250	44571	43903	43245	42597	41958	41329	40708	40097
31	47340	46628	45928	45238	44560	43892	43234	42586	41948	41318	40698	40087
32	47328	46616	45916	45227	44549	43881	43223	42575	41937	41308	40688	40076
33	47316	46604	45905	45216	44538	43870	43212	42565	41927	41298	40678	40066
34	47304	46593	45893	45204	44526	43859	43202	42554	41916	41287	40667	40056
35	47292	46581	45881	45193	44515	43848	43191	42543	41905	41277	40657	40046
36	47280	46569	45870	45182	44504	43837	43180	42533	41895	41266	40647	40036
37	47268	46557	45858	45170	44493	43826	43169	42522	41884	41256	40637	40026
38	47256	46546	45847	45159	44482	43815	43158	42511	41874	41246	40616	40016
39	47244	46534	45835	45147	44470	43804	43147	42500	41863	41235	40616	40006
40	47232	46522	45824	45136	44459	43793	43136	42490	41853	41225	40606	39996
41	47220	46510	45812	45125	44448	43782	43126	42479	41842	41214	40596	39985
42	47208	46499	45800	45113	44437	43771	43115	42468	41832	41204	40585	39975
43	47196	46487	45789	45102	44426	43760	43104	42458	41821	41194	40575	39965
44	47185	46475	45777	45091	44414	43749	43093	42447	41811	41183	40565	39955
45	47173	46464	45766	45079	44403	43738	43082	42436	41800	41173	40555	39945
46	47161	46452	45754	45068	44392	43727	43071	42426	41789	41162	40544	39935
47	47149	46440	45743	45057	44381	43716	43060	42415	41779	41152	40534	39925
48	47137	46428	45731	45045	44370	43705	43050	42404	41768	41142	40524	39915
49	47125	46417	45720	45034	44359	43694	43039	42394	41758	41131	40514	39905
50	47113	46405	45708	45022	44347	43683	43028	42383	41747	41121	40503	39895
51	47101	46393	45697	45011	44336	43672	43017	42372	41737	41111	40493	39885
52	47089	46382	45685	45000	44325	43661	43006	42362	41726	41100	40483	39874
53	47077	46370	45674	44988	44314	43650	42995	42351	41716	41090	40473	39864
54	47066	46358	45662	44977	44303	43639	42985	42340	41705	41080	40463	39854
55	47054	46346	45651	44966	44292	43628	42974	42330	41695	41069	40452	39844
56	47042	46335	45639	44955	44280	43617	42963	42319	41684	41059	40442	39834
57	47030	46323	45628	44943	44269	43606	42952	42308	41674	41048	40432	39824
58	47018	46311	45616	44932	44258	43595	42941	42298	41663	41038	40422	39814
59	47006	46300	45605	44921	44247	43584	42931	42287	41653	41028	40412	39804
60	46994	46288	45593	44909	44236	43573	42920	42276	41642	41017	40401	39794

APPENDIX 2.
CHART DATA USED IN THE TEXT

PERSONAL CHARTS		SOURCE
No.5	Queen Elizabeth II	Official Records
No.6	Duke of York (Prince Andrew)	Official Records
No.7	Duchess of York	Official Records
		(A.Q. Vol.60, No.1)
No.8	Princess Margaret	Official Records
No.9	M.D.	Mother
No.10	N.D.	Mother
No.18	Mary	From her
No.22	Susi	From mother
No.27	Ann	From mother
No.31	Helen	From her
No.35	Sally	From mother
No.38	Molly	From mother

Miscellaneous data:

Elizabeth of Austria	Notable Nativities
	(809 & M.A.)
Francis Joseph	(152)
Bullfighter	(063)
Lottery & Contest Winners No.1–5	American Book
	of Charts
No.6	American Astrology
	Nov. 1974

Natal Data

	(1)		(2)		(3)	
Time UT	09.05		11.50		09.08	
Date	12.6.29		29.8.28		28.6.25	
Lat.	51.31N		48.47N		51.10N	
Long.	00.20W		09.11E		07.04E	
Natal Sun	20.53.41	♓	05.52.11	♍	06.07.59	♋
Natal Moon	27.31	♌	15.40	♒	24.13	♍
RAMC	02.24.29		10.56.29		04.00.03	
Mean Sun	05.20.49		10.29.45		06.23.47	
Apparent Sun	05.20.21		10.30.38		06.26.43	
Asc.	22	♌	24	♏	9	♍
MC	8	♑	13	♍	2	♓
	Mary		*Susi*		*Ann*	
Natal Chart No.	18		22		27	

	(4)		(5)		(6)	
Time UT	06.45		01.40		15.30	
Date	23.3.1899		21.4.26		19.2.60	
Lat.	51.10N		51.30N		51.30N	
Long.	07.04E		00.08W		00.08W	
Natal Sun	02.26.15	♈	00.12.21	♉	00.00.09	♓
Natal Moon	17.22	♌	12.07	♌	25.29	♏
RAMC	19.15.26		15.32.58		01.23.51	
Mean Sun	00.02.10		01.53.30		21.54.23	
Apparent Sun	00.08.57		01.52.25		22.08.23	
Asc.	11	♉	21	♑	11	♌
MC	17	♑	25	♏	23	♈
	Helen		*Queen Eliz.II*		*Duke of York*	
Natal Chart No.	31		5		6	

Natal Data

	(7)		(8)		(9)	
Time UT	09.03		20.22		23.07	
Date	15.10.59		21.8.30		02.6.53	
Lat.	51.31N		56.57N		34.21N	
Long.	00.09W		03.00W		119.04W	
Natal Sun	21.15.38	♎	28.01.43	♌	12.04.56	♓
Natal Moon	06.38	♈	25.16	♋	18.48	♒
RAMC	10.35.00		18.07.42		07.55.11	
Mean Sun	13.32.36		09.57.42		04.44.28	

	(7)	(8)	(9)
Apparent Sun	13.18.35	10.00.49	04.42.20
Asc.	18 ♏	6 ♈	24 ♎
MC	7 ♍	2 ♑	27 ♋
	Duchess of York	Princess Margaret	MD
Natal Chart No.	7	8	9

	(10)	(11)	(12)
Time UT	04.00	09.00	23.10
Date	17.10.49	11.5.53	04.3.56
Lat.	34.09N	51.37N	51.30N
Long.	118.09W	00.17W	00.08W
Natal Sun	23.26.57 ♎	20.21.53 ♉	14.21.50 ♓
Natal Moon	18.25 ♌	25.37 ♈	19.29 ♐
RAMC	21.48.43	00.14.16	10.00.11
Mean Sun	13.41.19	03.15.25	22.50.43
Apparent Sun	13.26.48	03.11.41	23.02.24
Asc.	15 ♓	29 ♋	12 ♏
MC	25 ♒	4 ♈	28 ♌
	ND	Sally	Molly
Natal Chart No.	10	35	38

Mundane data	*Source*
World War I declaration	*The Home Fronts,* John Williams, Constable, 1972
Armistice signed	Ency. Brit.
World War II declaration	Contemporary reports
American Shuttle disaster	Current Press and TV reports.
Christa McAuliffe (shuttle victim)	AA Data section
Judy Resnik (shuttle victim)	AA Data section

Earthquakes
Nos. 1 and 2   Seismicity of the Earth,
                                 Gutenberg & Richter.
                                 Princetown University
                                 Press (1949)
No. 3   Earth Sciences,
                                 Seismicity of the Earth,

Mundane data	*Source*
	Unesco (1969)
No.4	MA Vol.30, No.3, 1933
No.5 and 6	Current Press reports

Mine disasters	*Source*
No.1 and 2	MA Vol.31, No.6, 1934

Explosions	
No.1	American Astrology, June 1957 (Garth Allen)
No.2	Current reports

Atomic bombs	
No.1	Sunday Times 16.11.80
No.2	Time noted from a British TV report, August 1985

London Air raid victims	
No.1	AQ Vol.21, No.1 1947
No.2–4	AQ Vol.25, No.2 1951

APPENDIX 3.

Abbreviations
AA   Astrological Association
AJ   Astrological Journal
AQ   Astrologer's Quarterly
MA   Modern Astrology (now defunct)

Terms
Ingress   Sun, Moon or planet's entry into a sign
LR   Lunar return
SLR   Lunar return (sidereal)
TLR   Lunar return (tropical)
MS   Mean Sun
RAAS   Right Ascension of the Apparent Sun
Radix   Radical or natal
SR   Solar return
SSR   Solar return (sidereal)
TSR   Solar return (tropical)
Solstice Sun's entry into Cancer (June) and Capricorn
          (December)
UT   Universal time (Greenwich Mean time)
LT   Local time

SIGNS AND SYMBOLS IN COMPUTER-DRAWN CHARTS

SIGNS		PLANETS	
Ar	Aries	So	Sun
Ta	Taurus	Me	Mercury

SIGNS		PLANETS	
Ge	Gemini	Ve	Venus
Cn	Cancer	Ma	Mars
Le	Leo	Ju	Jupiter
Vi	Virgo	Sa	Saturn
Li	Libra	Ur	Uranus
Sc	Scorpio	Ne	Neptune
Sa	Sagittarius	Pl	Pluto
Cp	Capricorn	Mo	Moon
Aq	Aquarius	Nn	North node
Pi	Pisces	As	Ascendant
		Mc	Midheaven

RAMC = Right Ascension of the Midheaven
        = Sidereal time

All the computer calculated charts are in terms of the
TROPICAL ZODIAC
using an Astrocalc program (see references)
on an Amstrad 6128 computer.

APPENDIX 4.

Astrological data:
Source: Modern Astrology, Vol. IX, 1912
Welsh Mining disasters

```
 1. 05.00 UT  24.  5.1901, 51.28N,    3.10W
 2. 07.40 UT  26.  8.1892, 51.36N,    3.35W
 3. 05.30 UT  27.  1.1896, 51.39N,    3.30W
 4. 01.20 UT  10.12.1880, 51.35N,    3.21W
 5. 18.30 UT  10.  3.1905, 51.50N,    3.30W
 6. 12.00 UT  11.  7.1905, 51.39N,    3.30W
 7. 13.30 LT   8.11.1867, 51.28N,    3.10W
 8. 07.20 LT  10.  6.1869, 51.28N,    3.10W
 9. 19.00 UT  18.  2.1887, 51.39N,    3.30W
10. 09.00 LT   1.12.1860, 51.35N,    3.00W
11. 01.20 UT  15.  7.1880, 51.35N,    3.00W
12. 10.30 LT  17.10.1863, 51.45N,    3.22W
```

Data collected by Arthur Mee from contemporary newspapers and records and published in the *Western Mail*. The times quoted are not specified precisely. As Greenwich Time became official in 1880, it is assumed that the earlier dates are in local time.

Californian Earthquakes
Source: The Seismicity of the Earth, UNESCO, 1953–1965

```
1. 19.56 UT 21.12.1954, 40.49N, 124.05W
2. 05.51 UT 24.  8.1954, 39.35N, 118.27W
3. 11.13 UT  6.  7.1954, 39.25N, 118.32W
4. 11.07 UT 16.12.1954, 39.20N, 118.12W
5. 14.35 UT 23.  6.1959, 39.05N, 118.49W
```

6. 19.44 UT 22. 3.1957, 37.40N, 122.29W
7. 07.23 UT   9. 4.1961, 36.41N, 121.18W
8. 23.34 UT 12. 1.1954, 35.00N, 119.06W
9. 21.32 UT   4. 4.1961, 33.48N, 118.12W
10. 02.01 UT   5. 9.1955, 37.22N, 121.47W

Mexican Earthquakes
1. 08.40 UT 28. 7.1957, 16.30N, 99.00W
2. 08.25 UT 26. 8.1959, 18.18N, 94.24W
3. 07.22 UT   6. 7.1964, 18.18N, 100.24W
4. 15.18 UT   5. 2.1954, 17.18N, 92.36W
5. 19.46 UT 23. 8.1965, 16.18N, 95.48W

BIBLIOGRAPHY
SUGGESTED READING AND REFERENCE MATERIALS

Books
Boyd, H., *The True Horoscope of the United States* (ASI Publishers, 1973).
Bradley, D., *Solar and Lunar Returns* (Sidereal) (Llewellyn Foundation of Astrological Research, 1950).
Fagan, C., *Zodiacs Old and New* (Anscombe, London, 1951).
——, *The Solunars Handbook* (Clancy Publications, 1970).
Fagan, C., and Firebrace, R., *A Primer of the Sidereal Zodiac* (Moray Series No.1, 1961).
Powell, R., and Treadgold, P., *The Sidereal Zodiac* (Anthroposophical Publications, 1979).
Rodden, L. M., *Profiles of Women* (American Federation of Astrologers, Inc. 1979).
——, *The American Book of Charts* (Astro-Computing Services, San Diego, 1980).

Journals
Astrology, The Astrologer's Quarterly, Astrological Lodge of London.
The Astrological Journal, Astrological Association.
American Astrology, Clancy Publications.
The FAA Journal, Federation of Australian Astrologers.
The Schneider-Gauquelin Research Journal, Paris, France. Vol.1 1982 to date contains valuable European time data.

Reference Materials
Astrocalc, British astrological software, 67 Peascroft Road, Hemel Hempstead, Herts., HP3 8ER, England.
Raphael's Ephemerides, 1860 to date, Foulsham.

Raphael's Tables of Houses for Northern Latitudes, Foulsham.

Raphael's Tables of Houses for Great Britain, Foulsham.

The American Ephemeris for the Twentieth Century (1900–2000) Neil Michelsen (Astro-Computing Services)

The American Sidereal Ephemeris (1976–2000), includes SVP condensed tables (1833–1976), Astro-Computing Services.

Longitudes and Latitudes Throughout the World (excluding the USA), E. Dernay (American Federation of Astrologers).

Longitudes and Latitudes in the USA, E. Dernay.

Time Changes in the World (excluding USA, Canada and Mexico), Doris Chase Doane (American Federation of Astrologers).

Time Changes in the USA, Doris Chase Doane (American Federation of Astrologers).

Time Changes in Canada and Mexico, Doris Chase Doane (American Federation of Astrologers).

World Almanac and Book of Facts, (Newspaper Enterprise Association Inc. New York). (Annual publication.)

INDEX